Precarious Ties

Precarious Ties

Business and the State in Authoritarian Asia

MEG RITHMIRE

OXFORD
UNIVERSITY PRESS

OXFORD
UNIVERSITY PRESS

Oxford University Press is a department of the University of Oxford. It furthers
the University's objective of excellence in research, scholarship, and education
by publishing worldwide. Oxford is a registered trade mark of Oxford University
Press in the UK and certain other countries.

Published in the United States of America by Oxford University Press
198 Madison Avenue, New York, NY 10016, United States of America.

Library of Congress Cataloging-in-Publication Data
Names: Rithmire, Meg E., 1982- author.
Title: Precarious ties : business and the state in authoritarian Asia / Meg Rithmire.
Description: New York, NY : Oxford University Press, [2023] |
Includes bibliographical references and index.
Identifiers: LCCN 2023011408 (print) | LCCN 2023011409 (ebook) |
ISBN 9780197697528 (hardback) | ISBN 9780197697535 (paperback) |
ISBN 9780197697542 (epub)
Subjects: LCSH: Industrial policy—Asia. | Authoritarianism—Asia. |
Patronage, Political—Asia. | Asia—Politics and government.
Classification: LCC HD3616.C63 R57 2023 (print) |
LCC HD3616.C63 (ebook) | DDC 338.95—dc23/eng/20230602
LC record available at https://lccn.loc.gov/2023011408
LC ebook record available at https://lccn.loc.gov/2023011409

DOI: 10.1093/oso/9780197697528.001.0001

Paperback printed by Marquis Book Printing, Canada
Hardback printed by Bridgeport National Bindery, Inc., United States of America

To the wonderful people who care for small children, especially the staff at Peabody Terrace Children's Center, Grace Foster, Ariela Weinbach, and Amelia Kraus

Contents

Tables

Figures

Acknowledgments

I spent summer of 2015 in Hong Kong, Singapore, and Indonesia, exploring materials for a project on transnational capital in Asia. On a very hot day in June, I crossed the border for a long day of meetings and took a break for lunch with a very wealthy entrepreneur in Shenzhen. During lunch, as I was freezing in an overly air-conditioned restaurant, my companion was sweating with increasing unease, watching his three phones as stock markets in Shenzhen and Shanghai were in free fall. He told me he had lost a considerable sum as we were eating, and I offered to get the bill. He said something along the lines of "No worries; this is basically a casino for me, and anyway I am sure the government won't let important firms really collapse." His comment did not seem surprising at first, but I returned to it again and again while watching the financial turmoil unfold over the next couple of years. I did end up writing a book somewhat about transnational capital in Asia, but not the one I expected to write. By the time of the book's completion, as the Chinese Communist Party was turning on capitalists once again and financial scandal contributed to political turmoil in Malaysia, I knew it was the right project.

The set of questions that would motivate this book emerged during my years as an assistant and associate professor at Harvard Business School. I would like to say the questions were all my own, but, alas, I cannot. Scholarly life in an interdisciplinary department and interaction with practitioners confront me with large, comparative, and temporally expansive questions about China. My students and colleagues puzzle over the long-term sustainability of debt in China, why firms look the way they do, and why Chinese entrepreneurs even bother when they can theoretically be expropriated by the state at any moment, to name a few. The more I tried to answer these questions, the deeper they revealed themselves to be. The ideas in this book would have never come to fruition without the general education I get (and try to give) in the classroom and the hallways of campus. I am grateful to my current and former co-teachers, including Rawi Abdelal, Rafael DiTella, Kristin Fabbe, Jeremy Friedman, Peter Katzenstein, Akshay Mangla, Vincent Pons, Sophus Reinert, Dante

Roscini (who taught me how to read a bank balance sheet at some pre-dawn hour), Gunnar Trumbull, Matt Weinzierl, and Eric Werker, who were all part of a mutual aid society of sorts. I have also been enriched by conversations with Alberto Cavallo, Matts Fibiger, Reshma Hussam, Charlotte Robertson, Marco Tabellini, Marlous van Waijenburg, and Jaya Wen. Several of my colleagues read parts of this book in progress. I thank Rawi Abdelal, Caroline Elkins, Kristin Fabbe, Charlotte Robertson, Gunnar Trumbull, Marlous van Waijenburg, Matt Weinzierl, and Jaya Wen for their critical help. Matts Fibiger not only read the work but also helped with sources for Indonesia. Sophus Reinert provided critical feedback and camaraderie. I owe a special debt to the late Julio Rotemberg, whose improbable intellectual mentorship enriched my life immensely. He told me that working on how businesspeople behave would be fun; as with most things, he was right.

Rick Doner introduced me to political economy and Southeast Asia when I was much younger and has encouraged me in the decades since. I will always be grateful to Elizabeth Perry for my training in Chinese politics and her good judgment and support; I will always be her student. It is my great fortune to be part of the larger Harvard China and Asia community. I am grateful to Bill Alford, Nara Dillon, Dinda Elliott, Mark Elliott, Bill Hsiao, Iain Johnston, Bill Kirby, Dan Murphy, Bill Overholt, Dwight Perkins, James Robson, Tony Saich, Michael Szonyi, Karen Thornber, Mark Wu, and Winnie Yip for engaging my ideas or helping me socialize them. I am especially delighted to benefit from a younger generation of Harvard China comrades: Arunabh Ghosh, Li Jie, Daniel Koss, Ya-Wen Lei, Yuhua Wang, Mark Wu, and David Yang. Roderick MacFarquhar and Ezra Vogel were sources of support and constructive challenge. I was lucky to learn from them as a student and be treated graciously as a colleague. We all miss them dearly. Warren McFarlan has been a booster, a mentor, and a mensch. Having his name on my card has elicited admiration from people I have met all over Asia, and it is a privilege to take on the mantle.

The research for this book took many years and spanned several countries. A leave year in 2016–2017 enabled me to spend time in at the Asia Research Institute at the National University of Singapore and in Shanghai. ARI was a terrific home in Singapore, and the NUS Southeast Asia and Chinese collection librarians were wonderfully helpful. Singapore was a great base for travel to Malaysia and Indonesia, where I was grateful to the many businesspeople, political elites, and bureaucrats who tolerated my slow education in Southeast Asian politics and business. I especially appreciate Essie Alamsyah, Khazanah

Nasional Berhad, Li-Kai Chen, George Hendrata, George Hendropropriyono, Jomo KS, Tom Lembang, Ray Pulungan, and Datuk Othman Yusoff for help in Indonesia and Malaysia. In China, I thank Nancy Dai, Huang Jingsheng, Dawn Lau, Lin Shu, Wang Yi, and especially Bonnie Cao at HBS's Asia Pacific Research Office, as well as scholars from the China Academy of Social Sciences, the Shanghai Academy of Social Sciences, Fudan, East China Normal, Peking, Tsinghua, Renmin, and Nanjing Universities for invaluable discussions and help in the field. The names of scholars, businesspeople, regulators, and citizens in China who helped me do not appear here, but I could not have written most of the other words without them.

My own collaborators over the last several years have contributed immensely to my own intellectual growth and to the research in this book. Chen Hao has been a thoughtful interlocutor and friend, and the research in the chapters on China would not have been possible without him. Margaret M. Pearson and Kellee S. Tsai have been mentors, partners, and inspiring examples in a great many things during an especially challenging time. Li Yihao literally traveled the earth with me, and it is a miracle his patience survived.

Harvard Business School invested considerable resources in this project. I thank the Department of Faculty Research and Development and especially the school's Global Research Fellowship for support on research and travel. Victoria Liublinksa and Christine Rivera from Research Computing Services lent their talents to this work, and the Baker Library team was professional, patient, and always helpful. I thank Alex Caracuzzo, Katy McNeill, Linda Rosen, Rhys Sevier, and James Zeitler for help in accessing, organizing, and visualizing data in these chapters. Lin Poping introduced me to the world of Chinese bond prospectuses. Richard Lesage and Ma Xiao-He from Harvard's libraries provided critical help in acquiring sources. Nancy Hearst did that and also read every single word of this book and cleaned up my mess of footnotes. I am so grateful for her editorial skills in addition to her wonderful library.

A small army of overqualified research assistants spent their valuable time helping me. These include Essie Alamsayah, Jamie Chen, Nathan Cisneros, Galit Goldstein, Irene Guo, David Hicks, Alexa Jordan, Yihao Li, Elizabeth Lively, Paul Sedille, Jing Shang, Mike Shao, Zhiming Shen, Leticia Smith, Seth Soderborg, Kaitlyn Sydlowski, Yuhao Wang, and Zhiying Xie. I am terrifically grateful to Angelin Oey and Liu Jingyu for their time and patience with Indonesian and Chinese materials respectively.

Many people read parts of this book and provided helpful feedback, though they surely do not agree with all of what follows. I thank Ling Chen,

Nara Dillon, Martin Dimitrov, Yue Hou, Chang-Tai Hsieh, Roselyn Hsueh, Yasheng Huang, Diana Kim, Arthur Kroeber, Doreen Lee, Maggie Lewis, Yi-Min Lin, Kristen Looney, Eddy Malesky, Dan Mattingly, Sean McGraw, Jonas Nahm, Barry Naughton, Jean Oi, Lynette Ong, Jen Pan, Tom Pepinsky, Maria Repnikova, Scott Rozelle, Tony Saich, Victor Shih, Yeling Tan, Ashutosh Varshney, Andrew Walder, Jeremy Wallace, Carl Walter, Saul Wilson, and Logan Wright. I also appreciate Tom Remington, who initially prodded me to focus on finance, and Adi Sunderam, who did his best to make sure I did not make mistakes on finance. Needless to say, he is not to blame if I did. I am especially grateful to Dan Slater and John Yasuda for engaging with the whole project so constructively. My special thanks to Stacy Tan for educating me about intricacies of China's financial regulation and, again, preventing me from making mistakes. David McBride from Oxford University Press supported this project from the very beginning and was patient with all my delays. Lyndsey Willcox and Sarah Antommaria provided invaluable logistical help on this and many things. Dave Barboza and Lin Zhang read the work, provided helpful feedback, and kindly contributed rich data.

For a book largely about dangerous and fragile relationships, I am fortunate to have strong ones. I am certain I taxed them all in writing this book. Jill Bolduc, Veronica Herrera, Ryan and Tammy Hickox, Brad Holland, Nia Maya James, Phil Jones, Rita Kraner, Didi Kuo, Kristen Looney, Sean McGraw, Jonas Nahm, Kang-Kuen Ni, Ann Owens, Christine Pace, and Annie Temple all helped me stay afloat and reminded me to play outside. My husband, Dave Hampton, left his job as a public interest lawyer for a year to allow us to spend time in Asia. Thank you for coming on this ride and for your patience with me as I did this work. My mother, Maxine Rithmire, mother-in-law, Betty Ford Hampton, and my brother-in-law, Jeff Hampton, took turns helping Dave while I was traveling. Dave and I are lucky to have this family. We lost my father, Jack, in 2020. He was the kind of man happy to watch the women around him shine, and his belief in me motivates me still.

My children, Theo and Maxine, actively impeded the completion of this book, but of course that is their job, and it is my absolute privilege to watch them do it so well. Raising them, especially in a pandemic, would not have been possible for us were it not for the community of people who care for them. These people also taught me how to parent and cared for me, too. For this, I will always be grateful to Peabody Terrace Children's Center, Ariela Weinbach, Grace Foster, and especially Amelia Kraus. I dedicate this book to them; my work is only possible because of theirs.

Abbreviations

1MDB	Malaysia Development Berhad (state-owned investment fund)
AFC	Asian Financial Crisis
BCA	Bank Central Asia
BDNI	Bank Dagang Nasional Indonesia
BEE	Bumiputera Economic Empowerment program
BEJ	Bursa Efek Jakarta (Indonesia Stock Exchange)
BERITA	British Malaysian Industry and Trade Association
BI	Bank Indonesia
BIS	Bank for International Settlements
BKPM	Investment Coordinating Board
BLBI	Bantuan Likuiditas Bank Indonesia
BMA	British Malayan Administration
BN	Barisan Nasional (National Front, Malaysia)
BPK	Supreme Audit Agency
BPPN	Badan Penyahayan Perbankan Nasional (Indonesian Bank Restructuring Agency)
BRI	Bank Rakyat Indonesia
BRI	Belt and Road Initiative
BTN	Bank Tabungan Negara (State Savings Bank)
BTO	bank takeover
CBE	commune and brigade enterprise (China)
CBRC	China Regulatory Banking Commission
CCDI	Central Commission on Discipline Inspection (China)
CDRC	Corporate Debt Restructuring Committee (Indonesia)
CEFC	China Energy Company, Ltd.
CFWC	Central Financial Work Commission (China)
CIC	Capital Issuance Committee (Malaysia)
CITIC	China International Trust and Investment Corporation (中信)
CMIG	China Minsheng Investment Group
CSRC	China Securities Regulatory Commission
DAP	Democratic Action Party (Malaysia)
DTC	deposit-taking cooperative
ECRL	East Coast Rail Link (Malaysia)
EPF	Employees Provident Fund (Malaysia)
FDI	foreign direct investment
FELDA	Federal Land Development Authority (Malaysia)

FI	financial institution
FYP	five-year plan
GLC	government linked corporation (Malaysia)
GLCT	Government Linked Companies Transformation Programme (Malaysia)
GLIC	government linked investment company
IBRA	Indonesia Banking Restructuring Agency
ICA	Industrial Coordination Act (Malaysia)
ICIJ	International Consortium of Investigative Journalists
IMF	International Monetary Fund
IOI	property development and palm oil plantation conglomerate (Malaysia)
JKSE	Jakarta Composite Stock Index
JSX	Jakarta Stock Exchange
KKN	corruption-collusion-nepotism
KLSE	Kuala Lumpur Stock Exchange (now known as Bursa Malaysia)
KMT	Guomindang, Nationalist Party (China)
KNB	Khazanah Nasional Berhad (Sovereign Wealth Fund) (Malaysia)
KPB	Konsortium Perkapalan Bhd (Malaysia)
KPK	Komisi Pemberantasan Korupsi (anticorruption commission, Indonesia)
KWAP	Retirement Fund Incorporated (Malaysia)
LGFV	local government financing vehicle (China)
LTAT	Armed Forces Savings Fund (Malaysia)
LTH	Pilgrim's Savings Fund (Malaysia)
M&A	merger and acquisition
MARA	Majlis Amanah Rakyat
MCA	Malayan Chinese Association
MCP	Malayan Communist Party
MIC	Malayan Indian Congress
MIDF	Malaysian Industrial Development Finance Berhad
MLB	Ministry of Land Resources (China)
MoF	Ministry of Finance (China)
MOFCOM	Ministry of Commerce (China)
MPAJA	Malayan People's Anti-Japanese Army
MUI	Malaysia United Industries
NEAC	National Economic Advisory Council (Malaysia)
NEM	New Economic Model (Malaysia)
NEP	New Economic Policy (Malaysia)
NOC	National Operations Council (Singapore)
NPL	nonperforming loan
NUS	National University of Singapore
OCBC	Oversea-Chinese Banking Corporation (Singapore)

OFDI	outward foreign direct investment
P2P	peer-to-peer lending
PAP	People's Action Party (Singapore)
PAS	Islamic Party of Malaysia
PBoC	People's Bank of China
PCMA	Perak Chinese Mining Association (Malaysia)
PERNAS	Perbadanan Nasional Berhad
PETRONAS	Malaysia's National Oil Company
PGRM	Parti Gerakan Rakyat Malaysia (Malaysian People's Movement Party)
PKI	Parti Kommunist Indonesia (Communist Party of Indonesia)
PKP	anticorruption commission
PKR	People's Justice Party (Malaysia)
PNB	Permodalan Nasional Berhad (Malaysia)
PPP	People's Progressive Party (Malaysia)
PRC	People's Republic of China
PSP	Soehargo Gondokusumo's Bank (Indonesia)
RHB	financial services group and bank (Malaysia)
RIDA	Rural Industrial Development Authority (Malaysia)
RoC	Republic of China
SAFE	State Administration of Foreign Exchange (China)
SASAC	State-Owned Assets Supervision and Administration Commission (China)
SDR	Special Drawing Rights
SEDC	State Economic Development Corporation
SEZ	special economic zone
SIP	Singapore-Suzhou Industrial Park (新加坡苏州工业园区) (China)
SME	small- and medium-sized enterprise
SOE	state-owned enterprise
TNI	Indonesian Republican Military Forces
TVE	town and village enterprise (China)
UEM	engineering company (Malaysia)
UI	Universitas Indonesia
UMNO	United Malay National Organization
WTO	World Trade Organization
YTL	construction company (Malaysia)

1

The Foundations of State-Business Relations in Authoritarian Asia

For most authoritarian regimes, whether political elites are able to control economic elites is a fundamental factor in the regime's survival and achievement. For all economies save those in which the state plans production and consumption, authoritarian rulers face the dilemma of needing to discipline but also to cultivate the business class. They must ensure that capitalists, who have substantial access to economic resources, do not organize against the regime, but excessive control of economic elites precludes them from investing in growth. For the past half-century at least, the vast majority of nondemocratic regimes have been in developing countries with at least partial market economies. As a result, political elites have faced demands to generate economic growth, but they have not entirely controlled whether and how their investments are allocated. Failing to strike a balance between disciplining and courting the business class can have catastrophic results for authoritarian rulers, either by generating political dissent, by precipitating economic crisis through capital flight, or through the kind of slow-churning economic stagnation that leaves one generation no better off than the last.

Capitalists in late-developing countries have not, in general, been agents of political liberalization.[1] Although a classical literature in social science credits the bourgeoisie with agitating for political democratization in the past, more contemporary portraits of the business class in authoritarian regimes have settled in the opposite direction, focusing on capitalists as a source of "authoritarian resilience." State-business relations in most developing countries are more often viewed as "money politics" or "crony

---

[1] Eva Bellin, "Contingent Democrats: Industrialists, Labor, and Democratization in Late-Developing Countries," *World Politics* 52, no. 2 (2000): 175–205; Eva Bellin, *Stalled Democracy: Capital, Labor, and the Paradox of State-Sponsored Development* (Ithaca: Cornell University Press, 2002).

Precarious Ties. Meg Rithmire, Oxford University Press. © Oxford University Press 2023.
DOI: 10.1093/oso/9780197697528.003.0001

capitalism" than as "no bourgeoisie, no democracy."[2] Scholars have focused on the roles of capitalists in corruption networks, enriching rulers and their families and securing privileged access for themselves at the expense of the society at large rather than their role in challenging political elites. I argue in this book that the empirical reality is somewhere in between. Although capitalists have not marched in the streets to take down autocratic regimes, they have contributed indirectly to many cases of regime change and collapse, either by precipitating economic crisis or by eroding regime legitimacy through extensive crony networks. In essence, business elites have generally been tied to autocrats, but those ties have been precarious.

This book answers a series of theoretical questions about the delicate relationship between capitalists and autocrats. What strategies do authoritarian political elites adopt to manage the business class? What kinds of strategies succeed, for example, to secure political stability and economic growth, and what kinds fail, either by stymieing economic growth or by generating regime instability? In pursuing these questions, I posit an additional empirical and theoretical puzzle: Why do elite relationships in authoritarian regimes so often begin as partnerships for growth but then disintegrate into corruption, authoritarian decay, and, frequently, regime collapse?

I explore these questions and this puzzle in the context of three authoritarian regimes in developing Asia: Indonesia under Suharto's New Order, Malaysia under the Barisan Nasional (BN), and China under the Chinese Communist Party (CCP). The political and economic experiences of these three Asian authoritarian regimes present numerous empirical puzzles. China under the CCP—the same regime that sought to exterminate the capitalist class between the 1940s and 1960s—has experienced dramatic economic growth and political stability since the market reforms began in 1978.[3] The BN in Malaysia, a coalition held together by a shared commitment to capitalism and fear of Communist movements and national disintegration, executed a decades-long policy of radical economic redistribution with relative success, all the while sustaining its monopoly on political

---

[2] This is Barrington Moore's famous statement. See Barrington Moore, *Social Origins of Dictatorship and Democracy: Lord and Peasant in the Making of the Modern World* (Boston: Beacon Press, 1996). As Kellee S. Tsai, *Capitalism without Democracy: The Private Sector in Contemporary China* (Ithaca: Cornell University Press, 2007), 5, points out, this statement is most frequently taken out of context; Moore is characterizing past roles rather than predicting a general role for capitalists.

[3] The 1989 Tiananmen protests can be considered the only time the CCP's monopoly on political control was challenged.

power. Meanwhile Suharto's Indonesia, a regime founded in part on a "beautiful friendship" between Suharto—the "father of development"—and a politically marginal but economically dominant group of Chinese capitalists, survived for over thirty years and did not collapse until following the Asian Financial Crisis in 1997–98, when the beautiful friendship unraveled rapidly with disastrous consequences for all.[4] Despite their different origins and orientations toward the business class, all three regimes have been characterized as facilitating a kind of "crony capitalism," or, in China's case, "crony communism."[5]

Why have regimes supposedly founded on alliances between autocrats and capitalists witnessed dramatic betrayals? Why has the regime with the most punitive history toward business elites outperformed others in both economic growth and political stability? Why did business-state relations in all three regimes come to be seen as "crony," and why do some crony arrangements generate growth and political stability, whereas others generate stagnation or crisis?

The answers to these questions, I argue, are uncovered by examining how different patterns of state-business relations come about and how, in turn, these patterns affect political stability and allocation of economic resources. Specifically, I show how political trust between groups of capitalists and autocrats, established during the regime-formation phase, and the coherence of those regimes' control of financial resources, which changes over time, generate different patterns of state-business relations. In addition to developing a theory on the origins of the patterns of state-business relations, this book offers conceptual development in characterizing state-business relations. I move beyond the blunt characterization of "co-optation" or cronyism to develop two models of relationships between capitalists and authoritarian regimes—mutual alignment and mutual endangerment—and generate hypotheses about their respective political and economic outcomes.

---

[4] The term "beautiful friendship" comes from Liem Sioe Liong, aka Sudono Salim, Suharto's top Chinese crony. Nancy Chng and Richard Borsuk, *Liem Sioe Liong's Salim Group: The Business Pillar of Suharto's Indonesia* (Singapore: Institute of Southeast Asian Studies, 2014), 2.

[5] On China, see Bruce J. Dickson, *Wealth into Power: The Communist Party's Embrace of China's Private Sector* (New York: Cambridge University Press, 2008); Minxin Pei, *China's Crony Capitalism: The Dynamics of Regime Decay* (Cambridge, MA: Harvard University Press, 2016); Andrew Hall Wedeman, *Double Paradox: Rapid Growth and Rising Corruption in China* (Ithaca: Cornell University Press, 2012).

The Limits of "Co-optation" and "Cronyism"

The issue of the power relations between capitalists and states has animated debates among social scientists and public intellectuals for centuries. Social theorists, especially those working in the Marxist tradition, have long argued that the capitalist class controls the state, but they have differed in their articulation of the mechanism by which this has occurred. A classic debate between Ralph Miliband and Nicos Poulantzas in the pages of the *New Left Review* in the 1960s over the means of bourgeois state capture laid the foundation for a more contemporary debate among social scientists about the relative importance of structural and instrumental power. Miliband, like C. Wright Mills, endeavors to show that members of the ruling class come from and share extensive social ties with economic elites, therefore compromising the autonomy of the state apparatus. Poulantzas's critique is that it does not matter who actually participates in governing the state apparatus because the function of the state in a capitalist system is to facilitate capital accumulation regardless of the articulation of interests.[6] Democratic and authoritarian regimes alike are alleged to be constrained by this "structural power" of capital, forced to capitulate to the interests of capital-holders or face the consequences of the withholding or withdrawal of investment.[7] With some exceptions, the focus on structural power has waned, in part because hypotheses about structural power are difficult to falsify and conceptions of power are overly blunt and predominantly unidirectional.[8]

An older literature on the instrumental or network power of business and capitalists has found a modern iteration in research on oligarchs. Mancur Olson predicted that capitalists would collude with political allies to form "distributional coalitions" to divert resources toward themselves and away

[6] Nicos Poulantzas, "The Problem of the Capitalist State," *New Left Review*, no. 158 (1969): 67; Ernesto Laclau, "The Specificity of the Political: The Poulantzas-Miliband Debate," *Economy and Society* 4, no. 1 (1975): 87–110, https://doi.org/10.1080/03085147500000002; Ralph Miliband, *The State in Capitalist Society* (New York: Basic Books, 1969).

[7] For a recent review, see Pepper D. Culpepper, "Structural Power and Political Science in the Post-crisis Era," *Business and Politics* 17, no. 3 (2015): 391–409, https://doi.org/10.1515/bap-2015-0031; Charles Lindblom, *Politics and Markets: The World's Political Economic System* (New York: Basic Books, 1977); Adam Przeworski and Michael Wallerstein, "Structural Dependence of the State on Capital," *American Political Science Review* 82, no. 1 (1988): 11–29, https://doi.org/10.2307/1958056.

[8] Culpepper, "Structural Power." See also David Vogel, "Political Science and the Study of Corporate Power: A Dissent from the New Conventional Wisdom," *British Journal of Political Science* 17, no. 4 (1987): 385–408.

from more socially beneficial uses, a phenomenon Jagdish Bhagwati calls "directly unproductive profit-seeking" and others may refer to more casually as "cronyism."[9] Indeed, social science research has substantiated the idea that political connections benefit firms. In contexts from Egypt to Indonesia and China, firms with identifiable political connections appear to be rewarded with greater profitability or greater access to resources when their friends are in power and they are punished by markets when their political connections are jeopardized.[10]

With a few exceptions, it is this particularistic power of capitalist elites, rather than the generalized structural power of capital, that has been the focus of political economy scholars in their attempts to explain why some authoritarian regimes in the developing world manage to generate growth and investment as well as variation in regime stability and longevity.[11] Unsurprisingly, a greater concentration of wealth in the hands of a small elite is argued to have a deleterious effect on both economic growth and political freedom and equality. A rich literature in economics has demonstrated that what is described broadly as "cronyism"—corrupt and personalistic connections to political leaders—diverts important resources and decreases efficiency in ways that reduce overall economic growth.[12] For their part, political scientists have examined the role of economic inequality and wealth concentration on political equality in democracies, arguing, as Jeffrey Winters has in the case of contemporary democratic Indonesia,

---

[9] Mancur Olson, *The Rise and Decline of Nations: Economic Growth, Stagflation, and Social Rigidities* (New Haven: Yale University Press, 1982); Jagdish N. Bhagwati, "Directly Unproductive, Profit-Seeking (DUP) Activities," *Journal of Political Economy* 90, no. 5 (1982): 988–1002.

[10] Ishac Diwan and Marc Schiffbaue, "Private Banking and Crony Capitalism in Egypt," *Business and Politics* 20, no. 3 (2018): 1–20, https://doi.org/10.1017/bap.2018.1; Raymond Fisman, "Estimating the Value of Political Connections," *American Economic Review* 91, no. 4 (2001): 1095–102, https://doi.org/10.1257/aer.91.4.1095; Rory Truex, "The Returns to Office in a 'Rubber Stamp' Parliament," *American Political Science Review* 108, no. 2 (2014): 235–51; Yue Hou, *The Private Sector in Public Office: Selective Property Rights in China* (New York: Cambridge University Press, 2019); Simon Johnson and Todd Mitton, "Cronyism and Capital Controls: Evidence from Malaysia," *Journal of Financial Economics* 67, no. 2 (2003): 351–82, https://doi.org/10.1016/S0304-405X(02)00255-6.

[11] For one such exception, see Jeffrey A. Winters, "Power and the Control of Capital," *World Politics* 46, no. 3 (1994): 419–52 and Jeffrey A. Winters, *Power in Motion: Capital Mobility and the Indonesian State* (Ithaca: Cornell University Press, 1996).

[12] Anne O. Krueger, "The Political Economy of the Rent-Seeking Society," *American Economic Review* 64, no. 3 (1974): 291–303, https://doi.org/10.2307/1808883; Raymond Fisman and Edward Miguel, *Economic Gangsters: Corruption, Violence, and the Poverty of Nations* (Princeton, NJ: Princeton University Press, 2008); Ishac Diwan, Adeel Malik, and Izak Atiyas, eds., *Crony Capitalism in the Middle East: Business and Politics from Liberalization to the Arab Spring* (New York: Oxford University Press, 2019). For a constructivist take, see Leonard Seabrooke, *The Social Sources of Financial Power: Domestic Legitimacy and International Financial Orders* (Ithaca: Cornell University Press, 2006).

that "extreme material inequality necessarily produces extreme political inequality."[13]

Ironically, while the larger literature on regimes in general has emphasized business power and constraints on the state, research on the political role of capitalists in contemporary authoritarian regimes has emphasized their apparent political docility. Eva Bellin argues that, in contrast to the capitalist classes in nondeveloped democracies who are said to have facilitated democratization and limits on state power historically, contemporary capitalist classes owe their success to states, rendering them dependent on authoritarian leviathans for their access to profits and their safety from demands from below.[14] A more recent fixation with "state capitalism," in which "the state acts as the dominant player and uses markets primarily for political gain,"[15] implies the impotence of the (nonstate) business class. Under state capitalism, private capitalists are envisaged as being "co-opted" by the state and therefore unable to pursue their own interests when they contravene those of the state.[16] In both cases, the unique power accrued by the state in "late development" renders contemporary business classes politically submissive relative to their historical counterparts.

The dual emphasis on "cronyism" and "co-optation" has created an image of business actors in authoritarian regimes as lackeys of their political counterparts, engaged in a project of mutual enrichment and invested in the perpetuation of political control by a small elite with whom they are connected. The assumption is that when political elites fall—and most inevitably do, like Mubarak in Egypt or Suharto in Indonesia or Marcos in the Philippines or the junta in Argentina—their cronies go down with them, like guilty bystanders in a process of regime change. We describe business elites as having "friends in high places" and assume mutual trust underlies their relationship of mutual enrichment. We think we know "cronyism" and "co-optation" when we see it; elites are cozy and engaged in mutual enrichment, and therefore business elites are secure and invested in the regime's perpetuation.

[13] Jeffrey A. Winters, "Oligarchy and Democracy in Indonesia," *Indonesia*, no. 96 (2013): 12. See also Jacob S. Hacker and Paul Pierson, *Winner-Take-All Politics: How Washington Made the Rich Richer—and Turned Its Back on the Middle Class* (New York: Simon & Schuster, 2010).

[14] Bellin, "Contingent Democrats."

[15] Ian Bremmer, *The End of the Free Market: Who Wins the War between States and Corporations?* (New York: Portfolio, 2010), 5.

[16] For a critique, see Margaret Pearson, Meg Rithmire, and Kellee Tsai, "Party-State Capitalism in China," *Current History* 120, no. 827 (2021): 207–13.

The problem with "cronyism" and "co-optation," however, is that as simplistic portrayals of political relationships, they lack sufficient nuance and therefore explain almost none of the drama that accompanies elite relationships between business and the state. Almost any wealthy elite in an authoritarian regime who is not actively fighting political elites can be called a "crony," but their identities and behaviors vary in important ways. For example, in the face of a crisis, some cronies rapidly betray their political patrons, while others shore up the regime's power.[17] Some regimes seem to have cronies intimately tied to specific political patrons, while other crony systems seem to have a more centripetal character. Mikhail Khodorkovsky, the former oligarch owner of Yukos Oil Company, was a crony of the Kremlin until he was its enemy, finding himself imprisoned in Siberia and his assets suddenly the property of the Russian state. Guo Wengui, a billionaire who obtained his wealth through close connections with the CCP, found himself in 2017 in a New York City penthouse apartment, decrying the corruption and theft of those at the apex of the CCP, that is, the very political patrons who helped him get rich. Yet for every Guo Wengui and Khodorkovsky, there are other "cronies" who stay rich and quiet and still others who find themselves sidelined or worse before they can attract international attention for renouncing their patrons.

If cronyism is too vague a characterization to explain variation in state-business relations across and within cases, "co-optation" is both vague and fundamentally misguided. To say that the business class is co-opted implies that their interests have been sufficiently served by the regime so as to extinguish their power to constrain it. The incorporation of business interests is not a one-off exchange of power; rather, business interests are continuously articulated in ways that shape the regime's power. Moreover, that business elites are temporarily satisfied with their prospects does not mean that they plan to always be so; in fact, most economic elites hedge their reliance on political elites, for example by hiding or expatriating assets, retaining damning information about politicians (*kompromat*), or simultaneously investing in relationships with sidelined elites. These iterated activities are dynamic, shaping and reshaping the elite power relations.

The difficulty with co-optation as a concept is that it reveals little about either the causes or the consequences of state-business political

---

[17] Stephan Haggard and Robert R. Kaufman, *The Political Economy of Democratic Transitions* (Princeton, NJ: Princeton University Press, 1995), 30, call this "authoritarian withdrawal."

arrangements. Noting that capitalists and autocrats seem to share common interests tells us nothing about how power relations work, what each side gains from cooperation, and the conditions under which each side's support for the other may disappear. Last, cronyism and co-optation are universal in authoritarian regimes with market activities, yet some regimes produce rapid and sustained economic growth and others produce far less desirable outcomes.

Capitalists and regimes are always "reciprocally interdependent," with political and business elites relying on one another for success or even survival.[18] But not all arrangements of interdependence produce similar outcomes. Some facilitate widely shared economic growth and prosperity, but others generate crisis or stagnation. And some elite relationships provide ballast for regime survival, while others feature elite betrayal or seem to presage regime decay. A better accounting of state-business relations would explain the origins and nature of state-business relations and what different patterns of relationships bode for important outcomes like regime stability and economic development.[19] This book aims to do exactly that.

The Argument

Based on a cross-national comparison of the Malaysian, Chinese, and Indonesia cases, I elaborate on two basic models of state-business relations in authoritarian regimes (see Table 1.1). The first, *mutual alignment*, obtains when an authoritarian regime cooperates with business, formally or informally, to pursue regime goals and to facilitate profits and growth for cooperating businesses. This pattern of relations is, to borrow terminology from biology, mutualistic: economic and political elites both benefit, but society also benefits because resources are channeled into (at least mostly) productive uses. The second, *mutual endangerment*, obtains when economic and political elites are entwined in corrupt dealings and invested in perpetuating each other's dominance primarily because any loss of power on one side would bring about the demise of the other. In this arrangement,

---

[18] Culpepper, "Structural Power."

[19] Rawi Abdelal, in "The Multinational Firm and Geopolitics: Europe, Russian Energy, and Power," *Business and Politics* 17, no. 3 (2015): 553–76, writes, "What is clear from decades of research . . . is that to ask the question of whether the state or the firm is the master of the other is to do irreparable damage to the nuances of their relations" (559).

Table 1.1 Patterns of State-Business Relations

	Characterization	Relationship with Society	Pathology	Observable Outcomes
Mutual Alignment	Regime and business cooperate to pursue regime goals and to facilitate profits for cooperative businesses	Mutualistic: society is recipient of some economic development	"Developmental paradox" of the authoritarian state	A period of strong growth, followed by: - Low private investment rates - Corruption - Inefficiencies of favored firms - Failed state attempts to shift development policy
Mutual Endangerment	Economic and political elites are entwined in corrupt dealings and face mutual demise	Competitive: elites divert and consume social resources	Inherent political and financial instability	- Capital flight / asset expatriation - Weaponized information - Looting

the relationship has deleterious effects on society; economic elites pressure political elites to channel resources and rents their way under the threat of mutual exposure, and political elites extort capitalists. Economic and social resources are allocated according to a short-term logic of political survival rather than toward long-term and socially beneficial investments. Moreover, both political and economic elites adopt strategies to manage the threat of mutual demise by hiding assets, sometimes by investing capital productively outside of the country and sometimes by squirreling away capital and assets via expatriation and theft. In both cases, domestic development suffers through capital flight and resource misallocation.[20]

Neither model of state-business relations is static. Rather, each generates destabilizing dynamics. In the case of mutual alignment, governments craft policies and institutions to benefit capitalists or at least certain capitalists, thereby nurturing a class of economic elites who develop the social,

---

[20] This is quite different from David Kang's elaboration of "mutual hostage" relations between a concentrated political elite and a concentrated economic elite that explains impressive economic growth alongside "money politics" in Korea. While I do not at all disagree with Kang's characterization of the Korean and Philippine cases, the theory focuses only on the social organization of political and economic elites and therefore cannot explain change over time within regimes. David C. Kang, *Crony Capitalism: Corruption and Development in South Korea and the Philippines* (New York: Cambridge University Press, 2002).

economic, and political power to make demands of the regime itself. This is what Eva Bellin describes as the "developmental paradox" of the authoritarian state: "The very success of the state's strategy leads to the demise of the state's capacity to dictate policy unilaterally."[21] Economic elites pursue rents through their connections with political elites, impeding efforts at economic reforms, raising barriers to entry for new firms, and dampening economic dynamism, all of which create political economies that appear "stuck" in a certain stage of development or mode of economic growth.

Mutual endangerment appears to be a stable mode of state-business interaction until one party fears the defection or loss of power of the other. Defection by either party, for example by behaving in a reckless way or by revealing knowledge of corruption, imperils both parties. In practice, then, both parties have incentives to defect or to hedge against defection, and a simple fear of defection can set off a dynamic unraveling of the relationship.[22] As we shall see, these dynamics are relatively easy to observe; if a specific political elite appears to be in danger, other elites tied to him will rapidly divest from him or betray him, thus furthering his demise. The introduction of political uncertainty, through crisis, anticorruption efforts, or any exogenous shock (e.g., a health crisis of a leader), is enough to unravel relationships that took decades to build.[23] Although economic elites rarely, if ever, actively pursue regime change, they act in ways that may unintentionally facilitate it, for example through capital flight and induced economic crises or by revealing damaging information about political elites. When state-business relations resemble mutual endangerment, economic elites and political elites have incentives to change the balance of power rather than to maintain it, lending inherent instability to the relationship.

Mutual endangerment manifests in three observable outcomes: the presence of capital flight or asset expatriation, the weaponization of information (revealing damaging information about other elites), and financial instability generated by malfeasance, fraud, and looting. All of these activities can be called "corruption," but they are specific activities that share an underlying political logic of short time horizons and a lack of trust in political elites. Also, each of these forms of corruption worsens the relations

---

[21] Bellin, *Stalled Democracy*, 4.

[22] Game theorists will recognize a simple prisoner's dilemma.

[23] In a seminal paper, Fisman finds that reports of Suharto's failing health prompted market responses for firms connected to him, meaning market participants also observed that political uncertainty about an elite jeopardizes his clients. Fisman, "Estimating the Value."

between political and business elites, exacerbating the financial crises and sometimes producing political instability. Capital flight, or the systematic expatriation of assets in pursuit of safety, is evidence of business elites' distrust of the political authorities, but it can also precipitate or hasten a financial crisis. The weaponization of information has clear and deleterious political and financial effects. While it is potentially stable if elites can hold one another hostage with mutually incriminating information, revelations trigger legitimacy crises for individual politicians and sometimes factions or entire ruling parties. "Mutual hostage" situations can unravel rapidly when parties perceive uncertainty or threat and defect, and the instrumental gains for one party for revealing corruption accumulate into generalized legitimacy crises. Finally, financial malfeasance and fraud, which I group under the term "looting," have a particular economic and political logic. To be sure, fraud happens in all sorts of places, but it becomes pervasive when economic actors have incentives to maximize current extractive value rather than to maximize the economic value of the firm.[24] Economists have focused on the macroeconomic or industry conditions that generate these incentives (weak regulation and moral hazard in the form of expected government bailouts), but I show that political conditions matter as well. Specifically, distrust of government and expectations of expropriation have the same effects as expectations of bailout.

These models are ideal types, and neither model is meant to characterize all state-business relations in a country. It is possible that some sectors of the economy, or some subnational geographies, appear to be in mutual alignment, while others look more like mutual endangerment. And, as we will see in the chapters that present the cases, state-business elites are aligned at some times and mutually endangered at others. The value in specifying these patterns is that they are predictive of the pathologies that develop from each model. I find that much of the drama of state-business relations—visible in anticorruption campaigns, reorganizations of the institutions that govern economies, policies toward globalization, and even ethnic riots—represents efforts by authoritarian regimes to address one pathology or the other. That is, authoritarian leaders attempt to free themselves from the grip of demanding capitalists and attain more autonomy, or they attempt to change

---

[24] George Akerlof and Paul M. Romer, "Looting: The Economic Underworld of Bankruptcy for Profit," *Brookings Papers on Economic Activity*, no. 2 (1993): 2. Here I focus on looting of nonstate firms by their own principals, not looting of the state.

the balance of power between economic elites and their own political elites when they fear that economic elites have gained the upper hand. The theory advanced in the book attempts to identify and account for the dynamics of state-business relations.

The central question, then, is, what accounts for the development of mutual alignment or mutual endangerment? I advance an argument that focuses on *political trust* and the *coherence of financial control* among the political elite.

Trust and Distrust between Political and Business Elites

Whether political and business elites trust one another affects their behavior, especially their reasons for cultivating closeness with one another. The concept of trust is foundational in social science, yet common definitions are elusive. I define trust as mutual expectations that parties in a relationship will cooperate rather than exploit each other's vulnerability.[25] Essentially, trust is an expectation of reciprocity. Vulnerability plays a key role in trust relations; if neither side is vulnerable, trust is not necessary for exchanges.[26] Vulnerability is inherent to the status of capitalists in authoritarian regimes. By definition, in almost all authoritarian states, independent institutions are insufficient to guarantee property rights and personal safety from the power of the state. Though vulnerability is pervasive in authoritarian regimes, its logic and magnitude nonetheless vary based on a regime's political economy, ideology, social relations, institutions, and state capacity. Vulnerability varies, and so does trust. Some vulnerable business elites enjoy consistent expectations of reciprocity with regime political elites, while others fear that political elites will exploit their vulnerability. Relations of trust are established across time, through iterative experiences of reciprocity or defection, and they frequently vary in issue area.[27]

---

[25] This definition draws on Charles Sabel's classic one, "mutual confidence that no party to an exchange will exploit the other's vulnerability." Charles F. Sabel, "Studied Trust: Building New Forms of Cooperation in a Volatile Economy," *Human Relations* 46, no. 9 (1993): 1133–70. This is a definition similar to those used in international relations, especially Andrew H. Kydd, *Trust and Mistrust in International Relations* (Princeton, NJ: Princeton University Press, 2018), 5–7. Many uses of trust in comparative politics focus on trust in institutions or generalized social trust; this book, however, focuses on trust between specific groups, or "expectation of another party in a transaction." Gregory A. Bigley and Jone L. Pearce, "Straining for Shared Meaning in Organizational Science: Problems of Trust and Distrust," *Academy of Management Review* 23, no. 3 (1998): 406.

[26] Bigley and Pearce, "Straining for Shared Meaning."

[27] Hardin, for example, discusses trust as "A trusts B to do X." Russell Hardin, *Trust and Trustworthiness* (New York: Russell Sage Foundation, 2002).

To understand trust and distrust between political and business elites, I focus on the phase of "regime formation," the time when "political actors struggle to define the boundaries and bases of the national political community."[28] For all three cases in this book, these political struggles involved violence, contestation over national inclusion, debates about whether and how to engage with the international community, and competing narratives about how to organize society for overall well-being. For each, the regime-formation phase concluded with definitive arrangements regarding whether capitalists—and which kinds of capitalists—would be included in or excluded from the ruling regimes.[29] That capitalists are politically marginal, that is, excluded from holding power, does not mean their interests cannot be incorporated into a regime's institutions or policies, but the relationship between the state and business will be marked by a mistrust that affects the adaptation strategies of each side. We may also find that, within the same country, some capitalists enjoy an included political status while the status of others may be marginal.

Trust affects how capitalists channel their demands and their expectations about the future. Marginal capitalists cannot guarantee that the regime will serve their interests. They lack formal channels by which to pursue their self-interest, such as advocating certain policies or seeking favorable treatment. They nonetheless do have access to the regime, but only through private and informal channels, generally out of the public eye via particularistic and personal relationships with political elites. Furthermore, marginal economic elites live with existential political threat; not only are they not able to guarantee that their interests will be included in the regime's policies, they also have no means to guarantee the safety of their property and, more importantly, their own freedom and security as well as that of their families. They thus depend on informal and personal relationships as the only likely path to protection.

In exchange for protection, economic elites typically offer myriad forms of kickbacks to political elites: cash or other goods, jobs or board member positions for associates and family members, and so forth. When business elites are politically marginal, these relationships are especially illegitimate

---

[28] Jason Brownlee, *Authoritarianism in an Age of Democratization* (New York: Cambridge University Press, 2007), 33.

[29] We might also think of political inclusion as whether or not economic elites are included in what Slater calls "protection pacts." As Slater observes, economic elites are likely to submit to state power when they fear the alternative to the regime (e.g., national disintegration, Communist revolution) is worse. Dan Slater, *Ordering Power: Contentious Politics and Authoritarian Leviathans in Southeast Asia* (New York: Cambridge University Press, 2010).

and, frequently, illegal. Thus a degree of secrecy characterizes state-business relations, wherein politicians protect business interests and economic elites cultivate ties with politicians behind closed doors and beyond public view. Secrecy, as economists have recognized, has distortionary effects on political economies: political elites design institutions and policies to maximize their potential for capturing value, and elite circles are closed to newcomers, stymieing change and innovation.[30] Secrecy also has an important political effect because it imbues information with political value; both political elites and economic elites hold information about corrupt dealings that may potentially be used to discredit or endanger others.[31] In other words, when capitalists are politically illegitimate, relationships with them automatically become *kompromat*.

Distrust also leads capitalists to be fearful of the future, a fact that impacts their investment decisions. Economic elites who, based on their past experiences, have reason to fear insecurity of person and property because of defection or attack will allocate resources to guard against this threat. Most often, they seek to hide or expatriate assets beyond the reach of untrustworthy autocrats. This has the effect of limiting resources available for domestic growth, and it also provides economic elites with a foothold outside the country, enabling them to rapidly turn against the regime when it is endangered. Other times, especially when their expectations of political instability or expropriation are acute, they turn to looting and financial fraud.

By contrast, capitalists with high political status can pursue their interests more or less openly, interacting with politicians and institutions in the public eye. The relative lack of secrecy removes from state-business relations the political use, or weaponization, of information. This does not mean that their arrangements are necessarily noncorrupt or good for society, but that state-business relations are not automatically illicit and economic elites are not forced to depend only on private relationships for protection. As a result, political elites have fewer opportunities to extort economic elites and economic

---

[30] Andrei Schleifer and Robert W. Vishny, "Corruption," *Quarterly Journal of Economics* 108, no. 3 (1993): 599–617.

[31] Lisa Blaydes, in *Elections and Distributive Politics in Mubarak's Egypt* (New York: Cambridge University Press, 2010), 10–11, argues that this dynamic was at work in Mubarak's Egypt: "By investing members of the rent-seeking elite in corrupt or, at the very least, below-board economic activity, members of this class become vulnerable to charges of economic crimes either under the current regime or under some future democratic or authoritarian government." In Egypt's case, Blaydes argues, parliamentary immunity induced rent-seeking elites to run for office, and these legislative links between business elites and the regime "bound" the parties to one another. I find that these relations develop well outside the context of authoritarian elections.

elites have fewer incentives to channel private benefits to political patrons. Business elites who trust political elites do not face an existential threat from the regime, and instead they sometimes have more to fear from regime collapse or democratization.[32] They are therefore less likely to invest in complex asset-hiding and expatriation strategies.

Moreover, trust between states and the business class tends to generate beneficial outcomes for society at large. As Ben Ross-Schneider and Silvia Maxfield synthesize in a review of the literature: "Trust increases the voluntary exchange of information, makes reciprocity more likely even without active monitoring and disciplining, and generally reduces uncertainty and increases credibility on all sides."[33] To be sure, trust between business and government is complex; in reality, trust is not something that either exists in full or is absent, but rather runs a spectrum and manifests differently in different aspects of the state-business relationship.[34] It is also a practice, as reciprocity or betrayal are repeated over time, of allowing relationships to accumulate trust or exacerbate distrust. My purpose here is not to be comprehensive in theorizing about trust but rather to highlight two possibilities in authoritarian regimes in which trust between state and business is either destroyed upon the regime's establishment or is well developed because of conditions of mutual reliance and regime inclusion.

Authoritarian Financial Systems

The phrase "Trust is good, but control is better," often attributed to V. I. Lenin, reflects a basic feature of interactions without trust: if parties do not trust one another to reciprocate and protect one another, some mechanisms

---

[32] Slater, *Ordering Power*, argues that economic elites opt to submit to an autocratic regime in a "protection pact" because they fear the alternative—democracy or national disintegration—much more. The circumstances that lead business elites to join a ruling authoritarian coalition in the first place cause them to fear its collapse.

[33] Ben Ross-Schneider and Sylvia Maxfield, "Business, the State, and Economic Performance in Developing Countries, " in Ben Ross-Schneider and Sylvia Maxfield, eds., *Business and the State in Developing Countries* (Ithaca: Cornell University Press, 1997), 14. See also Richard F. Doner, *Driving a Bargain: Automobile Industrialization and Japanese Firms in Southeast Asia* (Berkeley: University of California Press, 1991).

[34] For example, firms may fully trust the political elites to protect their property rights, but they may not trust them enough to share information about issues of business performance—say, labor conflicts or environmental regulations—because they do not trust that political elites will not use the information against them for political purposes. Again, see Doner, *Driving a Bargain*. In this book, trust in political elites is really about protection of property and self.

of discipline or monitoring—control—are required for the parties to work together. Most authoritarian regimes have tried to discipline business elites through state control over the financial system, the most important source of resources for business elites. I find that trust, or distrust, interacts with varying levels of control over the financial system to establish different patterns of state-business relations.

The structure of the financial system in any country affects the incentives and risks facing firms and the potential for government intervention in the national economy. A large literature in political economy examines the role of financial systems—essentially, the set of formal and informal institutions that govern the allocation of capital—in "late development," adjustment following economic crisis, and the ability of firms to innovate and engage in global supply chains.[35] The vast majority of this literature looks at the structure of financial systems in advanced industrial democracies or in "developmental states," yet the role of financial systems in structuring relationships between economic and political elites in authoritarian regimes is undertheorized.[36]

Financial systems in any regime are the main site of interaction between business and the state, and in authoritarian regimes financial systems are the main site of the struggle for power between economic and political elites. This perspective does not, of course, deny the importance of other sites of interaction. The control of land, as we shall see in the case of China, is another important site, and the dispensation of licenses and monopolies, especially relevant in Indonesia and Malaysia, may also define the terms of state-business relations. The value of examining financial systems is that they are universally important across political economies of different institutional structures, geography, or stage of development, and therefore they constitute an appropriate site of comparative inquiry for social scientists.

---

[35] Alexander Gerschenkron, *Economic Backwardness in Historical Perspective: A Book of Essays* (Cambridge, MA: Belknap Press of Harvard University Press, 1962); John Zysman, *Governments, Markets, and Growth: Financial Systems and the Politics of Industrial Change* (Ithaca: Cornell University Press, 1983); Peter A. Hall and David W. Soskice, eds., *Varieties of Capitalism: The Institutional Foundations of Comparative Advantage* (New York: Oxford University Press, 2001); Sylvia Maxfield, *Governing Capital: International Finance and Mexican Politics* (Ithaca: Cornell University Press, 1990); Jonas Nahm, *Collaborative Advantage: Forging Green Industries in the New Global Economy* (New York: Oxford University Press, 2021); Meredith Woo-Cumings, *Race to the Swift: State and Finance in Korean Industrialization* (New York: Columbia University Press, 1991).

[36] A major exception is the work by Jeffrey Winters on Indonesia. See Winters, *Power in Motion*. A large literature looks at the effects of politics on economic outcomes, for example the efficient or inefficient allocation of capital or the level of corruption, but few works examine the impact of financial systems on the longevity or capacity of authoritarian regimes.

Financial systems reflect political bargains, determining who controls the price of capital as well as who is able to obtain it.[37] In authoritarian regimes, control over the financial system therefore offers political elites opportunities to cultivate and empower favored economic actors and deprive disfavored ones, channel investment toward sectors or regions targeted for expansion, and ensure their own (ideally exclusive) access to rents. Authoritarian regimes cannot discipline economic elites without control over the financial sector, yet they face a dilemma. On the one hand, lax political control of the financial sector allows for the rise of economic elites beyond the disciplinary reach of the regime, the kinds of "untamed" oligarchs who can amass sufficient material resources to organize against the state or who can divert resources to subvert economic development goals.[38] On the other hand, an overly strong political hand in the financial sector defies market logic, allocating capital according to political criteria, expanding opportunities for rent-seeking and corruption, and, frequently, enhancing the probability of financial crisis.[39]

Ultimately, all autocrats—in fact, most governments—intervene in financial systems to channel investment and credit toward their preferred targets, be they favored firms and individuals or sectors and geographies. The literature on authoritarian regimes from Angola to Argentina is replete with examples of how autocrats have tapped into financial systems to enrich themselves and their families and to cultivate cronies, many of whom outlast the despotic regimes that created them. The variation lies not in whether the regimes intervene, but, rather, how they intervene and—the real puzzle—the source of discipline in financial systems structured by autocrats. Why are authoritarian financial systems not consistently a source of economic and eventual political instability, characterized by widespread misallocation of resources, predation, and rent-seeking?

---

[37] Zysman, *Governments, Markets, and Growth*. This characterization is based on Elliot Posner, "Sources of Institutional Change: The Supranational Origins of Europe's New Stock Markets," *World Politics* 58, no. 1 (2005): 9, http://dx.doi.org/10.1353/wp.2006.0021.

[38] Winters (among others) conceptualizes oligarchy as the "politics of wealth defense," and differentiates between tamed and wild oligarchs, or "whether the system of rule is powerful enough to control the behavior of oligarchs by imposing costs on their most pathological social behaviors" (36). Jeffrey A. Winters, *Oligarchy* (New York: Cambridge University Press, 2011).

[39] Indeed, a literature in economics has established that greater state control over financial systems, for example through industrial policy or capital controls that enable bank control, translates into more corruption. See Alberto Ades and Rafael Di Tella, "National Champions and Corruption: Some Unpleasant Interventionist Arithmetic," *Economic Journal* 107, no. 443 (1997): 1023–42, https://doi.org/10.1111/1468-0297.00204; Johnson and Mitton, "Cronyism and Capital Controls."

In any financial system in any society, discipline comes from some combination of markets and hierarchy. Markets, ideally, channel financial resources toward efficient uses and appropriately price risk. Yet even in systems in which market forces are given the greatest free hand, for example those with liberalized interest rates, competition among banks, and minority shareholder protections among other features, regulatory systems work to ensure that market participants do not manipulate financial systems to their advantage (e.g., rules against insider trading) and that participants and society at large shoulder appropriate levels of risk (e.g., macroregulation of bank balance sheets).[40] In authoritarian regimes, political elites are almost never willing to tolerate financial systems in which markets reign supreme over politics in allocating resources and pricing risk. Even in the most "capitalist" of authoritarian regimes, as we shall see in Suharto's Indonesia, political elites limit competition and structure financial systems so that they may exercise discretion in the allocation of credit and investment. Rarely, then, do market forces—especially domestic market sources—provide sufficient financial discipline in authoritarian regimes.

Instead, authoritarian financial discipline tends to come from political discipline, power by political elites that enables them to channel financial resources toward desired purposes *as well as* to monitor the recipients of those resources to ensure that risks remain in check and rents accrue to the "right" elites.[41] Financial systems in many authoritarian regimes rarely allocate any resources to economic growth; this is especially true in regimes with no political hierarchy at all, for instance, those helmed by kleptocratic families whose members compete with one another to treat the state's public and private financial systems as their own personal coffers. But when authoritarian

---

[40] David A. Moss, *When All Else Fails: Government as the Ultimate Risk Manager* (Cambridge, MA: Harvard University Press, 2002); Steven Kent Vogel, *Marketcraft: How Governments Make Markets Work* (New York: Oxford University Press, 2018).

[41] This argument echoes that made by Steven Solnick explaining why efforts to modernize and reform the Soviet bureaucracy precipitated breakdown rather than adaptation or evolution. He focuses on the breakdown in hierarchies, drawing on neoinstitutional concepts of principal-agent relations. When the structural characteristics that kept the incentive structures of midlevel and local bureaucrats in line with those above them no longer obtained, the Soviet bureaucracy succumbed to "opportunism from within" as those bureaucrats took advantage of better information and access to assets to pursue their own enrichment, the collective result of which was to subvert the system. The argument I make about financial systems is similar. Financial actors in authoritarian regimes—either firms that access capital or the bureaucrats and regulators who facilitate that access—will act opportunistically unless hierarchical power constrains them from doing so, especially when they are insulated from those market forces that would discipline their behavior. Steven Solnick, *Stealing the State: Control and Collapse in Soviet Institutions* (Cambridge, MA: Harvard University Press, 1998).

financial systems mobilize resources toward productive purposes—as they did in authoritarian "developmental states" and, at times and significantly, in all three countries under study here—they do so because ruling elites have political mechanisms to monitor resource allocations and to manage risk within financial systems.

In terms of the patterns of state-business relations articulated in the previous section, mutual alignment between economic and political elites is possible when economic elites access financial systems to invest and political hierarchies ensure that those investments generate social goods, meaning resources go toward mostly productive purposes and risk levels are appropriate. Mutual endangerment is possible when political control over the financial system breaks down, leaving the financial system vulnerable to predation or collusion between political and economic elites who divert financial resources toward their own personal enrichment and leave society at large to shoulder the risks generated by their activities. In societies in which trust between political and economic elites is endemically low, economic elites have incentives to divert and misallocate financial resources when they have access to them. As I show in the cases of Indonesia and China, this is because the time horizons of distrustful economic elites are short; for historical reasons, they are insecure about their safety and legitimacy over the long term, and therefore they use what they view as possibly temporary access to financial resources as opportunities to divert as many resources as possible and to secure those resources from threat, that is, by expatriating them. To further pursue security, these economic elites also nurture relationships with political elites, investing and implicating them in activities that are mutually enriching but also mutually endangering.

In all three cases, regimes began with political control over the financial sector and liberalized that control over time. They liberalized for similar reasons, namely, to address the pathologies inherent in mutual alignment and constrained by recessions or fiscal crises. They pursued greater private-sector entry and the loosening of state credit control in the financial sector to attempt to catalyze economic growth through greater allocation of resources to private business. Yet liberalization was partial in each case; markets were not permitted to discipline connected political and business elites, and regulatory apparatuses requiring transparency and impartial rule enforcement did not emerge. Liberalization, therefore, typically entails the growth of financial products and tools but without market or rule-of-law discipline, generating incentives to borrow heavily and abuse connections. Financial

Table 1.2 Typology and Cases

		Relations between Political and Business Elites	
Financial Control		Trust	Distrust
	Disciplined	**Mutual alignment:** (Malaysia, through 1998)	**Informal mutual alignment** (China, late 1970s–early 2000s; Indonesia, 1966–83) *or* unbridled state
	Partial liberalization	**Competitive clientelism:** (Malaysia, 1998–2018)	**Mutual endangerment** (China, post early 2000s; Indonesia, 1983–98)

crises (like those in Indonesia and Malaysia in 1997 and in China in 2015) are the result. In the wake of these crises, authoritarian regimes, if they survive, reimpose financial supervision, beginning the cycle anew.

Table 1.2 details how political trust and financial control interact to form patterns of state-business relations. When capitalists and political elites enjoy trust and the regime enjoys coherent control over financial resources, state-business relations follow a pattern of mutual alignment, meaning that policies, institutions, and processes are organized to serve the shared interests of both business and the state. This mutual alignment is similar to collusion in a prisoner's dilemma, with both business and the regime protecting one another's status. Like any relationship of reciprocity and cooperation, this does not mean that each side gets what it wants all the time but rather that parties protect one another's paramount interests; business elites do not threaten the regime, and the regime ensures basic protection of property and life for business elites.

When there is distrust but coherent financial control, the outcome can be either informal mutual alignment, whereby the regime's institutions and policies are informally organized to serve business, or unbridled state predation of business. These are, to be sure, two very different outcomes, but it is easy to see how either one is possible under these conditions. States can use their control of financial resources to organize themselves in ways that facilitate their goals. If the primary goal of the state is economic development, and political elites believe this is best accomplished through the growth of markets—as was the case in reform-era China and early in Suharto's New Order regime—then state-business relations can be organized to serve business, but only informally, that is, through interpersonal connections and outside the realm of the regime's institutional and legal system. If the regime's goals are not to effect overall economic development, however, its control of the financial sector and distrust combine to facilitate activities less desirable for the business class, such as simple enrichment of the ruling clique.[42]

Under partial financial liberalization, business and political elites can collude to exploit an undisciplined financial system. When these parties share trust, the outcome looks like "competitive clientelism," by which elites and their supporters "compete over special access to a limited set of state resources that they can distribute to their clients."[43] When distrust combines with fragmentation of control over financial resources, state-business relations can conform to a pattern of mutual endangerment.

It is worth highlighting several implications of this argument, all of which I offer here to foreshadow the substantive presentation of evidence. First, capitalists can be described as "co-opted," meaning their interests are incorporated into regime policies, whether they enjoy trust with political elites or not. Regardless of the nature of an authoritarian regime, business elites will pursue their interests—profits and safety—through alliances with political elites. Those alliances, or the nature of "co-optation," differ dramatically depending on the level of trust, with important and identifiable consequences for both economic growth and political stability. When political elites cannot guarantee profits for business elites, alliances begin to unravel. In this sense, capitalists cannot be co-opted; they support regimes when their interests are served by doing so, and they remove their support or hedge it when their interests are threatened.[44]

Second, ironically, capitalists can be endowed with more power to destroy those regimes from which they are excluded. When capitalists are

---

[42] Albertus, Fenner, and Slater remind us that "some of the world's most distributive regimes have been authoritarian." Michael Albertus, Sofia Fenner, and Dan Slater, *Coercive Distribution* (New York: Cambridge University Press, 2018). All three regimes under study here were growth oriented, and therefore I do not analyze any case of unbridled state predation.

[43] Ellen Lust-Okar, "Competitive Clientelism in the Middle East," *Journal of Democracy* 20, no. 3 (2009): 121; Lust-Okar focuses on elections in authoritarian regimes as the site of that competition, but elections are only one way in which elites compete for resources; they may also compete through behind-the-scenes factional conflict or public conflict over offices and appointments that does not involve elections. See also Richard F. Doner and Ansil Ramsey, "Competitive Clientelism and Economic Governance: The Case of Thailand," in Sylvia Maxfield and Ben Ross-Schneider, eds., *Business and the State in Developing Countries* (Ithaca: Cornell University Press, 1997), 237–76; Lindsay Whitfield, *Economies after Colonialism: Ghana and the Struggle for Power* (New York: Cambridge University Press, 2018).

[44] This is similar to the argument made in Bellin, "Contingent Democrats."

included in authoritarian regimes' coalitions—or "protection pacts"—it is usually because they fear the alternative to the authoritarian regime's expanded power: "endemic and unmanageable" threats to "their property, privileges, and persons from contentious politics."[45] Simply put, economic elites prefer to collaborate with a predictable power from above rather than to submit themselves to unpredictable demands from below. This is a form of reciprocity. Business elites may prefer a different organization of the economy, but they nonetheless trust political elites to return their cooperation. Precisely when the regime is weak, these included economic elites are most likely to invest in its continuance. The Malaysian case illustrates this logic perfectly: business elites partnered with the ruling coalition to implement decades of punitive policies because they had more to fear from national disintegration or unrestrained mobilization from below. By contrast, distrusting capitalists are less invested in the regime's survival. They may fear the regime as much as or more than they fear the alternative to the regime, and they allocate resources to address the threat that the regime poses. When the regime is weak, they are quick to turn against it, making it even weaker indeed. In the conclusion to this book, and in the chapters on Indonesia and China, I elaborate on this "disruptive" power of business, a form of power that business exercises that can imperil regimes and/or provide an impetus for states to develop new capacities to discipline business.

Third, state-business relations in authoritarian regimes are inherently unstable. Business elites are in more or less perpetual pursuit of advantages vis-à-vis competitors. If it is possible to gain advantage through connections with political elites, business elites will pursue those opportunities. Just as they pursue growth and advantage, economic elites are also concerned with self-preservation in the face of risk. Even though they feel safe in their relationship with political elites today, they anticipate a tomorrow in which such relationships may fail to protect them. In general, I find that capitalists large and small are more politically savvy than the social science literature gives them credit for. The constant maneuvering of economic elites precludes state-business relations from becoming settled or static in authoritarian regimes.[46] The "co-optation" view can misread state-business relationships as stable, which fails to account for change over time and the disintegration

---

[45] Slater, *Ordering Power*, 5.
[46] My dynamic approach is in contrast to explanations of state-business relations that focus on static social or economic conditions, e.g., Kang, *Crony Capitalism*.

of alliances. Viewing capitalists instead as savvy political actors in constant motion accounts for such instability.

Research Strategy and Data

The research strategy here employs a classic comparative historical analysis approach. I aim to provide a causal explanation by analyzing historical sequences and change over time while "engaged in systematic and contextualized comparisons of similar and contrasting cases."[47] The outcome to be explained is different patterns of state-business relations. As is clear from the above discussion, these different patterns of state-business relations affect macroeconomic and political phenomena. While I certainly engage these threads, I do not aim to offer a causal explanation of economic growth or regime stability; my primary goal is to understand the evolution of state-business relations. I also do not advance a general theory of state-business relations, that is, one that can explain patterns of corruption or the management of economic elites in all places in all times. The ideal typical models of state-business relations elucidated above—mutual alignment and mutual endangerment—may well describe patterns of elite interaction beyond the cases at hand. My more modest aim is to explain the historical evolution of these phenomena in three Asian regimes, which themselves comprise nearly two billion people and some of the most dynamic economies in the world.

These regimes have clear differences (see Table 1.3), especially in regime type. Although they are all long-lasting authoritarian regimes, China is a Leninist one-party state, while Suharto's New Order combined personalistic rule with a dominant party (Golkar) and military support, and Malaysia was, until 2018, a competitive authoritarian regime with a dominant party. The differences in power-sharing arrangements at the top are matched by vastly different economic and social structures. Ethnic heterogeneity overlaps with economic stratification to form "master cleavages"[48] in Malaysia and Indonesia; as a result, state-business relations and development efforts in

---

[47] James Mahoney and Dietrich Rueschemeyer, eds., *Comparative Historical Analysis in the Social Sciences* (New York: Cambridge University Press, 2003), 12–13.

[48] On the concept of "master cleavages," see Stathis Kalyvas, "The Ontology of 'Political Violence': Action and Identity in Civil Wars," *Perspectives on Politics* 1, no. 3 (2003): 475–94; Ashutosh Varshney, "Analyzing Collective Violence in Indonesia: An Overview," *Journal of East Asian Studies* 8, no. 3 (2008): 341–59.

Table 1.3 Cases and Outcomes

Case	Dates	Regime Type	Outcome
Indonesia: Suharto's New Order	1965–98	"Triple threat": combining single party, military rule, and personalism, but varying over time	Mixed developmental success; initial collusion between business and the state devolved into regime instability and collapse
Malaysia: Barisan Nasional	1958–2018	Single party / competitive authoritarian	Mixed development success; regime stability
China: Reform Era	1978–2001	Leninist single party	Development success; regime stability
China: Globalization Era	2001–18	Leninist single party	Development mixed (high growth with substantial misallocation); elite disintegration

Source: I draw on the classification of Barbara Geddes, "What Do We Know about Democratization after Twenty Years?," *Annual Review of Political Science* 2 (1999): 115–44, https://doi.org/10.1146/annurev.polisci.2.1.115; the concept of "competitive authoritarianism" comes from Steven Levitsky and Lucan Way, *Competitive Authoritarianism: Hybrid Regimes after the Cold War* (New York: Cambridge University Press, 2010). The New Order was not a stable regime, but rather changed over time as Suharto's relative dependence on foreign capital, domestic capital, resource rents, and global security arrangements fluctuated.

those countries have been intimately connected with questions of national integration and identity. China is certainly not ethnically homogenous, but ethnic politics have not, for the most part, affected state-business relations because of the systematic repression and economic exclusion of ethnic minorities. Colonial experiences, developmental starting points, religious diversity, and resource endowments also differ significantly among the three.

The countries do share important similarities. All three achieved modern nationhood around the same time and under similar conditions: order was established following important national conflict after the end of the Japanese occupation in World War II. The middle to late 1960s brought about mass mobilization, class and/or communal strife, and a traumatic repositioning of the state with regard to the business class. And all three countries—unlike the generation of countries that developed and democratized in the West— have wrestled with the pursuit of economic development and political stability during an era of open economies, with business communities linked to global supply chains and (at least somewhat) open flows of capital across borders. That states and capitalists both had to contend with global forces, and the threat of capital "exit" made the relationship between business and the state considerably more complex, as I will show.[49] Last, and most important for the questions at hand, economic elites in all three regimes became elites during the regimes' tenures, meaning that they all, in the broadest possible sense, owed their status and prosperity to the regime or the conditions created by the regime. Elites vary, of course, in how dependent they are on the state for resources, but none of the regimes in these cases can they be said to have gained wealth independent of the political regime.

The empirical data are, as one might expect with a project spanning sixty years and three countries, eclectic in both source and presentation. Material for the three chapters on China comes from fieldwork conducted between 2006 and 2019. I cite interviews with both economic elites (capitalists in a variety of firms) and government officials. Appendix, Tables D.3–D.4 details these interview subjects; for obvious reasons, these data are presented anonymously. I also rely extensively on Chinese-language written materials, including media reports, government white papers, yearbooks, gazetteers, and "gray literature" produced by think tanks, industry associations, and other nongovernmental groups. Chapters 5, 6, and 7 on China make use of original data on corporate ownership and corporate finance in China as well as data on the business connections of officials who were prosecuted during the anti-corruption campaign that began in 2013.

The material for the sections on Malaysia comes from interviews conducted with economic and political elites between 2016 and 2018. Details on these interviews are also included in Table D.2. To understand the role of Malaysian capitalists during the regime-formation phase, I draw on material from Chinese business associations, lineage organizations, and native place associations. I accessed most of these materials at the excellent Southeast Asia library collection at the National University of Singapore (NUS), which specializes in materials on overseas Chinese communities. I also relied on the NUS Singapore-Malaysia Collection for government documents related to economic planning and bureaucratic organization as well as for extensive materials on party organizations. The analysis for Malaysia (like that for China) extends to the present, including the surprising election of

---

[49] Winters, "Power and Control"; Woo-Cumings, *Race to the Swift*; Jeffry A. Frieden, *Debt, Development, and Democracy: Modern Political Economy and Latin America, 1965–1985* (Princeton, NJ: Princeton University Press, 2018).

2018, which saw Mohamed Mahathir, Malaysia's long-serving prime minister, dramatically return to power by ousting the United Malay National Organization (UMNO), the party that he had led for decades, and unseating Najib Razak, his own designated protégé.

My argument for the Indonesian case accords with much of the scholarship on the political economy of the New Order, though I draw on new sources available in the twenty years since Suharto's fall. These include newly published memoirs of business and some political elites as well as some Chinese-language resources typically overlooked by Indonesia specialists. Several trips to Jakarta and Sumatra between 2015 and 2018 afforded me opportunities to speak with prominent business elites. Some of these interviews are publicly available through Harvard Business School's Creating Emerging Markets project, and they are cited as such. Appendix, Table D.1 details both these interviews and private interviews.

Layout of the Book

This book is organized to show trust and financial control at work in creating patterns of state-business relations in Malaysia, Indonesia, and China. The first empirical chapter, Chapter 2, explores the foundations of political trust by looking at the historical relationship between capitalists and authoritarian regimes in Asia during the periods of regime formation. The three countries in this study exhibit important variation in political trust between capitalists and regimes, both across and within countries. The chapter explores critical antecedents to relationships between capitalists and the state—colonial arrangements, the Japanese occupation, and wars for independence—and the early decades of state-building and mass violence (the 1950s–1960s) to explain varying outcomes in political vulnerability and trust.

Capitalists in both Indonesia and China experienced political vulnerability, although for quite different reasons (Table 1.4). In China, the CCP came to power with a mandate to eradicate the capitalist class. It carried out this mission through land reform in rural China between the 1930s and the mid-1950s, through the (relatively peaceful) nationalization of urban business in the mid-1950s, and through the chaotic violence and persecution of capitalists—whether they were real capitalists, guilty by association, or only supposed—during the Cultural Revolution in the late 1960s. Capitalists, even those of the present generation, have historical memories of fear and

Table 1.4 Trust and Distrust in Malaysia, Indonesia, and China

	Political Trust	Mode of Incorporation for Vulnerable Capitalists	Historical Experience
Malaysia Chinese elites Chinese family/small- and medium-sized enterprises (SMEs)	Trust Distrust	Formal political infiltration of business	Emergency (1948–58) saw violence against owners of capital 1969 riots threatened national unity/ capitalists
Indonesia	Distrust	Fear and mutual endangerment	1965 mass murder Suharto periodically stoked riots to remind Chinese of their vulnerability
China	Distrust	"Vulnerable neglect" in the 1980s and 1990s (CCP ignores the private sector, but does not formally legitimize it and therefore retains the right to persecute). Formal legitimacy of capitalists in 2000, informal incorporation.	Revolution, postrevolution state-building, and Cultural Revolution brought extreme violence to real and suspected capitalists

a learned distrust of the CCP, and this distrust has shaped their practices and political orientations. In 2001, Jiang Zemin invited capitalists to join the CCP, something they had been doing informally since the late 1970s. Even though the formal political status of capitalists changed, a culture of marginality, self-reliance, distrust, and security through informal relationships had grown to characterize the community of private-sector capitalists. To be sure, Chinese capitalists have pursued power, at times fighting their way to the apex of the regime, but they have done so with a sense of vulnerability that affects the way they relate to political elites and the economic strategies they adopt.

In Indonesia, the preponderance of economic elites is ethnically Chinese, a demographic minority whose status in the Indonesian state and society has been uncertain and precarious over time. Suharto's New Order regime was established in 1965–66 on the heels of widespread state-sponsored violence against supposed Communists as well as against ethnic Chinese, whether or not these identities overlapped. The ethnic Chinese community lived with a distrustful dependence on the Suharto regime; Suharto cultivated Chinese economic elites because of their political vulnerability, and he periodically stoked violence to remind them of their reliance on him for protection. The endemic vulnerability of the ethnic Chinese capitalist class and its learned fear of the state shaped its economic and political interactions with the regime.

Malaysian elite Chinese capitalists, by contrast, developed trust—relations of reciprocity—with the regime's political elites. At the time of regime formation in the mid-1950s and again following ethnic riots in 1969, capitalist elites pursued inclusion in the regime's ruling coalition, even if it meant submitting to Malay political dominance and economic policies that would be transparently punitive to Chinese (and non-Malay) communities. As one scholar puts it, Chinese elites were part of a "coercive consociationalism," agreeing to accommodation on "essentially Malay terms."[50] This trust between economic elites and the Malaysian regime is a result of Malaysia's particular post–World War II and independence trajectory, marked by communal conflict, a Communist insurgency and counterinsurgency from 1948–58, and a resurgence of ethnic and class conflict in the late 1960s. I argue that class interests in Malaysia have been paramount; economic elites were far more fearful of uncontrolled demands from below than predictable (and malleable) demands from above. The experience of the Communist insurgency, in particular, which was dominated by ethnic Chinese, drove an indelible wedge into Malaysia's Chinese community, pitting urban and financial capitalists and large landholding capitalists against rural mining and plantation workers who would eventually become the urban bourgeoisie.

The historical foundations for political trust between elites in the three regimes having been laid, Chapters 3 through 7 present narratives about state-business relations as they evolved in Malaysia, Indonesia, and China. Table 1.5 summarizes how the ideal types developed in this chapter fit the cases.

In Chapter 3, I argue that the relationship between the Suharto regime and Chinese capitalist elites (*cukong* or *konglomerat* [conglomerate]) began with a brief phase of mutual alignment that rapidly deteriorated into mutual endangerment. A central theoretical puzzle in scholarship on the New Order is

[50] Diane K. Mauzy, "Malaysia: Malay Political Hegemony and 'Coercive Consociationalism,'" in John McGarry and Brendan O'Leary, eds., *The Politics of Ethnic Conflict Regulation* (London: Routledge, 1993), 110–11.

Table 1.5 The Cases and the Argument

		Political Trust	
Financial Control		*Trust*	*Distrust*
	Disciplined	Malaysia (through 1998)	China I
	Liberalization	Malaysia (1998–2018)	Indonesia China II

whether the state controlled capital or capital controlled the state.[51] Clearly, each held significant power over the other: Suharto needed capitalists to invest and grow the economy, and capitalists, especially Chinese capitalists, needed Suharto for protection. The question is not who had the upper hand but what was the nature of the exchange between business and the regime and what were the limits of mutual dependence for each side. I argue that generalized mistrust between Chinese capitalists and Indonesian authorities pervaded their relations after independence. Chinese Indonesians, for demographic, political, and historical reasons, never transcended "pariah" or outsider status, making it impossible for them to pursue safety through official political forums. Nonetheless, as I detail in Chapter 2, the war for independence from the Dutch afforded several Chinese elites opportunities for close alliance with Indonesian political elites, and this pattern of particularistic political alliances between economic and political elites defined the New Order. Pervasive distrust predisposed state-business relations toward mutual endangerment, but early New Order macroeconomic policies, which preserved capital openness and an independent financial sector, created conditions for mutual alignment by allowing capitalists a degree of distance from the state in exchange for investing domestically.[52] Over time, however, the regime's approach to economic control changed dramatically.

---

[51] Some scholarship (Thomas B. Pepinsky, *Economic Crises and the Breakdown of Authoritarian Regimes: Indonesia and Malaysia in Comparative Perspective* [New York: Cambridge University Press, 2009] and Winters, *Power in Motion*) suggests that mobile capital, especially Chinese-controlled and foreign capital, exercised a profound constraint on the regime. Others have suggested that the Suharto regime represented a "fusion" of state authority and bourgeois interests (Richard Robison and Vedi R. Hadiz, *Reorganising Power in Indonesia: The Politics of Oligarchy in an Age of Markets* [London: Routledge Curzon, 2004]).

[52] This was the period of the so-called Berkeley Mafia, during which a group of mostly US-trained economists were quite influential within the regime in pursuit of free market policies. Bradley R. Simpson, *Economists with Guns: Authoritarian Development and U.S.-Indonesian Relations, 1960–1968* (Stanford: Stanford University Press, 2008).

During the first twenty years of Suharto's New Order, capital was allocated through five dominant state-owned banks that were shielded from foreign competition but were controlled by a tight political hierarchy, with Suharto and his inner circle at the apex. Several Chinese Indonesian economic elites close to Suharto operated banks in their conglomerate networks, but these private banks were tightly regulated, restricted in how they could allocate assets and how many branches they could open. Over the course of the 1980s and especially after 1988, the regime deregulated the financial system, both opening to foreign competition and encouraging greater competition in the sector by liberalizing interest rates and macroprudential regulation. Over the course of the next several years, economic elites—Chinese and "native" Indonesian—became entangled with members of Suharto's family and inner circle. They launched business ventures that took advantage of their privileged access to financial resources and the implicit assumption of risk on behalf of the state in a pattern emblematic of mutual endangerment. An existential political threat, realized during periodic outbursts of violence against Indonesia's ethnic Chinese and the community's reliance on Suharto for protection, incentivized economic elites to expatriate assets before and, especially, during the crisis. Unlike in its neighbor, Suharto's cronies turned against the regime with great speed at the onset of the crisis, precipitating rapid collapse of the country's currency and financial system and, eventually, the regime itself.[53]

In Chapter 4, I argue that the Malaysian regime has effectively disciplined the capitalist class throughout its tenure, extracting political fealty while also pursuing the regime goals of ethnic redistribution and economic growth. I track how business elites' historic fear of ethnic mobilization and unpredictable redistribution led them to capitulate to the BN's program of Malay dominance and predictable, if coercive, redistribution. Specifically, I track how elite, urban Chinese business leaders supported the BN's policies, and I document the failed efforts at resistance, by small to medium business owners, the urban merchant class, and rural Chinese capitalists.

The UMNO's experiment in transforming the economic balance of power in society was founded on control of the financial system. The regime established rules about the distribution of credit as well as large

---

[53] My argument about Malaysia and Indonesia is similar to, but ultimately slightly different from, Thomas B. Pepinsky, "Capital Mobility and Coalitional Politics: Authoritarian Regimes and Economic Adjustment in Southeast Asia," *World Politics* 60, no. 3 (2008): 438–74 and Pepinsky, *Economic Crises*.

government-linked investment companies (GLICs) to channel investment to entrepreneurs of choice (in this case, ethnic Malays and trusted non-Malays) and to act as trustee owners of society's wealth on behalf of the capital-poor Malay masses. Until the push for privatization in the 1980s and early 1990s, the state had the power to both allocate capital and monitor its recipients. The privatization push, executed under expectations that a new class of economic elites cultivated by the state would both be loyal to the regime and manifest evidence that its policies had worked, instead generated economic elites with political patrons and little oversight. This pattern of state-business relations is captured by the term "competitive clientelism." But Malaysia's regime survived the Asian Financial Crisis as a result of the political loyalty of business elites who turned to, rather than against, the regime in the midst of economic and political crisis. In the aftermath of the crisis, the regime reconstituted state control through corporate governance mechanisms, reasserting and expanding GLIC control and oversight. But long-term mutual alignment in Malaysia has eroded both the power of business elites to allocate investments based on the pursuit of profit and the ability of the state to achieve its economic goals. Malaysia's growth patterns thus conform to the "developmental paradox" of the authoritarian state.

Chapters 5 through 7 cover China since the beginning of the reform and opening period of 1978. I argue in Chapter 5 that a mutual alignment of interests between the CCP, low-level bureaucrats, and the private sector characterized the Chinese political economy for the first two decades of the reforms (1978–98). But China's private entrepreneurs famously experienced discrimination and exclusion from the financial sector. During the first two decades of reform, the vast majority of the country's financial resources— which were ample, thanks to capital controls and high domestic savings rates—flowed to China's state sector. As a result, private enterprises relied on self-financing mechanisms, either retained earnings or what Kellee Tsai calls "back-alley banks," informal financial relations that were fiercely competitive and in which discipline was maintained through social networks and relations of trust.[54] The resources in China's formal financial system flowed disproportionately to the state sector, where we can see the political hierarchy mechanism at work. Indeed, as we might expect and as a generation of political economy work on partially reformed state socialism suggests, state

[54] Kellee S. Tsai, *Back-Alley Banking: Private Entrepreneurs in China* (Ithaca: Cornell University Press, 2002).

agents abused their privileged access to the financial system to promote investment, generating bouts of inflation and resource misallocation. Such activities were reined in through political hierarchies, as the CCP drew on its own internal disciplinary measures (as opposed to interest rates or market discipline) to contract lending and direct investment.[55] The mutual alignment era was characterized by financial exclusion but a practical embrace of the private sector.

Toward the late 1990s and in the early 2000s, discipline in both the public and the private financial systems broke down. In China's public finance system, tax recentralization disconnected local officials from the firms in their jurisdictions, and the rise of land finance introduced an alternative source of investment and self-enrichment for local officials. In the financial system, institutional reforms to expand equity markets and introduce a bureaucratic— as opposed to a party-driven—regulatory system to govern banks and other nonbank financial institutions diminished CCP political control but did not replace it with either market discipline or rule of law. Economic elites grew through the privatization of state assets and by operating in the disciplinary interstices of the financial system. They cultivated relationships with multiple political elites and their families, who benefited financially from the growth of these firms but also found themselves implicated in their activities and therefore invested in their survival. In other words, gaps in the political control of public finance and the financial system enabled the rise of mutual endangerment as well as massive financial risks in both the public and nonpublic sectors. I call this process "elite disintegration." Chapters 5, 6, and 7 describe these processes and interpret Xi Jinping's sweeping anticorruption efforts as an attempt to reassert political control over both public- and private-sector elites. A major part of the efforts by the Xi Jinping administration to expand its control over economic elites has been through the mechanism of corporate governance, a phenomenon I demonstrate in Chapter 7.

The final chapter concludes by exploring the implications of the experience of state-business relations in authoritarian Asia for debates about the power of business, the role of the state in the economy, and the moral economy of capitalism in different regimes.

---

[55] Yasheng Huang, *Inflation and Investment Controls in China: The Political Economy of Central-Local Relations During the Reform Era* (New York: Cambridge University Press, 1996).

2

The Origins of Trust and Distrust

The Making of Capitalist Classes in Asia, 1945–1970

> Routines are based on interpretations of the past more than
> anticipations of the future.
>
> —Barbara Levitt and James March, "Organizational Learning"[1]

Mochtar Riady was born in 1929 in Malang, East Java, to first-generation Chinese immigrant parents who had recently arrived from Fujian province in Mainland China. Riady would eventually establish and head the Lippo Group, one of Indonesia's largest conglomerates, with business interests that ranged from banking to retail to natural resources. During the New Order, Riady enjoyed a close relationship with Suharto, and he was frequently summoned to Suharto's residence for private conversations.[2] Before Riady went into business, however, he had almost become a Chinese Communist guerrilla. On his telling, his experiences protesting Dutch rule as an Indonesian high-school student led him to study in Nanjing at National Central University after the end of World War II, during which time he developed a serious interest in Marxism. This history "contributed to my belief that the great problems of the world all stemmed from imperialism and that only the Communist Party could save mankind."[3] But for a late-arriving letter from his girlfriend (and eventual wife) begging him not to leave by boat for Tianjin to travel to Yan'an, Riady would have been a Chinese Communist guerrilla rather than an elite Indonesian capitalist.

[1] Barbara Levitt and J. G. March, "Organizational Learning," *Annual Review of Sociology* 14, no. 1 (1998): 319–40, at 320, https://doi.org/10.1146/annurev.so.14.080188.001535.

[2] Mochtar Riady, *My Life Story* (Singapore: Wiley, 2017), 112. In the 1980s, Riady, in partnership with Sudono Salim (Liem Sioe Liong), owned the Bank of Central Asia, in which Suharto's children held minority stakes. Riady's Chinese name is Li Wenzheng, or Li Mong Ding in Xinghuanese dialect.

[3] Ibid., 21.

Precarious Ties. Meg Rithmire, Oxford University Press. © Oxford University Press 2023.
DOI: 10.1093/oso/9780197697528.003.0002

Although a surprising number of Asia's postwar capitalist elites share Riady's experience in conflicting loyalties, his story is not representative of the region's business elites.[4] Rather, it encapsulates two dynamics that have shaped the political identities of capitalists in both China and Southeast Asia, namely, the status of ethnic Chinese as economically dominant minorities and the rise and rule of the People's Republic of China (PRC). The combination of these forces generated a particular politics of capitalism in Southeast Asia: authoritarian regimes were established to oppose the threat of communism, yet domestic capitalists found themselves on the outside of the political mainstream because of their ethnic identity, specifically their Chineseness. Events in China itself—the revolution in the late 1940s and the chaotic violence of the Cultural Revolution in the late 1960s—raised the stakes for ethnic and ideological conflicts elsewhere in Asia. Ethnic Chinese outsiders who had entertained thoughts of "return"[5] to China saw that pathway foreclosed as their extended families suffered persecution for having overseas relatives. At the same time, the radicalism in Mao's China fueled anticommunist fervor throughout Asia, lending a ready narrative to political entrepreneurs who sought to exploit ethnic tension or ideological strife for political gain.

The outcome is ironic. On the one hand, authoritarian regimes founded on the basis of anticommunism had only tenuous relationships with their own domestic capitalist classes, while, on the other hand, an eventual capitalist class with deep ties to the Communist Party emerged in China. This political distance between ruling elites and economic elites in Asia has had a lasting effect on state-business relations and on the legitimacy of business in the region because it has shaped trust, or expectations of reciprocity, and a belief that one side will not exploit the vulnerability of the other.[6] The vulnerability of business classes in authoritarian Asia was an outcome of historical processes, both those that produced authoritarian political structures and those that generated political and social distance between societies and

[4] Other regional business elites who were sympathetic to the Chinese Communist Party (CCP) include Tan Kah Kee, the Singapore-born "George Washington of the Overseas Chinese," who died in Mainland China in 1961.

[5] I do not use "return" literally because, in fact, many ethnic Chinese in Southeast Asia had never been to Mainland China, having been born in their countries of residence, often many generations removed from China. Even among those groups, however, ties to China could remain strong. Gungwu Wang, *Don't Leave Home: Migration and the Chinese* (Singapore: Times Academic, 2001); Gungwu Wang, "Chinese Politics in Malaya," *China Quarterly*, no. 43 (1970): 1–30.

[6] See Charles F. Sabel, "Studied Trust: Building New Forms of Cooperation in a Volatile Economy," *Human Relations* 46, no. 9 (1993): 1133–70, https://doi.org/10.1177/001872679304600907; Andrew H. Kydd, *Trust and Mistrust in International Relations* (Princeton, NJ: Princeton University Press, 2018).

capitalists. Trust between business and political elites was produced itera-
tively over time, and the crucibles of revolution, nation-making, and political
mobilization would end with ideas and expectations about reciprocity that
would shape economic behaviors over the long term.[7]

This chapter deals with the region as a whole and with each individual
country's trajectory from the eve of World War II through the mass violence
of the 1960s. In recent years, historians of Mainland China have shown great
interest in the ways in which that country's sizable diaspora exercised influence over pivotal moments in Chinese history. From the 1911 and 1949
revolutions to the excesses of the Maoist period and China's re-engagement
with the global economy that began in the 1980s, the Chinese diaspora has
served as a critical conduit of ideas and resources in both directions; Shelly
Chan uses the term "diaspora moments" to describe junctures at which "diaspora rises to the level of major discussions, demanding a response from
leaders and institutions."[8] In explaining the evolution of state-business relations, I engage the reverse of diaspora moments: pointing to junctures at
which events in Mainland China intersected with events in Southeast Asia
to force pivotal moments of choice for state and society alike.[9] Specifically,
the timing of the Japanese Occupation of China served to connect dispa-
rate groups of ethnic Chinese in Southeast Asia, and the establishment of
the PRC in 1949 and the onset of the Cultural Revolution in 1966 interacted
with critical moments in Malaysian and Indonesian political history to turn
ethnic Chinese toward identification with those nations.

The process of regime formation, from the late 1940s to the late 1960s,
produced distrust between most state and business elites in Indonesia

[7] On trust as learned, see Adam B. Seligman, *The Problem of Trust* (Princeton, NJ: Princeton
University Press, 2000); Niklas Luhmann, *Trust and Power*, trans. Christian Morgner and Michael
King (Malden, MA: Polity Press, 2017); James S. Coleman, *Foundations of Social Theory* (Cambridge,
MA: Belknap Press of Harvard University Press, 1994).

[8] Shelly Chan, *Diaspora's Homeland: Modern China in the Age of Global Migration* (Durham,
NC: Duke University Press, 2018), 13. See also Glen Peterson, *Overseas Chinese in the People's
Republic of China* (London: Routledge, 2012); Min Ye, *Diasporas and Foreign Direct Investment in
China and India* (New York: Cambridge University Press, 2014); You-tien Hsing, *Making Capitalism
in China: The Taiwan Connection* (New York: Oxford University Press, 1998); Shelly Chan, "The Case
for Diaspora: A Temporal Approach to the Chinese Experience," *Journal of Asian Studies* 74, no. 1
(2015): 107–28.

[9] Here, the chapter takes cues from the emerging "Cold War studies" approaches to regional history
that seriously consider China's trajectory and geopolitics in shaping domestic realities in Southeast
Asia in particular. See Jeremy E. Taylor, "'Not a Particularly Happy Expression': 'Malayanization' and
the China Threat in Britain's Late-Colonial Southeast Asian Territories," *Journal of Asian Studies* 78,
no. 4 (2019): 789–808; Jeremy Friedman, *Shadow Cold War: The Sino-Soviet Competition for the Third
World* (Chapel Hill: University of North Carolina Press, 2015).

and China and a level of trust in Malaysia. In China, the immediate postrevolutionary period of state-building established a pattern of accommodation-reprisal between capitalists and the new regime. Repeated experiences of brief accommodation followed by persecution combined with CCP political practices—namely, campaigns—to inculcate a distrust of political elites. Instead of learning to expect reciprocity or cooperation for complying with the demands of political elites, capitalists developed short time horizons and learned a repertoire of behaviors I call "adept dissimulation," riding the waves of radicalism and changes in regime priorities by appearing to accommodate demands but all the while hedging and prioritizing self-protection.[10] In Indonesia, ethnically Chinese capitalists were social and political outsiders. Chinese business elites would become close to Suharto, but only because they were vulnerable. Suharto cultivated economic elites who relied on him for protection of life and property. Like their counterparts in China, they did not trust that Suharto would always return their cooperation, hedging by distributing their assets and wielding threats against political elites. In Malaysia, a protracted fight against a Communist insurgency and an episode of ethnic conflict that threatened the country's survival convinced elites of different ethnic groups that they could trust one another to cooperate rather than to risk national disintegration and more punitive demands from below.

This chapter is organized to identify the critical antecedents and critical junctures that produced both vulnerability and trust or distrust among business classes in Asia.[11] The regime-formation period was a critical juncture for each country during which violence and mobilization resulted in lasting expectations about power-sharing and trust. But similar violence, for example communal conflict in Malaysia and Indonesia, constituted antecedent experiences of colonization, war, and decolonization that interacted with regime formation to differently shape trust.

---

[10] This term from Gordon A. Bennett, *Yundong: Mass Campaigns in Chinese Communist Leadership* (Berkeley: Center for Chinese Studies, University of California, 1976), 87.

[11] Dan Slater and Erica Simmons, "Informative Regress: Critical Antecedents in Comparative Politics," *Comparative Political Studies* 43, no. 7 (2010): 886–917. Slater and Simmons define "critical antecedents" as "factors or conditions preceding a critical juncture that combine with causal forces during a critical juncture to produce long-term divergence in outcomes" (889). Critical junctures are "periods in history in which a specified causal force pushes multiple cases onto divergent long-term pathways or pushes a single case onto a new political trajectory that diverges significantly from the old" (888). See also Paul Pierson, "Increasing Returns, Path Dependence, and the Study of Politics," *American Political Science Review* 94, no. 2 (2000): 251–67.

Foundations of Vulnerability: Class and Race in Postwar Asia

It is the consensus of nearly every historian of Asia that the experience of Japanese Occupation—whether it was fourteen years (in China) or three years (in most of Southeast Asia)—fundamentally transformed the region. Victor Purcell, a participant in much of the region's wartime and postwar experience as Britain's agent in Malaya, has written: "The Pacific War created an entirely new pattern in Southeast Asian politics—so much so that the observer who was fairly closely in touch with the situation in 1940 would, if he did not return to Southeast Asia until 1948 and had not kept himself up to date with a close study of reports, find himself unable to recognize what he saw."[12] In China, the Japanese Occupation facilitated the success of the CCP vis-à-vis the Nationalists and until this day serves as a historical scar in the collective memory of China's twentieth century, one that exemplifies the pain that results from state weakness. The failure of the Guomindang (KMT) Nationalist regime to effectively rout the Japanese and the rural wartime practices of the CCP contributed to the latter's success in the subsequent civil war and its claim to revolutionary legitimacy.[13] For different reasons in each of the countries in this study, the experience of Japanese Occupation produced social divisions and cohesions that had long-term impacts on the organization of state-business relations in the respective regimes.

Three outcomes of the Japanese Occupation were especially relevant for the longer-term construction of state-business relations: one, the generation of solidarity among the overseas Chinese populations, both within countries and across them; two, the amplification of ethnic conflict and development of competing postwar nationalisms; and, three, the role of the Occupation in unsettling prewar economic orders. Taken together, the first two outcomes positioned ethnic Chinese capitalists as threatening outsiders in the states that would form in Southeast Asia, and the third would determine who constituted the postwar capitalist class.

---

[12] Cited in Jeff Goodwin, *No Other Way Out: States and Revolutionary Movements, 1945–1991* (New York: Cambridge University Press, 2001), 72. For more on Purcell, see C. A. Bayly and T. N. Harper, *Forgotten Wars: Freedom and Revolution in Southeast Asia* (Cambridge, MA: Belknap Press of Harvard University Press, 2007). On the Japanese Occupation as an interlude, see Diana S. Kim, *Empires of Vice: The Rise of Opium Prohibition across Southeast Asia* (Princeton, NJ: Princeton University Press, 2020).

[13] Chalmers A. Johnson, *Peasant Nationalism and Communist Power: The Emergence of Revolutionary China* (Stanford: Stanford University Press, 1962); Elizabeth J. Perry, "Studying Chinese Politics: Farewell to Revolution?," *China Journal*, no. 57 (2007): 1–22.

Nationalism within overseas Chinese communities in Southeast Asia was by no means born during the war against Japan, but the nature of Chinese orientations changed significantly during that period. The competition for loyalty and resources of the overseas Chinese began in the late Qing, as the empire turned from distrusting emigrants to embracing them as part of the "self-strengthening" policy. Both the very late Qing (1909) and the Republic that replaced it extended citizenship to overseas Chinese through *jus sanguinis* (right of blood) citizenship principles, which would create conflicting loyalties for Chinese communities throughout the region as their countries of residence struggled to define the scope of their national movements and incipient states.[14] The Guomindang fought to organize Chinese populations in Southeast Asia, especially in British Malaya, but it was not until the Japanese invasion of the Mainland that these groups would "reorient their activities away from their own local problems and towards 'saving' China from the Japanese."[15] The war "generated an unprecedented wave of nationalism and patriotism" among Southeast Asian Chinese, and the Nanyang National Salvation Movement unified Chinese within and across Southeast Asian territories, providing a much-needed source of funding and resources to the Mainland and constituting an extraterritorial battleground in which the KMT and CCP would fight for influence and loyalty.[16]

Furthermore, if the Chinese in the Dutch Indies and British Malaya held more narrow identifications with native place, lineage, or language communities, their experiences under Japanese Occupation facilitated a more Pan-Chinese identity. The brutality of the Japanese treatment of Chinese made no distinction among them, and the displacement and migration of Chinese communities, especially in Malaya, frayed some social bonds and forced the forging of new bonds. New social and political organizations formed during the Occupation, including resistance groups, new smuggling networks, and Japanese-sponsored *kumiai* (cooperative syndicates), brought Chinese out of their traditional communities and into situations in which they would interact and identify with larger groups of Chinese.[17]

---

[14] See Peterson, *Overseas Chinese*, 15–17; Philip A. Kuhn, *Chinese among Others: Emigration in Modern Times* (Lanham, MD: Rowman & Littlefield, 2008); Gungwu Wang, *A Short History of the Nanyang Chinese* (Singapore: Eastern Universities Press, 1959).

[15] Peterson, *Overseas Chinese*, 17.

[16] Yōji Akashi, *The Nanyang Chinese National Salvation Movement, 1937–1941* (Lawrence: Center for East Asian Studies, University of Kansas, 1970), 15.

[17] See Victor Purcell, *The Chinese in Malaya* (New York: Oxford University Press, 1948), 241–62.

Second, and relatedly, the withdrawal of the Japanese at the end of the war left political uncertainties and competing nationalisms in all three countries under study. As many historians of the period have argued, nationalism(s) were solidified in the postwar period as, in Odd Arne Westad's words, "All over Asia indigenous elites hoped to fill the power vacuum that a Japanese defeat would create."[18] In China, as Westad details, the withdrawal of the Japanese left the Guomindang significantly weakened, but the years between 1945 and 1949 would be filled with choice and contingency as the KMT and CCP fought for territorial and ideological control of the Chinese Mainland. The perceived inefficacy of the KMT in fighting the Japanese and handling their withdrawal served to bolster the Communists and erode support for the Nationalists. In the realm of economic management in particular, the KMT's mishandling of alleged "collaborators" in the business community and the experience of hyperinflation encouraged even capitalists to consider the CCP as a better alternative.[19]

In Southeast Asia, the Japanese Occupation destroyed the myth of the supremacy of colonial rulers, who, in both the Dutch and British cases, were quickly felled by the invading Japanese. In both Malaya and Indonesia, some elements of the indigenous populations (i.e., non-Chinese residents) "openly welcomed" the Japanese Occupation, either because they expected that Japanese rule would be better, or at least no worse, than their present occupiers or because, especially in the Malay case, they anticipated that the Japanese would aid their efforts to overcome Chinese economic dominance.[20] In the Indonesian case, they were wrong: Japanese Occupation was far harsher than Dutch rule for a far greater swath of the population. Kahin credits the Japanese with a "tremendous increase in national consciousness and the will to political independence"; the Occupation fostered a solidarity among Indonesians that had eluded leaders of the nationalist movement prior to 1942. The harshness of the Occupation affected peasants, provided a source of anti-Western ideology, created a class of educated youth displaced from their homes and capable of organizing, and drew Indonesians

[18] Odd Arne Westad, *Decisive Encounters: The Chinese Civil War, 1946–1950* (Stanford: Stanford University Press, 2003), 19.

[19] Suzanne Pepper, *Civil War in China: The Political Struggle, 1945–1949*, 2nd ed. (Lanham, MD: Rowman & Littlefield, 1999), attributes so much to the KMT's mishandling of the takeover that she calls it "the beginning of the end" (7).

[20] Victor Purcell, *South and East Asia since 1800* (Cambridge: University Press, 1965), 178. See also George McTurnan Kahin, *Nationalism and Revolution in Indonesia* (Ithaca: Cornell University Press, 1952), 100.

into technical and administrative positions, a source of mobility they feared giving up with the return of Dutch rule.[21]

In the Malayan case, however, they were somewhat right: the Japanese "regarded the Chinese in general as their enemies," and they treated them brutally, at times because of suspected Communist sympathies but at times for no reason other than ethnicity.[22] Accounts of the Occupation in Malaya report "a programme of brutality, torture and arbitrary execution against whole communities, and this programme had been implemented with casual efficiency by the Imperial Forces whenever there was nothing better to do."[23] Many Chinese abandoned rubber plantations, which were all but destroyed due to low prices as a result of the Depression, and urban areas for subsistence farming, instead squatting on higher ground land or clearing plots in jungles.[24] This population of displaced Chinese would, several years after the war's end, become critical to the efforts by both Communist insurgents and those trying to stop them. Other Chinese were recruited by the British to resist the Japanese. During the Occupation, the British anti-Japanese efforts found common cause with the Malayan Communist Party (MCP) to form the Malayan People's Anti-Japanese Army, which comprised Communists as well as "staunch anti-Communists" who had been either KMT supporters stranded in China or "civilians in Malaya before the war, businessmen, or, more often than not, policemen."[25]

Immediately upon the withdrawal of the Japanese in 1945, those who had formed a tenuous alliance during the Occupation found themselves enemies once again, and those whose social tensions were exacerbated during the Occupation—namely, Malays and Chinese—found themselves in "the hellish fires of political anarchy and communal chaos."[26] I am certainly not the first to argue that this communal chaos would cast a long shadow on state and society in its wake.[27] In addition to shaping state

[21] Kahin, *Nationalism and Revolution*, 128–33.

[22] Purcell, *South and East Asia*, 178.

[23] Donald Mackay, *The Malayan Emergency, 1948–60: The Domino That Stood* (Washington DC: Brassey's, 1997), 12. See also Bayly and Harper, *Forgotten Wars*, 24–25. The most extreme manifestation of Japanese brutality toward Chinese took place in Singapore: the *sook ching* ("purification by elimination") massacre, in which fifty thousand lives were taken in Singapore as the Japanese army eliminated anyone suspected of sympathies with China.

[24] Bayly and Harper, *Forgotten Wars*, 108, state that one out of every five Malayans was a squatter in 1945.

[25] Ibid., 37–38.

[26] Dan Slater, *Ordering Power: Contentious Politics and Authoritarian Leviathans in Southeast Asia* (New York: Cambridge University Press, 2010), 75.

[27] Among others, Dan Slater argues that postwar patterns of contentious politics can explain both state strength and regime type across Southeast Asia, and Bayly and Harper, *Forgotten Wars*, xxviii,

strength, regime type, and more, the postwar, preindependence years were also important for class-based political alliances. In Malaysia, the specter of ethnic conflict and national disintegration threatened Chinese elites, but so too did class-based political violence that originated, for the most part, within their own ethnic group. These combined threats persuaded business elites to ally with Malay political elites, accepting Malay political hegemony in exchange for formal representation within the ruling coalition and in the state.

The Indonesian economic order underwent a more gradual change during and right after the war, but one no less important for its postindependence landscape. Historians of Indonesia have argued that Dutch colonial practices impeded the creation of an indigenous bourgeoisie. A combination of the privileged entrance of advanced enterprises from the metropole in the late nineteenth and early twentieth centuries, plantation economies that entrenched precapitalist social structures and expatriated capital to Holland, and reliance on Chinese traders and tax farmers denied indigenous Indonesians opportunities for capital accumulation and laid the groundwork for antipathies between Indonesians and Chinese, who were able to insert themselves into Dutch economic networks and rely on kinship networks and become capitalists.[28] During the Japanese Occupation, however, the balance of power *within* the Indonesian Chinese community would change. Dutch withdrawal dimmed the fortunes of *peranakan* Chinese (Straits-born Chinese), many of whom spoke Dutch and had assimilated into colonial society, while the *totok* communities, more recent arrivals from Mainland China, emerged newly prosperous. These recent arrivals had no relationship with the Dutch, and many instead learned Javanese; they benefited from the rising importance of highly personal, trans-Straits smuggling networks during the Japanese Occupation and later during the revolution.[29] The new

frame their sweeping history of 1945–49 as "Asia's time of revolution," during which regimes and long-lasting social cleavages took shape from unimaginably open political landscapes following Japan's withdrawal.

[28] See Richard Robison, *Indonesia: The Rise of Capital* (Sydney: Allen & Unwin, 1986), 3–4. See also J. H. Boeke, *Economics and Economic Policy of Dual Societies, as Exemplified by Indonesia* (New York: International Secretariat, Institute of Pacific Relations, 1953); Ann Laura Stoler, *Capitalism and Confrontation in Sumatra's Plantation Belt, 1870–1979*, 2nd ed. (Ann Arbor: University of Michigan Press, 1995); J. A. C. Mackie, ed., *The Chinese in Indonesia: Five Essays* (Honolulu: University Press of Hawai'i, 1976).

[29] Peck Yang Twang, *The Chinese Business Elite in Indonesia and the Transition to Independence, 1940–1950* (New York: Oxford University Press, 1998), 13, 70–110, finds that, in addition to smuggling, Japanese-founded *kumiai*, or cooperatives, likely expanded Chinese business networks

class of *totok* (recent migrant) business elites that emerged in this period would form alliances with Indonesian political elites after the war and supply the class of *cukong* (cronies) during Suharto's New Order.

The regime-formation periods in all three countries intersected with one another in critical and often underappreciated ways. One British planter and soldier offered this observation:

> In one South East Asian country after another resurgent nationalism was showing an unnerving readiness to cross borders. . . . Most ominous of all, in China Mao Tse Tung was clearly winning the war against the Kuomintang forces . . . and no one could tell how soon he might be in a position to start spreading the Revolution to other lands. Already there were signs of this in Malaya: amongst the Chinese community, supporters of Mao and the Kuomintang were already at each others' throats and the killing had started.[30]

Ethnic Chinese communities throughout Southeast Asia experienced microcosms of the Chinese civil war after the war against Japan concluded. For many Southeast Asian Chinese elites, the CCP's victory in 1949 foreclosed the possibility of "return" to China, raising the stakes of the struggle for citizenship and inclusion in what would become Malaysia and for informal alliances with nationalists in Indonesia, where the Chinese minority was not sizable or politically palatable enough to hope for formal political representation. The combination of the KMT's economic ineptitude and the treatment of ethnic Chinese abroad persuaded many Mainland Chinese elites to gradually accept the ascendancy of the CCP. Across the region, capitalists were preparing for the emergence of regimes in which their interests would be underrepresented and their lives and property would be threatened. As the next sections discuss, their particular efforts at adaptation would establish patterns of state-business relations that proved durable for decades.

---

and put Chinese and Indonesians together in business operations, facilitating a closeness that would be important in the years to come. On prewar Chinese smuggling, see Eric Tagliacozzo, *Secret Trades, Porous Borders: Smuggling and States along a Southeast Asian Frontier, 1865–1915* (New Haven: Yale University Press, 2005), especially chap. 6.

[30] Mackay, *The Malayan Emergency, 1948–60*, 51.

Capitalist Insiders and Outsiders

How these capitalist classes navigated the processes of civil conflict, revolution, and the establishment of authoritarian regimes greatly determined
their inclusion in the nascent regime or foreclosed such a possibility. Before
the following sections look deeply at the experiences of capitalists in China,
Malaysia, and Indonesia, this section sketches the outcomes and variations
among the cases. Table 2.1 outlines the argument.

Unsurprisingly, capitalists suffered the most extreme political exclusion
and learned the greatest distrust of political elites in China, where the CCP
effected a peasant-led Communist revolution in 1949. Many capitalist elites
(or at least their families)—those with sufficient assets to be considered on
a national scale—fled China on the eve of the revolution to resettle in Hong
Kong or Taiwan. Those who remained weathered the successive campaigns
and radicalism of the CCP's first two and a half decades in the same way
that all Chinese citizens did: by learning to anticipate political headwinds,
adapting themselves to the language and performative requirements of the
new regime, and sublimating their skills into activities that would aid the regime and their own self-preservation.

Importantly for my argument, Chinese capitalists were not liquidated as
a class. Rather, capitalism itself was eliminated (at least officially) in a piece-
meal fashion during the first decade of the PRC, and capitalists were given
opportunities to remake themselves into politically useful subjects of the
new revolutionary regime. Many did so with enthusiasm. Nonetheless, the
immutability of one's class background left capitalists, no matter how well
they anticipated and adapted, vulnerable to bouts of radicalism and reprisal.
They suffered repeatedly and considerably between the revolution and the

Table 2.1 Political Inclusion of Capitalists

Country	Trust	Reason	Mode of incorporation
Malaysia	Yes	Elite Chinese distrust of lower-class Chinese demands	Formal political participation
		Fear of ethnic conflict and national disintegration	
Indonesia	No	Chinese ethnic outsiders; the New Order was a racially exclusive regime	Personalistic dependence on regime insiders
China	No	Anticapitalist regime	Vernacular, informal

end of the Cultural Revolution and learned to distrust the CCP even as they adapted to it and joined it. These memories of persecution and vulnerability inform capitalists' perceptions of their political status in reform-era China, where adaptation strategies are generally similar to those of the Maoist era. What appears as closeness to the regime, co-optation, or "red capitalism" is in fact a strategy on the part of vulnerable and excluded capitalists to best access information about policy and politics and to protect themselves from what they know to be a capricious and punishing regime.

Indonesian capitalists of Chinese descent were excluded from political power in Suharto's New Order, and a generalized distrust between Chinese capitalists and the regime pervaded state-business relations. I describe the distrust as "generalized" because specific capitalists held quite close relationships with specific politicians, including Suharto himself and members of his family. These particularistic mutual dependencies should be interpreted as evidence of business's political exclusion, and adaptation to vulnerability, rather than its political power within the regime. Suharto's *cukong* depended on his personal protection to insulate them from a threatening military and a society that was deeply distrustful toward and prone to periodic and generalized violence against Chinese. The New Order was born of violence; the state both conducted and tolerated violence toward suspected Communists and Chinese communities, whether they overlapped or not. The vulnerability of Chinese capitalists was built into the logic of the New Order: Suharto relied on ethnic Chinese capitalists for access to capital and investment, and the capitalists in turn relied on Suharto for protection, a fact of which he reminded them by periodically stoking violence.[31] That these capitalists depended entirely on Suharto (or his allies and family members) for protection incentivized them to pursue security through investments abroad. Ultimately, when Suharto and his immediate allies were endangered, these capitalists fled Indonesia, with disastrous consequences for the economy and the regime, as we shall see in the next chapter.

Malaya's Chinese capitalists faced threats of political and economic vulnerability during the long process of decolonization. They found themselves on the outside of both a Malay-centric conception of the nation and

---

[31] Here I follow several scholars who similarly assess the Suharto regime. See Thomas B. Pepinsky, *Economic Crises and the Breakdown of Authoritarian Regimes: Indonesia and Malaysia in Comparative Perspective* (New York: Cambridge University Press, 2009); Robison, *Indonesia*; Slater, *Ordering Power*; Ross H. McLeod, "Soeharto's Indonesia: A Better Class of Corruption," *Agenda* 7, no. 2 (2000): 99–112; Jeffrey A. Winters, *Power in Motion: Capital Mobility and the Indonesian State* (Ithaca: Cornell University Press, 1996).

of (predominantly Chinese) class-based demands for redistribution and Communist revolution. Rather than investing in particularistic relationships like their Indonesian counterparts, and no doubt aided by their more substantial numbers, Malayan Chinese elites chose to ensure that they were not politically excluded from the regime.[32] They were convinced that without political inclusion—formal political representation among the parties in government—they could not guarantee their well-being. The development of this "anti-Communist Chinese bourgeoisie" shaped a long history of state-business relations.[33] Malaysian Chinese capitalists bore the costs for formal political power as the perpetual junior partner of the Malay-dominated (i.e., dominated by the United Malays National Organisation [UMNO]) coalition: they agreed to the UMNO's demands for ethnic redistribution to benefit Malays, able to shape some of the implementation around the edges but unable to challenge Malay economic and political hegemony.

In all three cases, vulnerable capitalists submitted to majority views on how the regimes would be structured and the plans for national development that took shape under those regimes. Their means of submission and strategies for survival as vulnerable capitalists in unfriendly regimes differed in important ways, as I detail in the next sections. The circumstances by which each group was rendered vulnerable are critical antecedents to how they would interact with new authoritarian regimes during the periods of state-building and mass violence that characterized the 1950s and 1960s.

China: Distrust and Adept Dissimulation

Many accounts of capitalism in the PRC start with the story of Rong Yiren, mostly because his trajectory seems unique, but in fact it is a sort of elite analogue of the experience of nearly every capitalist in the PRC. On the one hundredth anniversary of Rong's birth in 2016, Zhang Dejiang, then a member of the Politburo Standing Committee of the CCP, described him paradoxically: "Comrade Rong was one of modern China's leading businessmen, an

---

[32] Gungwu Wang writes, "The forceful Chinese communal identity developed for political purposes in Malaysia could not be found anywhere else because no other Chinese community was large enough to share power with the indigenous peoples even to a limited extent," in Gungwu Wang and Jennifer Wayne Cushman, *Changing Identities of the Southeast Asian Chinese since World War II* (Hong Kong: Hong Kong University Press, 1988), 4.

[33] Donald Nonini, *Getting By: Class and State Formation among Chinese in Malaysia* (Ithaca: Cornell University Press, 2015), 36.

outstanding national leader, a mighty patriot, and a soldier of communism."[34] Rong was born into a cotton, flour, and textile family empire in 1916. While most of his family fled the Mainland for Hong Kong on the eve of the revolution, Rong stayed to manage the family business. During the Mao era, he was at the apex of a group of high-profile capitalists, based mostly in Shanghai, who worked closely with the CCP to aid the new regime in everything from tax collection to commercial and industrial planning to evangelizing the revolution in and outside China's borders.[35] Rong himself served in the party-state under Mao, including as vice mayor of Shanghai.

Rong, and most like him, suffered during the Cultural Revolution. He was beaten, detained, and sent to work as a janitor, but he survived and was rehabilitated under Deng Xiaoping. In 1979, with Deng's order to be "boldly creative," he founded the China International Trust and Investment Corporation (中信), which grew into one of the world's largest conglomerates and holding companies. Rong served as vice president of the PRC under Jiang Zemin and died a billionaire in 2005.[36] Rong's experience at the pinnacle of both wealth and power is unique, but his story of adaptation and survival is one familiar to most who lived through those times.

Consider Mr. Fang, an entrepreneur I met in Shenzhen in 2015. At the time, Mr. Fang was the head of a number of businesses, but I met him due to his association with a High Technology Zone outside of a major city, where he ran a logistics business. I asked what the "high tech" content of his business was, and he responded that although he does help some factories with automation and digitization, he calls the business a "technology company" because this is the best way to receive tax benefits and critical inputs like water, power, and land from the local government. He proudly explained that he is highly capable of understanding and benefiting from local policy: in the 1980s, he had a collectively owned "town and village enterprise" (TVE) to afford experimentation with capitalism and private enterprise under a safe corporate form. In the 1990s, his company was registered as a "foreign-invested enterprise" to benefit from preferential policies toward foreign capital (which, for him, was his own capital routed through

---

[34] 张德江 (Zhang Dejiang), "在纪念荣毅仁同志诞辰100周年座谈会上的讲话" (Speech at the Symposium Honoring the One Hundredth Anniversary of the Birth of Comrade Rong Yiren), April 26, 2016, http://www.xinhuanet.com//politics/2016-04/26/c_1118744840.htm.

[35] Christopher R. Leighton, "Revolutionary Rich: Red Capitalists under Mao," ms.

[36] David Barboza, "Rong Yiren, a Chinese Billionaire, Dies at 89," *New York Times*, October 28, 2005, https://www.nytimes.com/2005/10/28/obituaries/rong-yiren-a-chinese-billionaire-dies-at-89.html.

Hong Kong), and at the time of our meeting he was reaping the benefits associated with China's high-tech push.[37]

Rong and Fang share a great deal in common: the ability to anticipate changes in political mode or direction, to collect information on policy in order to adjust to it, and to forge alliances with relevant political elites, whether high or low, to protect themselves should the political tides shift against them. These skills are far from extraordinary in China, especially among the generation of Chinese who lived through the Maoist era, during which time mass mobilization campaigns (群众运动) constituted the primary mode of politics and site of social relations for Chinese citizens. Campaigns have two faces. On the one hand, they are disruptive, drawing on revolutionary political traditions to mobilize masses and the entire political system to achieve concrete policy objectives. On the other hand, campaigns are routinized, involving "organization, planning, and repetition."[38] Campaigns involve setting ambitious targets at the top, and implementation is left to all levels of the political hierarchy. Officials execute campaigns in a politicized atmosphere, with periods of extreme mobilization and propaganda followed by excessive overcompliance, denouement, and recalibration.[39]

As a number of scholars have documented for students, workers, and peasants during this era, campaigns required extraordinary exertion on the part of those inside and outside the party-state.[40] Survival, even for ordinary citizens, required staying abreast of "changing winds," "tides," or "waves

[37] Interview, June 21, 2015, Shenzhen. On TVEs, see Jean Oi, *Rural China Takes Off: Institutional Foundations of Economic Reform* (Berkeley: University of California Press, 1999). See also Yasheng Huang, *Capitalism with Chinese Characteristics: Entrepreneurship and the State* (New York: Cambridge University Press, 2008). On foreign direct investment round-tripping, see Yasheng Huang, *Why Is There So Much Demand for Foreign Equity Capital in China? An Institutional and Policy Perspective* (Cambridge, MA: Weatherhead Center for International Affairs, Harvard University, 1999).
[38] Tyrene White, *China's Longest Campaign: Birth Planning in the People's Republic, 1949–2005* (Ithaca: Cornell University Press. 2006), 7–8.
[39] Several scholars in the sociological tradition have sought to model the phases of campaigns. See G. William Skinner and Edwin A. Winckler, "Compliance Succession in Rural Communist China: A Cyclical Theory," in Amitai Etzioni, comp., *A Sociological Reader on Complex Organizations*, 2nd ed. (New York: Holt Rinehart and Winston, 1969), 410–38.
[40] Andrew G. Walder, *Communist Neo-traditionalism: Work and Authority in Chinese Industry* (Berkeley: University of California Press, 1986); Elizabeth J. Perry and Xun Li, *Proletarian Power: Shanghai in the Cultural Revolution* (Boulder, CO: Westview Press, 1997); Andrew G. Walder, *Fractured Rebellion: The Beijing Red Guard Movement* (Cambridge, MA: Harvard University Press, 2009); Thomas P. Bernstein, "Leadership and Mass Mobilisation in the Soviet and Chinese Collectivisation Campaigns of 1929–30 and 1955–56: A Comparison," *China Quarterly*, no. 31 (1967): 1–47; Thomas P. Bernstein, "Mao Zedong and the Famine of 1959–1960: A Study in Wilfulness," *China Quarterly*, no. 186 (2006): 421–45; Kristen E. Looney, *Mobilizing for Development: The Modernization of Rural East Asia* (Ithaca: Cornell University Press, 2020).

of assault" as campaigns unfolded. Whether through "compliance cycles," "life plans" for "getting along and getting ahead," or "adept dissimulation," Chinese of all walks of life became skilled at navigating political uncertainty and mobilization.[41] Campaigns have changed in the post-Mao period, but they have not disappeared. The post-Mao CCP has approached policy arenas, from population control to rural modernization to party discipline, through the use of campaigns. Not all are "mass mobilization" campaigns, requiring intense action on the part of Chinese citizens at the grassroots, but they do require action on the part of social elites in addition to party-state officials.[42]

As nearly every narrative of the Chinese reform era and its economic achievements points out, the introduction of capitalism in China came not through legal or institutional innovations and guarantees but rather through informal encouragement and creative experimentation at all levels of the Chinese polity and society. The adaptive skills that capitalists, and eventual capitalists, acquired in navigating Chinese politics before and after Mao facilitated their survival in the absence of institutional and legal protections.[43] Capitalists in China like Mr. Fang above have adopted the same strategies in weathering markets that they learned in weathering campaigns: appear to align oneself with the highest political goal of the moment, creatively disguise one's pursuits, forge alliances with those in power to access protection, and, critically, avidly collect information and remain vigilant in case of dramatic shifts in favor or permissibility.

Scholars of Chinese politics have focused on "co-optation" as an explanation for why capitalists in the post-Mao period have not been harbingers of democracy or even a more liberal form of capitalism. This work has focused on the ways in which private entrepreneurs seem to hold few liberal

[41] Skinner and Winckler, "Compliance Succession"; Michel Oksenberg, "Getting Ahead and Along in Communist China: The Ladder of Success on the Eve of the Cultural Revolution," in John Wilson Lewis, ed., *Party Leadership and Revolutionary Power in China* (New York: Cambridge University Press, 1970), 304–47; Bennett, *Yundong*, 87.

[42] Kristen E. Looney, "China's Campaign to Build a New Socialist Countryside: Village Modernization, Peasant Councils, and the Ganzhou Model of Rural Development," *China Quarterly*, no. 224 (2015): 909–32, https://doi.org/10.1017/S0305741015001204; Looney, *Mobilizing for Development*; Elizabeth J. Perry, "From Mass Campaigns to Managed Campaigns: 'Constructing a New Socialist Countryside,'" in Sebastian Heilmann and Elizabeth J. Perry, eds., *Mao's Invisible Hand: The Political Foundations of Adaptive Governance in China* (Cambridge, MA: Harvard University Asia Center, 2011), 30–61; Andrew Mertha, "'Stressing Out': Cadre Calibration and Affective Proximity to the CCP in Reform-Era China," *China Quarterly*, no. 229 (2017): 64–85; White, *China's Longest Campaign*.

[43] These adaptive behaviors, Kellee Tsai argues, have not only protected capitalists themselves but also have changed the regime endogenously. See Kellee S. Tsai, "Adaptive Informal Institutions and Endogenous Institutional Change in China," *World Politics* 59, no. 1 (2006): 116–41.

preferences and on their formal connections to the regime itself, whether they are former officials who "jumped into the sea" (下海) to pursue business or entrepreneurs who later joined the CCP or served the state in an official capacity, for example in local or national people's congresses.[44] Bruce Dickson summarizes: "China's capitalists are increasingly being integrated into the political system and have little incentive or inclination to change the status quo under which they have prospered."[45]

To be sure, capitalists in China are superficially aligned with the regime. Many are card-carrying members of the CCP and join organizations up and down the political hierarchy—from the National People's Congress to local chambers of commerce to industry associations—that are organized to serve the purposes of the state rather than to represent the interests of business. They frequently wax poetic about the party and its leaders. Jack Ma, founder of Alibaba, remarked in 2017: "Today's China, the era of today, is the best time to be doing business. . . . The work of China's clean and honest government has attracted the attention of the world: there's no country on earth like this."[46] A mere year later, he said that "2018 was indeed a difficult year," and the years to come "could be even more difficult."[47] Ma would be stepping down from the helms of the company he founded, sparking speculation that conflict with Xi Jinping's government, especially its ambitions to take greater control of the technology sector, precipitated the end of Ma's career. Two years later, the state fined Ma's company and took steps to reorganize it.[48]

---

[44] Bruce J. Dickson, "Cooptation and Corporatism in China: The Logic of Party Adaptation," *Political Science Quarterly* 115, no. 4 (2000–2001): 517–40; Bruce J. Dickson, *Red Capitalists in China: The Party, Private Entrepreneurs, and Prospects for Political Change* (New York: Cambridge University Press, 2003); Margaret M. Pearson, *Joint Ventures in the People's Republic of China: The Control of Foreign Direct Investment under Socialism* (Princeton, NJ: Princeton University Press, 1991); Margaret M. Pearson, *China's New Business Elite: The Political Consequences of Economic Reform* (Berkeley: University of California Press, 1997); Kellee S. Tsai, "Capitalists without a Class: Political Diversity among Private Entrepreneurs in China," *Comparative Political Studies* 38, no. 9 (2005): 1130–58; Kellee S. Tsai, *Capitalism without Democracy: The Private Sector in Contemporary China* (Ithaca: Cornell University Press, 2007); Yue Hou, "Participating for Protection: Legislatures, Private Entrepreneurs, and Property Security in China," unpublished ms., 2017; Rory Truex, "The Returns to Office in a 'Rubber Stamp' Parliament," *American Political Science Review* 108, no. 2 (2014): 235–51.

[45] Bruce J. Dickson, *Wealth into Power: The Communist Party's Embrace of China's Private Sector* (New York: Cambridge University Press, 2008), 28.

[46] Josh Horwitz, "Jack Ma Has Some Thoughts on China's 'Clean' Communism and the US's Divided Politics," *Quartz*, November 30, 2017, https://qz.com/1142604/jack-ma-has-some-thoughts-on-chinas-clean-communism-and-the-uss-divided-politics/.

[47] Quoted in Yue Hou, "The Private Sector: Challenges and Opportunities During Xi's Second Term," *China Leadership Monitor*, no. 59 (March 2019), https://www.prcleader.org/past-issues.

[48] See Margaret Pearson, Meg Rithmire, and Kellee Tsai, "Party-State Capitalism in China," *Current History* 120, no. 827 (2021): 207–13.

Ma's experience under Xi illustrates the problem with co-optation as a concept. It purports to deduce preferences of actors (in this case, entrepreneurs) by observing their public actions and affiliations in restricted political environments. That they join official organizations or display loyalty to the ruling party simply tells us that they know how to behave in order to protect themselves and to gather information about the business environment, skills that Chinese have honed since dawn of the PRC. "Co-optation" reveals little to nothing about the private strategies of vulnerable capitalists, the durability of their apparent alliance with the regime, or the substance of what either the state or capitalists get from these arrangements.[49]

Instead of having been effectively co-opted, Chinese capitalists during the reform era have adhered to a script written decades earlier. They remain close to the party not because they trust it but because they do not trust it. A pattern of accommodation-reprisal was established during the period of regime formation, which began in 1949 and spanned the early years of state-building in the 1950s through the Cultural Revolution of the 1960s, teaching Chinese capitalists and would-be capitalists that the party would appear to accommodate them to accomplish its goals (growth, peace, state-building, acquiring logistical knowledge), but it could also turn on them at any moment. Lived and intergenerational experiences of suffering and persecution have produced three important elements of state-business relations in China that have continued into the reform era. First, a generalized wariness of the Chinese party-state and impulses toward self-protection amid distrust; second, learned strategies of feigned loyalty (表现) and cultivating closeness to power to collect information about political headwinds; and, third, short time horizons, as citizens have learned to live with the possibility of change and reversal in the political and economic spheres.

Capitalists after the Revolution

The Chinese Communist revolution was gradual and geographically variegated, with different regions undergoing "liberation" at different times and

---

[49] Capitalists' apparent support for the regime is similar to preference falsification. Timur Kuran, *Private Truths, Public Lies: The Social Consequences of Preference Falsification* (Cambridge, MA: Harvard University Press, 1995). For evidence of preference falsification in China, see Junyan Jiang and Dali L. Yang, "Lying or Believing? Measuring Preference Falsification from a Political Purge in China," *Comparative Political Studies* 49, no. 5 (2016): 600–634.

in processes that adapted to local circumstances. While the CCP benefited from the Guomindang's incredible mismanagement of the economy to gain acceptance among even unlikely social groups (i.e., business), it also faced extreme challenges to rehabilitate national and local economies. Meeting such challenges required a strategic accommodation of capitalists during the years immediately following the revolution; Mao's widely circulated slogans included "Develop production; make the economy prosper; consider both the public and private sectors; and benefit both labor and capital."[50] Initial accommodations, however, were followed with psychologically and socially intense campaigns targeting capitalists in the early 1950s and nationalization ·in the late 1950s.

Upon "liberation" of various cities, many capitalist families chose to emigrate or hedged their political futures by sending parts of the family abroad (e.g., to Taiwan, Hong Kong, or Southeast Asia), while keeping some foothold in the Mainland. These choices were complex and idiosyncratic for different families, but the regional timing of China's Communist revolution—amid war and revolution throughout East and Southeast Asia—required political savviness and risk management on the part of economic elites near and far.[51] Those who remained in China were initially treated well by the new regime. The CCP made a distinction between "national" (民族资本家) and "bureaucratic comprador" (买办官僚资本家) capitalists, rewarding the former with new roles in the new China. But even the national capitalists accommodated by the CCP would have to navigate early campaign waves and the sensitive process of nationalization.

Kenneth Lieberthal's classic study of the revolution in Tianjin illustrates how the political waves were experienced during the early PRC period in one of China's largest and most economically advanced cities. After initial efforts to effect revolution in the city were deemed to be too much and too fast, the CCP's second-ranking leader, Liu Shaoqi, was dispatched to the city in the spring of 1949—six months before the fall of nearby Beijing—to recalibrate the party's management. Liu's strategy was to demobilize society, defuse antagonism between social groups (principally, labor and capital), and establish a top-down and carefully paced revolution. Accommodating the capitalist

---

[50] Kenneth Lieberthal, *Revolution and Tradition in Tientsin, 1949–1952* (Stanford: Stanford University Press, 1980), 30.

[51] Siu-lun Wong, *Emigrant Entrepreneurs: Shanghai Industrialists in Hong Kong* (New York: Oxford University Press, 1988); Taomo Zhou, *Migration in the Time of Revolution: China, Indonesia, and the Cold War* (Ithaca: Cornell University Press, 2019).

class was a key goal, both to prevent southward capital flight (to Hong Kong and areas still controlled by the Nationalists) and to facilitate much-needed economic growth and tax revenue consolidation. Liu promised a gradual expansion of the public sector without negatively affecting the private sector, the ability to retain "reasonable" profits, and adherence to fair labor dispute arbitration procedures.[52] Politically, very few capitalists were branded as counterrevolutionaries, and the party took serious measures to improve management of the city's mills and factories by convening trade conferences on production and marketing. In short, the general strategy and specific policies of the early PRC period were aimed to "persuade the Tientsin bourgeoisie that they had a future worth contemplating in the New China" and "enlist the help of industrialists and businessmen in rehabilitating the city's devastated economy."[53]

The initial accommodation of capitalists was short-lived. The onset of the early PRC's first wave of political campaigns, the three- and five-antis (三反五反) in 1952, introduced capitalists (among others) to the existential threat that the new regime would pose. Lieberthal describes the effects of the five-antis campaign, which specifically targeted capitalists, through the case of a chemical company manager in Tianjin. After several years of having little knowledge of the new regime and its policies save a noticeable improvement in the economy, a campaign "work team" arrived at the firm toward the end of 1951 and thus began "by his own account, the most traumatic experience in his [the chemical company manager] life."[54] The manager was detained for months of interrogations, confessions, accusations against other businessmen, and struggle sessions with employees. In the end, the firm was designated a "basically law-abiding firm," like most in the city; less than 6 percent of the city's enterprises were designated as "seriously" or "completely" lawbreaking; the chemical company's manager attributed his firm's relative safety to his cooperative attitude during the campaign.[55] The psycho-social, and ultimately political, effects of the campaigns were profound. They drove an indelible wedge between social groups, established the power and normative dominance of the CCP, and introduced the need to appear aligned with the regime's goals to survive.

[52] Lieberthal, *Revolution and Tradition.*
[53] Ibid., 45–46.
[54] Ibid., 32. Work teams (工作队) are the classic means of campaign implementation. See Elizabeth J. Perry, "Missionaries of the Party: Work-Team Participation and Intellectual Incorporation," *China Quarterly,* no. 248 (S1) (2021): 73–94.
[55] Lieberthal, *Revolution and Tradition,* 139 and 168.

Socialization and State-Building

By the mid-1950s, capitalists and other social groups in China had learned that adapting to politics was paramount. After the five-antis campaign, several national leaders went to "great lengths" to comfort the capitalists and restore the economy. In 1953, Li Weihan put forward the idea of a "joint state-private enterprise" (公私合营企业) as a means of nationalization, and from 1953 to 1956, factory owners themselves played a "surprising role" in facilitating the transition to socialism.[56] Some had encountered economic or labor management difficulties in the hybrid system, while others feared that political denunciation would be worse than expropriation.[57] Industry associations encouraged firms to "get it over with," and the PRC government promised to provide some compensation, retain staff, and pay comparable wages after nationalization. As Robert Cliver notes, "Once it became clear, however, that all private factories would be 'transformed' regardless of their internal conditions, factory owners rushed to demonstrate their enthusiasm for joint operations—whether sincere or not."[58] The son of a prominent Shanghai capitalist, Zhang Naiqi, said the same: "For the five antis, everyone felt we must give in, to delay would make trouble, so just finish this matter. For entrepreneurs at this moment, there was a lingering fear. Many people looked forward to socialist transformation; if the firm doesn't do it, it will be done to you, so let us get rid of this matter."[59]

The experience of Li Kangnian, a high-profile capitalist in Shanghai whose renowned National Goods Company (国货公司) was nationalized in the early 1950s after it fell on hard times, exemplifies the dynamic of accommodation-reprisal. Li was supposedly "not very keen on politics, but under the new regime he worked hard to learn the vocabulary of the official

---

[56] Robert K. Cliver, "Surviving Socialism: Private Industry and the Transition to Socialism in China, 1945–1958," *Cross-Currents: East Asian History and Culture Review* 4, no. 2 (2015): 698.

[57] On the problems generated by hybrid "state capitalism," see Bennis Wai-yip So, "The Policy-Making and Political Economy of the Abolition of Private Ownership in the Early 1950s: Findings from New Material," *China Quarterly*, no. 171 (2002): 682–703. See also Qi Zhang and Mingxing Liu, *Revolutionary Legacy, Power Structure, and Grassroots Capitalism under the Red Flag in China* (New York: Cambridge University Press, 2019), 90–93, who suggest that in Zhejiang, following the five antis in which corrupt cadres who "colluded" with the capitalists were punished, businesses were fined so heavily that they were essentially forced to sell to the state at depressed prices.

[58] Cliver, "Surviving Socialism": online text, at https://cross-currents.berkeley.edu/sites/default/files/e-journal/articles/cliver.pdf.

[59] "五反"这个事儿，大家都觉得得让一步，搞得太急会出乱子，所以这个事儿就缓了。这一下子对企业家来讲，心有余悸。很多人很盼着搞社会主义改造，企业不做了，都给你们，我把这个事儿摆脱了吧——这个心思已经出来了，" http://www.mingjinglishi.com/2013/05/1953.html https://history.sohu.com/s2013/huiketing01/.

ideology to demonstrate his progress. Obviously, he was aware that although the Communist Party did not trust businessmen, political performance was the prerequisite for bargaining with the government."[60] Li became a delegate to the Shanghai People's Congress, where, in 1957, he advocated changes to the state plan to accommodate capitalists after nationalization. During the 1956–57 period of relatively open political discourse known as the "Hundred Flowers,"[61] his request to extend state payments for private property was widely discussed. But the opening was short-lived; during the 1957 antirightist campaign, in which the state turned on many of those who had spoken up during the "Hundred Flowers," Li was an immediate victim; he, several family members, and those who had allied with him were all labeled "rightists" and denounced, and their extended families were given class labels that would haunt them for decades.[62]

The cycle of pragmatic accommodation followed by politicized reprisal culminated in the Cultural Revolution. Between 1966 and 1976, even the "reddest" of China's "nationalist capitalists" faced abuse, loss of property, and threat to life. Private businesspeople and those with "bad class backgrounds" were among the first victims of the Red Guards, who targeted "class enemies" for "offenses" that went back decades.[63] Many of their stories have been chronicled in vernacular and even official narratives of that decade of state-sponsored terror.[64] My point here is not to provide such a chronicle nor to emphasize the severity of the violence. My argument is not that capitalists, past or future, real or alleged, were persecuted or stamped out but rather that the Cultural Revolution imprinted the capriciousness of the regime on its subjects. Unlike the grassroots violence that produced regimes in Malaysia and Indonesia in the late 1960s, China's period of violence was long and variegated, marked by repeated cycles of radicalism and reversal. The Cultural Revolution itself lasted ten years and was, as I describe above, preceded by

---

[60] Xiaohong Xiao-Planes, "Buy 20 Years," *European Journal of East Asian Studies* 13, no. 2 (2014): 220–21.

[61] Mao's exhortation was, "Let a hundred flowers bloom, let a thousand schools contend." On this, see Roderick MacFarquhar, *Contradictions among the People, 1956–1957* (New York: Columbia University Press, 1974).

[62] 李传芳, 董芷林, 杨之立 (Li Chuanfang, Dong Zhilin, Yang Zhili), "追忆我的伯父'大右派'李康年" (Recalling My Uncle "The Great Rightist," Li Kangnian), 世纪 (Century), no. 3 (2015): 12–16.

[63] Roderick MacFarquhar and Michael Schoenhals, *Mao's Last Revolution* (Cambridge, MA: Belknap Press of Harvard University Press), chap. 15, "Cleansing the Class Ranks."

[64] Ibid.; 王年一 (Wang Nianyi), 大动乱的年代 (A Decade of Great Upheaval) (郑州：河南人民出版社, 1988); Jisheng Yang, *The World Turned Upside Down: A History of the Chinese Cultural Revolution*, trans. Stacy Mosher and Guo Jian (New York: Farrar, Straus and Giroux, 2020); Frank Dikötter, *The Cultural Revolution: A People's History, 1962–1976* (New York: Bloomsbury, 2016).

seventeen years of acceleration and détente, the rhythm of campaigns. In culmination, by the time that the market reforms were officially embraced, Chinese citizens, whether they had been capitalists or would eventually become capitalists, were acclimatized to political adaptation and "adept dissimulation" as a survival strategy and way of life.[65]

Capitalism, as contemporary historiography has obsessively pursued, was far from obliterated, even at the height of Maoist state socialism. Meticulous work with local-level prosecution data on informal markets and profiteering has exposed extensive capitalist activity throughout the Maoist era, and especially during the anarchy of the Cultural Revolution.[66] Practices varied throughout China, of course, but evidence abounds that local-level alliances between officials and citizens facilitated market activity and illicit commerce. Zhang Qi and Liu Mingxing show that it was in those places where such alliances were most prominent that the earliest and most extensive emergence of private business of the reform era was seen.[67] This period of regime formation in Communist China did not eliminate capitalism, and really may have never sought to, but it produced learned political behaviors that would shape capitalist practices present and future.

The common wisdom is that market reforms would have not been possible without the cataclysm of the Cultural Revolution.[68] Perhaps it is true that the total disintegration of society indeed made it possible, even inevitable, for China's leaders to imagine a future path involving markets and relying on the capitalists they had both accommodated and punished. But the behaviors and strategies that Chinese citizens had learned to survive the Mao period did not die with him, even as the PRC gradually embraced capitalists. On the contrary, the "adept dissimulation" persisted into the early and heady

---

[65] Andrew Walder's ethnographic work with industrial workers demonstrates that the socialist workplace experience habituated workers to displays of loyalty (表现). His later work on students during the Cultural Revolution shows that many students embraced radicalism as a sort of defensive or preemptive compensation for their "bad" class backgrounds. Walder, *Communist Neotraditionalism*; Walder, *Fractured Rebellion*.

[66] Adam K Frost, Zeren Li, and Yasheng Huang, "Anarchy and Capitalism in China's Cultural Revolution," working paper, 2021, https://scholar.harvard.edu/adamkfrost/publications/anarchy-and-capitalism-chinas-cultural-revolution.

[67] Zhang and Liu, *Revolutionary Legacy*.

[68] Roderick MacFarquhar expresses this "truism": "No Cultural Revolution, no reform." https://www.scmp.com/comment/insight-opinion/article/1076451/long-shadow-cultural-revolution.   In the conclusion to their book on the Cultural Revolution, MacFarquhar and Schoenhals, *Mao's Last Revolution*, state: "In the succeeding quarter-century, Mao's worst revisionist nightmare has been realized, with only himself to blame. Deng will get historians' credit for the capitalist-style modernization of China ("reform"—*gaige*) and its incorporation into the wider world ("opening"—*kaifang*), but it was Mao's disastrous enactment of his utopian fantasies that freed Deng's mind from Communist orthodoxies" (459).

decades of market reforms, during which time the political legitimacy of capitalists and markets remained uncertain. As I discuss in Chapter 5, private ownership had neither a legal foundation nor a political blessing but rather emerged informally, shifting its shape as businesspeople did what they had always done, whether they had been capitalists or students or children before 1978: they "smelled the wind and adapted" (闻风而动), placing themselves informally, and then formally, close to power so as to protect themselves from it.

These learned behaviors matter tremendously for how business is practiced in China today, both enhancing the competitive dynamism of and constraining the worldviews of participants. Expertise in discerning trends, shape-shifting, and adapting quickly have no doubt contributed to the innovative capacity of Chinese businesses, especially as they have inserted themselves into global supply chains and, notoriously, mimicked and even stolen intellectual property. Management literature is replete with adjectives to describe firms that seem best prepared to weather market and sectoral changes: agile, nimble, flexible, adaptive, and so forth. These are the same descriptors one could apply to successful navigators of China's Mao-era (and beyond) political turmoil. To be sure, staying alive in a capricious authoritarian regime is far from a sufficient condition for competitive entrepreneurship, but the practice of politics at the time of the survival and emergence of capitalism in China affected its character. At the same time, the "pervasive uncertainty" that incentivized adaptation also produced short time horizons for those who remained or became private-sector entrepreneurs. As I detail in Chapters 5 and 6, endemically short time horizons, because one cannot know when political winds will change and when efforts may be worth nothing or worse, generate sets of behaviors that militate against sustainable business development and political stability.

Even as they endeavored to be insiders, China's early capitalists would be outsiders. They knew the regime would tolerate them and make use of their talents when it suited the party-state's goals, but they also knew that the regime could turn against them at any time. Liu Hongsheng, a prominent Shanghai industrialist whom Zhou Enlai managed to recruit to return to the Mainland after he had fled to Hong Kong, said in 1949: "The Communists will never be our real friends."[69] Although he returned from Hong Kong

[69] Sherman Cochran, "Capitalists Choosing Communist China: The Liu Family of Shanghai, 1948–1956," in Jeremy Brown and Paul G. Pickowicz, eds., *Dilemmas of Victory: The Early Years of the People's Republic of China* (Cambridge, MA: Harvard University Press, 2010), 365.

and attained national fame and leadership as a patriotic capitalist, Liu was humiliated and hounded during the Cultural Revolution, during which time his second son committed suicide. He publicly made the case that the CCP's communism was not incompatible with capitalism, but he privately still harbored distrust.[70] Ultimately, he was right on both counts.

Malaysia: Vulnerability with Reciprocity

> I therefore hope that every member of our community will ask himself what he can do for his country and his Party rather than what his country and his Party can do for him. . . .We must at all times remember that political power is the only means of guaranteeing our economic and even cultural survival and political power can only come from the masses.[71]
>
> —Tan Siew Sin, twenty-fifth anniversary of the
> Malayan Chinese Association

Malaysia is the only country under study in which the period of state formation facilitated the growth of political trust between powerful political and business elites. Malaysia's postwar tumult—the decade-long "emergency" that pitted a predominantly ethnically Chinese Communist insurgency against British and Malayan forces and the formidable challenge to the consociational Malaysian regime presented by the 1969 elections and their aftermath—convinced Chinese (and Indian) business elites that submitting to harsh, but predictable, demands from above was preferable to subjecting themselves to unpredictable demands from below. They feared massive redistribution, an end to national integrity, or both.[72]

---

[70] See also Sherman Cochran, *The Capitalist Dilemma in China's Communist Revolution* (Ithaca: Cornell University Press, 2014).

[71] Tun Tan Siew Sin, "Foreword," MCA Twenty-Fifth Anniversary Souvenir Publication, 1974 (NUS Singapore-Malaysia Collection).

[72] This argument accords with those made by Case and Slater on the foundations of the Malaysian regime. Slater argues that Malaysian Chinese joined "protection pacts" with Malay elites that formed a basis for authoritarian stability. The argument I make differs slightly from that of Pepinsky, *Economic Crises and the Breakdown of Authoritarian Regimes*, in that I argue that elite Malaysian Chinese capitalists were part of the ruling coalition in Malaysia. Pepinsky and I agree, however, that they were not powerful parts of that coalition; my explanation for their lack of power is that their support for the ruling regime was quite high and they were willing to accept the more punitive policies of the state.

I focus on a central puzzle in Malaysian politics and political economy: How and why did electoral gains by "ethnically Chinese" political parties in 1969 translate into incredibly punitive policies toward those groups, and why did the Chinese business community fail to challenge those policies over the next two generations? I find that Chinese business elites, fearful of their coethnics' demands from below and committed to Malaysian citizenship as roads to China closed in the late 1940s and again in the late 1960s, submitted themselves to Malay elites, acquiescing to punitive economic policies in exchange for guarantees of political inclusion.[73] In short, they preferred reciprocity on unequal terms.

The Emergency, 1948–1957

That the experience of Japanese Occupation and its immediate aftermath produced competing ethnic nationalisms in Malaya remains an unquestioned conclusion of nearly every historian analyzing the period. A focus on the ethnic element of postwar conflict in Malaysia, however, obscures the importance of class conflict, especially in the "emergency" conflict between the MCP and the last remnants of the British imperial regime that ended in the independence of Malaya in 1957. This conflict defined the scope of political participation for lower-class Chinese, producing a new political geography of the Chinese Malaysian experience that set the stage for the political conflict—electoral and otherwise—that marked the first two decades of Malaysian independence.

Malaya after the Japanese exit and before the state of emergency in 1948 experienced the sort of flourishing of ideas about the structure of the polity and society that is only possible in the context of radical change in power and authority. The ease with which the Japanese had routed the British in Malaya and Singapore cast a long shadow over the moral authority of British imperial power in the region. The British returned to the arc of settlements that would become Malaysia after the war, but they found themselves inserted into an unfamiliar world of contestation over political and economic power.

---

[73] Donald Nonini, in the introduction to his ethnography of cultural politics and class within a Chinese Malaysian community in Penang, argues that class conflict has been neglected from studies of ethnic politics in Malaysia. His three-decade study of "infrapolitics" in Penang yields similar insights on the critical role of class in dividing political loyalties among Malaysian Chinese. Nonini, *Getting By*. See also David Brown, *The State and Ethnic Politics in Southeast Asia* (London: Routledge, 1994).

The alliances they made with Chinese guerrillas to fight the Japanese would be tested in postwar labor struggles, and British notions of how to organize a Malayan polity would meet resistance among groups for whom the struggle for representation and power was existential.

The goals of the British Malayan Administration (BMA) were many: to manage the establishment of peace in Malaya that was imagined to be requisite for its freedom and, critically, to re-establish industrial activity and commodity production, the latter a critical source of much-needed dollars for the British Empire in its postwar rebuilding efforts.[74] The BMA found common cause with several local industrialists, bringing exiled Chinese businesspeople back from abroad and embracing forms of grand and petty corruption that, in the view of some historians, constitutes a form of "crony capitalism" so blatant that locals dubbed it the "Black Market Administration."[75] In addition to this attenuating legitimacy for the BMA, wide swaths of the Malay Peninsula were essentially stateless, run by remnants of the Malayan People's Anti-Japanese Army.

In this context, with uncertainty over political ideologies and ethnic power-sharing, the BMA was pursuing a "fashioning of a 'Malayan' national identity," taking up "nation-building with evangelical fervor."[76] Efforts at "nation-building" would include a tentative tolerance of the Communists as long as they appeared to agitate through formal institutions and various proposals for a post-British Malaya. The first, the 1946 Malayan Union, would grant equal rights and citizenship to most residents—Chinese, Indian, and Malay—of the Malay Peninsula. The opposition from ethnic Malays and the sultans who occupied exalted positions was swift and serious. A budding movement of nonreligious and nonsultan Malay elites coalesced behind Onn bin Jaffar and his UMNO. The UMNO was fatally wounded by the refusal of the Malays to participate and recognize the polity's authority. In 1948 it was replaced by the Malayan Federation, which mandated that fifteen continuous years of residence in Malaya be required for citizenship. In effect, the Federation exiled many Indian and Chinese in situ as it placed Malays at the center of the emerging polity.[77]

[74] On the importance of Malaya for British fiscal policy, see Caroline Elkins, *Legacy of Violence: A History of the British Empire* (New York: Alfred A. Knopf, 2022), esp. chaps. 9, 10. Elkins also discusses the "civilizing" justification of British postwar violence in Malaya and elsewhere. See also Bayly and Harper, *Forgotten Wars.*

[75] Elkins, *Legacy of Violence,* 101, 108–9.

[76] Elkins, *Legacy of Violence,* 99–100.

[77] James P. Ongkili, *Nation-Building in Malaysia, 1946–1974* (New York: Oxford University Press, 1985).

Issues of class, labor, and capital were also sources of tremendous political contestation. As ethnic and political conflict seemed to be exploding at the grassroots across the peninsula, the BMA and others were attempting to contain large-scale conflict in formal institutions. The MCP was pursuing its objectives through labor organization and activism rather than through violence. Strikes, drawing on established organizations and repertoires of activism and protest that pervaded Malaya before the Japanese invasion, were prevalent in urban areas. Chinese clan and guild networks among the imported workers who staffed Malaya's rubber plantations, transport hubs, and industrial enterprises played especially important activist roles.[78] The BMA and industrial elites, however, were unyielding to labor demands; colonial authorities painted unions as politically ambitious and implacable, responding with arrests, deportations, and violence.[79] In June 1948, fed-up organizers struck a plantation, killing three Caucasian managers. For the next decade, the MCP and its sympathizers became involved in a Maoism-inspired guerrilla insurgency against British security forces that sought to both protect the empire's critical economic assets in Malaya and exterminate the threat of communism in the peninsula as the global Cold War was emerging.

The Emergency is typically depicted as an ethnic civil war as much as a Communist insurgency. While it is true that the MCP was dominated by ethnic Chinese, it was not merely an ethnic insurgency, a fact illustrated by the deep opposition to the insurgency that came from elite Chinese. Tan Siew Sin, who would serve as minister of finance for fifteen years under the National Front (BN, Barisan Nasional) said of the Emergency in 1986, "That very nearly sealed the fate of the Chinese, because the British then regarded most Chinese in this country either as Communists or at the best, Communist sympathizers. There was even talk of deporting 500,000 Chinese squatters back to China for aiding the Communists."[80] The Malayan Chinese Association (MCA) was founded in this context in 1949 to amalgamate

[78] See Yuen Tai, *Labour Unrest in Malaya, 1934–1941: The Rise of the Workers' Movement* (Kuala Lumpur: Institute of Postgraduate Studies and Research, University of Malaya, 2000). See also Meredith Weiss, *Protest and Possibilities: Civil Society and Coalitions for Political Change in Malaysia* (Stanford: Stanford University Press, 2006), chap. 3.

[79] Bayly and Harper, *Forgotten Wars*, 205–9.

[80] "The Role of the MCA in Malaysia," speech by Tan Siew Sin (President of the Malaysian Chinese Association) to the Historical Society of the University of Malaya, September 10, 1965, 7 (NUS Singapore-Malaysia Collection). Such deportations did occur. Caroline Elkins estimates that there were at least twenty-five thousand deportations; she also cites British officials who have estimated as many as forty thousand. See Elkins, *Legacy of Violence*, 12.

Chinese ethnic and guild associations in opposition to the MCP and to represent the interests of Malayan Chinese in the forging of a new state. In the words of Tan Cheg Lok, a MCA founder, the goal of the MCA was to "foster and to engender a truly Malayan outlook, consciousness and patriotism among the domiciled Malayan Chinese in order to forge and fortify their ties with this country and unity as an integral part and parcel of the Malayan people, and to help develop their sense of civil responsibility, duty and obligation to their country of adoption."[81] The MCA would garner a membership of over 150,000 within a year, attracting support from urban business-oriented Chinese groups and undertaking substantial welfare efforts for both urban and rural Chinese to expand support. Lotteries would fund investment in so-called New Villages—settlements for the vast number of landless Chinese "squatters" who, whether by force or allegiance, provided aid to the MCP.[82]

The Emergency, its effect amplified by its timing in relation to the Chinese Mainland, was a crucible in which the political affiliations of Chinese economic elites were formed. The rise of an anti-imperialist and Communist "new China" generated an urgency on the part of both late colonial elites and Chinese bourgeoisie to promote a Malaysian identity and belonging for Malaysians of Chinese descent. Historians debate the relative importance of Chinese propaganda, British imperial forces, and, more broadly, geopolitical and domestic factors in shaping these identities, but there is a great consensus that Malayan Chinese business elites embraced "Malayanization" as a direct reaction to the threat of communism near and far.[83] Chinese establishment figures and economic elites would invoke the Emergency for decades to come, especially during moments of disunity and crisis within the Chinese community, which were many. At an MCA meeting in March 1968, Tan Siew Sin said, "It is doubly important that the majority who are loyal

[81] Quoted in Anna Belogurova, "The Malayan Communist Party and the Malayan Chinese Association: Internationalism and Nationalism in Chinese Overseas Political Participation, c. 1920–1960," in Leslie Hames and Elisabeth Leake, eds., Decolonization and the Cold War: Negotiating Independence (London: Bloomsbury, 2015), 135. Tan Cheng-Lock's efforts to form an MCA failed in 1948, but they succeeded in 1949 because of intervention by the Emergency. Lim San Kok, "Some Aspects of the Malayan Chinese Association, 1949–69," Journal of the South Seas Society 26, no. 2 (1971): 31–48 (NUS Singapore-Malaysia Collection).

[82] Tan Siew Sin, "Role of the MCA," 8; Belogurova, "Malayan Communist Party," 134.

[83] Anna E. Belogurova, The Nanyang Revolution: The Comintern and Chinese Networks in Histories, Cultures, Identities: Studies in Malaysian Chinese Worlds (Singapore: Singapore University Press, 2019); Taylor, "Not a Particularly Happy Expression"; Fujio Hara, "Malayan Chinese and China: Conversion in Identity Consciousness, 1945–1957" (Tokyo: Institute of Developing Economies, Occasional Paper no. 33, 1997); T. N. Harper, The End of Empire and the Making of Malaya (New York: Cambridge University Press, 1998); Wang, "Chinese Politics in Malaya."

should show under no uncertain terms that they thoroughly disapprove of the small minority. . . . Disapproval unless something more than neutrality or even silent disapproval in the face of the Communist threat which, though not really apparent to the public, is nonetheless real and ever present. . . . In short, *bumiputeras* [ethnic Malays and, later, other indigenous peoples] of Chinese origin should show that they are as loyal to this country as any other *bumiputera*."[84]

This formal participation approach was forged in the early 1950s in municipal elections, during which the MCA would join UMNO to form, along with the Malayan Indian Congress, the Alliance. Contestation on both sides—from members of the MCA who demanded more concrete citizenship assurances and from UMNO elites who resisted multiethnic participation— troubled the Alliance's performance in its early years, but it nonetheless grew through contestation in local elections. In the first elections for the Legislative Council in 1955, Malays would form the overwhelming majority in fifty out of fifty-two districts, but Tunku Abdul Rahman, the head of the UMNO and an advocate of both a noncommunal view of Malayan politics and Malay dominance, convinced his party to hold fifteen seats for Chinese representatives. This pattern of politics, by which Chinese establishment elites would accept Malay political dominance in exchange for a formal seat at the table, characterized Malaysian political norms after independence.

This was also written into the formal constitution of the newly independent state. Article 153 gave the king of Malaysia the duty to "safeguard the special position of the Malays" through quotas and various forms of preferential treatment (most of which I address in the next chapter). In exchange, the question of citizenship for Malayans of Chinese and Indian descent was settled, as was the question of Chinese-language education in the new state. In the MCA's own statement: "The MCA spent more than four months in bargaining before a compromised memorandum. . . . Indeed, the MCA had done its utmost on these issues. The MCA proceeded very carefully, in the spirit of sacrifice and mutual cooperation, to safeguard the vital interests of the Chinese and the Indians, who have adopted Malaya as their country. As a result of the MCA's efforts, thousands upon thousands of Chinese have acquired citizenship and obtained a rightful place under the Malayan sun. It could be said that the MCA had saved thousands upon thousands of Chinese

---

[84] Tun Tan Siew Sin, "The Challenge Ahead," March 23, 1968, speech at the MCA General Assembly, Kuala Lumpur, 11–12 (NUS Singapore-Malaysia Collection).

from their plight."[85] The point is not that the MCA is right about its role and the benefits of its approach, but that elite Malayan Chinese saw these compromises as the foundation of their safety.

The newly independent state, however, would face a turbulent first few decades. The incorporation of Sabah, Sarawak, and Singapore in 1963 to form Malaysia would change the ethnic balance of power and introduce a new force of Chinese power in the form of Lee Kuan Yew's People's Action Party (PAP). The more moderate MCA, again holding dear its politics of accommodation with the UMNO and the Tunku-led Alliance, fielded candidates in Singapore, and Lee, in turn, fielded PAP candidates on the peninsula. This aggressive politics proved too severe a threat to Malaysia's delicate balance, resulting in Singapore being kicked out of the Federation in 1965. But rising dissatisfaction with the representation of Chinese interests, and especially those of working-class and rural Chinese, would dislodge the grand bargain of Malaysian politics and generate violence within just a few years.[86]

May 13 and After

The 1969 elections and their aftermath constituted a critical juncture in the young Malaysian polity: the consociational bargain between communal elites suffered a dramatic blow in federal elections when the predominantly ethnically Chinese parties gained seats at the expense of the MCA and other members of the Alliance. The Democratic Action Party (DAP) and Gerakan, both formally progressive/left, multiracial parties with strong support from urban Chinese in particular, made surprising gains, partly by campaigning against *bumiputera* privileges and claiming to be more legitimate representatives of grassroots Chinese interests than the elite MCA, but the Alliance still retained a parliamentary majority. Nonetheless, the election results were popularly received as a major blow to the Alliance; Gerakan and DAP rallies in Kuala Lumpur and other urban centers quickly turned into ethnic rioting in May 1969. The violence and destruction etched a lasting scar on the Malaysian political conscience and contributed to a new grand bargain and role for the Malaysian state in the economy and society.

---

[85] MCA Twenty-fifth Anniversary Souvenir Publication, 1974, 2 (NUS Singapore-Malaysia Collection).

[86] G. P. Daniel, *Dr. Ling Liong Sik and the Politics of Ethnic Chinese Unity* (Selangor Darul Ehsan, Malaysia: Times, 1995); Ongkili, *Nation-Building in Malaysia*.

Understandably, because they translated into ethnic rioting and a massive project of redistribution with an ethnic logic, the 1969 elections are interpreted as evidence that the ethnic balance of power in postindependence Malaysia was untenable. This is certainly the interpretation Mahathir himself has articulated for decades.[87] A closer look at events preceding the elections, however, suggests an important additional interpretation: a confluence of economic troubles uniquely affected middle- and lower-class Malaysian Chinese, who voted against the MCA both because they resented the MCA's domination by Chinese economic elites and because economic hardships were exacerbating resentment against Malay privileges. In short, the 1969 elections reflected both the fragility of an ethnically heterogeneous society and class conflict among Malaysian Chinese. Understanding the class dimension helps make sense of why the business class would further embrace Malay political dominance—even "coercive redistribution"—in the aftermath of the violence.[88]

Economically, the 1960s were hard on urban and rural lower-class Chinese communities. In rural areas, many Chinese who had been forcibly resettled into the "New Villages" found their communities underinvested. Poor upkeep and a lack of economic opportunities prompted both resentment of federal elites and urbanization. The latter combined unhappily with already high unemployment rates in many urban areas. In Penang, elimination of the Free Port Status in 1969 precipitated an unemployment rate of over 15 percent.[89] Before that, the collapse of rubber and tin prices—rubber at a nineteen-year low—and production during the late 1950s and early 1960s forced Chinese plantation workers off the rural plantations and into the cities.[90] At an MCA meeting in March 1968, a year before the election violence, then head of the MCA, Tan Siew Sin, acknowledging widespread economic discontent

[87] For example: "Malaysia's second great post-War crisis occurred with race riots in Kuala Lumpur on May 13, 1969. . . . And to ensure there would be no recurrence of such riots we implemented the New Economic Policy (NEP) aimed at eradicating poverty regardless of race and the elimination of the identification of race with economic functions." Dr. Mahathir Mohamad, "Malaysia: Bouncing Back from the Brink," speech delivered at the World Economic Forum Annual Meeting in Davos, Switzerland, January 29, 1999, in Hashim Makaruddin, ed., *Selected Speeches of Dr. Mahathir Mohamad*, vol. 2: *Managing the Malaysian Economy* (Subang Jaya, Selangor: Pelanduk, 2000), 49.

[88] Michael Albertus, Sofia Fenner, and Dan Slater, *Coercive Distribution* (New York Cambridge University Press, 2018).

[89] Neil Khor, "Watching Penang 'Grow,'" March 3, 2008, https://www.malaysiakini.com/opinions/79059; Penang Chamber of Commerce, 110th Anniversary Publication, 2013.

[90] The drop in prices was most severe for tin in the late 1950s, pushing rural Chinese into the cities as dredging and mining production collapsed. Production levels did not recover until 1968. Perak Chinese Mining Association, *37th Anniversary Publication*, 1972, 40–43.

among Chinese communities, said, "When it is remembered that all these things have happened within less than one year, it is not too much to claim that a society which can take these shocks and yet remain on an even keel must necessarily be a strong and stable one."[91]

But it would not prove to be strong and stable enough. In the 1969 elections, ethnic Chinese parties campaigned against MCA candidates, demanding a less conciliatory tone on everything from Chinese-medium education to special economic privileges for Malays. The more moderate DAP argued that "the have-nots in Malaysia are of all races. They are found in rural areas as well as urban slums," while the People's Progressive Party (PPP) more aggressively challenged Malay privileges.[92] The DAP and PPP bested MCA candidates in urban areas, traditionally the party's stronghold; only thirteen out of thirty-three candidates won, and two cabinet-level ministers (commerce and industry, and welfare services) lost.[93] The Alliance maintained its electoral majority, but lost substantial ground, the majority of it to insurgent Chinese parties.[94] MCA elites attributed the defeat to a combination of economic disenfranchisement for many Chinese and growing concerns that they would be politically disenfranchised in a Malay-dominated state, exacerbated by the "subtraction" of Chinese-dominated Singapore.[95] (See Table 2.2.)

The 1969 elections ended in rioting and violence. Victory rallies held by insurgent parties sparked counter-rallies, and violence erupted on May 13, 1969, lasting for days. Hundreds were killed and many neighborhoods of Kuala Lumpur and other cities were destroyed. The military, which was called in the evening the violence broke out, took days to regain control of the capital. Many feared the riots were a fatal blow to the nation, one that, after all, had already endured two decades of political tumult. Parliamentary

---

[91] Tun Tan Siew Sin, "The Challenge Ahead," March 23, 1968, speech at the MCA General Assembly, Kuala Lumpur, 2 (NUS Singapore-Malaysia Collection).

[92] Both were essentially Chinese parties. The DAP was the successor to the Singaporean PAP. The DAP manifesto is quoted in Ongkili, *Nation-Building in Malaysia*, 200.

[93] MCA 25th Anniversary Souvenir Publication, 1974 (NUS Singapore-Malaysia Collection).

[94] Overall, the Alliance lost twenty-three seats from the 1964 general election, fourteen of which were lost by MCA candidates.

[95] Ongkili, *Nation-Building in Malaysia*, 193–95. The MCA's own historical narrative is that economically aggrieved, newly urbanized Chinese were susceptible to Socialist and Communist overtures with ethnic content. I do not mean to argue that economic grievances among Chinese were the only issues. The 1967 law designating Malay as the only official national language and the end of "confrontation" with Indonesia, and the national unity it produced, were important factors. My aim is to show that class considerations within the Chinese community affected the outlook of business elites in particular.

Table 2.2 MCA Performance in 1959, 1964, and 1969 Elections

	1959		1964		1969	
	Contested	*Won*	*Contested*	*Won*	*Contested*	*Won*
Seats						
Federal	31	19	33	27	33	13
State	78	59	82	67	80	26
Votes received (% of total)						
State		16.29		17.39		12.71
Federal		14.82		18.68		13.50

Source: Loh Kok Wah, "The Politics of Chinese Unity in Malaysia: Reform and Conflict in the Malaysian Chinese Association 1971–73," ISEAS Occasional Paper no. 70, 8 (NUS Singapore-Malaysia Collection).

democracy was suspended. Tun Abdul Razak, inheriting leadership of the UMNO and the country from Tunku and following a playbook very similar to Tunku's reaction to the violence in 1948, vested power in a National Operations Council, a nine-member committee modeled on the Operations Council during the Emergency.[96]

As the MCA and the Alliance regrouped, the lesson they took from the May 13 violence was that Malaysian society had to be radically transformed if the country were to hold together. The 1957 bargain saw Chinese citizenship exchanged for recognition of Malay privileges and hegemony. Ironically, in the aftermath of a Chinese working-class electoral insurgence that shook the foundations of the Alliance and challenged this bargain, the Alliance adopted a solution that would exacerbate, rather than accommodate, the demands of the insurgents. The New Economic Policy (NEP), adopted in 1971, sought to economically empower Malays and create a society in which race was disassociated from economic function or geographic location. The MCA, having lost an election for accommodating Malay demands, was fully on board.

Chinese business elites and Malaysian political elites had two reference points for the violence of 1969, both terrifying. One was the recent domestic past, the vision of a nation embroiled in class and ethnic conflict and unable

---

[96] Ongkili, *Nation-Building in Malaysia*, 203–15. See also Abdul Razak bin Dato' Hussein and Haji Tun, *The May 13th Tragedy: A Report* (Kuala Lumpur: National Operations Council, 1969); Tunku Abdul Rahman, *May 13: Before and After* (Kuala Lumpur: Utusan Melayu Press, 1969).

to hold together. The second reference was the even more recent and on-going regional political context: namely, the violence against Indonesians of Chinese descent in Malaysia's neighbor and the height of radicalism in Mainland China during the throes of the Cultural Revolution. As the next section details, Indonesia's postindependence political trajectory entailed an unusual tolerance for a wide array of ideas about what form the nation and state should take, but it ended with extreme violence against Communists, real and suspected, and Chinese Indonesians, whether those two identities overlapped or not. The fate of Chinese Indonesians, already changing their names and eliminating Chinese-language and cultural havens, loomed large in the minds of Chinese elites and would become a recurring theme in MCA exhortations to maintain a political voice: "The plight of the Chinese in the neighbouring territories is attributed mainly to their failure in recognizing the importance of this move [to join the Alliance], and to their refusal to join in with the natives in the struggle for independence. The consequences are quite clear."[97] At the same time, especially for business elites, the route to Mainland China was closed. Families with overseas relatives, especially capitalist relatives, were punished in the radicalism and anarchy of Maoist mobilizations.

The best choice Malaysian business elites had to preserve their assets and safety was to accept, even facilitate, "coercive redistribution" and maintain political insider status so as to shape the details of implementation. In the thick of rank-and-file frustration with the NEP in the late 1970s, the chairman of the Malaysian Chinese Chamber of Commerce said: "We all know if we do not have a political status in the government; we have no guarantee of our economic safety. . . . We must encourage the fight for political representation in every area and increase our voice in the government (within the orderly processes of democratic institutions)."[98] This commitment to political inclu-sion fomented political trust between Chinese business elites and the BN for decades to come. As the next chapter shows, family businesses and small and medium firms bristled for generations at the NEP and Malay hegemony, but,

[97] "Why You Should Join the MCA," speech by Enche Khaw Kai Boh, Minister of Local Government and Housing and MCA Vice President, March 15, 1968, Collected MCA Pamphlets (NUS Singapore-Malaysia Collection).

[98] Speech of the Chairman, Malaysian Chinese Chamber of Commerce, Malaysian Chinese Economic Conference, Report on Conference Proceedings, April 9, 1978 (Kuala Lumpur Federal Hotel). 马来西亚中华工商联合，全国华人经济大会。 报告录 (NUS Singapore-Malaysia Collection).

without support from the economic elites, they had little choice but to accept this dominant feature of Malaysian politics.

Indonesia: Engineering Vulnerability and Closeness without Trust

> The Chinese here in Indonesia are considered more the businesspeople, right? So [Indonesians] always look at the Chinese as being the ones who make money. And I think that perspective always tied on with the fact that you are Chinese—you are the one who makes money, you make as much profit as you can here in Indonesia. So trying to change that perception—it takes a lot of effort for me to show that I'm actually not just here to make money. Right? That I am here to also contribute to our country.[99]

> I always believed that as an Indonesian Chinese, especially, I am in a sensitive position. We are a racial and religious minority. I am Christian. I am non-Muslim. And I'm of Chinese race. The protection of Indonesian Chinese or minorities is not purely depending on the law, even though we have anti-discrimination laws. I always share with my fellow colleagues that for the Chinese people, Chinese-Indonesian people, what can protect us is our behavior. It's not purely dependent on the anti-discrimination law. You have to have proper behavior as well. . . . I like to show my sympathy for this nation, that I want to be a proper businessman.[100]

As the above quotations show, Indonesians of Chinese heritage occupy a position of political and social marginality. These sentiments, expressed nearly two decades after Indonesia's transition to a multiparty democracy, reflect a very long history of political exclusion and vulnerability accompanied by economic success.[101] This dual status—economically privileged, politically marginal— was both harnessed and nurtured by Indonesia's authoritarian rulers, including

---

[99] Interview with Shinta Widjaja Kamdani, Jakarta, November 28, 2016, Creating Emerging Markets Oral History Collection, Baker Special Collections, Harvard Business School.

[100] Interview with Dato' Sri Prof. Tahir, Jakarta, January 24, 2017, Creating Emerging Markets Oral History Collection, Baker Special Collections, Harvard Business School.

[101] It must be said that not all Indonesians of Chinese heritage have met with economic success.

the Dutch imperial regime and Suharto's New Order. For the Dutch, nurturing a class of ethnic Chinese middlemen proved to be a useful strategy for enabling economic extraction and political repression, an "intermediary economic force in the process of mercantile extraction" whose "insulation from the local population made them vulnerable and dependent."[102] This lack of an indigenous bourgeoisie and political uncertainty for Chinese communities are common to the colonial heritage of both Malaysia and Indonesia. But the fact that there were smaller numbers of Chinese in Indonesia (roughly 5 percent of the population) and the particular events in the Indonesian revolution and the founding of the New Order would alienate ethnic Chinese business elites from politics. While Malaysian Chinese elites pursued and maintained political inclusion and submitted to punishing economic policies, Chinese Indonesian business elites depended informally on the Suharto regime and particularistically on political elites for protection. The result was a form of mutual dependence between Suharto and the *cukong*, but one built on unequal vulnerability, distrust, and threat of defection.

The Uncertain Status of Chinese Indonesians

The early to mid-twentieth century was an "age of movements" (*pergerakan*) in Indonesia, where expressions of communism, Islam, secular nationalism, and more all circulated, overlapping and contradicting one another even within the same circles.[103] Expressions of nationalism, with the exception of communism, almost universally excluded Indonesians of Chinese descent, distinguishing sharply between the *bangsa Indonesia* (Indonesian people or nation) and "minorities of foreign descent."[104] Revolutionary violence was typically accompanied by property damage to Chinese shops and neighborhoods, both organized violence carried out by the Indonesian Republican Military Forces and spontaneous violence in the absence of state authority and protection.[105]

---

[102] Robison, *Indonesia*, 19. On the lack of an indigenous bourgeoisie in Indonesia, see Jan H. Boeke, *Economics and Economic Policy of Dual Societies, as Exemplified by Indonesia* (New York: International Secretariat, Institute of Pacific Relations, 1953).

[103] See John Thayer Sidel, *Republicanism, Communism, Islam: Cosmopolitan Origins of Revolution in Southeast Asia* (Ithaca: Cornell University Press, 2021).

[104] Herbert Feith and Lance Castles, comps., *Indonesian Political Thinking, 1945–64* (Ithaca: Cornell University Press, 1970), 340.

[105] Zhou, *Migration*, 18; Mary F. Somers Heidhues, *Peranakan Chinese Politics in Indonesia* (Ithaca: Southeast Asia Program, Cornell University, 1964); Twang, *Chinese Business Elite*, 155–62.

Nevertheless, the Chinese played a role in the revolution. Though many *peranakan* Indonesian Chinese were associated with embracing Dutch rule, the socially and economically rising *totok* groups found common ground, if not common cause, with Indonesian revolutionaries. Chinese intermediaries were critical to providing basic supplies for the revolutionary forces against the Dutch. During the revolution, and especially during the Dutch blockade, transnationally connected groups of Chinese were able to get commodities from Indonesia—rubber, spices, and more—to regional markets in exchange for much-needed cash and to get necessary goods to the revolutionary fighters. Importantly, it was the less embedded *totok* communities, especially Chinese immigrants from Fujian, who both had the transnational contacts and were uninvested in Dutch networks, that emerged as allies of the revolutionary forces.[106] This relationship foreshadowed ones to come. For example, Liem Sioe Liong, better known as Sudono Salim, the New Order's top *cukong*, first met Suharto in the hills of central Java during the revolution. Liem supplied basic goods to the soldiers, and "the trust that Liem earned with some of Suharto's top aides came in handy after Suharto became president and was looking for businessmen to work with."[107]

When the Dutch finally transferred sovereignty in 1949, the status of Chinese of Indonesian descent remained unsettled. A 1929 law from the Nationalist government in Mainland China designated all overseas Chinese as citizens, a practice that persisted through wartime and into the birth of the PRC. Republic policies in the early 1950s distinguished between citizens and aliens, and therefore the issue of citizenship formalization became urgent. Eventually, a 1955 treaty between the PRC and Indonesia allowed about half of the 2.5 million or so Indonesians of Chinese descent to either renounce their Chinese citizenship and declare Indonesian citizenship, "return" to China, or remain an alien in Indonesia.[108] At the same time that the treaty was finally being implemented in 1960, the Republic was also adopting a ban on retail trade by "aliens" in small towns and rural areas, an effort to "attack the traditional Chinese role as middleman" between agricultural producers and export markets and Indonesian consumers and imported goods. The ban, accompanied by violence and a deteriorating balance of interests in

---

[106] Twang, *Chinese Business Elite*, chap. 6.

[107] Nancy Chng and Richard Borsuk, *Liem Sioe Liong's Salim Group: The Business Pillar of Suharto's Indonesia* (Singapore: Institute of Southeast Asian Studies, 2014), xiii.

[108] There is no "official" number for the size of the Chinese community. Skinner estimates between 2.3 and 2.6 million, and the PRC embassy in Jakarta estimates 2.7 million in 1957. See Zhou, *Migration*, 5–6, and Somers Heidhues, *Peranakan Chinese Politics*, 13–14.

the unstable years of parliamentary democracy, prompted many *totok* and *peranakans* to leave Indonesia.

The retail ban reflected contestation over the economic role of the Chinese in the 1950s. The "Assaat" movement, which demanded preferential treatment in economic affairs for *pribumi*, was initiated in the mid-1950s. In a famous speech, Assaat, a leader of the Masjumi party and chairman of the All-Indonesia National Economic Congress, gave formal voice to the political views held by many:

> *Totok* father, *totok* mother, capital from his father. Such a man is a foreigner. Socially and economically, he is still part of the Chinese *totok* community; yet he could become an Indonesian citizen. Do these people feel themselves Indonesian? Do they feel one with the Indonesian people? Would they be prepared to defend the interests of Indonesia if there was a dispute with another country, even if it was the Chinese People's Republic or Taiwan? . . . If we give in now, then the revolution which has claimed the lives of hundreds of thousands of Indonesians will have been in vain. Economically, we will still be oppressed by the Chinese.[109]

The crisis of 1959–60 forced hundreds of thousands of Chinese from rural areas into cities and still others to "return" to the PRC.[110]

Thus, as Indonesian democracy seemed existentially challenged by centrifugal tendencies, so too did Indonesians of Chinese descent. On the eve of the violence of 1965, the Communists appeared to be the only major political-ideological group to embrace the Chinese cause. As has been well documented, the Parti Kommunist Indonesia, or PKI, founded a year before the CCP as Asia's first Marxist party, was close to the PRC even as relations between the two countries were tenuous.[111] The PRC, like the Republic of China before it, was vocal in defending the interests of the Chinese in Indonesia, but it was unable to demand much from the Sukarno government without alienating it.[112] Again, the intersection of Indonesian domestic

---

[109] Assaat, "The Chinese Grip on Our Economy," speech to the All-Indonesian National Importers Congress, March 1956. Full text of *Badan Pekerdja KENSI Pusat* (Central Working Committee of the All-Indonesia National Economic Congress) (Djakarta: Djambatan, 1957), can be found in Herbert Feith and Lance Castles, comps., *Indonesian Political Thinking, 1945–1965* (Ithaca: Cornell University Press, 1970), 343–46.

[110] Zhou, *Migration*, chap. 6.

[111] Jeremy Friedman, *Ripe for Revolution: Building Socialism in the Third World* (Cambridge, MA: Harvard University Press, 2021).

[112] Zhou, *Migration*.

politics with Chinese politics proved to be consequential for the Indonesians of Chinese descent. Ironically, the group that had been most associated with economic dominance would also be associated with a domestic Communist movement, a combination that produced cataclysmic violence during the bloody birth of Suharto's New Order.

Violence and the Birth of the New Order

The opaque and bizarre events that led to Sukarno's loss of power and Suharto's capture of power are the subject of an increasingly rich body of literature among contemporary historians. What is known is that a group of military officers attempted a poorly devised coup, murdering several generals and throwing their bodies in a ditch in suburban Jakarta in the early hours of October 1, 1965. Within hours of the announcement by the insurgents that they had taken control of strategic locations in Jakarta, Suharto, who was commander of the Army's Strategic Reserve, had wrested control over the army and was set to destroy the insurgents. Generations have speculated about the powers behind the coup, whether Suharto himself had advance knowledge, and what role external powers, chiefly the PRC, may have had. What is abundantly clear is that the September 30 Movement (Gestapu), as it would become known in Indonesia, was the "pretext" for mass violence against real, or suspected, Communists in Indonesia, and a wide swath of other victims, including ethnic Chinese. Suharto's fight against the PKI would constitute the New Order's founding myth, an existential battle for the survival of Indonesia, and would justify Suharto's concentration of power and enable his regime to garner support from global anticommunist allies.

The mass violence that racked Indonesian society in 1965 and 1966 was both chaotic and organized, a state-sponsored period of terror during which the Indonesian Armed Forces murdered hundreds of thousands of people, mostly executing detainees, and tens of thousands more were murdered in the climate of chaos, conflict, and suspicion that the violence produced.[113] As with most violent convulsions in Indonesian society, those of Chinese

---

[113] John Roosa, *Pretext for Mass Murder: The September 30th Movement and Suharto's Coup d'État in Indonesia* (Madison: University of Wisconsin Press, 2006); Jess Melvin, *The Army and the Indonesian Genocide: Mechanics of Mass Murder* (London: Routledge, 2021); Jemma Purdey, *Anti-Chinese Violence in Indonesia, 1996–1999* (Honolulu: University of Hawai'i Press, 2006).

descent were targeted, whether because the chaos offered opportunity for retribution for long-held grievances, because the PKI was the most prominent political organization friendly to the Chinese, because communism was associated with the PRC, or because of some combination of these things. The violence was astounding. The first waves in 1965 and 1966 targeted PRC-associated organizations and individuals. Zhou Taomo finds that "aliens" were asked to hang PRC flags on their homes and businesses to indicate that they were not nationals and therefore outside of the political conflict only to find the flags led armed groups directly to them.[114] After the massacres had mostly annihilated the PKI and its sympathizers, ethnic Chinese were targeted en masse, and various Chinese organizations were declared linked to the PKI and attacked.[115] The violence against Chinese groups had a political logic in the founding of the New Order; the military exacted a campaign of existential fear on Chinese communities to both discipline them and consolidate the new regime.[116]

In the regime's shuddering, violent birth, ethnic Chinese were decidedly on the outside of formal politics in Suharto's New Order. Their status as outsiders would be formalized during the regime's early period, with Chinese-language schools and organizations banned and ethnic Chinese citizens forced to adopt Indonesian names. The formal exclusion and perennial threat of violence was a foundation of Suharto's regime. In the same way that the murders in 1965 and 1966 were officially blamed on the spontaneous eruption of violence but were in reality orchestrated carefully by the military, Suharto assured Chinese elites that only he and the army could protect them from violence while simultaneously stoking it to maintain fear and control. As in 1959–60, many Chinese Indonesians relocated to the PRC, where they were received as heroes but then thrown into China's own ongoing political chaos at the outset of the Cultural Revolution. Business elites, in contrast, did not have such a choice; they had assets to lose in Indonesia and faced the threat of persecution in China, which was experiencing its own cataclysmic violence in the form of the Cultural Revolution.

Chinese economic elites would prove to be the perfect cronies for Suharto, political outsiders unable to mobilize against him. Although individual elites would come to depend closely on Suharto and his family—relationships

---

[114] Zhou, *Migration*, 183.

[115] This included Baperki (the Consultative Council for Indonesian Citizenship) and its Universitas Res Republik (Res Publica University).

[116] Zhou, *Migration*; Melvin, *The Army*.

I detail in Chapter 4—their status in the New Order was always precarious. Relationships between political elites and business elites were built not on trust but on fear of defection. Endemic vulnerability shaped corporate forms, economic behaviors, and political relationships for the next thirty years, incentivizing Chinese elites to depend particularistically on Suharto and his associates but also to hedge by endangering those same elites and distributing assets beyond the reach of the regime. These elites would build empires under Suharto, all the while acting as if they could not really trust him to protect them. Eventually, their expectations were self-fulfilling. They had no formal political power in the New Order, but the withdrawal of their support for Suharto in the form of capital exodus during the Asian Financial Crisis would prove among the regime's fatal blows.

Conclusion: Capitalism's Precarious Legitimacy

Alfred Chandler's history of American capitalism describes a process by which business elites eclipsed political elites as the most legitimate economic decision-makers as firms "acquired functions hitherto carried out by the market." The federal government, by contrast, was a legitimate economic actor only insofar as firms and managers were unable to produce growth and stability: "Government officials had no intention of replacing the managers as the coordinators of current demand and allocator of resources for the future. They acted only when the activities of the corporate managers failed to maintain full employment and high demand. The federal government became a coordinator and allocator of last resort."[117] The social and political effects of the high legitimacy of the business class are readily apparent in the United States. Policies are routinely criticized as overly prescriptive or interventionist in processes that ought to be left to capitalists as the primary actors, and any program that seems to connote government ownership or industrial policy is quickly dismissed, by some, as illogical or potentially distortionary.

The process of regime formation in the countries under study here produced the opposite outcome: capitalists emerged as actors without political or social legitimacy, while governments were endowed with legitimate power to manage

[117] Alfred D. Chandler, *The Visible Hand: The Managerial Revolution in American Business* (Cambridge, MA: Belknap Press of Harvard University Press, 1977), 1, 497.

economies. Again, the sources of capitalist illegitimacy varied, as did the willingness of business elites to submit to the power of the state, and these varying outcomes mattered in the establishment of patterns of state-business relations that would endure for decades. In Malaysia, Chinese business elites submitted to Malay political hegemony and, eventually, a program of coercive redistribution for fear that political exclusion posed an existential threat. In Indonesia and China, capitalists learned to cloak their pursuits in the language of nationalism and rely on particularistic relationships with political elites for safety. At the same time, they learned to fear the state, and they developed worldviews, manifest in economic behaviors and firm structures, that reflected these fears.

The business elites under study here made political choices based on a transnational, regional logic as well as a national one. The trajectories of these three countries intersected in consequential ways. Contestation over Chinese nationalism and global communism was refracted through local ethnic struggles and imperial relations in Southeast Asia. Overseas Chinese communities in Malaya and Indonesia faced uncertainties on all sides: whether they would be citizens of new states and what shape those states would take, and what would "China" be if they chose to "return" or emigrate there. The CCP's victory in the Mainland and the targeting of capitalists and those with family overseas during the Cultural Revolution affected the choices available to Malaysians and Indonesians of Chinese descent. Anthony Reid writes that the Maoist period "rendered the ancestral land unusually unattractive as a magnet of focus of loyalty. The idealistic youth who 'returned' in the 1940s to build a fatherland they had never known suffered miseries that became known in the diaspora."[118] Within Southeast Asia, the contrasting fates of Chinese communities in Indonesia and Malaysia led each community to further embrace its own realities. The violence of the May 13 riots paled in comparison to the mass murders in Indonesia at the New Order's birth, but the Indonesian experience shaped the worldviews of the Malaysian Chinese elites: accept Malay hegemony, or things could get much worse. For their part, Indonesian elites sought special relations with Suharto to protect themselves from both violence and expropriation. The contrasts would resurface again during the late 1990s' Asian Financial Crisis, and with similar effects.

---

[118] Anthony Reid, "Entrepreneurial Minorities, Nationalism, and the State," in Daniel Chirot and Anthony Reid, eds., *Essential Outsiders: Chinese and Jews in the Modern Transformation of Southeast Asia and Central Europe* (Seattle: University of Washington Press, 1997), 60.

Albeit for different reasons and through different pathways, the capitalism that would take shape in much of the region was one that would privilege national interests, even nationalism, over private economic interests. I have focused on the ways in which business elites grew to harbor trust or distrust for political elites, but trust goes both ways. Capitalists were not trusted to act in the national interest. Even where capitalism was enthusiastically embraced after protracted and violent struggles against communism, states were imbued with power to tame business elites. For their part, business elites acknowledged, and to varying degrees accepted, the circumscription of their autonomy. But the varying degree of acceptance matters. In essence, Malaysian elites submitted to reciprocity, accepting the state's authority over the economy and expecting state protection and inclusion. Chinese and Indonesian capitalists, however, never expected the state to return their co-operation and therefore they never really submitted, instead hedging their activities and becoming adept at pursuing their own interests regardless of the regime's priorities.

3

Mutual Endangerment in Indonesia

State-Business Relations with Distrust

I give witness
That this country is the country of officials and bureaucrats.
The *priyayi* [Javanese noble] culture of old times
Is patched up with new fancy [touches].
Like the traditional princes,
The new princes ally with foreign *cukongs*,
Monopolize the means of production and the power of distribution.
The *pribumi* traders,
Can just sell services or become peddlers . . .
Like elephants,
State officials control all grass and leaves.
Needs are produced,
But social mobility is victimized;
Life becomes languid and jammed.
Security is maintained,
But the people are strained and bridled;
Life becomes depressed without choice.

. . . .

I give witness
That the elephants can change themselves into Mastodons . . .

. . . .

I give witness.
If Doomsday ever comes in this country,
Then it will happen,
Not with a sign of a beggar's uprising,
Not because of a poet's protesting verses,
Or a natural disaster,
But it will happen with the sign of Mastodons fighting one another.
— Rendra, "Witness to Mastodons," December 9, 1985[1]

[1] The poem, read by the Rendra, the author, at a rally in 1985, was transcribed and translated
via audio recording in Yoon Hwan Shin, "Demystifying the Capitalist State: Political Patronage,

Precarious Ties. Meg Rithmire, Oxford University Press. © Oxford University Press 2023.
DOI: 10.1093/oso/9780197697528.003.0003

Indonesia was home to many scandals in the twilight years of Suharto's New Order. One, in particular, was made into a Hollywood film in 2016 and involved several former North American heads of state and a fake gold discovery. As one might expect from this description, the story is complex and fascinating: a Filipino geologist working for a small Canadian prospecting firm claims to have discovered what would have been one of the world's largest gold mines in a remote part of Kalimantan. After years of squabbling among international mining firms and Indonesian ministries and business elites, it turns out that the geologist had faked the discovery, but, in the meantime, the stock of the Canadian prospecting firm had ridden a colossal wave.

Much about the episode is emblematic of the late New Order: foreign and domestic firms were jockeying to link arms with Suharto's children to secure their part of the windfall, Suharto's children were competing with one another to grab a larger piece of the pie, some technocratic elements of the state were hopelessly committed to bureaucratic procedures, and various prominent business leaders were ready to pounce on the findings in whatever way they could. Before the fraud was exposed, the major drama involved Bob Hasan, an ethnic Chinese businessman with ties so close to Suharto that he was frequently called the "first friend," outmaneuvering Minister of Mines and Energy Ida Bagus Sudjana to secure a large stake in the mine for his own company.[2] Hasan had Suharto's ear, but he used another tool in his arsenal to sideline Sudjana. Hasan was the owner of an Indonesian magazine, *Gatra*, which, at the height of negotiations and while Sudjana was abroad, published an article suggesting that Sudjana had embezzled 40 billion rupiah from a state-owned coal company. The article prompted a hearing in the Indonesian House of Representatives and, although Sudjana claimed he had transferred the funds to shield them from "wasteful bureaucrats," the floodgates were open for a wave of testimonies about corruption and favoritism in the country's natural resource management.[3]

Bureaucratic Interests, and Capitalists-in-Formation in Soeharto's Indonesia," PhD dissertation, Yale University, 1989, 129–31.

[2] Sudjana had allied with a more established Canadian mining company, Barrick, which was left empty-handed in the final deal. Hasan would go on to be the sole ethnic Chinese Indonesian to hold a cabinet position under Suharto, but only during the last two months of the regime.

[3] For details on the story, see Brian Hutchinson, "Rags & Riches: The Story Behind Bre-X's Roller Coaster Ride," *The Calgary Herald*, March 29, 1997: B8.; Jennifer Wells, "Greed, Graft, and Gold," *Mclean's* 110, no. 9 (1997): 38–45; Jeffrey Bell, Christine Dinh-Tan, and Philip Purnama, "Busang (A): River of Gold," HBS Case 798-002 (May 1997); Jeffrey Bell, Christine Dinh-Tan, and Philip Purnama, "Busang (B): River of Gold," HBS Case 798-003 (October 1997); and Jeffrey Bell, Jeffrey,

The above details may seem salacious or exceptional, but they relay the underlying logic of state-business relations in the late New Order and illustrate a pattern I identify as mutual endangerment, in which relations among business elites and political elites are fundamentally organized to plunder state resources and create mutually incriminating webs. Mutual endangerment entails corruption, but more specifically it involves extensive capital flight or asset expatriation, weaponized information, and the widespread presence of fraud, malfeasance, and looting. This is precisely what occurred during the collapse of Suharto's regime during the Asian Financial Crisis (AFC) of 1997–98. By its third decade, the regime had been thoroughly hollowed out by military misadventures, endemic corruption, elite infighting, and the tapering of international support following the end of the Cold War.[4] In a sense, its demise was overdetermined, since very few military dictatorships headed by a single man could have been expected to retain power for a fourth decade amid an unprecedented currency crisis.[5] Most accounts of Suharto's demise examine the crisis, looking to either institutions or coalition politics to explain why it was managed so poorly that it became an existential political crisis in the country.[6]

This chapter examines the regime's demise, but only as a secondary outcome. The primary question is this: Why and how did Suharto's relationship

Christine Dinh-Tan, and Philip Purnama, "Busang (C): River of Gold," HBS Case 9-798-004 (September 1997).

[4] Benedict Anderson, "Exit Suharto," *New Left Review*, no. 50 (March–April 2008): 27–59. On the importance of the Cold War to the regime, see Matthias Fibiger, *Suharto's Cold War: Indonesia, Southeast Asia, and the World* (New York: Oxford University Press, 2023).
[5] Mark J. Gasiorowski, "Economic Crisis and Political Regime Change: An Event History Analysis," *American Political Science Review* 89, no. 4 (1995): 882–97, https://doi.org/10.2307/2082 515; Stephan Haggard and Robert R. Kaufman, *The Political Economy of Democratic Transitions* (Princeton, NJ: Princeton University Press, 1995); Ora John Reuter and Jennifer Gandhi, "Economic Performance and Elite Defection from Hegemonic Parties," *British Journal of Political Science* 41, no. 1 (2011): 83–110, https://doi.org/10.1017/S0007123410000293.
[6] The preeminent works here are Thomas B. Pepinsky, *Economic Crises and the Breakdown of Authoritarian Regimes: Indonesia and Malaysia in Comparative Perspective* (New York: Cambridge University Press, 2009) and Andrew J. MacIntyre, *The Power of Institutions: Political Architecture and Governance* (Ithaca: Cornell University Press, 2003). Both take a comparative approach and agree that Indonesia's response displayed excessive policy volatility, enabling the crisis to rapidly consume the economy and generate insurmountable political pressure for Suharto's resignation. MacIntyre looks to the explanatory role of political institutions, arguing that an extreme concentration of power in the person of Suharto himself carried "powerful . . . potential for policy instability" (91). Pepinsky also blames policy volatility and ineffectiveness, but he argues that the inclusion of Chinese business elites with mobile assets forced the regime to maintain capital account openness during the crisis, exacerbating capital flight and explaining the policy volatility.

with the domestic business class, long touted as close and mutualistic, un-ravel in the 1990s? The roots of the AFC, as refracted through Indonesia's political economy, were laid well before 1997. The crisis, and the regime's response, were manifestations of mutual endangerment, and this form of state-business relations emerged in the 1980s and 1990s as the Suharto regime liberalized the financial sector. In Chapter 1, I argue that mutual endangerment only obtains when relations between business and political elites are characterized by distrust. Indonesia's most dominant economic elites were ethnic Chinese Indonesians (hereafter Chinese),[7] who were excluded from power in the country because of politically engendered distrust and the specific narratives of the New Order. The New Order was founded on anti-Chinese and anti-Communist sentiment, and the events of September 30, 1965 were invoked endlessly as a crucible through which an independent and stable Indonesia was forged.[8] The history of violence, as well as the ever-present threat of further violence, produced existential political vulnerability for Chinese business elites, a status that made them attractive sources of economic support for Suharto because they could not amass independent political power.[9]

Business elites cultivated close ties with Suharto out of vulnerability and desire for protection rather than any true fealty. During much of the New Order, Suharto and elite Chinese businessmen, the *cukong*, were mutually aligned. The *cukong* depended on Suharto and his control over the military for safety and for resources to grow their wealth and businesses. Suharto depended on the *cukong* as a source of investment capital, business know-how, and international connections. The distrust between the two, however, was realized immediately in the form of an open capital account. There are a number of factors that influenced the regime's early, and unusual at the time, decision to open its capital account, including the role of Western-trained "orthodox" economists and the desires and demands of international

---

[7] I refer to Indonesians of Chinese descent as "Chinese" in this chapter. In so doing, I follow usage in the secondary literature, using the term to refer to ethnicity rather than national identity.

[8] John Roosa, *Pretext for Mass Murder: The September 30th Movement and Suharto's Coup d'État in Indonesia* (Madison: University of Wisconsin Press, 2006); Fibiger, *Suharto's Cold War*.

[9] This view of Suharto's relationship with the Chinese business elites is nearly universally embraced in the literature. Ross McLeod, "Soeharto's Indonesia: A Better Class of Corruption," *Agenda* 7, no. 2 (2000): 106, writes: "Given the Chinese Indonesian minority's vulnerability to outbreaks of mob violence and to extortion by neighborhood thugs, they could always be expected to pay in various ways for protection." See also Richard Robison, *Indonesia: The Rise of Capital* (Sydney: Allen & Unwin, 1986); Jeffrey A. Winters, *Power in Motion: Capital Mobility and the Indonesian State* (Ithaca: Cornell University Press, 1996).

creditors and donors on whom the regime depended.[10] Undeniably, how-ever, the *cukong* were reassured by their access to capital mobility that served as a safety valve solution to political vulnerability at home.

Openness to global capital markets was matched with tight control over the domestic financial system during the first decade and a half of the New Order. The Indonesian government had extensive access to international aid, credit, and development assistance. This access was a result of the regime's apparent embrace of global capitalist orthodoxy and its staunch anticommunism during the height of the Cold War. The regime also had access to resource rents: the state-owned oil company, Pertamina, was ap-parently immune from the lean government orthodoxy that was applied to general issues of macroeconomic management, and its revenues were used for political patronage until and after the company nearly defaulted in the mid-1970s. After resource rents and international largesse were less forth-coming, however, Suharto and his team of economic advisers turned to fi-nancial deregulation as a solution. The introduction of competition in the financial sector, and deregulation in other sectors, was meant to mobilize more investment capital and to discipline state-owned banks. These goals were achieved, but liberalization of the financial sector also brought about mutual endangerment. Business elites, abetted by regime insiders and espe-cially Suharto's children, engaged in financial fraud and looting at society's expense. Some had expectations that they would be bailed out, and others had such low expectations and short time horizons that they pursued imme-diate extractive value in firm financial arrangements. Self-dealing was perva-sive, and the regime was in a financial death spiral by the 1990s, well before the Thai bhat was devalued and the AFC was set in motion.

My purpose in this chapter is not to provide a novel account of the New Order nor to comprehensively explain its achievements, failures, or de-mise. Instead, the chapter aims to explain why the New Order began with mutual alignment between business and political elites and ended in de-structive betrayal and crisis—fighting among mastodons. I begin where Chapter 2 ends: the founding of the New Order and the alienation of Indonesians of Chinese descent. Although Suharto and Chinese elites were allies, their ties were precarious, each party loyal to goals they held above

---

[10] For the best account of this policy decision, see Jeffrey M. Chwieroth, "How Do Crises Lead to Change? Liberalizing Capital Controls in the Early Years of New Order Indonesia," *World Politics* 62, no. 3 (2010): 496–527, https://doi.org/10.1017/S0043887110000110.

their mutual arrangements and dependent on one another only out of a sense of mutual threat. I then narrate the attenuation of financial discipline. As in the Malaysian case, initial financial control on the part of the state was dismantled in the pursuit of capital mobilization after the fiscal crisis. Unlike Malaysia, however, distrustful elites abused state access and international markets to loot, expatriate assets, and hold one another hostage with mutually incriminating information. Late New Order Indonesia is a paradigmatic case of mutual endangerment.

State (Re)building: Economic Orthodoxy and an Alienated Capital Class

The New Order was founded in violence and amid the economic wreckage of Sukarno's Guided Democracy. Macroeconomic stability was an immediate concern of the new regime: taming inflation and addressing the country's debt load were the most urgent tasks.[11] The new regime would also seek legitimation via distance and contrast with Sukarno's economic policies, which had embraced state ownership and heavy-handed state intervention in the name of countering neocolonialism and dependence (NEKOLIM, in Sukarno's parlance) by developing domestic capabilities. A distrust of the domestic business class undergirded Sukarno's approaches.[12] By contrast, the New Order would be a beacon of orthodox economic policy in its management of the macroeconomy. Suharto's embrace of Western-trained economists and orthodox ideas, especially about capital account openness and strict inflation targeting, has been the subject of a good deal of scholarship on the New Order.[13] But the orthodox economists and their ideas would dominate only in the realms of macroeconomic management (e.g., the Ministry of Finance, Bank Indonesia [BI, the central bank], and Bappenas [Ministry of National Development Planning]), leaving trade and industrial

[11] Winters, *Power in Motion*; Radius Prawiro, an architect of the New Order's economic management who served as governor of Bank Indonesia, minister of finance, and coordinating minister variously from the 1970s through the 1990s, reflects: "The New Order staked its existence on its ability to build the Indonesian economy. If it failed in this effort, its credibility and the basic platform on which it was founded would have been destroyed." See Radius Prawiro, *Indonesia's Struggle for Economic Development: Pragmatism in Action* (New York: Oxford University Press, 1998), 80.

[12] Robison, *Indonesia*, 37.

[13] See Bradley R. Simpson, *Economists with Guns: Authoritarian Development and U.S.-Indonesian Relations, 1960–1968* (Stanford: Stanford University Press, 2008); Chwieroth, "How Do Crises Lead."

Table 3.1 Credit by Source Prior to Liberalization, 1974–1983 (billions of rupiahs)

Source	1974	1975	1976	1977	1978	1979	1980	1981	1982	1983
BI (direct credits)	231	894	1,212	1,229	1,935	2,163	2,454	2,649	2,771	2,356
State commercial banks	1,136	1,602	2,007	2,267	2,832	3,270	4,295	5,881	8,031	9,787
National private banks	89	133	197	257	366	493	711	1,081	1,554	2,294
Foreign banks	117	122	150	184	262	342	414	548	666	862

Source: Wing Thye Woo, Bruce Glassburner, and Anwar Nasution, *Macroeconomic Policies, Crises, and Long-Term Growth in Indonesia* (Washington, DC: World Bank Comparative Macroeconomic Series, 1994), 20, and verified by BI statistics.

policy to those who leaned more toward economic nationalism, resulting in a "complex mix of liberalization and interventionism."[14]

The financial system remained dominated by the state. Banking acts in 1967 and 1968 split the single "superbank" formed under Sukarno into Bank Indonesia and five state-owned banks, a state-owned savings bank, and a state development bank (Bapindo).[15] Tight state ownership of banks, selective credit allocation, and the use of credit ceilings (for sectors and firms) determined by the BI constituted relatively strict financial discipline through the early 1980s. Foreign and domestic private banks operated in a limited fashion, but they were also subject to credit ceilings, and the total volume of lending in the country remained under control. Bapindo and the five state commercial banks supplied more than 80 percent of financial assets in the 1970s; in 1982, they provided 72 percent of working capital and 95 percent of investment capital[16] (Table 3.1).

Several credit schemes targeted smallholder agriculture or indigenous business and had strict collateral requirements and due diligence processes. In practice, many of these loans likely did not reach their stated

[14] Chwieroth, "How Do Crises Lead," 514.

[15] Each of the five commercial banks had a specific purpose. Bank Rakyat Indonesia was for rural development and smallholder agriculture; Bank Bumi Daya for estate agriculture and forestry; Bank Negara Indonesia for industry; Bank Dagang Negara for mining; and Bank Ekspor-impor for exports. Wing Thye Woo, Bruce Glassburner, and Anwar Nasution, *Macroeconomic Policies, Crises, and Long-Term Growth in Indonesia, 1965–90* (Washington DC: World Bank Comparative Macroeconomic Series, 1994), 19–20.

[16] Ibid., 90.

targets and instead were diverted, either to so-called Ali Baba business partnerships (in which Chinese and *pribumi* actors colluded) or through more classic forms of patronage.[17] Equity markets were underdeveloped during the first half of the New Order. The Jakarta Stock Exchange (JKSE) was closed in 1958 and did not reopen until 1977. By 1986, only twenty-four equity stocks and three bonds were listed on the exchange; sixteen of the equity listings were foreign companies, and all of the bonds were for public enterprises.[18]

In describing this financial system as "disciplined," I do not mean that it allocated resources according to some ideal efficiency logic or absent of corruption, but rather that resource distribution was firmly in the hands of the regime and subject to the New Order's political priorities. In fact, the period of financial political discipline was also one of misallocated assets that one scholar called a "better class of corruption."[19] Specifically, the military was the recipient of a large amount of the regime's largesse, and it was granted the independence to undertake its own financial endeavors. The vast majority of the early New Order credit went to rice farmers through Bulog, the agency responsible for rice price stability.[20] Default rates for small-scale entrepreneurs and agricultural smallholders were high (around 60 percent in the 1970s), state banks required bailouts (e.g., Bank Bumi Daya in 1977), and a World Bank study estimates that, for some years in the 1970s, during the height of the oil boom, state banks overall showed a 0 percent return on capital.[21] This economic inefficiency, however, was politically expedient. Harold Crouch famously described the flow of resources to key groups in a way that enriched key players as "neo-patrimonialism," combining a traditional

---

[17] Ibid., 21; see also Winters, *Power in Motion*, 111, who reports that the high collateral and requirements for self-provided capital effectively limited loans to Chinese and Alibaba-type businesses. Also noteworthy is that many of the oil boom-era credit schemes reserved for indigenous Indonesians were announced in 1974 following the Malari riots, during which protests against Japanese or foreign dominance in the economy turned into anti-Chinese riots. See Andrew J. MacIntyre, "The Politics of Finance in Indonesia: Command, Confusion, and Competition," in Stephan Haggard, Chung H. Lee, and Sylvia Maxfield, eds., *The Politics of Finance in Devveloping Countries* (Ithaca: Cornell University Press,1993), 142; Robison, *Indonesia*, 147–68; Winters, *Power in Motion*, 108–10.

[18] Woo, Glassburner, and Nasution, *Macroeconomic Policies*, 23.

[19] McLeod, "Soeharto's Indonesia," 105: "Soeharto always took the long-term view, in which sustained growth was essential to the flow of rents and, consequently, to his hold on power. In this sense, Indonesia under Soeharto was 'blessed' with a better class of corruption than many other countries—and, indeed, than under his predecessor, Sukarno, whose regime came to be characterized by such excessive government intervention and corruption that entrepreneurship was largely stifled."

[20] On this especially see MacIntyre, "Politics of Finance."

[21] Woo, Glassburner, and Nasution, *Macroeconomic Policies*, 92.

Javanese politics of elite co-optation and mass exclusion with the project of authoritarian modernization.[22]

The early New Order (1966–83) combined hierarchical control over the financial sector with pockets of discretion for critical actors. Pertamina, the state oil company under the control of General Ibn Sutowo, was always beyond the view of the economic orthodoxy that was applied to the country's macroeconomic governance, providing a source of soft revenues and patronage resources for the regime. Many accounts portray the company in the early 1970s as something close to the "Mafia-like" firms I describe in Chapter 6 on China, riddled with corruption and hollowed out by everyone within the corporate hierarchy angling for a cut of revenue.[23] It is also noteworthy that the company was imagined as a "nationally integrated economic unit," a conglomerate with diversified activities to rival Chinese-run businesses.[24] A massive debt crisis in 1975 laid bare the extent of corruption and mismanagement and also caused the state's debt to balloon as it bailed out Pertamina.

The country's more orthodox economic planners saw Pertamina as "an accident waiting to happen," even a "quasi national treasury" beyond their purview.[25] The Pertamina "accident" indeed occurred, but careful macroeconomic management confined the damage as the country took on substantial external debt in bailing out the company. The Pertamina drama shows the dynamics of the lack of financial discipline. The company openly defied state regulations, limiting corporate risk and borrowing in short- and long-term markets and from foreign institutions when it could not meet its wants domestically.[26] Its immunity from political rebuke and discipline enabled it to engage in the sort of financial alchemy and mismanagement that is typical of moral hazard. Pertamina's problems, however, did not include fraud and malfeasance, weaponized information, or asset expatriation because the firm's managers were political insiders with expectations of political safety. Instead, the company is a site of the kind of internal relations and relations with outside players that are better described as "competitive clientelism,"

[22] Harold Crouch, "Patrimonialism and Military Rule in Indonesia," *World Politics* 31, no. 4 (1979): 571–87.

[23] Adrian Vickers, *A History of Modern Indonesia* (New York: Cambridge University Press, 2005).

[24] Woo, Glassburner, and Nasution, *Macroeconomic Policies*, 55–56.

[25] Prawiro dubs the conglomerate a "state within a state" or "Indonesia's other development agency," and argues it is appropriately imagined as a "venture capital" undertaking. Prawiro, *Indonesia's Struggle*, 104–5. See also Winters, *Power in Motion*, 8–92.

[26] Prawiro, *Indonesia's Struggle*, 106.

various groups competing to manipulate state resources for patronage and political favor. As I detail in Chapter 4 on Malaysia, this is the mode of state-business relations I expect when financial discipline is absent but political trust remains.

Enterprises in the 1970s and early 1980s complained of "liquidity crises," and debates about whether domestic economic growth had been sacrificed for orthodox macroeconomic control were vocal, but they were universally won by those who advocated tight financial control.[27] That the financial system worked for the regime and credit was tightly regulated meant that private-sector firms either self-funded or depended on very close ties to the state. For the large, Chinese-dominated conglomerate firms, the answer is really both. They were able to access state finance, but indirectly and only by currying favor with political elites. Most credit dispensed to the nonstate sector was project- rather than firm-based, and therefore firms that wanted state-credit access pursued projects the state also wanted. The largest of the Chinese-controlled *konglomerat*, including Salim, Ometracto, Raja Garuda Mas, Sinar Mas, and others, either got their start with large state-backed projects or saw their empires expand through such projects.[28] By December 1978 most of the banks' credits were estimated to fall under the control of the conglomerates or other conglomerate-linked companies, even after several policies were designed to increase allocations to *pribumi* businesspeople.[29]

The *konglomerat* also financed their growth with borrowings from abroad. They famously depended on transnational finance networks, especially in the 1960s and early 1970s as the Indonesian economy was recovering and capital for private business was scarce. Transnational investors, typically wealthy ethnic Chinese networks in Hong Kong, Singapore, and even the Philippines, imposed discipline on borrowers in Indonesia in a variety of ways. Trading required iterative relationships with global counterparties, and finance and other business activities were intertwined. One Indonesian businessman describes how he financed an expansion into mining with capital from Hong Kong business connections

---

[27] Ibid. See also Simpson, *Economists with Guns*.

[28] Interviews, November 2016 through January 2017; see Appendix A; Nancy Chng and Richard Borsuk, *Liem Sioe Liong's Salim Group: The Business Pillar of Suharto's Indonesia* (Singapore: Institute of Southeast Asian Studies, 2014); Christian Chua, "Defining Indonesian Chineseness under the New Order," *Journal of Contemporary Asia* 34, no. 4 (2004): 465–79.

[29] Dorodjatun Kuntjoro-Jakti, "The Political-Economy of Development: The Case of Indonesia under the New Order Government, 1966–1978," PhD dissertation, University of California, Berkeley, 1981, 96.

who were also his suppliers for an import business and potentially his buyers for exports from the new expansion.[30]

The Indonesian financial system imposed state-directed discipline on the country's private sector for the first few decades of the New Order. The state monopolized domestic finance and enjoyed mechanisms by which it could monitor business and tether the private sector's interests to its own. Business elites depended on relationships with political elites to grow, and the tight financial control combined with business's vulnerability, which I discuss next, rendered the private sector subservient to the state.

Cronyism without Trust

A central argument in this book is that in many authoritarian regimes and for different reasons economic elites live with existential threat. The dynamics of that threat are rather obvious: any authoritarian regime strong enough to repress, expropriate, or endanger economic elites presents an ever-present threat to their existence, so economic elites adopt strategies to secure themselves. In most contexts, this includes particularistic relationships with political elites in which protection is supplied by political elites in exchange for economic support, either investment in targeted areas or personal enrichment, and frequently both.[31] While popular portrayals of these elite relationships tend toward the simplistic in arguing that economic elites are "puppets" of dictators or, conversely, political leaders are held "in the pockets" of economic elites, in reality the mutual dependence affords power to both sides.[32] The apparent closeness between Suharto and Chinese elites

---

[30] Interview, Jakarta, November 2016.

[31] Sometimes these relationships are referred to as "clientelism" or "instrumental friendships," in which economic resources are exchanged for political support. Particularistic relationships among elites in authoritarian regimes can be a form of clientelism, but I prefer not to use this term because of its deep association with voting. In the Malaysian case, I argue that "competitive clientelism" characterizes elite relations without pervasive distrust. See Allen Hicken, "Clientelism," *Annual Review of Political Science* 14, no. 1 (2014): 289–310; James C. Scott, "Patron-Client Politics and Political Change in Southeast Asia," *American Political Science Review* 66, no. 1 (1972): 91–113, https://doi.org/10.2307/1959280; Edward Aspinall, Meredith L. Weiss, Allen Hicken, and Paul D. Hutchcroft, *Mobilizing for Elections: Patronage and Political Machines in Southeast Asia* (New York: Cambridge University Press, 2022).

[32] Abdelal writes: "What is clear from decades of research, however, is that to ask the question of whether the state or the firm is the master of the other is to do irreparable damage to the nuances of their relations." See Rawi Abdelal, "The Multinational Firm and Geopolitics: Europe, Russian Energy, and Power," *Business and Politics* 17, no. 3 (2015): 553–76, https://doi.org/10.1515/bap-2014-0044.

was based on the former threatening and exploiting the vulnerability of the latter. The fundamental distrust between political and business elites shaped the New Order.

Chinese business elites in Suharto's Indonesia were paradigmatic vulnerable elites. Their ethnic outsider status, and the history of their tenuous status in independent Indonesia, foreclosed the possibility of their grasping formal political power, making them attractive elites to cultivate because they could not challenge the political elites for power. In Chapter 2 I discuss how the New Order was born in violence against Indonesians of Chinese descent (among others). What followed was a program of forced assimilation (*assimilasi*). A 1966 directive encouraged Chinese to adopt Indonesian-sounding names, and a 1967 directive essentially prohibited Chinese cultural practices. Chinese-medium schools and business associations were closed, and visible signs of Chineseness, including Chinese characters and celebration of Chinese holidays, disappeared from visibility in Indonesian life.[33] The new regime justified many of these moves by pointing to the specter of violence and the supposed connections among China, ethnic Chinese, and the PKI (Communist Party of Indonesia).[34] Yet they also voiced concern about racism and ethnic conflict in Indonesia, often citing (and reproducing) widely held negative views of Chinese.[35] The regime saw its purview as both protecting the nation from the threat posed by Chinese and, to an extent, protecting Chinese (and national) stability from the threat posed by their pariah status.

---

[33] Chua, "Defining Indonesian Chineseness."

[34] For example, the 1967 mandate to create the State Committee for Chinese Affairs (Panitia Negara Urusan Tjina) states that Chinese citizens had become a national issue meriting special attention due to *gestapu* and the PKI ("Guidance on the Chinese Issue," *Sekkab*, April 1967, Indonesian National Archives). A report from the Political Bureau of the Committee for the Formulation of Chinese-Related Policies (Kelompok Politik—Panitia Perumus Kebidjaksanaan Penjelesaian Masalah Tjina) similarly associates solving the "Chinese problem" through assimilation with the preservation of social stability (August 6, 1967).

[35] These include views of Chinese "exclusive" behavior (favoring Chinese networks and excluding outsiders), suspect political allegiances, fundamental self-interest (contrasted with the interests of the state or nation), and more. A 1967 memo from the Political Bureau of the Committee for the Formulation of Chinese-Related Policies (Kelompok Politik—Panitia Perumus Kebidjaksanaan Penjelesaian Masalah Tjina) states: "It can be said that generally they are still viewed as a moneygrubbers, disrupters of the economy, smugglers, bribers who should always be distrusted— which in turn incites feelings of jealousy and emotional suspicion and makes them the main target of many actions and policies" (*Sekkab*, August 6, 1967, Indonesian National Archives).

The threat of anti-Chinese violence, even in the context of the New Order's fixation with social stability, was real.[36] The periodic riots and pogroms that marked the colonial and independence periods persisted under Suharto, but violence seemed more like a lever the regime could manipulate than a pressure cooker it could not control. Some have argued that Suharto and elements of the regime even stoked ethnic violence to remind the vulnerable populations of their dependence on him and on the military under his control, a tactic used by Dutch rulers as well.[37] Chinese Indonesians lived with existential vulnerability during the New Order era and beyond. Many with means retained exit options, including homes and even citizenship in Singapore or Hong Kong. More than a few interviewees indicated that their families had purchased their own planes primarily to facilitate an easy escape from Jakarta if necessary.[38] Business practices, too, incorporated existential vulnerability and distrust. Many Chinese businessmen enjoyed access to overseas financing networks, a reason Suharto depended on them during the regime's early days when investment capital for the private sector was generally scarce. But throughout the 1970s and 1980s, capital went both ways, as conglomerates pursued overseas assets as a form of safety, as I detail in the section on asset expatriation below.

The political relationships between Suharto and Chinese businessmen were built on the endemic vulnerability of the latter. The relationships were distrustful and particularistic rather than principled or multiparty (like Slater's "protection pacts").[39] As such, commitments were thin, and each side was incentivized to hedge against defection or failure of the other. The *cukong* planned for a world

---

[36] Varshney estimates, based on local newspaper data on violence, that the "master cleavage" in Indonesian society between Christians/Chinese and Muslims/*pribumis* was "almost certainly" deadlier than the master cleavage between Hindus and Muslims in India, a startling statement. See Ashutosh Varshney, "Analyzing Collective Violence in Indonesia: An Overview," *Journal of East Asian Studies* 8, no. 3 (2008): 343.

[37] Winters, *Power in Motion*, 77 n. 82, writes: "These eruptions of violence against the ethnic Chinese have been occurring fairly regularly in Indonesia for more than two hundred years. . . . Indonesian leaders of state (who all receive important political money from ethnic Chinese financiers) have adopted the old Dutch tactic of routinely unleashing society's deep resentment of this minority as a way of reminding them of their precarious position."

[38] Interview, Jakarta, November 2016. Well into Indonesia's second democratic decade, such fears persisted. During the fall of 2016, when large-scale protests over comments by the Chinese Indonesian governor of Jakarta shook the city, one wealthy Chinese family bought plane tickets to Singapore each morning just in case protests were to turn into violent riots.

[39] Dan Slater, in *Ordering Power: Contentious Politics and Authoritarian Leviathans in Southeast Asia* (New York: Cambridge University Press, 2010), 109, states that Chinese business elites individually allied themselves with government insiders rather than forming the kind of collective "protection pacts" that laid a foundation for the strong states and durable regimes in Singapore and Malaysia.

without Suharto and pursued self-protection in the event he could not protect them, and Suharto pursued the expansion of businesses, including military-led businesses and some *pribumi* businesses, to have other allies.

Economically, the regime's tight control over the financial sector limited the maneuvering space for vulnerable elites in the first two decades of the New Order, and the terms of particularistic exchange within these thin friendships were clear. Suharto offered protection and privileged access to resources (including monopoly licenses, tariff protections, resource rents, and so forth) and Chinese elites invested in critical industries and channeled financial benefits to well-placed individuals, including Suharto's family members.[40] As the regime's financial control attenuated in the late 1980s and 1990s, the regime lost its ability to discipline business elites, and the latter no longer relied on the regime for resources to expand their businesses and personal wealth. The combination of fundamental distrust with financial loosening opened opportunities for business elites to engage, fully rationally, in the kinds of economic fraud and malfeasance and excessive risk behavior that would endanger the regime.

A "Decade of Deregulation": Indonesia in the 1980s

The process of financial liberalization in Indonesia shares much in common with that in Malaysia during the same time period (1980s–1990s). Both regimes were prompted to deregulate their financial sectors in the wake of the global decline in commodity prices and the domestic fiscal and macro-economic reverberations they caused. The 1980s ushered in an economic era of liberalizing reforms more generally, a "decade of deregulation," as Hadi Soesastro described it.[41] In addition to the financial sector, *deregulasi* efforts affected tax collection, customs management, and trade. In each sector, reforms were designed to stimulate private investment and to enable the state to better capture the gains of the economic activity.[42] For our

---

[40] Pepinsky, *Economic Crises*, 58.

[41] M. Hadi Soesastro, "The Political Economy of Deregulation in Indonesia," *Asian Survey* 29, no. 9 (1989): 853.

[42] Tax reforms included streamlined and simplified collection and overall tax-rate reductions. Customs changes were dramatic, with the government eliminating its own customs service and in its stead installing a Swiss firm, an effort to reduce corruption. Trade reform entailed reduced licensing and import restrictions, and several efforts were designed to attract more foreign investment. Robison, *Indonesia*; Prawiro, *Indonesia's Struggle*; Hal Hill, *The Indonesian Economy in Crisis: Causes, Consequences, and Lessons* (New York: St. Martin's Press, 1999). For detailed discussions of the changes in taxes especially, see Winters, *Power in Motion*, 170–91.

purposes, it is noteworthy that, while the reforms were accurately portrayed as "pro-capital" or business friendly, they nonetheless presented challenges to economic actors who were used to privileged access to rents. Dual desires to generate more economic competition in protected sectors and to nurture the rise of an indigenous (*pribumi*) business class threatened Chinese *konglomerat* incumbents. Chinese capitalists made haste to benefit from financial reforms, and they did so in a general climate of competitive pressure and uncertainty about their economic futures.[43] For vulnerable capitalists, liberalizing reforms presented a mixed bag that would be destructive for the economy: more freedom to participate in financial innovation amid threats to their survival. As monopoly licenses and guaranteed profitability in real sectors seemed to recede, finance appeared as a set of opportunities to pursue profits and personal wealth.[44]

Financial Liberalization

Indonesia's era of financial liberalization began in 1983. A decline in global prices of oil in 1982 put pressure on both the financial and fiscal systems. The price drop clearly threatened state revenues, but it also caused a reduction in the liquidity credits to state banks, causing outflows to the few private banks that existed at the time (fewer than fifty) and endangering the position of the state banks. The government faced the choice of further subsidizing state banks or enabling them to compete. The financial-sector problems were but one manifestation of what was perceived to be a larger, more systemic problem in the Indonesian economy, namely, excessive government intervention enabled by oil revenues: "The fading of the prosperity fostered by oil revenue emphasized the importance of encouraging economic growth through efficient allocation of investment

---

[43] Indeed, Robison predicted conflict among classes and subclasses (especially among capitalists) over the benefits of a newly liberalized economy. He argued that the "pact of domination" between the politico-bureaucrats and leading domestic groups (read: Chinese conglomerates) had been breached (*Indonesia*, 67–71). This chapter says little about conflicts within society, however, as I am focusing on how the Chinese capitalists responded to the changes.

[44] Woo, Glassburner, and Nasution, *Macroeconomic Policies*, state that the proportion of items covered by import license requirements fell from 32 percent in the mid-1970s to 22 percent by the end of 1987. They further state (102) that the Chinese elites were the biggest losers of these reforms, as family members of high-ranking officials still retained their licenses. Bouts of reforms of import-license requirements continued into the early 1990s.

funds."[45] Indeed, oil earnings peaked in 1981–82 at $19 billion and would fall to less than half of that ($6.9 billion) by 1986–87. Over the course of the early 1980s, the "authority of liberal economists" grew alongside a sense that the country had to change course to survive.[46]

An initial set of reforms in 1983 inaugurated Indonesia's age of deregulation in the financial sector. Credit ceilings were abolished, rates on deposits and loans were deregulated, and direct lending from the BI was substantially reduced.[47] The 1983 reforms had an almost immediate impact: one study estimates that lending by domestic private banks increased 90 percent and that by state banks increased by 42 percent in the first fifteen months after the reforms.[48] Liberalization was met with enthusiasm, both domestically and internationally. International financial institutions and those who staffed them rewarded Indonesian policymakers with the esteem they valued, and the domestic business class seemed to clamor for more and more liberalization.[49]

Yet reforms went slowly and intentionally to "accommodate political problems" and enable the development of macroeconomic tools to manage a newly active and diverse financial landscape.[50] Politically, the reforms stood to deprive the state and groups within the state of their access to resources to be distributed to various constituent groups. Economically, the reforms generated substantial monetary growth—the intent of the reforms—but they required, in particular, new means of managing external balances. The BI was quick to develop a few new tools, including monetary instruments and new claims on the BI itself that it would use to affect interest rates and manage liquidity. But the 1980s nonetheless saw damaging bouts of currency outflows. In 1984, and again in 1987, fears of a devaluation contributed to capital flight and liquidity concerns, and on both occasions the state intervened by directing state banks to purchase BI securities. These "Sumarlin shocks,"

---

[45] Ibid., 92.

[46] MacIntyre, "Politics of Finance," 144. Clearly the external shock of oil price declines coincided with a global neoliberal moment, during which developed countries were undertaking "liberalizing" reforms and privatization, and advice from global institutions pushed in such a direction. The reforms also came with a change in the BI governor, but both Adrianus Mooy and Rachmat Saleh were liberal economists of the "UI" (Universitas Indonesia) school. All $ amounts are USD unless otherwise indicated.

[47] Hill, *Indonesian Economy in Crisis*, 35–36; MacIntyre, "Politics of Finance," 144; David C. Cole and Betty F. Slade, *Building a Modern Financial System: The Indonesian Experience* (New York: Cambridge University Press, 1996); Prawiro, *Indonesia's Struggle*.

[48] Anne Booth, "Survey of Recent Developments," *Bulletin of Indonesian Economic Studies* 20, no. 3 (1984): 1–35.

[49] See the seminal account by Robison, *Indonesia*, especially Part III. See also Soesastro, "Political Economy of Deregulation," 865.

[50] Ali Wardhana, a former coordinating minister for economic affairs and a force behind deregulation, justified gradualism for these reasons. See Soesastro, "Political Economy of Deregulation," 854.

named after the minister of finance, J. B. Sumarlin, worked to stem currency pressures, but they retained the air of direct state economic intervention.[51]

A later set of reforms in October 1988—which would become known as "Pakto 88"—constituted what one economist called "the most decisive financial policy of the decade."[52] This package of reforms removed barriers to financial participation and competition that had stood for decades: all domestic banks could establish new offices and branches, state firms could deposit up to 50 percent of their assets in nonstate banks, nonbank financial institutions were permitted to take deposits, and reserve requirements were cut from 15 percent to 2 percent. Pakto 88 also placed a 15 percent tax on bank deposits to push capital into the newly revitalized Jakarta Composite Index (JKSE), and a December 1988 set of reforms further liberalized the stock markets.[53] The goal of the reforms was "the development of long-term sources of finance" for domestic firms as well as the development of new financial services.[54]

Effects of the Reforms

The impact of the late 1980s suite of reforms was rapid and substantial. As Table 3.2 shows, a massive expansion of the private sector in banking shifted assets away from state banks such that, by December 1994, more than half of the country's banking sector was in private hands. The number of private banks was 64 in 1987 and 166 by 1994, with the number of private branches multiplying six times during the same period (Table 3.3). And while overall lending expanded, Tables 3.2 and 3.3 indicate that it was decisively driven by the nonstate banks.

Even more specifically, the late 1980s and early 1990s saw a marked expansion of large conglomerate firms within the financial sector. Many of the largest conglomerates included financial firms prior to Pakto 88, but they were used as self-financing tools and their activities were constrained. Immediately after the liberalization, as well as before in anticipation, business

[51] Hill, *Indonesian Economy in Crisis*, 35–36; Cole and Slade, *Building*, 52–53.

[52] Hill, *Indonesian Economy in Crisis*, 36.

[53] Ibid., 35–36. Paket December eased rules for listing in Jakarta, permitted exchanges in several provincial cities, and removed a 4 percent limit in the fluctuation of listed shares. Prawiro, *Indonesia's Struggle*, 239–44; Cole and Slade, *Building*, 93–94.

[54] Soesastro, "Political Economy of Deregulation," 864–65.

Table 3.2 Shares of Bank Assets by Type of Ownership, 1983–1994 (%)

Ownership	March 1983	December 1988	December 1994
Government*	80.2	71.0	47.0
Private domestic	11.2	24.0	44.3
Foreign and joint venture	8.6	5.0	8.7

Source: Bank Indonesia derived from bank balance sheet data, via David Cole and Betty F. Slade, "Financial Development in Indonesia" (Cambridge, MA: Harvard Institute for International Development, Development Discussion Paper, no. 336, 1990), 22.
*Government banks include state commercial banks, Bapindo (Bank Penbangunan), and regional development banks.

Table 3.3 Bank Growth, 1987–1994

	Number of Banks							
	1987	1988	1989	1990	1991	1992	1993	1994
State Banks								
Banks	7	7	7	7	7	7	7	7
Offices	830	852	922	1018	1044	1066	1076	1171
Rate of credit growth (%)			38.4	35.2	11.8	14	5.2	11.8
Private Banks								
Banks	64	63	88	106	126	141	158	166
Offices	504	559	1,238	2,052	2,639	2,747	2,926	3,203
Rate of Credit Growth (%)			73.5	88.1	19.6	1.2	42.7	46.7
Foreign and Joint Venture Banks								
Banks	11	11	23	28	39	30	39	40
Offices	21	21	38	48	53	61	75	83
Rate of credit growth (%)			62.8	98.3	37.8	9.6	24.5	23.7
Regional Development Banks								
Banks	27	27	27	27	27	27	27	27
Offices	233.0	262.0	304	352	408	425	426	431
Rate of credit growth (%)			35.9	41.7	13.6	15.3	18.0	22.8
Total credit growth			48.2	54.2	16.3	8.9	19.9	27.3

Source: BI statistics, via Cole and Slade, "Financial Development in Indonesia," 114, 62.
Note: State banks include Bapindo and Bank Tabungan Negara (BTN, a state savings bank). Private banks include private savings banks. Offices include branches and sub-branches.

groups pursued financial firms to compete in the new sector. "They opened new branches at a rapid rate, initiated new deposit schemes offering both high interest rates and attractive lottery schemes, sought foreign-exchange licenses if they did not already have them and rapidly expanded overseas operations, and expanded their loan and investment portfolios at rates that precluded prudent evaluation."[55] A private evaluation in 1990 found that the largest twenty-five private banks had expanded their assets by an average of 220 percent between 1988 and 1990, four had asset growth of over 300 percent, and three had asset growth greater than 600 percent.[56]

Sinar Mas's Bank International Indonesia upgraded its status immediately to access foreign borrowings and to set up a joint venture with Fuji Bank. The Astra Group moved its Bank Summa's headquarters from Germany to Jakarta to reorient it as a domestic bank, and it also acquired Bank Agung Asia, which had been struggling. The Lippo Group kept its international arm (First Pacific) separate from its domestic business, but it quickly expanded the services and products it offered through Lippo Bank.[57] Lippo offered high-profile products, including new savings deposit accounts with prize money, attracting a wave of new customers and excitement about the sector. The Jan Darmadi Group acquired Bank Pan Indonesia and Bank Susila Bhakti in the mid-1980s in anticipation of the liberalization.[58] Bank Danamon was taken over in the late 1980s when Usman Admadjaja's Kali Raya Sari Group entered finance.

Competition was immediately fierce, and the entry of Chinese firms was high profile. Issues of "conglomeration" in financial services started to attract media and public comment, as did the ever-present racial element.[59] The Indonesian public watched Chinese firms grow at astonishing rates in the late 1980s and 1990s, and backlash was inevitable. For example, an issue of the weekly magazine *Tempo* in 1993 noted the growth in assets of Chinese-owned conglomerates during the late 1980s and early 1990s, and it suspected

[55] Cole and Slade, *Building*, 136.
[56] Ibid., 146n. Moreover, the private banks were most highly leveraged.
[57] Yuri Sato, "The Development of Business Groups in Indonesia: 1967–1989," in Takashi Shiraishi, ed., *Approaching Suharto's Indonesia from the Margins* (Ithaca: Cornell University Press, 1994), 148–50.
[58] CISI Raya Utama, PT, *A Study on the Top-200 National Private Business Groups in Indonesia, 1989* (Jakarta, 1989), 235. See Appendix A.
[59] Sato, "Development of Business Groups"; Harold Crouch and Hal Hill, eds., "Indonesia Assessment 1990: Proceedings of Indonesia Update Conference, October 1990," Indonesia Project, Department of Economics and Department of Political and Social Change, Research School of Pacific Studies, Australia National University, 1990; MacIntyre, "Politics of Finance," 163.

that the owners were likely to take earnings from Indonesia and invest them in their "motherland" (i.e., Mainland China).[60] Indonesian officials often remarked to members of the foreign business and financial communities that privatization would have been faster in the early 1990s if they did not fear the excessive concentration of assets in the hands of Chinese firms and the political backlash brought about by such concentration.[61]

By the 1990s, by many accounts, Indonesia's financial sector was one of the world's most liberal.[62] Yet that liberalization was not accompanied by effective regulation. The BI, used to strict credit ceilings and controlled interest rates, did not have the supervisory capacity to evaluate bank activities. A brief debate about deposit insurance concluded by rejecting the idea because policymakers feared it would invite moral hazard, especially in a context in which regulators could not overpower political elites and their connections.[63] A suite of laws in the early 1990s did aim to develop modern accounting systems and prudential regulation, for example placing limits on self-dealing and caps on the share of loan assets that banks could concentrate in individual borrowers (20 percent) or affiliate groups (50 percent). But the ability to enforce these regulations was immediately imperiled, as even state banks could not comply with many regulations.[64] Even some architects of financial liberalization acknowledged that private banks had long been the source of funds for business groups, that for years the BI had issued circulars for years to discourage self-dealing with no impact, and that "early reports on some trial efforts" were "not encouraging" in the 1990s.[65]

Indonesia's equity markets experienced a similar expansion during financial liberalization. By May 1990, the number of firms listed on the

[60] "Kalau Modal Minggat ke Negeri Orang" [When Capital Flees to the People's Homeland], *Tempo*, April 10, 1993; see also the "Greater China and Overseas Chinese" column, *Tempo*, October 1993; November 20, 1993.

[61] Proceedings from the Economist Conference: Roundtable with the Government of Indonesia, March 19–21, 1995, Grand Hyatt, Jakarta, Conclusions Paper Summary, 19 (in National University of Singapore closed stacks). It is worth noting also that government officials declared that they would prefer foreign buyers in the privatization of PT Indosat, PT Telkom, and several mining firms.

[62] Jonathan Pincus and Rizal Ramli, "Indonesia: From Showcase to Basket Case," *Cambridge Journal of Economics* 22, no. 6 (1998): 725, https://doi.org/10.1093/cje/22.6.723.

[63] See Hill, *Indonesian Economy in Crisis*, 36; Soesastro, "Political Economy of Deregulation," 862; Prawiro, *Indonesia's Struggle*, 244; Cole and Slade, *Building*, 92.

[64] Cole and Slade, *Building*, 24, 133, write that although state banks were restructured to address risk, such moves only caused a further outflow of assets to the private sector. Formal limits on self-dealing and concentration were issued in the banking law of 1992. In addition to the limits on concentration, banks were barred from lending more than 5 percent of their portfolio to their own commissioners, shareholders, or other affiliates. See also Ross H. McLeod, "Indonesia's New Banking Law," *Bulletin of Indonesian Economic Studies* 28, no. 3 (1992): 107–22.

[65] Cole and Slade, *Building*, 133.

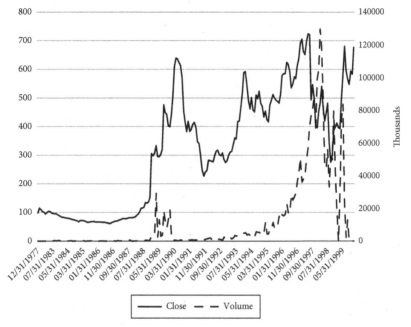

Figure 3.1 Jakarta Stock Exchange Composite Index and Volume, 1977–2000
Source: Global Financial Data, accessed 2021.

Jakarta Stock Exchange and the volume of daily equity trading turnover had tripled compared to May 1989.[66] The early 1990s equities markets had all the markings of a postshow rock band hotel party in which everyone seeks a thrill under the implicit assumption that someone else will pay for it and clean up the mess. Radius Prawiro writes that the country was swept up in *demam bursa*, or "stock market fever": "For a brief period from 1989 to 1990, virtually the entire nation was fixated on the stock exchange. The exchange seemed to be a machine for generating overnight millionaires."[67] A first bubble emerged and burst by 1990. (See Figures 3.1 and 3.2.) In an effort at professionalization, the exchange was privatized in 1992, creating PT Bursa Efek Jakarta (BEJ), but by 1993, the exchange was again overheating.

Companies issued at quite high prices, yet their issuances were oversubscribed. In 1993, a stock market surge had ordinary Jakarta citizens making

[66] "Jakarta Bourse Looking Up," *South China Morning Post*, May 13, 1990.
[67] Prawiro, *Indonesia's Struggle*, 364.

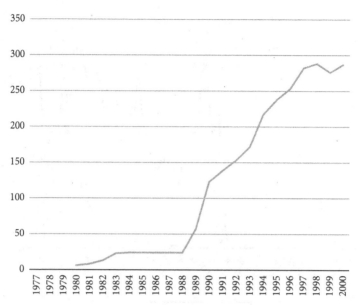

Figure 3.2 Number of Firms Listed, Jakarta Stock Exchange, 1977–2000
Source: Meridian Securities Market, *World Stock Exchange Fact Book, 2015* (2016). Accessed 2021.

money as *jockis* (jockeys), waiting in line for application forms for newly offered shares.[68] Large conglomerate firms entered the nonbank financial sector with enthusiasm. According to a survey of the two hundred largest firms in Indonesia in 1991, thirty new securities firms were founded after the 1988 reforms.[69] By 1995, at least forty-six securities companies were owned by large conglomerates.[70] The *konglomerat* also listed on domestic exchanges, raising capital via listings but retaining majority family control in most cases. In 1989 Liem Sioe Liong (Sudono Salim)'s Indocement (one of Indonesia's largest cement producers) was given a special exemption from the requirement that a firm must demonstrate three years of profit before listing; the firm had been bailed out by the state in 1985 when a collapse in property prices exposed questionable corporate finance practices. The issuance was large enough ($335 million, around 30 percent of the total JKSE

[68] "Jakarta Jockeys Act as Market Stand-Ins," *Wall Street Journal* (European Edition), October 22, 1993, 22.
[69] CISI Raya Utama, *Top-200*. See Appendix A.
[70] Andrew Rosser, *The Politics of Economic Liberalisation in Indonesia: State, Market and Power* (Richmond, Surrey, UK: Curzon, 2022), 210–13.

market capitalization at the time) to allow a major shareholder to divest, and state financial institutions bought the shares.[71] The entire transaction was underwritten by Danareksa, the state-run shareholding firm, thus generating accusations that all parties conspired to set prices.[72] In 1990, Astra listed 12.4 percent of its holding company, and the Soeryadjaya family retained 76 percent control.[73] Barito Pacific, the timber conglomerate run by Prajogo Pangestu, offered $200 million in the summer of 1993 after it was rumored to owe more than $380 million, but in the absence of a public declaration of assets and liabilities. The issuance was twenty-four times oversubscribed, and the price jumped 53 percent on the first day, partly on news that a state agency had bought a large stake in the company, a revelation that was met with outcry about corruption and cronyism.[74]

Endemic corruption did not appear suddenly in Indonesia upon financial liberalization. Rather, these practices were embedded in the nature of the New Order, but they took on a new logic and moral economy in the 1980s and 1990s. The patrimonialism and hierarchical flow of resources that characterized intrastate relations bound together powerful political actors in relations of dependence and a sense of mutual threat and benefit. For the most part, capitalists were allowed access at the margins: a handful of ethnic Chinese businessmen were allowed to be close to power because they posed no political threat and had access to external sources of investment that would be useful for Suharto's developmental agenda. They benefited from some access to state resources, but faced meaningful constraints on their financial behavior especially, and on how much risk they could generate for the macroeconomy. Before the era of deregulation, it was generally

---

[71] Steven Jones, Christopher Huny, and Richard Borsuk, "Indonesia Cement Firm's Huge Offering on Jakarta Exchange Stirs Sharp Debate," *Wall Street Journal*, November 13, 1989; Richard Borsuk, "Indonesia's Biggest-Ever Share Offering Succeeds but Falls Below Expectations," *Wall Street Journal*, November 17, 1989.

[72] Cole and Slade, *Building*, 211. The state pension funds, PT Aspen and PT Taspen, purchased most of the shares and were urged to do so to ensure that the IPO was fully subscribed. Rosser, *Politics of Economic Liberalisation*, 95.

[73] Richard Borsuk, "Astra's First-Half Earnings Drop 67%," *Asian Wall Street Journal*, September 17, 1992, 3.

[74] The agency was PT Taspen, the state civil-service pension fund, which privately paid $185 million for 20 percent of Barito Pacific. The deal prompted outcry about collusion. Many analysts were convinced that Barito Pacific would be allowed to make an IPO despite secrecy and clear financial problems because of Prajogo's connections to Suharto and his children. Richard Borsuk, "Outcry Unlikely to Hinder Barito Pacific's Stock Issue," *Wall Street Journal* (Asia Edition), July 16, 1993, 1; Robert Steiner, "Barito Pacific IPO Takes Shape in Jakarta," *Asian Wall Street Journal*, August 10, 1993, 9; "Business Brief—PT Barito Pacific Timber: Indonesia Firm's Share Offer is 24 Times Oversubscribed," *Wall Street Journal*, September 10, 1993, A7B; Rosser, *Politics of Economic Liberalisation*, 101–2.

the state itself (or some actors within the state, e.g., Pertamina) that took on the most financial risk simply because it could. Distrust between the state and ethnic Chinese businessmen was evident before the financial reforms in the structure of their businesses (e.g., overseas assets) and the education and residency behavior of Chinese families. But the liberalization of the financial sector removed what discipline remained within Indonesia's elite business class. To be sure, some firms would remain embedded in global supply chains and focused on core competencies, but many others were incentivized to exploit the financial system for gains as opportunities presented themselves and constraints were few.

The Moral Economy of the Late New Order: Mutual Endangerment

By the 1990s, Suharto had been in office a quarter-century and was growing old and infirm with no plans in place for succession. As the decade wore on, Suharto's health seemed tenuous, and many, but not all, in Indonesia and the region expected the New Order might be in its final years. As late as 1996, one of the country's most astute observers noted "Suharto's tightening grip" on the messy social and political environment that characterized the 1990s.[75] Late New Order Indonesia was plagued by labor activism, student activism, protests against the repression of those activists, political violence, and the coalescence of many of the demands for reform in the *Reformasi* movement.[76] Conflictual and destructive state-business relations were among the regime's many problems and would contribute to Suharto's demise. To be sure, business elites did not join university students and others in the street protests that precipitated the general's resignation in May 1998, but their actions contributed directly to the financial crisis that unveiled the regime's dysfunction and a cascade of corruption scandals that had eroded legitimacy over the preceding decade.

[75] R. William Liddle, "Indonesia: Suharto's Tightening Grip," *Journal of Democracy* 7, no. 4 (1996): 58–72. Liddle had written in 1992 that the regime seemed to be weakening in the face of democratic pressures, but later he argued that Suharto had regained control over elites and especially the military.

[76] See Doreen Lee, *Activist Archives: Youth Culture and the Political Past in Indonesia* (Durham, NC: Duke University Press, 2016); Meredith L. Weiss, *Protest and Possibilities: Civil Society and Coalitions for Political Change in Malaysia* (Stanford: Stanford University Press, 2006); Edward Aspinall, *Opposing Suharto: Compromise, Resistance, and Regime Change* (Stanford: Stanford University Press, 2005).

The moves toward financial deregulation in the 1980s combined with endemic distrust and uncertainty to create conditions of mutual endangerment in state-business relations. The late New Order political economy was one of short time horizons and pervasive predation by actors both inside and outside the state. The three manifestations of mutual endangerment—asset expatriation, weaponized information, and extensive fraud and malfeasance, or "looting"—were widely visible. Some elements of each of these dynamics were present before the 1990s. Chinese conglomerates, for example, had pursued overseas assets since the regime was founded, a mark of the generalized distrust between the state and the business elites and the vulnerability of the latter. But the liberalization of the financial sector offered opportunities for vulnerable and distrustful business elites to plunder and incentives to loot, to maximize the present extractable value of their domestic firms at the expense of society and their own long-term solvency. Political ties were precarious for politicians and clients alike, incentivizing both parties to extract as much value from political protections as possible in the short term.

These dynamics proved mutually accelerating: the more that elites expatriated assets and perpetrated fraud and malfeasance, the weaker the regime became, incentivizing them to further pursue those same activities. Some have argued Suharto's fall was an exercise in self-fulfilling prophecies because everyone thought that Suharto could not handle a macroeconomic crisis, so they reacted to the crisis with behavior (capital flight, strategic bankruptcy, and looting) that exacerbated the crisis and made it politically disastrous.[77] Mutual endangerment is the political version of a self-fulfilling prophecy: firms and political elites behave as if tomorrow is uncertain, and loose financial controls enable them to access destructive weaponry.

Asset Expatriation

For almost the entire New Order, an open capital account enabled the holders of mobile capital, chiefly foreign investors and Chinese capitalists, to transfer assets into and out of the country at will. As scholarship on the New Order has argued, the regime's commitment to openness reassured foreign and Chinese capitalists and rendered the government vulnerable to the

[77] McLeod, "Soeharto's Indonesia"; George Fane and Ross H. McLeod, "Lessons for Monetary and Banking Policies from the 1997–1998 Economic Crises in Indonesia and Thailand," *Journal of Asian Economics* 10, no. 3 (1999): 395–413.

maneuverings of mobile asset holders.[78] In reality, each party was vulnerable to the other, but one can imagine the profound unwillingness of the Chinese capitalists in particular to allocate substantial assets within Indonesia without some path of escape should politics turn against them. The body of work that emphasizes the differences in preferences between holders of fixed versus mobile assets, however, overlooks that decisions about asset investment are endogenous to politics. Simply put, assets do not choose people, but rather capitalists cultivate asset profiles.

The Chinese capitalists who emerged during the course of the New Order pursued a portfolio of assets and investments based on their political vulnerability. While much is made of their ability to withdraw assets, they also invested in substantial fixed assets inside Indonesia. Sudono Salim, Suharto's closest ally and Indonesia's richest man by far, built his empire on flour milling, cement, and food processing, all lines of business he entered with Suharto's help, but then he quickly sought diversification. He registered companies in Singapore in the 1960s to both take loans and protect assets outside the country, and, after 1971, he "actively pursued geographic expansion beyond Indonesia so that not all eggs were in one basket."[79] Each of the top thirty conglomerates in 1991 held substantial fixed assets in addition to mobile assets. In fact, most of the conglomerates had their start in fixed assets, especially the export of raw materials and/or the import and distribution of goods (e.g., cigarettes, automobiles, and electronic goods). By the 1990s, conglomerates that were dependent on fixed assets (especially plantations and distribution monopolies) had diversified into finance, the most mobile industry of all. (See Appendix A.)

Large Indonesian firms, especially Chinese-controlled firms, diversified their assets abroad early and often in order to manage risk.[80] They both hedged domestic risks and retained a credible threat of capital exit in order to ensure Suharto's friendliness. As conglomerates gained increasing access

---

[78] Winters, *Power in Motion*; Pepinsky, *Economic Crises*. The account of the early New Order decision to open the capital account in 1971, in Chwieroth, "How Do Crises Lead," is definitive, though it downplays the role that Chinese capitalists had in demanding this policy.

[79] Chng and Borsuk, *Liem Sioe Liong's Salim Group*, 17. They add, "After Suharto fell in 1998, Salim's eggs outside Indonesia proved very helpful to efforts to deal with debts and keep Salim in Indofood."

[80] In fact, before Chinese conglomerates gained access to mobile capital, they only had access to fixed capital. Winters, *Power in Motion*, chap. 2, finds that Chinese capitalists failed to achieve interest representation early in the New Order because their assets were relatively fixed and they posed no credible threat. Robison, *Indonesia*, 43, reports that in 1952 almost one-fifth of the plantations on Java were owned by Chinese.

to mobile assets when they entered finance in the late 1980s and early 1990s, asset expatriation accelerated. As it accelerated, the macroeconomic stability and political stability of the New Order attenuated, manifesting the spiral dynamics characteristic of this form of state-business relations. Pressure on the exchange rate from capital flows, driven by both domestic and foreign investors, produced more than a few episodes of instability and devaluation. The threat of devaluation and anxieties about how macroeconomic challenges were managed begot further incentives to expatriate assets. Politically, asset expatriation compounded corruption scandals in the regime; as its legitimacy was damaged and various parties seemed to get away with expatriating assets, others were further incentivized to do so as well. Anticipation of regime uncertainty incentivized asset expatriation, and asset expatriation then enhanced regime uncertainty.

It is well documented in the secondary literature that domestic instability, communal violence in particular, contributed to bouts of asset expatriation.[81] A great deal of Chinese capital understandably left in the middle to late 1960s amid the political violence, and a 1968 law sought to allow it to be repatriated with "no questions asked" about the source.[82] It is also well documented that communal violence accelerated in the 1990s. Scholars disagree over whether the rise in violence is best attributed to the weakening of the military as peacekeeper or to Suharto's embrace of Islamist groups in the early 1990s, but, whatever the cause, vulnerable Chinese, who were primarily Christian, saw their faith in regime protection shaken.[83] For example, riots in North Sumatra (Medan) in the spring of 1994 led to immediate expatriation of as much as $200 million. One prominent Indonesian businessman reflected that people like him "can easily go abroad as they have money."[84]

Asset expatriation facilitated looting, much of which I describe below. Access to the financial system combined with pathways out of Indonesia enabled abuse of state and firm assets in pursuit of personal wealth. In February 1994, in the "Golden Key" scandal, the owner of the Golden Key company, Eddy Tansil, was revealed to have disappeared overseas with

[81] Pepinsky, *Economic Crises*; Chua, "Defining Indonesian Chineseness"; Robison, *Indonesia*.

[82] This was the Domestic Investment Law of 1968. "Long-term deposits" (*deposito berjangka*) were allowed with no declaration of information on the source of the funds. This was a concession to Chinese Indonesians, whose investment the new regime needed. Winters, *Power in Motion*, 77.

[83] Yuhki Tajima, *The Institutional Origins of Communal Violence: Indonesia's Transition from Authoritarian Rule* (New York: Cambridge University Press, 2014); Varshney, "Analyzing Collective Violence"; Jacques Bartrand, "Ethnic Conflicts in Indonesia: Models, Critical Junctures and the Timing of Violence," *Journal of East Asian Studies* 8, no. 3 (2008): 425–49.

[84] "Government Hopeful Riot Won't Hit Investment," *Jakarta Post*, August 1, 1996.

hundreds of millions of dollars borrowed from Bapindo.[85] Such a brazen act is clearly a reflection of contentious state-business relations and a lack of discipline over the financial sector, but asset expatriation does not only include absconding with assets acquired illegally. Endangered business elites, like Salim, also make legitimate investments abroad.

In the late 1980s and 1990s, these investments accelerated among nearly all of Indonesia's conglomerates. After 1992, outward direct investments from Indonesia went from nothing to an average of $600 million per year through 1997. [86] Corporate filings data show that of the top thirty conglomerates by asset size owned by Chinese-Indonesian individuals, all had overseas firms in 1990, and among them, the group controlled at least 300 firms (215 nontrading firms). Of the nontrading firms, dominant sectors included real estate and finance, in addition to the more standard business lines relevant to the firms' core competencies (e.g., shipping, oil and gas, textiles). Notably, most overseas assets, especially in real estate and finance, were located in Singapore, Hong Kong, the OECD countries, or tax havens such as the Cayman Islands and Panama. (See Appendix A for details on data collection and Figure A.1 for an example of corporate profile of a firm. Note these data only include corporate assets, not personal assets, and only assets identifiable and listed in corporate reports; therefore it is likely these data considerably underestimate the extent of outward investments.)

Weaponized Information

Mutual endangerment differs from mutual alignment in that corrupt dealings between and among business and political elites are secretive and existentially high stakes. Chinese capitalists in Indonesia, similar to capitalists in reform-era China, faced a harsh formal business environment because, as a matter of policy, they were excluded from many credit schemes. They thus depended on informal relationships with political elites to access finance, permits, and licenses and to enforce contracts, or otherwise engage in business transactions. Relationships were not always secretive, especially at the

---

[85] Charles Enoch, Barbara Balden, Olivier Frécaut, and Arto Kovanen, "Anatomy of Banking Crises: Two Years of Living Dangerously, 1997–1999," International Monetary Fund Working Paper WP/01/52, 2001, https://www.imf.org/external/pubs/ft/wp/2001/wp0152.pdf.

[86] Balance-of-payments data, via Economist Intelligence Unit. Note also that, despite the open capital account, Indonesia's errors and omissions (money entering and leaving illegally) was always high, averaging over 1 percent of GDP in the 1980s and the precrisis 1990s.

outset of the New Order but also through to the end. Suharto's "beautiful friendships" with various *cukong*, especially Sudono Salim, occurred in the public eye and were designed as partnerships for growth. Unlike late reform China, it was widely known that various Chinese business elites enjoyed license monopolies (e.g., Bob Hasan's plywood empire, Salim's flour milling and cement monopolies) and that Suharto's own family members were constructing business empires. And the famous "foundations" (*yayasans*), run by members of Suharto's family or other high-level or retired officials, controlled various firms and insisted on minority shareholding in or donations from others.[87]

Yet many relationships were secretive, especially among lower-profile members of the political elite, including regulatory officials. As state control over financial resources attenuated, relations among business elites and between business and the state became less hierarchical and dependent and more weblike and obfuscated. Business actors enmeshed political elites in their networks and vice versa, not only to access resources but also to protect themselves by holding incriminating information about others. In particular, as asset expatriation and looting accelerated, savvy business elites made sure that powerful political officials were implicated in their actions so that they would remain beyond reproach.

Financial enmeshment with the Suharto family became a sort of "continuous nuisance" to the private sector in the late New Order.[88] As was the case with the (eventually bogus) gold mine that begins this chapter, connections with one or more of Suharto's children (or his cousin, Sudwikatmono) seemed increasingly required for success in business on any scale. This would be especially true of financial institutions, where both parties would be impressed into fraud and malfeasance. Salim's Bank Central Asia (BCA) was partially owned by Suharto's eldest daughter (Tutut) and his second son (Sigit). Until the late 1980s, Mochtar Riady of Lippo Group, an experienced banker and *konglomerat* head, co-owned BCA, but he divested as the bank deepened its ties with Suharto's children. Riady thought the combination would be dangerous for the bank's health because of pressure to engage in excessive risk and self-dealing.[89] In addition to BCA, Tutut held shares in

---

[87] Shin, "Demystifying the Capitalist State," 131; Robison, *Indonesia*, 65.

[88] Shin, "Demystifying the Capitalist State," 131.

[89] Interview, Mochtar Riady, Jakarta, November 2016; ownership data from corporate filings (see Appendix A).

Barito Pacific's Bank Yama and Bank Surya, affiliated with the Ongko Group, which was co-owned by Sudwikamono.[90]

As the *konglomerat* entered the financial sector en masse, they also entered hand in hand with one another. Weblike relations and collusion among large conglomerates are a hallmark of mutual endangerment; plenty of economies are dominated by large business groups, but in most places they compete fiercely with one another for access to preferential policies and resources as well as for market share and profits.[91] When elites are commonly threatened, however, they have better incentives to collude in webs of self-protection. Indeed, connections among large *konglomerat* expanded during liberalization-era Indonesia. Many of the top groups began to cooperate on large projects, particularly real estate and industrial investments that required substantial capital.[92] But they also began to cofound new businesses; for example, the Rajawali Group, which held assets in television, real estate, banking, and more, was founded in the 1980s jointly between the Gajjah Tunggal, Ometracto, and Danawarsa groups along with Bimantara, the media group of Suharto's son.[93] Figures 3.3 and 3.4 present a visualization of these ties in the early 1990s. Figure 3.3 displays connections among the top two hundred business groups as determined through corporate filings, and Figure 3.4 shows the most densely connected groups in more detail. As evident in the figures, many of the country's largest firms were enmeshed with one another and with political elites. My argument is that many of these connections were based not solely on trust and cooperation but also on a desire to bind fates as a form of protection.

---

[90] Corporate profiles from CISI Raya Utama, BPPN annual reports, and Rosser, *Politics of Economic Liberalisation*. See Appendix A.

[91] Competition, rather than collusion, characterizes relationships between conglomerates (e.g., *chaebol and keiretsu*) in developmental states such as Korea and Japan. Relations with state entities were close, but large conglomerates competed fiercely to be selected as winners and to be given critical resources from state industrial planners. See David C. Kang, *Crony Capitalism: Corruption and Development in South Korea and the Philippines* (New York: Cambridge University Press, 2002); Yong-Chool Ha and Myung-Koo Kang, "Creating a Capable Bureaucracy with Loyalists: The Internal Dynamics of the South Korean Developmental State, 1948–1979," *Comparative Political Studies* 44, no. 1 (2010): 78–108; Ha-Joon Chang, *The Political Economy of Industrial Policy* (New York: St. Martin's, 1994); Eun-mi Kim, *Big Business, Strong State: Collusion and Conflict in South Korean Development, 1960–1990* (Albany: State University of New York Press, 1997); Jong-sung You, "The Changing Dynamics of State-Business Relations and the Politics of Reform and Capture in South Korea," *Review of International Political Economy* 28, no. 1 (2021): 81–102. On keiretsu in Japan, see Chalmers A. Johnson, *MITI and the Japanese Miracle* (Stanford: Stanford University Press, 1992), 203–7.

[92] For example, a major real estate development project in metro Jakarta (Bumi Serpon Damai) was undertaken by the Jaya, Sinar Mas, and Salim groups. Sato, "Development of Business Groups."

[93] Cisi Raya 200; see Appendix A.

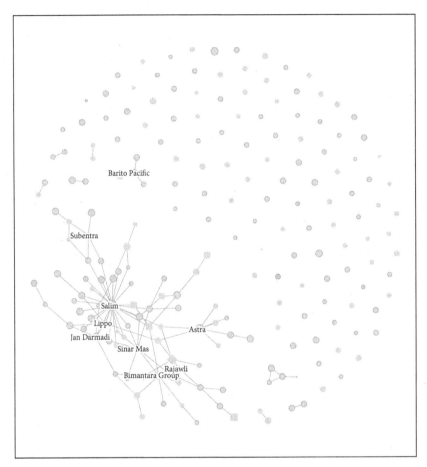

Figure 3.3 Network Map of Company Connections, Top Two Hundred
Conglomerates

As the density of connections intensifies, so too does information about
the wrongdoings and positions of others. Information can be weaponized
against business and political actors alike, and this was frequently done
during the late New Order and during its dissolution. The weaponization
of information is visible not only in strategic leaks and revelations but also
in curious episodes of restraint, as political elites are precluded from going
after business elites for fear of mutual demise. The sections below describe
multiple episodes of too-late discoveries of financial malfeasance or mismanagement; banks and other firms were frequently in precarious positions

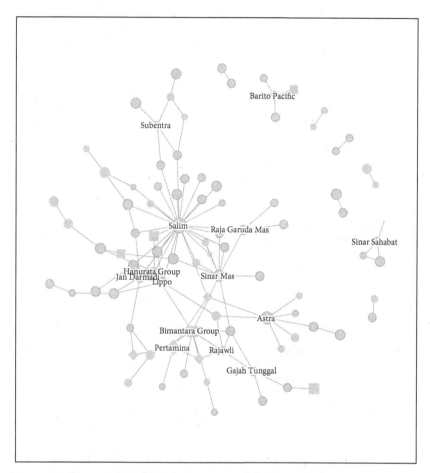

Figure 3.4 Network Map of Conglomerates with Connections

Note: The unit of analysis is the firm, and two firms are considered to have a link if they were co-invested, were known to exchange ownership in other firms, or were listed by corporate analysts as having "close" relations in 1991. The size of the nodes indicates asset size in 1991 (log scale). The shape of the nodes indicates the firm owner's political category: circles are nonstate business groups, squares are business groups owned by Suharto's family, and diamonds are military firms. See Appendix A.

Source: Author database of top conglomerates, via corporate filings and profiles, including CISI Raya Top 200 conglomerates; profiles of businessmen, *Conglomerat Indonesia*; Andrew Rosser, *The Politics of Economic Liberalisation in Indonesia: State, Market and Power* (Richmond, Surrey, UK: Curzon, 2022); and BPPN.

and visible to regulatory officials for years before the public was made aware. Even when "technocratic" regulatory officials wanted to take action against problematic firms, they found themselves restrained because political elites would be implicated.

Looting

One puzzle in firms' economic behavior, evident in the late New Order and in contemporary China, is why firms pursue economic behaviors that seem to destroy their businesses. These behaviors include accruing substantial and insurmountable debt, expanding rapidly into business lines well beyond their core competencies, overpaying for domestic and (especially) foreign assets, and risking bankruptcy. These activities are not simply "corruption," though corruption is involved; for example, political relationships enable firms to access credit despite poor fundamentals. Instead of pursuing rents and special resources that ensure long-term market dominance, these firms seem to invert expectations of rational economic behavior, leading to tenuous and often lethal economic positions. Following Akerlof and Romer, I call this "looting," whereby managers have incentives to maximize the current extractable value of their firms at the expense of their long-term viability and at great cost to society, and firm behavior generates losses that exceed the gains looters achieve.[94] Akerlof and Romer focus on moral hazard, or expectations of bailouts, as the mechanism that drives inverted economic behavior in situations ranging from the US savings and loan crisis of the 1980s to the financial crisis in Chile. But expectations of impunity for bad behavior (e.g., bailouts) are only one mechanism through which market participants discount the value of future revenue: expectations of political demise generate the same incentives. In the context of mutual endangerment, both mechanisms are at play. Politically connected firms expect that the government will step in when they falter, producing a moral hazard mechanism. And vulnerable firms fear that their political connections may disappear, incentivizing them to adopt short time horizons and to focus on extraction and self-protection. In fact, they know the case to be one or the other: either they can expect a government bailout through their political connections or they face political threat, and both expectations generate looting incentives. Further, looting interacts with weaponized information: many firms enmesh political elites in corrupt relations to wield information against them and to demand impunity and/or bailouts.

---

[94] George A. Akerlof and Paul M. Romer, "Looting: The Economic Underworld of Bankruptcy for Profit," *Brookings Papers on Economic Activity*, no. 2 (1993): 1–73, https://doi.org/10.2307/2534564.

Looting incidents appear in all sorts of political economies and for various reasons.[95] But late New Order Indonesia and contemporary China were home to widespread looting as a political phenomenon that spanned sectors and intensified quickly once it appeared. In essence, looting was endemic to the political economy and it snowballed: once a few market participants invert their economic behaviors and enmesh one another in activities to loot, such behaviors metastasize through the economy.[96] And once a few participants appear to get away with looting, the incentives to model are amplified. Several episodes in financial markets in the early 1990s illustrate looting dynamics that would accelerate as the decade wore on.

Bank Duta and Bank Summa

In May 1990, Bank Duta, a national, private bank owned by three foundations (*yayasan*) chaired by Suharto, listed on the JSX, earning $120 million for 20 percent of its ownership.[97] Within a few months, in September 1990, the bank was revealed to have incurred foreign-exchange losses of $300 million, and several *yayasan* rescued the bank.[98] That the bank had been able to "conceal huge losses from future shareholders during a public share offering" caused anger at Bapepam, BI, and other financial custodians for failing to properly monitor and regulate.[99] The losses were from off–balance sheet foreign-exchange transactions, and very little information was made public.[100] The foreign-exchange losses were compounded by discoveries that the bank had deposited dollars in the National Bank of Kuwait. "There is widespread suspicion . . . that Bank Duta's foreign-exchange dealers were trading extensively on their own account and for wealthy individual clients."

---

[95] I am not arguing that political distrust is a necessary condition for looting. A lack of financial discipline seems to be a condition, but looting incidents occur in regimes with rule of law and protections for business, e.g., the savings and loan crisis in the United States.

[96] Akerlof and Romer ("Looting," 3) recognize a similar dynamic: "Looting can spread symbiotically to other markets, bringing to life a whole economic underworld with perverse incentives. The looters of the sector covered by the government guarantees will make trades with unaffiliated firms outside this sector, causing them to produce in a way that helps maximize the looters' current extractions with no regard for future losses. Rather than looking for business partners who will honor their contracts, the looters look for partners who will sign contracts that appear to have high current value if fulfilled but that will not—and could not—be honored."

[97] Adam Schwarz, "Caveat Rupiah: Indonesian System's Weaknesses Revealed by Forex Loss," *Far Eastern Economic Review* 149, no. 38 (September 20, 1990): 105.

[98] Hill, *Indonesian Economy in Crisis*, 36.

[99] Richard Borsuk, "Jakarta Limits Scope of Private Exchange," *Wall Street Journal*, April 20, 1992; "Jakarta Market's New Look Full of Future Promise," *South China Morning Post*, August 23, 1992. See also Rosser, *Politics of Economic Liberalisation*, 99–100.

[100] Woo, Glassburner, and Nasution, *Macroeconomic Policies*, 95.

Those clients, it was rumored, did not pay up when losses were incurred. The bank regularly flouted rules about foreign-exchange exposure, engaging in foreign-exchange positions that dwarfed the capital of the bank: "That's suicide for a bank that size," a banker is quoted as saying.[101] One reason BI was not able to observe the bank's position was that the bankers kept no records of their activities, allegedly throwing tickets "in drawers" as if they were exchanging play money.[102]

Some foreign bankers called Indonesian banks "unsophisticated" in their foreign-exchange dealings, but the Bank Duta episode illustrates the logic of looting. The *yayasan* injected sufficient capital to save the bank, fulfilling the expectations of bankers, managers, and "wealthy clients" that they could take money earned partly through public listings and behave as they pleased with relative impunity.[103] The lack of basic professionalism and "suicidal" behavior was, in fact, a sort of bankruptcy for profit, as some individuals benefited from personal positions in risky exchanges while generating losses for society.

Two years later, a large private bank associated with the Soeryadjaya family's Astra conglomerate, the country's second largest, was closed after it had incurred large debts (hundreds of millions of dollars) from rapid expansion in property and other ventures.[104] Astra founder William Soeryadjaya's eldest son, Edward, had expanded Summa after buying Bank Agung Asia, a failing domestic bank, in 1989 and moving the headquarters of his Germany-based Bank Summa to Jakarta. The bank's assets surged more than tenfold between 1989 and 1991, making huge loans to other members of the Summa Group, which invested in real estate at peak market. Problems in the bank's governance had been an open secret for at least two years: One banker is quoted saying, "The level of mismanagement at Summa was astounding. A large proportion of the loans were also made to intra-group companies on an unsecured, totally nonsensical basis. Abuses were rife."[105]

BI authorities had set a deadline for the Soeryadjayas to inject capital into the bank, and, when they failed to do so, they revoked its license and closed

---

[101] Schwarz, "Caveat Rupiah," 105–6.

[102] Ibid., 106.

[103] The board of directors and board of commissioners were all fired, but no individual was held legally accountable and no funds were recovered. Ibid., 105–6. The bank's treasurer and vice president, Dicky Iskandar Di Nata, was sentenced to ten years in jail on corruption charges, but most people saw him as a scapegoat. Rosser, *Politics of Economic Liberalisation*, 72.

[104] Borsuk, "Astra's First-Half Earnings," 3.

[105] Tony Shale, "Top-Level Shakeout Needed to Mend the Financial System," *Euromoney*, June 1993, 55.

the bank in December 1992. BI and Ministry of Finance officials wanted Summa's closure to be a "benchmark" for other banks to reduce moral hazard, but the Soeryadjaya family did not face significant penalties.[106] In fact, Astra's next move was viewed by many as a backdoor bailout. Shortly after Summa's liquidation, 16.5 percent of Astra was listed (earning $200 million) in the JSX's largest-ever posted trades.[107] Danareksa, the state-owned shareholding firm that had monopolized the JSX before the late 1980s, bought the shares and sold them to a state pension fund.[108] Edward Soeryadjaya departed for Germany and was never held accountable for flouting regulations, and the Astra Group expanded its assets and profits in the years that followed. The Summa episode was a benchmark, but one that only deepened incentives for looting. The long liquidation process entailed "public protests and street demonstrations directed against the BI," all of which "reinforced BI's view that bank closures should be avoided at almost all cost."[109] These lessons were not lost on market participants, who would engage in ever-riskier behavior with the expectation of personal profit and impunity.

Liberalized rules for lending enabled both private entry into banking and the self-dealing that ensued, and loosened rules that governed credit extension of state banks (these included the elimination of credit ceilings and looser requirements for collateral and investment self-financing). In June 1993, a list of twenty-six business groups alleged to hold "doubtful or bad" debts to state banks, only one of which was not found to be "deeply mired in non-performing loans and technically insolvent," circulated in Jakarta.[110] The list's origins were never verified; some alleged that the BI itself circulated the list to exert pressure on the business groups to pay, but the BI denied it was the source and had to work to reassure markets that bad debt was not a real threat. Collecting debt was difficult for anyone in the legal environment

[106] Julia Leung, "Indonesian Banks Pay for Their Growth Binge," *Wall Street Journal*, December 16, 1992, 13. BI governor Mooy said that the closure "represents a sea change for Indonesia's financial regulation" and "will be looked at as a benchmark for years to come."

[107] "International Brief—PT Astra International: Family Sells Two Big Blocks of Auto Company's Shares," *Wall Street Journal*, November 16, 1992, C11.

[108] Richard Borsuk, "Indonesian Unit Trust Buys 11% of Astra for $126 Million," *Wall Street Journal* (European Edition), December 30, 1992, 7.

[109] Enoch et al., "Anatomy of Banking Crises," 24; Rosser, *Politics of Economic Liberalisation*, 73–74, notes that concerns about contagion were also acute because two banks connected with Suharto's relative (Sudwikatmono), Bank Surya and Bank Subentra, were threatened.

[110] Cole and Slade, *Building*, 138–39. They state that preliminary findings of a report commissioned by Marie indicated that "a limited number of conglomerates, often with strong political connections, had been able to obtain large loans from the state banks on which they paid no interest or return on principal."

of the 1990s, but connected firms were particularly difficult to discipline because of their air of political impunity. The 1993 list included many of the
country's largest groups and also Bimantara, the group belonging to Suharto's
son. An editorial in the *Jakarta Post* captured the sentiment of systemic disciplinary failures: "Those businessmen are only the small fry and the big
fish may never be caught."[111] The excessive debt and refusal to pay follow
the dynamics of mutual endangerment perfectly. State bank officials and "big
borrowers" allegedly colluded to "bypass normal credit analysis," allowing
large firms to balloon in size and in the risk they posed to the state. As in
China in the 2000s, bank directors earned commissions on loans, and most
actors were beyond legal or market discipline, so incentives pushed toward
lending and borrowing in amounts as great as possible.[112]

"The Worst Exchange in the World": The JSX Unbound
Within a few years, the explosion of activity on the "once comatose" Jakarta
Stock Exchange was not simple irrational exuberance; rather it had all
the hallmarks of coldly rational fraud and malfeasance. As early as 1991,
concerns that, in the words of one Indonesian scholar, company reports were
Indonesia's "most creative fiction" writing, were scaring off investors and
turning the "sexiest" market in Asia into an "ugly duckling."[113] Companies
were inflating earnings and issuing at "wildly inflated values" and then experienced sell-offs when they reported substantially lower real earnings (these
include Argo Pantes, a textile firm connected to The Ning King's Damatex
Group, and Sampoerna, a cigarette company). But a lack of regulations to
protect investors meant that companies benefited from listing at inflated
prices and investors could not recover. One securities investor at the time
estimated that as much as a quarter of the money raised through stock sales
was "being stashed in bank accounts."[114] Another tactic was for companies
to "change their minds" about capital needs and uses after issuance; investors
expected their funds to go to capital investments, but companies would

[111] Quoted in Richard Borsuk, "Indonesian Banks Come Under Scrutiny: Talk of Bad Debts at
State-Owned Lenders Prompts Calls for Cleanup," *Wall Street Journal* (Asia Edition), July 2, 1993. See
also Cole and Slade, *Building*, 95; Rosser, *Politics of Economic Liberalisation*, 76–78.
[112] Quote from Rizal Ramli, a managing director of a private economics consultancy, in Borsuk,
"Indonesian Banks." This was frequently called "memo lending," when bank officials extended credit
without any proper evaluation process. Shale, "Top-Level Shakeout," 56.
[113] Hadi Soesastro goes on to say of company reports: "You should see them—lots of pictures, fan-
tastic write-ups, but they are not accurate. . . . Here, numbers do lie." Quoted in Cait Murphy, "Hard
Times on the Jakarta Exchange," *Asian Wall Street Journal*, November 14, 1991.
[114] Ibid.

Table 3.4 Indonesian Chinese-Owned Conglomerates in Top Fifty National Firms by Asset Size, with Financial Firms

Conglomerate	Owner	Bank Connections*	Bank Outcome in AFC	Connections
Astra	William Soeryadjaya	Bank Summa	†Closed in 1992, insolvent	
Bank Bali	Djaja Ramli	Bank Bali	Receivership	Sinar Sahabat, Batamtex
Barito Pacific	Prajogo Pangestu	Bank Andromeda Bank Universal Bank Yama	Liquidated in 1998; Bambang sued Ministry of Finance and immediately opened Bank Alfa in same building Recapitalized	Citra Lamtoro (Tutut, Suharto's daughter) Bimantara (Bambang, Suharto son) Djajanti
Bira	Atang Latief	Bank Bira		
Bob Hasan	Bob Hasan	Bank Umum Nasional	Frozen in 1998; defrauded the IRBA	Ongko, Wanandi
Djarum	Robert Budi Hartono		†Took shares of BCA during the crisis	
Gajah Tunggal	Nursalim	Bank Dagang Nasional Indonesia	BTO; Nursalim fled and refused to cooperate with IBRA	Salim, Ometracto, Bimantara
Jan Darmadi	Jan Darmadi	Bank Pan Indonesia		Salim, Lippo, Djata
Kali Raya Sari	Usman Admadjaja	**Bank Danamon** Bank Delta	BTO; not cooperative with the IBRA	Salim
Lippo	Mochtar Riady	Bank Lippo	Recapitalized	Salim
Metropolitan	Ciputra	Bank Metropolitan	Suspended in 1999	Salim
Modern Photo	Samadikun Hartono	**Bank Modern**	BTO; Hartono fled, not cooperative with the IBRA	
Ometracto	Ferry Teguh Santoso	**Bank Tiara Asia**	BTO	Gajjah Tunggal, Sinar Mas, Bimantara (Bambang)
Ongko (Arya Upaya)	Kaharuddin Ongko	Bank Surya Nusantara **Bank Umum Nasional** Bank Arya	BTO Suspended in 1998; hostile IBRA relationship Suspended in 1999	Bob Hasan, Wanandi

Table 3.4 Continued

Conglomerate	Owner	Bank Connections*	Bank Outcome in AFC	Connections
Panin	Mu'min Ali	Panin Bank	Survived without BLBI	Lippo, Jan Darmadi
Raja Garuda Mas	Sukanto Tanoto	Bank Tani Nasional		Salim, Sinar Mas, STTC, Satya Djaya Raya
Rodamas	Tan Siong Kie	Bank Buana Indonesia		Sigit (Suharto's son), Tutut (Suharto's daughter)
Salim	Liem Sioe Liong	**Bank Central Asia Bank Danamon**	BTO BTO	Sinar Mas Kali Raya Sari
Sinar Mas	Eka Tjipta Widjaja	Bank Internasional Indonesia	Recapitalized	Salim
Sinar Sahabat	Sukanta Tanudjaja	Bank Bali	BTO	Bank Bali
Tahija	Julius Tahija	Bank Niaga **Bank PDFCI**	BTO BTO	Soedarpo
Wanandi	Wanandi family	Bank Umum Nasional	Suspended in 1998; hostile IBRA relationship	Bob Hasan, Ongko

Sources: Andrew Rosser, *The Politics of Economic Liberalisation in Indonesia: State, Market and Power* (Richmond, Surrey, UK: Curzon, 2022), 209–10; affiliate and identity data are from Cisi Raya Study on Top 200 Indonesian Conglomerates (1990), Cisi Raya Study on 200 Prominent Indonesian Businessmen (1990). Bank outcome data and BLBI loans from BBPN (IBRA) Annual Reports. See Appendix A, Figure A.1.
* Bold type indicates banks that received BLBI loans in excess of 500 percent of their equity.
† Closed prior to the AFC.

redirect the funds into property speculation or overseas ventures.[115] Other forms of fraud were more pedestrian; in 1992 and 1993, the operator the JSX suspended several brokerage firms after they were discovered to have been trading fake share certificates or even using phony checks to purchase shares. In 1993, four firms colluded to defraud investors of at least $5 million, and

[115] "Growing Pains of a Changing Market," *South China Morning Post*, August 17, 1991. See also Rosser, *Politics of Economic Liberalisation*, 98–99.

the BEJ suspended trading on one stock until all fake certificates could be accounted for.[116]

In 1992, the JSX was dubbed by *Forbes* as one of the two worst exchanges in the world (alongside Norway's) and described by Standard & Poor's as "totally unregulated."[117] To be sure, Indonesia's banking and equities markets lacked effective regulation, but the problems were political rather than technical. Even when regulations were crafted to limit self-dealing and facilitate prudential oversight, they were flouted by public and private actors alike. Mutual endangerment makes the enforcement of rules on the books nearly impossible because public and private agents are entwined in corruption and malfeasance. Indeed, there is every signal that the country's technocrats at the Ministry of Finance, BI, and Bapepam wanted to rein in the fraudulent behavior but were incapable of doing so. In 1995, a capital market bill aimed to protect investors by requiring listing companies to disclose financial circumstances and by holding directors and commissioners accountable for inaccurate or misleading information.[118] And by 1996, Bapepam was trying to tighten requirements for securities firms; 70 of the 197 firms with a JSX seat had lost money in 1995, a curious outcome given that the country was growing at 7 percent.[119]

Nonetheless, episodes of malfeasance and corruption continued. A blatant episode of insider trading of a bank's shares (Bank Mashill, whose securities firm had been suspended over counterfeit scrips in 1993) in April 1996 was made possible by poor surveillance of unusual trading. Officials lamented that the increased trading volume might be attributed to brokerage houses having "played their own portfolios" rather than adding new clients.[120] As

---

[116] "Jakarta Exchange Suspends 4 Brokerage Firms," *Wall Street Journal* (European Edition), April 6, 1993; "Jakarta to Let Foreigners Own More Shares," *Wall Street Journal* (Asia Edition), April 30, 1993. See also Rosser, *Politics of Economic Liberalisation*, 107–9.

[117] "Jakarta Battles to Restore Lost Image," *South China Morning Post*, October 18, 1995. Much of the commentary at the time included discussions of the lack of regulation. See Soesastro, "Political Economy of Deregulation"; Michael Shari, "Calls for More Liquidity and Tighter Rules in Jakarta," *South China Morning Post*, April 2, 1994; Ross McLeod, "Indonesia's Economic Performance: An Assessment," *Journal of Asian Business* 12, no. 4 (1996): 71–83; Alex Low, "Indonesian Banking: An Exercise in Reregulation of Deregulation," *James Cook University Law Review* 4 (1997): 39–67. Technocrat participants in Indonesia's liberalization efforts also desired more regulation. See Prawiro, *Indonesia's Struggle*; Cole and Slade, *Building*.

[118] "Government Introduces Stock Exchange Bill to Protect Investors," *Jakarta Post*, March 30, 1995, 9.

[119] "Government to Tighten Control of Brokerage Companies," *Jakarta Post*, January 15, 1996.

[120] "JSX Formulating System to Protest Public Interests," *Jakarta Post*, June 5, 1996, 11. Mashill was owned by Lakop Group, itself affiliated with several other conglomerates (including Sinar Sahabat, Bank Bali, and Bamatex). Rosser, *Politics of Economic Liberalisation*, 211; Appendix A.

would be the case in China twenty years later, decisions about regulators and regulations became embroiled in weaponized information. In 1996, the politics of selecting the JSX president became acrimonious and personal, with letters circulating that attacked potential candidates with allegations of corruption.[121]

A particularly prominent securities firm, called the "underwriter to the stars" for its association with many of the country's highest profile issuances, illustrates the dynamics of mutual endangerment.[122] PT Makindo, founded in the late 1970s by a Chinese businessman, was frequently accused of winning underwriting contracts because of its willingness to abet fraud and embezzlement. The firm seemed especially willing to sell underpriced and early shares to political and business elites, many of whom would then resell on secondary markets after share prices had increased. Between 1993 and 1996, Makindo was accused of self-dealing in underwriting the Barito Pacific issuance (illegally allocating shares to its own managing director, a relative of the founder), allocating shares to connected individuals (including members of the Suharto family) in the listing of the state-owned BNI in 1996, and similar actions in an issuance for Telkom (a state-owned enterprise). Despite public outcry and private resistance from other business elites and some efforts to investigate, senior government officials appeared to protect the firm from legal scrutiny because of the involvement of prominent political elites.[123]

Within two years, the JSX would be closed for several months, dozens of banks would enter state receivership, and large firm networks would collapse amid one of the worst financial crises in modern history. With mounting evidence that political relationships precluded proper regulation of banks and equities as well as protection of minority shareholders, the onset of the crisis prompted a massive withdrawal of funds from banks and sell-offs on the JSX. Crisis dynamics snowballed. Banks that had occupied precarious financial positions for years became even more precarious amid the collapse of the rupiah and public demands for withdrawals. Mobile capitalists, including domestic businessmen, hastened to expatriate what assets they had, with incentives for looting intensifying after 1997. The crisis ended the New Order.

---

[121] "Only 39% of JSX Shareholders Eligible to Nominate Directors," *Jakarta Post*, March 6, 1996, 8; Rosser, *Politics of Economic Liberalisation*, 118–20.

[122] *Far Eastern Economic Review*, July 27, 1995, quoted in Rosser, *Politics of Economic Liberalisation*, 109.

[123] Rosser, *Politics of Economic Liberalisation*, 109–11.

Spiraling: Mutual Endangerment and Crisis

Mutual alignment and mutual endangerment are both unstable forms of state-business relations in the sense that they generate endogenous political and economic dynamics that push each party to change. Mutual alignment can facilitate political elites' ability to discipline business elites—making them behave in ways that accord with the regime's goals—but so too can it generate economic stagnation, meaning challenges to "upgrading" economies or promoting higher levels of economic development. We see that this was the case during the first two decades of Indonesia's New Order. The government's tight control over the financial sector allowed it to distribute gains to political supporters. The country grew, even dramatically, but it was reliant on the export of natural resources. When those resources disappeared, the pathologies of mutual alignment became problematic. The financial system was good at facilitating political patrimonialism but weak at allocating resources toward dynamic sectors or igniting domestic investment. The regime responded by pursuing financial-sector liberalization alongside a suite of other reform measures as state-business relations veered toward mutual endangerment. The critical difference is evident in that firms, even and especially connected firms, engaged in activities that contravened the interests of the regime, pursuing speculative ventures, generating bubbles, looting their own firms, squirreling assets abroad, and taking on systemically risky debt.

Mutual endangerment entails inherent political and economic instability. To be sure, the New Order had experienced no small amount of economic disruption, having been born in hyperinflation and undergone painful exchange-rate adjustments and a wrenching state firm debt crisis (Pertamina). But the financial instability in the 1980s and 1990s was systemic and cumulative rather than episodic or isolated. As the above section reveals, manifestations of mutual endangerment (asset expatriation, weaponized information, and looting) were widespread political phenomena rather than actions attributable to a few bad actors. Indonesia's experience during the AFC that began in 1997 further illustrates the dynamics of mutual endangerment in two ways. First, looting and asset expatriation contributed to the crisis itself, and, second, the dynamics of mutual engenderment spiraled during the crisis, ensuring that the crisis was far worse in Indonesia than in places where such a form of state-business relations did not exist, notably Malaysia.

The causes, nature, and lessons of the AFC are the subject of a wide and multidisciplinary literature, one I need not rehash here. Generally, policymakers and scholars alike emphasize both the political issues and the economic fundamentals to explain the onset of the crisis and its regional contagion.[124] The political science literature on the crisis tends to examine how the crisis refracted through a diverse set of regimes and political economy arrangements.[125] In this chapter as well as Chapter 4, I offer a political explanation for why capitalists in Malaysia and Indonesia behaved differently during the crisis (as opposed to explaining government action alone). Indonesia's capitalists accelerated the crisis by rapidly deploying assets abroad and intensifying their looting as the Indonesian government tried to address the collapse of the financial sector. These actions contributed directly to dramatic rounds of depreciation for the rupiah, the BI's depletion of reserves, catastrophic inflation, and perceptions of mismanagement and corruption that decayed the regime's legitimacy.

To be clear, my argument is not that either the behavior of business elites or mutual endangerment on their own caused Suharto's downfall.[126] But I do posit a counterfactual, which is that if the *konglmerat*, in particular, had turned toward the regime rather than away from it, as their Malaysian counterparts did, it is possible that the crisis would not have been as severe and perhaps even survivable (if accompanied by effective management of Suharto's declining health and succession). Clearly, this counterfactual

---

[124] Wing Thye Woo, Jeffrey D. Sachs, and Klaus Schwab, eds., *The Asian Financial Crisis: Lessons for a Resilient Asia* (Cambridge MA: MIT Press, 2000); Paul Krugman, "What Happened to Asia?" (January 1998), http://web.mit.edu/krugman/www/DISINTER.html; T. J. Pempel, ed., *The Politics of the Asian Financial Crisis* (Ithaca: Cornell University Press, 1999); Giancarlo Corsetti, Paolo Pesenti, and Nouriel Roubini, "What Caused the Asian Financial and Currency Crisis? Part I: A Macroeconomic Overview," NBER Working Paper no. 6833 (December 1998) and "Part II: The Policy Debate," NBER Working Paper no. 6834 (December 1998). My approach has much in common with that of Haggard, who focuses on state-business relations, and especially the "capture" of financial liberalization processes, as a cause of the crisis. Stephan Haggard, *The Political Economy of the Asian Financial Crisis* (Washington, DC: Institute for International Economics, 2000).

[125] Pepinsky, in *Economic Crises*, for example, examines why Malaysia's BN was able to react coherently and decisively to the crisis, enabling the regime to retain power, while Indonesia fared so differently. His key argument is that the New Order's support coalition comprised mobile capital (*konglomerat*) and fixed capital (politico-bureaucrats), and therefore the regime's response to the crisis vacillated between trying to satisfy these groups as well as international financial institutions (the IMF), but they ultimately failed. By contrast, the Malaysian regime's coalition included fixed capital and labor, and so it imposed capital controls, managed the crisis, and retained power. MacIntyre, *The Power of Institutions*, points to different political institutional architectures to explain the differing responses in Thailand, the Philippines, Indonesia, and Malaysia.

[126] Such a claim would deny the substantial efforts by indigenous businesspeople; students; civil society actors, including opposition political parties such as Megawati's Partai Demokrasi Indonesia; and vocal public critics, all of whom contributed to the fall of the New Order. See Lee, *Activist Archives*; Weiss, *Protest and Possibilities*.

cannot be empirically tested; I reason this way only to clarify my argument about different crisis behaviors in different modes of state-business relations. In addition, the crisis behavior of the *konglomerat*, as well as businesspeople connected to Suharto's family, demonstrates how looting can come from expectations of demise just as well as from expectations of bailout. Behaving as if the autocrat will fall can indeed contribute to such an outcome.

Looting Accelerates

Indonesia's high-growth economy, the darling of foreign investors and macroeconomic analysts, entered an unexpected free-fall after the devaluation of the Thai bhat engulfed the wider region in twin financial and currency crises. Initial expectations were that Indonesia would not be as badly hit: even in fall 1997, the "almost universally-held analysis" was that the country's problems were purely from contagion, that the "underlying economy was basically sound," and that "confidence-building measures," like bank bailouts and macro adjustments, would suffice.[127] Less than a year later, however, in May 1998, students had occupied parliament, Suharto had resigned, food-price inflation was up more than 50 percent, and ethnic conflict and riots had plagued Jakarta and other cities. Many prominent Chinese individuals and families fled Indonesia in 1998, some permanently. The macroeconomic analysis, and even the political understandings, failed to account for the precarity of ties—the deep distrust and the proclivity of elites to turn against the regime. The measures meant to restore confidence instead facilitated accelerated looting.

In the summer of 1997, domestic debt troubles prompted currency attacks, first in Thailand and then, toward the end of the year, throughout the region. The BI spent $1 billion to defend the rupiah, ultimately allowing the currency to float on August 14. In less than two months, the rupiah had lost nearly one-third of its value, and Suharto turned to the International Monetary Fund for help. A series of IMF agreements brought an estimated $40 billion in loans for Indonesia from international financial institutions and other countries in exchange for wrenching domestic liberalization measures, including canceling several megaprojects, privatizations, elimination of monopolies (e.g., for cloves and plywood), ending consumer subsidies, and

---

[127] Enoch et al., "Anatomy of Banking Crises," 9, 11.

generally the removal of economic privileges for the politically connected. These programs clearly threatened the New Order's political foundations, and therefore met with significant resistance from both inside and outside of the state. Over the course of late fall 1997 and during the first several months of 1998, Suharto attempted to navigate between increasingly strict IMF demands and domestic constituencies. Each time, Suharto's reform commitments wavered at the implementation stage as the IMF became more demanding, eventually culminating in a third package in April 1998. Various signals indicated that the terms of the package, which entailed significant liberalization measures, including elimination of monopolies and privatization efforts, would hold.[128]

Throughout the crisis, both while Suharto remained in power and after he stepped down, the state's efforts to manage the banking crisis and defend the currency failed as business actors took advantage of the policies to enrich themselves. The main means of extending help to the country's troubled banks during the crisis was a liquidity provision program run by the BI (Bantuan Likuiditas Bank Indonesia, BLBI). In contrast to sudden closures and high interest rates, the BLBI program offered deposit guarantees and liquidity to troubled banks.[129] The theory of mutual endangerment would predict that these resources were quickly turned into personal assets of capitalists with short time horizons, and indeed, the BLBI funds were rapidly abused. The "great majority" of BLBI funds, which totaled Rp144.5 trillion, more than 15 percent of Indonesia's GDP in 2002, went to connected financial firms, either conglomerates, those associated with Suharto's family, or both.[130] Salim's BCA alone received nearly Rp53 trillion, and many other banks received loans in excess of 500 percent of their equity (see Table 3.4).[131]

Such a tremendous expense would make sense if it worked to stabilize banks' balance sheets and return public confidence, but the BLBI program

---

[128] For example, monopolies on cloves and plywood that benefited Tommy Suharto and Bob Hasan (who in March had become minister of trade and industry) were dismantled, signaling that the IMF had won. Rosser, *Politics of Economic Liberalisation*, 181.

[129] Haggard, *Political Economy*, 66–69; Donald Hanna, "Restructuring Asia's Financial System," in Wing Thye Woo, Jeffrey D. Sachs, and Klaus Schwab, eds., *The Asian Financial Crisis: Lessons for a Resilient Asia* (Cambridge MA: MIT Press, 2000), 57. In November 1997, the government abruptly closed more than a dozen financial institutions, yet there was still no deposit insurance scheme in place. Though the closed banks were smaller ones, fears of further closures decreased public confidence in the financial system.

[130] Haggard, *Political Economy*, 76; Rosser, *Politics of Economic Liberalisation*, 174–76; Pepinsky, *Economic Crises*, 94–97. Total BLBI figure from the 2002 Indonesia Bank Restructuring Agency (Badan Penyahayan Perbankan Nasional, or BPPN) Annual Report, 15.

[131] The Salim Group received Rp52,726,575 million according to the 2002 BPPN Annual Report.

did the opposite. Recipients were incentivized to "create deficits" on their balance sheets so as to be eligible for funds, which they used to rescue other endangered firms in their groups or even to squirrel away assets overseas.[132] BI liquidity rose continuously, accelerating as the Indonesian Banking Restructuring Agency (IBRA) assumed control of more banks and Suharto's grip on power weakened. The BI was "in effect financing speculative attacks on itself."[133] Looting began early in the crisis and continued until resources were gone. The IBRA team formed by the BI in the first round of bank closures in 1997 immediately found that the productive and lucrative assets of the banks had already disappeared. One national magazine wrote of Hendra Rahardja, the owner-turned-fugitive of Bank Harapan Sentosa, "Thieves are smarter than cops. Knowing that he was being chased by law enforcement, he would deposit some of his stolen goods with friends and relatives before he was caught. His goal is to prevent these looted goods from being confiscated in their entirety."[134] Most of Rahardja's assets were transferred to Australia and Hong Kong; Rahardja's brother, Eddy, had similarly looted state assets during the Golden Key scandal of 1994.

The BLBI resource drain was classic looting: conglomerates had incentives to invert their own firms' economic health for personal gain, and government officials abetted them in doing so. The aftermath of the crisis revealed the extent of the looting. In March 2000, fifty-seven individuals from the BI, Ministry of Finance, IBRA, and private banks were accused of colluding to "defraud the government of Indonesia through their liquidity provisions" and conspiring to exchange assets that were overvalued to "pay back" loans.[135]

The IBRA spent years attempting to recover its lost resources. It would take the closure of over forty-eight banks during the crisis or the freezing or re-capitalization of several others (see Table 3.4). Early IBRA annual reports cite the impossibility of obtaining documentation for rapid transactions during the crisis and also convey efforts to recover assets from the shareholders of the liquidated banks.[136] The largest obligors were the major work of the IBRA, as 1,874 people or entities, fewer than 2 percent of the total number of debtors, owed more than Rp50 billion each and the twenty largest obligors

[132] Pepinsky, *Economic Crises*, 96–97.

[133] Haggard, *Political Economy*, 67.

[134] "Perburuan Menyelamatkan Aset Bank" [The Rush to Save Bank Assets], *SWA Magazine*, no. 08/XV/22 (April–May 1999).

[135] Pepinsky, *Economic Crises*, 105.

[136] 1999 BPPN Annual Report, 12.

accounted for Rp61.9 trillion.[137] Hundreds of these were designated as "noncooperative" and taken to court over the course of several years.[138] Others swapped corporate assets to repay BLBI obligations, generating years of conflict over the valuation of those assets and the ability of state authorities to dispose of them under crisis conditions. As late as 2002, the IBRA stated that "144.5 trillion of taxpayers' money was lost to Bank Indonesia liquidity assistance (BLBI) that was provided to insolvent banks during the financial crisis and banking collapse of 1998 and 1999. . . . And it is probably safe to say that a sizable portion of it may never be recovered."[139]

The precise reason that the funds were not recovered was that they had been stolen and expatriated. The case of Sjamsul Nursalim, head of Gajah Tunggal and Bank Dagang Nasional Indonesia (BDNI), is among the most famous. Nursalim received Rp28.49 trillion of BLBI funds intended to rescue BDNI but is alleged to have redirected those resources toward related firms within Gajah Tunggal. Nursalim himself departed for Singapore ("hopped it to Singapore," in the language of one of Indonesia's weekly newspapers) in 1998, along with the rest of his family and a significant fortune, and for years was noncooperative with the IBRA's efforts to recover the funds.[140] Initial promises to settle within four years went unfulfilled; by 2002, the government had recovered only Rp17.6 trillion from thirty-three "big fish" debtors who owed Rp130.6 trillion. Shareholder agreements proved to be difficult to enforce because debtors were willing to take advantage of legal loopholes and pledged corporate assets that had declined in value, while their personal cash on hand may have been sufficient to settle but was beyond the reach of the state. In a story with nearly fictional absurdity, Nursalim insisted his debts had been settled because he had pledged assets on paper, but he never actually transferred the assets.[141] The IBRA "closed" with Nursalim while he still apparently owed Rp4.58 trillion, causing a corruption trial for the former IBRA chairman. In 2021, the anticorruption commission (Komisi

---

[137] Ibid., 23.

[138] By 2002, those designated as "noncooperative" included Ciputra's Bank Metropolitan, Soehargo Gondokusumo's Bank PSP (Dharmala Group), and others. 2002 BPPN Annual Report, 35.

[139] 2002 BPPN Annual Report, 42. The Supreme Audit Agency (BPK) also concluded that "the majority of BLBI funding was actually used for the interests of individual groups, including securities transactions, covering debts and loan expansions." Karaniya Dharmasaputra and Agus S. Riyanto, "Debt: After the Carrot, Use the Big Stick," Tempo, April 1, 2002.

[140] Dharmasaputra and Riyanto, "Debt."

[141] Ibid. The legal details involve IBRA agreements drafted by consultants in Singapore with insufficient knowledge of the Indonesian legal system and also the brazen willingness of the debtors to refuse cooperation.

Pemberantasan Korupsi, KPK) dropped the long-standing corruption case against Nursalim, the first time it had ever done so.[142]

Hokiarto, the main shareholder of Bank Hokindo and a rather flashy business figure of the late New Order, also engaged in activities that typify looting and mutual endangerment before and during the crisis. He was involved in one of the New Order's most famous corruption episodes, a land swap with Bulog that resulted in a prison sentence for Tommy Suharto, his transition to fugitive, a lifting of that sentence, and assassination of the judge in the trial, earning Tommy a fifteen-year prison sentence. The 1995 land swap involved Bulog, the state logistics agency, and companies run by Tommy Suharto and Hokiarto. The day after Beddu Amang became head of Bulog in 1995, he signed an agreement with companies run by Tommy Suharto and Hokiarto to swap land with Bulog in which the state suffered a significant loss (at least Rp95.5 billion). On paper, Hokiarto's company also suffered a loss because he had borrowed from a state bank to finance the transaction and did not repay the loan. In a series of trials from 1999 through 2002, all parties denied corruption on the grounds that their companies all suffered losses, but the viability of their firms was not the point of the transaction. Hokiarto was acquitted in 2002 partly because the government could not make a clear case of how the parties benefited from the corruption. But the facts indicated that state banks and Bulog had financed land acquisitions and overpayments for the two businessmen.[143] Hokiarto also owed Rp339 billion to the IBRA in BLBI funds received by his Bank Hokindo, for which he appears to never have cooperated in paying.[144]

Bob Hasan, nicknamed the country's "first friend" because of his closeness with Suharto and the only Chinese to hold political office in the New Order (Hasan had converted to Islam), was also alleged to have pilfered assets from his own banks during the crisis. Hasan co-owned Bank Umum Nasional (alongside two other prominent *cukong*, Ongko and Wanandi), which was frozen in 1998. Hasan initially pledged his own personal assets to cover borrowings from the BLBI funds, but later he repeatedly delayed

[142] Fana Suparman and Heru Andriyanto, "KPK Drops Corruption Case against Tycoon Sjamsul Nursalim, Wife," *Jakarta Globe*, April 1, 2021, https://jakartaglobe.id/news/kpk-drops-corruption-case-against-tycoon-sjamsul-nursalim-wife.

[143] S. Happy, Rommy Fibri, and Agus Hidayat, "Heads . . . Not Guilty, Tails . . . Not Guilty," *Tempo*, October 15, 2001; "Verdicts: Appeals All Round," *Tempo*, November 19, 2001; Ardi Bramantyo, "Corruption: An Eye for an Eye," *Tempo*, September 2, 2002; "Hokiarto's Lucky Break," *Tempo*, September 16, 2002.

[144] Status of Return of Liabilities to Shareholders (as of December 31, 1999), in "MSAA: The Unfinished Agreements," *Tempo*, October 1, 2000.

meetings with the IBRA and attempted to defraud it by offering assets that were either pledged elsewhere, worthless, or both.[145] Hasan was criticized by the media after Suharto's fall, alongside Nursalim, Hartono (Modern Group), and others for "corruption-collusion-nepotism" and pilfering his own bank and bringing his company to ruin while his personal assets seemed not to be at risk.[146] Hasan was eventually convicted of corruption and fraud not for his actions during the crisis but for defrauding the state in a forest-mapping scheme prior to 1997. [147] The IBRA and legal officials commented that Hasan would not cooperate in recovering state assets because he knew he would eventually be jailed; the "Bob Hasan route" was to be "incarcerated in jail but not repaying a single rupiah of the nation's money."[148]

It is tempting to see much of the looting activity as caused by ineffective bankruptcy laws, for example, laws that allowed assets to be transferred out of failing firms and to be unrecoverable from individual owners. During the financial turmoil in China in the mid-2010s, when similar looting and asset expatriation occurred, Chinese officials blamed the same legal loopholes for this behavior. But the looting occurred before the crisis and the impending bankruptcy, and it was caused by underlying political incentives and motivations as well as legal permissiveness. Indonesian business elites had short time horizons and expectations of eventual bailout or demise, both of which made their seemingly irrational business activities politically rational indeed.

Abandoning Political Friends

One of the most illustrative episodes of the late New Order was the Suharto family's final and public effort to convince business elites to commit to the regime. The "Love the Rupiah" campaign, which was spearheaded by Tutut and eventually became the "Love Indonesia Movement," beseeched the country's residents to donate cash and precious metals to the BI to protect the value of the rupiah from free fall. Tutut and others publicly handed over some of their own dollar-denominated assets, but business elites were unconvinced

---

[145] Rosser, *Politics of Economic Liberalisation*, 187; 2001 BPPN Annual Report.

[146] "Tolonglah! Saya Tidak Punya Apa-Apa Lagi" [Please! I Do Not Have Anything Anymore], *SWA Magazine*, no. 22/ XIV/ 29 (October–November 1998).

[147] Richard Borsuk, "Fixing Up the Joint: Crony Stays Busy behind Bars," *Wall Street Journal*, August 13, 2003, A1.

[148] Dharmasputra and Riyanto, "Debt."

by the campaign. Media coverage of these affective efforts to manage the crisis turned into attacks on the Chinese conglomerates for failing to convert their holdings. The blame was politically helpful to Suharto's family and the politico-bureaucrats whose assets were not so easily converted abroad, but it is also true that the *konglomerat*, who had long held exit options, accelerated their use of such options as the crisis deepened, causing it to deepen even further.

In January 1998, business elites were summoned to meetings with BI officials (including Governor Soedradjad himself), and they were phoned by military officials and encouraged to convert their dollar holdings to rupiah. The officials expressed public frustration with their refusal.[149] Privately, Chinese business elites saw the regime, as well as the economy, in free fall and they feared for far more than merely their assets. One such elite who had moved to Singapore in 1998 reflected: "It did not seem possible for the old man to hold onto power. Then what would happen to us? Would the military protect our homes? No. If the country fell to the mobs, we knew we would be the first targets. And we were right."[150] Indeed, attacks on Indonesians of Chinese descent accelerated during the final months of the New Order, culminating in the extreme violence of May 1998. May 1998 would prove to be the final exit for many business elites, both because of the violence and because of the anticipation that Suharto's demise would mean their own.[151]

What if the *konglomerat* elites had indeed spent the last months of 1997 and the first few months of 1998 converting their foreign assets to rupiah? One can imagine that confidence in the banking system and the regime might not have collapsed, the rupiah might have held more of its value, and the social frustrations that exploded on the streets of Jakarta and elsewhere would have perhaps simmered but would have been less combustible. Such a thought experiment, however, seems absurd. Though "mobile" (Chinese) capitalists may have been a crucial part of Suharto's power base, they could not on their own hold on to power and defend their interests, and instead they relied on others to do so. Specifically, they depended on relationships with Suharto and his family to shield themselves from public scrutiny and ire. Political elites and business elites were mutually embedded to enrich

---

[149] Pepinsky, *Economic Crises*, 114–15, 171–73.

[150] Interview, Singapore, October 2016.

[151] Pepinsky, *Economic Crises*; Chua, "Defining Indonesian Chineseness." Pepinsky sees late spring 1998 as the turning point for the regime, the moment when fixed (politico-bureaucrats and *pribumi*) capital and mobile capital (Chinese *konglomerat*) split and the New Order coalition dissipated.

themselves and to protect themselves, but the unraveling proceeded rapidly once it began. Fundamental vulnerability caused business elites to go from being political friends to becoming fugitive businesspeople during the crisis, making the crisis deadly for the regime.

Conclusion: Suharto's Precarious Ties

By early 1998, Suharto had gone from the "father of development" (*Bapak Pembanguan*) to the "father of bankruptcy" (*Bapak Pembangkrutan*).[152] Unable to discipline his former friends before or during the crisis, he stepped down within months, amid widespread calls for his resignation, economic free-fall, and public disorder and violence. Suharto immediately handed power to Habibie, who was later compelled to allow democratic elections that would cement the country's regime change. The democratic Indonesia built in the wake of the New Order bears the scars of mutual endangerment. The vast majority of commentary on the country's political economy, and even political equality, has centered on the concept of oligarchy, observing that many of the same figures who dominated the New Order economy dominate contemporary Indonesia as well.[153] Their conglomerates are managed professionally or by the next generation of family members, who often reside in Singapore or Hong Kong, with some of their parents unable to return to Indonesia for fear of prosecution. The early years of post–New Order Indonesia were marked by elite uncertainty over what to do with Suharto, his family, and his cronies. Some, like Tommy Suharto and Bob Hasan, were tried and convicted for corruption or related crimes, but others remain powerful in politics and business to this day.

Surely, some of the continuity between past and present can be attributed to the sense of mutual destiny shared by elites that precluded them from prosecuting one another. It is easy to see how regimes that collapse in mutual endangerment but do not experience total revolution carry forward elements of oligarchic power. New holders of power hesitate to investigate and prosecute elements of the ancien régime because of their connections and

---

[152] Anderson, "Exit Suharto."

[153] Richard Robison and V. R. Hadiz, *Reorganising Power in Indonesia: The Politics of Oligarchy in an Age of Markets* (London: RoutledgeCurzon, 2004); Jeffrey Winters, *Oligarchy* (New York: Cambridge University Press, 2011); Jeffrey Winters, "Oligarchy and Democracy in Indonesia," *Indonesia*, no. 96 (2013): 11–33; see also Michele Ford and Thomas Pepinsky, eds., *Beyond Oligarchy: Wealth, Power, and Contemporary Indonesian Politics* (Ithaca: Cornell University Press, 2014).

potentially devastating information. Indeed, the early years after Suharto's fall saw exhortations for the new leaders to "take it easy" on members of Suharto's family and others.[154] And while family patriarchs like Sjamsul Nursalim were beyond reach out of the country, the government refrained from going after their assets via their family members who remained in Indonesia. One former anticorruption commission (KPK) staffer commented that family members remained off-limits as long as most of the extended families, both state and business, contained guilty parties.[155]

And, of course, capitalists retained structural power in a regime that may have changed but still needed investment.[156] The process of recovering or repatriating capital that fled the country during the dissolution of the New Order remains a central element in Indonesian politics. In 2016 and 2017, under President Joko Widodo (Jokowi), the country launched a "tax amnesty," allowing Indonesians with large amounts of capital outside the country to repatriate it at quite low rates (2 percent for early entrants and 4 percent for second-phase entrants). The program was criticized both in Indonesia and abroad for rewarding tax cheats, but policymakers saw it as the only way to attract domestic investment and to increase the country's tax base at a critical moment.[157] Three-quarters of the repatriated funds came from Singapore, and 87 percent of the Rp135 trillion ($9 billion) raised was from individuals, with the remaining 13 percent from large firms.[158] Most of those who repatriated assets did so because their account information would soon become available to the Indonesian government as part of an "automatic exchange of information" agreement in early 2017.

This chapter has focused on the elements of decay and distrust that characterized the regime's political economy in the decade prior to its collapse and that indeed contributed to Suharto's dramatic demise. Salacious details of corruption and fraud may contribute to a sense that the New Order was yet another tragically unaccountable regime that squandered the resources of the country it was charged with leading. In the end, then, it is worth reminding ourselves of the substantial economic achievements of the

---

[154] Pepinsky cites a taped conversation between Habibie and a newly appointed attorney general in which Habibie asks that the attorney general "take it easy" on Suharto. Habibie also seemed to rescue firms close to him, although these tended to be *pribumi* firms (like Bakrie). *Economic Crises*, 188–89.

[155] Interview, Jakarta, January 2017.

[156] This reason for retained oligarchic power is the focus of Robison and Hadiz, *Reorganising Power in Indonesia*; Winters, *Oligarchy*.

[157] Interview, Tom Lembong, chair of Investment Coordinating Board (BKPM), October 2016.

[158] Christine Lewis, "Raising More Public Revenue in Indonesia in a Growth and Equity-Friendly Way," OECD Working Paper no. 1534 (February 2019), 11, https://doi.org/10.1787/a487771f-en.

regime. Between 1966 and 1997, Indonesia grew at an average rate of nearly 6 percent per year, the poverty rate went from 60 percent to 13 percent by one measure, and the country experienced both an economic boom led by natural resource extraction and a substantial industrialization that benefited its nascent middle class.[159] Mostly for its orthodox macroeconomic policy but also for its developmental achievements, the New Order was a darling of global financial institutions. To be sure, the New Order did engage in violence, both literally and figuratively, toward segments of the Indonesian population whose experiences have been neglected in this chapter in favor of its focus on business elites and the state. Therefore, I do not pretend to comprehensively evaluate the regime's performance, nor is that the task of political science scholarship. Instead, I emphasize that the regime ended differently than it began. It began by simultaneously disciplining and cultivating economic elites, and it ended in an onslaught of corruption during a financial crisis generated by behaviors that business elites adopted rationally in the context of their political vulnerability, distrust, and access to financial resources. Indonesia's trajectory from growth to collapse and Suharto's pathway from father of development to father of bankruptcy reveal the benefits of theorizing more precisely about the modes of state-business relations beyond the broad categories of cronyism and corruption. The chapter also reveals the ironic power possessed by vulnerable and distrustful elites, an idea I will revisit in the chapters on China.

[159] See Hal Hill, *The Indonesian Economy since 1966: Southeast Asia's Emerging Giant* (New York: Cambridge University Press, 1996); Donald Greenlees, "Suharto's Legacy of Development and Corruption," *New York Times*, January 28, 2008, https://www.nytimes.com/2008/01/28/world/asia/28iht-suharto.1.9542684.html.

4

Mutual Alignment and Competitive Clientelism in Malaysia

The Barisan Nasional (BN) coalition led Malaysia, an ethnically diverse country in developing Asia, for sixty years through episodes of ethnic riots and financial instability that proved deadly for other regimes.[1] A large literature examines this authoritarian durability in Malaysia and has generated two prominent explanations. First, at the popular level, the BN endured because of the consistency of Malay support, especially from rural Malays who benefited from the BN's economic programs.[2] Second, at the elite level, the regime-formation phase produced both "protection pacts" among elites and a strong political party that effectively managed elite conflict, aided by classic "competitive authoritarian" tactics that emboldened the ruling party.[3] These explanations for authoritarian durability, however, should not obscure the substantial vicissitudes in Malaysian politics. That the regime held power for more than half a century does not mean it did so with ease or without challenge. On the contrary, the BN endured, sometimes barely, despite considerable challenges to its rule, including insurgent parties, internal conflicts, economic downturns, and steady declines in its electoral

---

[1] As Chapter 2 narrates, the Alliance was the progenitor of the BN and similarly comprised the Malaysian Chinese Association (MCA), Malayan Indian Congress (MIC), and the dominant United Malay National Organization (UMNO) party. For the sake of simplicity, I use the BN to refer to both the Alliance and the BN. The BN lost the 2018 elections to a coalition of opposition parties, Pakatan Harapan, led by the BN's longest-serving prime minister, Mohamad Mahathir. Mahathir's government lasted less than two years before the coalition fell into political crisis. This chapter covers the period between 1958 and 2018.

[2] Thomas B. Pepinsky, *Economic Crises and the Breakdown of Authoritarian Regimes: Indonesia and Malaysia in Comparative Perspective* (New York: Cambridge University Press, 2009); Thomas B. Pepinsky, "Interpreting Ethnicity and Urbanization in Malaysia's 2013 General Election," *Journal of East Asian Studies* 15, no. 2 (2015): 199–226; Michael Albertus, Sofia Fenner, and Dan Slater, *Coercive Distribution* (New York: Cambridge University Press, 2018).

[3] Jason Brownlee, *Authoritarianism in an Age of Democratization* (New York: Cambridge University Press, 2007); Stevan Levitsky and Lucan Way, *Competitive Authoritarianism: Hybrid Regimes after the Cold War* (New York: Cambridge University Press, 2010); Dan Slater, *Ordering Power: Contentious Politics and Authoritarian Leviathans in Southeast Asia* (New York: Cambridge University Press, 2010).

Precarious Ties. Meg Rithmire, Oxford University Press. © Oxford University Press 2023.
DOI: 10.1093/oso/9780197697528.003.0004

performance. In 2018, after several years of scandal and elite defections, the BN lost power and the country plunged into a period of political turmoil and uncertainty.

Amid its political triumphs and challenges, the BN also presided over one of the most dramatic programs of state-led economic development and redistribution in Asia, carried out by a staunchly anticommunist regime and with considerable economic achievements. But, like its political tenacity, the BN's economic record features considerable blemishes, namely, moments of economic crisis, such as the 1997 Asian Financial Crisis (AFC), long periods of stagnation, and innumerable episodes of corruption and scandal.

This chapter explains these political vicissitudes and mixed economic achievements in terms of state-business relations. Malaysia under the BN went through cycles of state control and loss of control over the financial sector. In terms of the models presented in this book, it vacillated between mutual alignment and competitive clientelism, in which economic elites compete with one another for resources from the state and political elites compete for support from economic elites.[4] Mutual endangerment, the most destructive form of state-business relations, never fully obtained in Malaysia because business elites cooperated with political elites and expected cooperation in return. With very few exceptions, Malaysia's business elites did not have incentives to pursue behaviors, such as asset expatriation,[5] information weaponization, and looting, that characterize mutual endangerment and make it so destructive. In fact, while mutual endangerment makes crises spiral quickly as economic actors abandon regimes and hasten toward safety, during period of crisis in Malaysia, business elites turn toward the state for security.

---

[4] My definition is closest to that used by Doner and Ramsay in their description of Thailand's political economy, in which "intra-elite rivalries led to a competitive rather than a monopolistic market for state-supplied goods and services" (239). See Richard F. Doner and Ansil Ramsay, "Competitive Clientelism and Economic Governance: The Case of Thailand," in Sylvia Maxfield and Ben Ross-Schneider, eds., *Business and the State in Developing Countries* (Ithaca: Cornell University Press, 2018), 237–76. Whitfield's book on industrial policy in Ghana describes competitive clientelism more generally as a pattern of politics in developing countries in which there is "a large group of fragmented political elites who enter shifting alliances to form a coalition strong enough to govern the country and the state apparatus," in Lindsay Whitfield, *Economies after Colonialism: Ghana and the Struggle for Power* (New York: Cambridge University Press, 2018), 5. She argues that forms of competition and clientelism differ across regimes. In Ghana, competitive clientelism produced political stability but ineffective industrial policy, whereas Doner and Ramsay, "Competitive Clientelism," argue that the dynamics in Thailand facilitated development.

[5] They did diversify their businesses by investing abroad, a phenomenon I address below. Outward foreign direct investment (FDI) is not the same as capital flight, and it was mostly pursued in concert with the regime and its own development and diplomatic goals.

Although mutual alignment and competitive clientelism do not produce the spiraling dynamics and perverse incentives of mutual endangerment, they do have other pathologies evident in patterns of development in Malaysia. As I argue in Chapter 1, mutual alignment portends the "paradox of the developmental state": the business elites nurtured by state resources and policies are the very same ones who oppose new policy directions, primarily because reforms or new directions may endanger their rents.[6] Politically, as we will see in the case of the United Malays National Organisation (UMNO) and especially Malay business elites, many attempts at liberalization stalled as they generated opposition from elites and fears of political consequences for the party. Economic stagnation is evident in low productivity and low rates of private investment, outcomes we see during periods of high regime control over the financial sector. Competitive clientelism, in contrast, resulted when the government loosened control over the financial sector, for example through privatization and liberalization drives. The intention of those policies was to produce Malay business elites and dynamism through more private control over the economy, but then the regime lost its easy access to economic resources it needed for political power (in funding election campaigns) and could not effectively discipline the financial behavior of economic actors. Instead of stagnation, competitive clientelism produced corruption and economic mismanagement, punctuated by crisis.

Malaysia's political economy, like its polity, is fragmented. Malay economic elites were nurtured by the BN and came to limit maneuverability in economic policy, but the same cannot be said of the ethnic Chinese business class. As I argue in Chapter 2, the Chinese population itself was importantly fragmented, with capital-owning elites enjoying trust and inclusion among the Malay political elites. The bulk of Malaysians of Chinese descent, however, were rural dwellers who were forcibly settled in the New Villages during the emergency, or urban small-scale entrepreneurs, often owning family firms. These groups were hostile to the BN throughout; they dealt the Malaysian Chinese Association (MCA) a nearly deadly blow in 1969 and bitterly opposed the program of state-sponsored growth and redistribution that emerged in the wake of May 13. This group is frequently written out of prominent accounts of Malaysian politics: they are not part of UMNO's political machine and their opposition did not amount to a significant challenge to

---

[6] Eva Bellin, *Stalled Democracy: Capital, Labor, and the Paradox of State-Sponsored Development* (Ithaca: Cornell University Press, 2002).

the UMNO's dominance. But this political ostracization held economic consequences: they were never part of the mutual alignment of interests between business and the state, leaving the Malaysian economy dominated by foreign-owned multinationals or behemoth domestic firms with low levels of innovation and high dependence on the state. This is an exceptional contrast, as we shall see, to the reform-era Chinese economy, in which growth and dynamism came from vast numbers of small and medium-sized (SME), nonstate firms that were financially independent from the state, motivated to compete quickly, and subject to strict forms of market discipline. Malaysia's Chinese-led SMEs were subject to harsh market and political discipline, but they suffered from poor incentives, creating an urban SME sector that was competitive, but small and prone to underinvestment.

A thorough account of the BN's political path and economic record should attend to variation in state-business relations across groups and across time. I describe the BN's sixty-year tenure in these terms, showing how political inclusion of economic elites shaped behaviors and kept big business close to the state and how varying levels of financial control explain economic stagnation, crisis, and corruption. I pay particular attention to the form of state financial control in Malaysia, which is large-scale state shareholding through the deployment of "government-linked investment companies," or GLICs. The GLICs were the primary mechanisms of effecting the New Economic Policy (NEP), the BN's state-sponsored redistribution and growth program, and their varying importance is closely connected with the economic and political outcomes of interest. When the GLICs have been most prominent in the Malaysian economy, political elites have exercised strong control over business, but the Malaysian economy lacked dynamism and was prone to corruption scandals. When the GLICs retreated, business elites were more difficult to discipline and took financial risks that have produced instability.

The chapter is organized to illustrate these arguments, as captured in Table 4.1. The next section begins where the second chapter left off, with the launch of the NEP in the aftermath of the 1969 election violence. The following sections show variation in financial control during the NEP "high tide" (1971–83), a period of engineered liberalization (1983–98), which was punctuated by the financial crisis followed by a period of reasserted state corporate governance control (2001–18). The final section looks at Malaysia's recent economic and political turmoil in terms of state-business relations.

Table 4.1 Characterizing State-Business Relations in Malaysia

Time Period	Mode of State-Business Relations	Economic Outcomes	Financial Dynamics	Precipitating Event
1958–69	Laissez-faire	Growth with inequality	Foreign domination	Independence
1971–85	Mutual alignment	Growth dominated by large firms	State control through state shareholding	May 13 riots
1985–97	Competitive clientelism	Growth, corruption, financial crisis	Privatization, liberalization	Fiscal concerns, low growth, recession
2001–10	Mutual alignment	Stagnation	Increased state shareholding	Asian Financial Crisis
2010–18	Competitive clientelism	Financial crisis, corruption	Mixed; shareholding for many and loss of discipline for others	Stagnation of post- AFC period

Malaysia's Second Grand Bargain

In the aftermath of the 1969 election violence, Malaysia's political elites struck a "grand bargain" that would structure Malaysia's politics and economy for the next five decades. UMNO leaders and Chinese business elites collectively saw the violence as the outcome of an unequal society, one in which race was inexorably associated with economic function. As long as Malays occupied both rural villages and the lower end of the socioeconomic spectrum and Malaysians of Chinese descent occupied cities and were owners of capital and industrial and commercial assets, Malaysia's society would not attain stability and the polity could not hold.[7] Ironically, given the electoral gains of pro-Chinese parties opposed to special privileges for Malays, the lesson learned among elites was that the country could not hold together without a radical change in the distribution of economic power.

As I argue in Chapter 2, Chinese business elites, represented by the establishment Chinese political party and member of the Alliance, the MCA,

---

[7] This view is on full display in Mahathir's essays "What Went Wrong?" and "The Malay Economic Dilemma," in Mohamad bin Mahathir, *The Malay Dilemma* (Singapore: Asia Pacific Press, 1970), 4–15 and 32–61, respectively.

continued to advocate for accepting Malay hegemony and reversing Chinese economic dominance because it feared demands from below and political disintegration more than predictable demands from above. The MCA also saw the bargain as the only terms on which Malaysians of Chinese descent could share formal political power, which it felt was the only guarantee against an existential threat for the larger community.

Practically, elections were suspended and the country was ruled by the National Operations Council for two years after 1969. By the early 1970s, the Alliance, which would take a new form in the BN, took several steps to establish a new set of political expectations. First, the coalition became more encompassing so as to co-opt erstwhile challengers; Gerakan (one of the 1969 insurgent, mostly Chinese, parties), among others, joined the BN. But the incorporation of potential challengers entailed their acceptance of Malay hegemony and UMNO leadership. A National Consultative Council was formed to prepare the Rukunegara (Basic Principles of the State), and legislation made debate about issues related to Malay special rights, among other things, illegal.[8] These incorporations and prohibitions paved the way for the NEP, a set of economic policies that aimed to overhaul the country's socioeconomic dynamic.

The NEP was introduced in 1970–71 with the "two-pronged objective of eradicating poverty, irrespective of race, and restructuring Malaysian society to reduce and eventually eliminate the identification of race with economic function."[9] The framing of the NEP, especially initially, was more about equity through growth than about redistribution, but the policy was clear from the outset that the goal was to advance the economic status of the country's ethnic Malays.[10] The government's goal was that *bumiputeras* (ethnic Malays and, later, other indigenous peoples) would own and manage 30 percent of the nation's industrial and commercial assets. In 1969, that number

---

[8] For example, speech challenging non-Malay citizenship, Islam, and the national language was prohibited. See Meredith Weiss, *Protest and Possibilities: Civil Society and Coalitions for Political Change in Malaysia* (Stanford: Stanford University Press, 2006), 86; James V. Jesudason, *Ethnicity and the Economy: The State, Chinese Business, and Multinationals in Malaysia* (New York: Oxford University Press, 1989), 77.

[9] Razak Abdul, *The Second Malaysia Plan, 1971–1975: A Critique*, ed. Hussein Syed Alatas (Singapore: Occasional Paper no. 15, Institute of Southeast Asian Studies, 1972), foreword.

[10] "The Outline Perspective Plan for 1971–1990," in *Third Malaysia Plan 1976–80*, at https://www.epu.gov.my/sites/default/files/2021-05/FirstOutlinePerspective.pdf sets forth plans to "achieve the goals of the NEP on the basis of sustained economic growth." Edmund Terence Gomez and K. S. Jomo, *Malaysia's Political Economy: Politics, Patronage, and Profits* (New York: Cambridge University Press, 1997), 24.

was 1.5 percent (Tables 4.2 and 4.3 show these metrics over time). Non-*bumiputera* Malaysians were to own 40 percent, ideally at the expense of foreign capital, which dominated the economy through the 1970s.[11] The Second Malaysian Plan, published in 1971, clearly stated that the goal was to create "a full-fledged Malay entrepreneurial community within one generation."[12]

The mechanisms of the NEP, and therefore the political economic architecture of the country, would change over time, but several features were established at the outset. One such feature was quotas for most public institutions and large firms to increase *bumiputera* representation and ensure that participation in most parts of society reflected the country's racial makeup. Another was a variety of programs to train and educate *bumiputeras*, alongside quotas in educational institutions, to inherit and steward a greater share of the country's economic resources. As they are elsewhere, quotas were controversial in Malaysia, but the most contested and complex elements of the NEP were those that sought to transform extant firms and generate new sources of wealth for *bumiputeras*. Because the assets owned by *bumiputeras* were so few at the outset of the NEP (2.4 percent for 56 percent of the population), the government took a heavy-handed role in owning and investing in assets with an eye to developing a crop of indigenous business elites to whom those assets might be transferred in the future. In short, the Malaysian state would act as a "trustee" for *bumiputera* wealth development, which required an expansive presence in corporate governance and as a provider of capital.[13] I elaborate on the regime's management of the financial sector in the next section.

The government was to establish firm control over the country's ample natural resources, for example through the 1974 National Petroleum Act,

---

[11] See J. J. Puthucheary, *Ownership and Control in the Malayan Economy: A Study of the Structure of Ownership and Control and Its Effects on the Development of Secondary Industries and Economic Growth in Malaya and Singapore* (Singapore: Eastern Universities Press, 1960); Mah Hui Lim, *Ownership and Control of the One Hundred Largest Corporations in Malaysia* (Kuala Lumpur: Oxford University Press, 1981).

[12] Abdul, *Second Malaysia Plan*, 47.

[13] On "equity restructuring by trusteeship," see MCA Economic Congress, March 3, 1974 (NUS Singapore-Malaysia Collection); *The Chinese Community towards & beyond 1990 in Multi-racial Malaysia: A Political Seminar* (Kuala Lumpur: Ibu Pejabat MCA, 1987[?]); Collected MCA Materials, June 28, 1987 (NUS Singapore-Malaysia Collection). The Second Malaysia Plan, 1971–1975, established extensive institutional changes to allow the government to "undertake commercial and industrial ventures on behalf of the Malays and other indigenous peoples" (52). See also Ozay Mehmet, *Development in Malaysia: Poverty, Wealth, and Trusteeship* (London: Croom Helm, 1986); Edmund Terence Gomez, "The Rise and Fall of Capital: Corporate Malaysia in Historical Perspective," *Journal of Contemporary Asia* 39, no. 3 (2009): 345–81.

Table 4.2 Asset Ownership by Ethnic Group

	1969	1970	1975	1980	1985	1990	1995	1999	2006	2008
Bumiputera individuals and trust agencies	1.5	2.4	9.2	12.5	19.1	19.2	20.6	19.1	19.4	21.9
Chinese	22.8	27.2	NA	NA	33.4	45.5	40.9	37.9		36.7*
Indians	0.9	1.1	NA	NA	1.2	1	1.5	1.5		
Others	—	—	—	—	—	—	—	0.9		
Nominee companies	2.1	6	NA	NA	1.3	8.5	8.3	7.9		
Locally controlled firms[†]	10.1	—	—	—	7.2	0.3	1	—		
Foreigners	62.1	63.4	53.3	42.9	26.0	25.4	27.7	32.7		41.4*

Source: Economic Planning Unit, "Seventh Malaysia Five Year Plan, 1996–2000" (Putrajaya) at https://www.epu.gov.my/en/economic-developments/development-plans/rmk/seventh-malaysia-plan-1996-2000 and Economic Planning Unit, "Eight Malaysia 2001–2005" (Putrajava), https://www.epu.gov.my/en/economic-developments/development-plans/rmk/eight-malaysia-plan-2001-2005; Edmund Gomez, "Malaysian Business Groups: The State and Capital Development in the Post-Currency Crisis Period," in Sea-Jin Chang, ed., *Business Groups in East Asia: Financial Crisis, Restructuring, and New Growth* (Oxford: Oxford University Press, 2006), 124; Economic Planning Unit, "Tenth Malaysia 10th MP" (Putrajava), at https://www.epu.gov.my/en/economic-developments/development-plans/rmk/tenth-malaysia-plan-10th-mp.

* For 2008, the number is for "non-*bumiputera*" rather than Chinese and Indian disaggregated. Foreigners are listed as "others."

[†] Companies whose ownership could not be disaggregated further or assigned to specific ethnic groups.

Table 4.3 Asset Ownership by Group

	1970	1990	2000	2008
Bumiputera	2.4	19.3	18.9	21.9
Non-*bumiputera*	34.3	46.8	41.3	36.7
Others	63.3	33.9	39.8	41.4

Source: Economic Planning Unit, "Tenth Malaysia 10th MP" (Putrajava), at https://www.epu.gov.my/en/economic-developments/development-plans/rmk/tenth-malaysia-plan-10th-mp, 146.

which established Petronas (Malaysia's national oil company). Resource company acquisitions mostly targeted foreign-owned firms, but the Industrial Coordination Act (ICA) of 1975 and the purview of the Capital Issuance Committee (CIC) were to hit closer to home for non-*bumiputera*-owned domestic firms. The ICA concentrated power to distribute licenses for manufacturing firms in the hands of the government and stipulated that distribution would be "consistent with national economic and social objectives and would promote the orderly development of manufacturing activities." In practice, this stipulation meant that the government was to enforce the goal of every manufacturing enterprise having 70 percent Malaysian ownership and 30 percent *bumiputera* ownership, and the government was to enjoy "all-encompassing control and regulation of the industry."[14] In tandem, the ICA and CIC required firms, even family firms, to recruit *bumiputera* owners in order to procure a license or to expand capital investment. Because they were perceived as a means of limiting the expansion of Malaysian Chinese capital, these institutions were to become major sites of confrontation over the NEP between the government and the Malaysian Chinese community.

Mutual Alignment: Reciprocity and Adaptation under the NEP

> The MCA is committed to work with the Barisan Nasional system, for it believes that in the present-day context of Malaysian politics, political power can only be maintained through a partnership with a moderate Malay party, i.e., UMNO.
> —YB Dato' Dr. Ling Liong Sik, deputy minister of education[15]

During the NEP's first decade or so, relations between Malaysia's business elites—meaning the wealthiest Chinese groups and the emergent Malay business class—and the regime can be characterized as mutual alignment, by

---

[14] Nobuyuki Yasuda, "Malaysia's New Economic Policy and the Industrial Co-ordination Act," *Developing Economies* 29, no. 4 (1991): 334. See also Gomez and Jomo, *Malaysia's Political Economy*, 42. The CIC was established in 1968, and during the early period of the NEP it required 30 percent *bumiputera* ownership for securities issuance. In 1992, the CIC was replaced by the Securities Commission.

[15] Malaysian Chinese Association, "The Role of the MCA: Towards the Next Century," MCA Political Seminar: Democracy and the MCA, Collected Speeches, October 27, 1985 (NUS Singapore-Malaysia Collection).

which political elites and business elites cooperated, formally or informally, to pursue regime goals and to secure profits and growth for cooperating businesses. The cooperation, built on trust and reciprocity, was based on acceptance by some Chinese elites, but by no means all Chinese, that radical distributive measures were necessary to hold the country together and that cooperation with the BN would be to their benefit. The regime accommodated cooperative elites, making use of its discretion over NEP implementation to forebear where it could. And business elites accepted constraints on their choices and found paths to profits, even to growth, in sectors and through investments that did not challenge the basic goals of the NEP.

Though Chinese business groups would eventually demand repeal of the ICA, the act was amended several times.[16] These changes, the result of bargaining between Chinese businesses and the regime, would essentially make enforcement of the NEP particularistic and ad hoc, giving the government broad discretion over who received licenses and how the mandates of the NEP would interact with development and political imperatives. The Malaysian Chinese Chamber of Commerce was at the forefront of the contestation from the Chinese business community. An exchange between Mahathir, then minister of trade and industry, and the Malaysian Chinese Chamber of Commerce at a 1978 conference is instructive. Meeting disgruntled representatives from various Chinese chambers, Mahathir gave a rigorous defense of the NEP and also suggested that exceptions to its implementation were possible, particularly if investment levels were especially high (i.e., for large-scale projects). He also suggested that opponents of the NEP might be passed over for consideration as domestic joint-venture partners for foreign investors.[17] The chairman of the Chamber of Commerce wielded his own set of threats: "The government cannot force private companies to invest, but we need incentives so that the government can realize its objective of growth and development." As attacking the NEP was considered a crime, representatives

---

[16] For example, in 1977 and 1979. The first amendment exempted stock ownership requirements for investments of less than RM500,000, essentially exempting Chinese family-owned firms. Yasuda, "Malaysia's New Economic Policy," 36.

[17] Mahathir said, "If an element of the implementation has a problem, the government can consider exceptional measures," intimating that a lower level of scrutiny over ownership shares would be applied to large investments, and he said, "Opponents of the NEP are impeding the government's efforts to attract foreign capital and to invest in development, and this is an unhappy affair. Perhaps these opponents are even responsible for the recent drop in FDI. This will badly influence local economy, since FIEs are required to have local partners." Malaysian Chinese Chamber of Commerce, Malaysian Chinese Economic Conference, Report on Conference Proceedings (Kuala Lumpur, Federal Hotel), April 9, 1978.

were careful in the delivery of their critiques, but the slate of proposals for the consideration of the regional chambers included "encouraging the government to reconsider any laws and regulations that inhibit or direct private investment, for example industrial coordination measures."[18]

The discretion over implementation allowed the government flexibility to accommodate domestic non-Malay businesses. For example, the ICA proved difficult to implement in the manufacturing and trading sectors, where Chinese (and Indian) firms dominated. Trade organizations objected and investment plateaued. To accommodate the desire for economic growth and the demands of the sector, various officials became personally responsible for promoting industry, and they were given wider discretion over NEP rule implementation. Formally, the restructuring requirements were relaxed for "existing companies."[19] This discretion meant that non-*bumiputera* businesses would indeed rely on political officials to navigate the NEP period, and the regime would ensure that loyal firms and those pursuing the developmental goals of the state were given a wider berth. This discretion facilitated cooperation and reciprocity, especially among elites.

At the outset of the NEP and throughout its first two decades, the MCA would continue to emphasize the importance of formal political representation (and thus to advocate acceptance of Malay political hegemony and the basic program of the NEP).[20] It would also focus on poverty reduction measures for rural Chinese and encourage Chinese businesses to scale up. In the early 1970s, a quarter of the population of Chinese Malaysians remained in the New Villages, which some had likened to "prison camps" at the time of their establishment in the 1950s and since then had fallen into further disrepair.[21] Agricultural asset ownership was dominated by foreign firms (51.6 percent)

马来西亚中华工商联合会, 全国华人经济大会。报告录 (吉隆坡: 马来西亚中华工商联合会, 1978), 4–5.

[18] Ibid., 8–9.

[19] Yong Poh Kon, "Economic Challenges of the 1980s," paper prepared for the "Seminar on Challenges of the 1980s," MCA, May 25, 1980, 3.

[20] For example, the MCA's 1975 Economic Congress statement included the following: "We . . . recognize that the Chinese Community has the responsibility, together with other Malaysians, to contribute to the task of nation-building. . . . We believe that effective steps must be taken to ensure that the goals set for the Chinese community under our National Plan are achieved so that the nation's economic cake is equitably shared by the various communities." MCA, 1974 Economic Congress Materials, March 3, 1974 (NUS Singapore-Malaysia Collection).

[21] Population data from YB Enick Richard Ho Ung Hun (MCA MP Sitiawan), November 29, 1973; Malaysia Chinese Association, "A Collection of Speeches by MCA Members of Parliament Delivered at the Dewan Rakyat on the Mid-Term Review of the Second Malaysia FYP, 1971–1975" (NUS Singapore-Malaysia Collection). See Meredith L. Weiss, "Legacies of the Cold War

and Malays (48.4 percent) because of historical patterns of landownership.[22] The MCA—the representative of elite Chinese business and establishment politics—took the NEP's promise of eradication of poverty irrespective of racial status as an invitation to advocate for small-scale rural industrialization in the New Village areas and for more land to be opened up to Chinese rural dwellers to "soften the effects of inflation" and urban poverty.[23] The MCA would push state investment agencies to support poor Chinese, specifically through land allocation. The threat of leftist movements continued to loom. As one MCA member of parliament said: "The danger of the revival of communist insurrection still lurks in our country. The Government's concern and active participation to help the have-nots and the setting up of industries in the poor areas to create jobs for them will be the best means to combat poverty in the urban and rural sectors and eventually achieve eradication of poverty irrespective of race."[24]

The second MCA response was to promote "modernization" of Malaysian Chinese businesses, meaning a turn away from small and medium-sized family businesses and toward large firms. Dr. Neo Yee Pan, who would hold a variety of cabinet positions and eventually become acting MCA president during a party crisis in the 1980s, said in 1974: "If we really want to advance our economic position in the next decade or so, we must break away from the traditional family business practices and collectively effect the formation of big corporations. We must branch out in all spheres of businesses and not just majoring in the retail and wholesale businesses. We should modernise our business techniques. The Chinese community should view the formation of large corporations as our two-pronged strategy to achieve business ownership and employment creation."[25]

---

in Malaysia: Anything but Communism," *Journal of Contemporary Asia* 50, no. 4 (2020): 520–22, https://doi.org/10.1080/00472336.2019.1709128.

[22] Malaysia Chinese Association, Economic Congress Materials, March 3, 1974 (NUS Singapore-Malaysia Collection).

[23] Ibid. See also speech by YB Enick Tiah Eng Bee (MP Kluang Utara), November 28, 1973, Malaysian Chinese Association, "A Collection of Speeches by MCA Members of Parliament Delivered at the Dewan Rakyat on the Mid-term Review of the Second Malaysia FYP, 1971–75" (NUS Singapore-Malaysia Collection). The MCA undertook these efforts in part because of constant agitation within the party from below and challenges, electoral and otherwise, to the MCA from other parts of the Chinese community.

[24] Mr. Chin Hon Ngian (MCA Sec Johore), "The Advancement of Life Chances of Have-nots with Special Reference to the Chinese Have-nots," MCA, 1974 Economic Congress Materials, March 3, 1974 (NUS Singapore-Malaysia Collection).

[25] Dr. Neo Yee Pan, "The Role of Chinese Business in the Context of Our National Objectives," MCA 1974 Economic Congress Materials, March 3, 1974, 4–5 (NUS Singapore-Malaysia Collection).

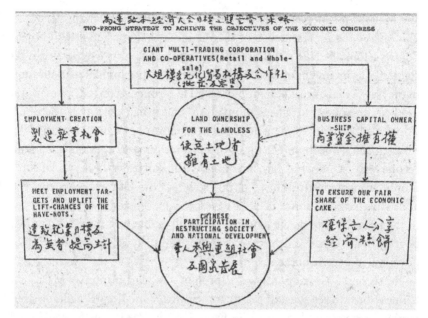

Figure 4.1 MCA Proposal for Managing Chinese Business under the NEP
Source: Malaysian Chinese Association, 1974 Economic Congress.

Together, land redistribution to rural Chinese and the creation of large, Chinese-owned corporations would ensure a "fair share of the economic cake" for the Chinese community in the context of the NEP (see Figure 4.1). The target of the NEP, many in the MCA argued, should be foreign-owned business, which, as every public speech took pains to point out, indeed dominated the economy of the 1960s and early 1970s. MCA elites and Chinese business communities advocated forced joint ventures with domestic firms and encouraged Chinese business owners to establish joint ventures with Malay newcomers.[26] It is not difficult to see the self-interest in the party's response to the NEP. The focus on lifting up the Chinese "have-nots" could address the

[26] For example, YB Enick Lim Pee Hung (MCA MP)) said in November 1973: "I am however concerned that the share of cap ownership of the non-Malays may be stagnated in the face of heavy influx of foreign investment in this sector. In the long-term interest of our nation it would be unwise to let foreigners dominate our economy. I must therefore strongly urge the Government to encourage not just joint-ventures between state-owned corporations and foreign firms but joint-ventures among state-owned corporations, non-Malay participation and foreign firms as well," in Malaysia Chinese Association, "A Collection of Speeches by MCA Members of Parliament Delivered at the Dewan Rakyat on the Mid-term Review of the Second Malaysia FYP, 1971–1975," 15–16 (NUS Singapore-Malaysia Collection).

grievances of those who voted for the insurgent Chinese parties in 1969, and very large corporations stood to benefit precisely the elites who comprised the MCA. Moreover, a hierarchically organized Chinese Malaysian economy would cement the MCA's leadership over the communal group and facilitate patron-client relations in delivering votes.

To be sure, the MCA's poor performance in 1969 generated a reckoning on its role within the Chinese community and a revitalization of its efforts to achieve Chinese unity. Up to 1969, differences within the Chinese business community played out in electoral politics. During the first decades after the devastating riots, however, that conflict—really a conflict between Chinese Malaysians with different class statuses—would play out within the party.[27] In the early 1970s, efforts at Chinese unity within the MCA would appeal to members of Chinese business and ethnic associations who remained ambivalent about the MCA at best and hostile at worst. Nonetheless, the MCA worked to reach out to the grassroots, including through a rural task force focused on Perak state, which both had the largest Chinese population of any state and was the site of the worst MCA defeat in 1969. Newer, up-start leaders organized under the banner of the "Malaysian Chinese Liaison Committee for National Unity" under MCA auspices, but not all leaders were part of the MCA. Incorporation of the upstarts would generate concern among the old-guard business leaders that the MCA was straying too far, prompting a round of purges. The MCA would never fully gain the support of nonelite Chinese, and the coalitional and electoral politics of the following decades would lay bare the thin grasp the BN had on less well-off Chinese communities.

An established "old guard" of Chinese business elites joined the MCA in accepting the NEP and submitting to UMNO's political hierarchy and program of coercive distribution. For the most part, they had little choice. The horrific events in Indonesia provided a worst-case scenario about the status of Chinese minorities in Southeast Asia, and, as I argue in Chapter 2, the idea of Mainland China as a possible future was diminished by the late 1960s as political radicalism seized that country. Not all Chinese business elites, however, tolerated UMNO's demands. Substantial capital flight in the 1970s and 1980s mostly ended up in Singapore, where Chinese elites enjoyed connections and found safety in that country's ethnic composition and

[27] Loh Kok Wah, "The Politics of Chinese Unity in Malaysia: Reform and Conflict in the Malaysian Chinese Association, 1971–1973," 1982 (NUS Singapore-Malaysia Collection).

state-driven developmentalism that embraced the economic elites.[28] Among those who remained, strategies to build and maintain business empires under the NEP involved close and publicly acknowledged political connections, such as board memberships, with political elites. The next few decades would be characterized by what feels like a familiar dance of "crony" state-business relations as Chinese capitalists pursued safety through connections. As the centrality of the MCA within the BN declined, and the NEP threatened the safety of non-*bumiputera* capitalists, those businessmen sought protection through clientelistic relationships with Malay political elites.

In addition to the MCA, the Chinese business community in Malaysia was organized through intermediary associations that represented business interests and more. While Chinese organizations were banned in Indonesia and industry and trade associations were essentially appendages of the state in China, Malaysian civil society organizations were mostly quite independent, with long histories of interest organization and representation. In Chapter 2 I discuss the union landscape in preindependence Malaya; capital interests were similarly organized, especially in local chambers of commerce and peak industry associations. Moreover, though they did not represent business interests per se, it is worth acknowledging that a wide range of civil society groups in Malaysia served to organize the Chinese community, including churches, native place organizations, charity and volunteer societies, lineage clan organizations, secret societies, and various combinations of the above. Most of these civil society organizations, and especially those that were business oriented, were dominated by local or sectoral elites who had a history of working with Malay and colonial political elites to protect their interests.[29] When the NEP came along, those organizations engaged with political elites once again in familiar ways to protect their interests.

The mining sector is instructive. Malaysia's tin resources were concentrated in Perak state near Ipoh and the Kinta River valley where, preindependence, both European and Chinese owners operated the mines. Commodity price fluctuations, especially during the Great Depression and the Emergency period, produced cooperation in the industry among those groups and with the government. Various groups, including the Perak Chinese Mining Association (PCMA), joined together to form the Kinta Valley Home Guard

[28] Morgan Guaranty estimated a total of $12 billion in capital flight between 1976 and 1985, cited in Gomez and Jomo, *Malaysia's Political Economy*, 43.
[29] Weiss, "Legacies of Cold War."

to provide protection to miners and property, purchasing arms, ammunition, and training from the local and British authorities.[30] The trust forged between the state and owners of capital during that period structured the way that the mining associations adapted to the NEP, namely, aggregating interests and cooperating with the state. In 1972, the minister of primary industries exhorted the Chinese miners to work with "those with land titles" (aka Malays) with the "vast experience, know-how, and capital" they had "accumulated over the years. Your co-operation . . . will go a long way to benefit not only all those concerned in producing tin but also in achieving the goal of the Second Malaysia FYP of distributing the wealth of the nation to as many people as possible."[31] Association officials, for their part, encouraged cooperation as well by drawing on a long history of resilience and cooperation:

> During that time the mining industry in Perak was confronted with many difficulties, including a world war and a long, drawn-out internal struggle against terrorist activities which threatened to dislocate the mining operations altogether. . . . I sincerely hope that the PCMA will do their best to help our Malay brothers to participate in the mining industry by giving them the technical expertise which our Perak miners have acquired through hard labor and sweat during these thirty-seven years.[32]

Local association officials, one after another, spoke about the need for cooperation and agglomeration, moving from "family affairs" to "syndication," and the risks of becoming "neglected and overburdened by the imposition and implementation of inconsiderate or harsh legislations."[33] As the availability of mining land declined and the government exercised strict control over licenses, miners worked through business associations and within the NEP framework to ensure compliance and access to necessary resources. The tone of the speeches by industry association officials, much like the tone of the MCA representatives, indicates a potentially restive audience. Indeed, the small-scale, family-run mining outfits, like their urban commercial

---

[30] Foreword from president of the PCMA, Hew Chai Kee, in 霹雳华人矿务公会卅七周年纪念特刊 (Perak Chinese Mining Association), 曾文福, 主编霹, 37th Anniversary Publication (伊藤: 霹雳华人矿务公会, 1972), 12–17.

[31] Minister of Primary Industries Tuan Haji Abdul Bin Mahmu, in ibid., 6.

[32] President of All-Malaya Chinese Mining Association, Senator Dato' Chan Kwong Hon, in ibid., 7.

[33] Message from the president of the Miners' Association of Selangor, Negeri Sembilan, and Pahang, in ibid., 9; Kee, foreword, in ibid.,12.

counterparts, were likely opposed to opening their businesses to cooperation with landed Malays, but their opposition could amount to little when
the leadership of the country's civic, business, and political organizations
comprised elite Chinese who advocated cooperation and acceptance of the
NEP and Malay political hegemony.

In fact, though the early NEP period was a difficult one for small-scale,
non-*bumiputera* business, it was not so difficult for many elite Chinese firms.
These firms, many founded and run by notable businessmen who gained
prominence in the "unfettered economic environment" that preceded 1969,
or even in 1958, saw their assets grow and also change composition as the
government focused on growing Malay wealth.[34] The section "Reconstituting
Financial Discipline" below examines the top one hundred firms in Malaysia
during the 2000s, a number of which are Chinese-owned firms with a mul-
tigenerational history in the country, such as Hong Leong, IOI (property
development and palm oil plantation conglomerate), Genting, and YTL
Group (construction). These firms are deeply diversified and indeed have
been so for decades. Such diversification is partly expected of large business
groups in emerging markets, but it also has roots in firms' strategies to adapt
to the NEP.[35] As government efforts took on various industries, including
nationalizing foreign firms and devising plans to challenge Chinese dominance in other firms (e.g., natural resources, manufacturing, retail, imports,
and so forth), incumbent firms diversified to hedge risks. A typical strategy,
deployed, for example, by Khoo Khay Peng's Malaysia United Industries
(MUI), was to pursue sectors, such as real estate and finance, in which firms
could expect short-term gains, and to grow via acquisitions so as to avoid the
regulatory burdens from establishing new firms.[36] Other Chinese-led firms
pursued sectors, such as gambling or gaming, that were off-limits to Malays
for cultural or religious reasons.

In fact, Chinese ownership over national wealth increased during the
1970s (from 30.4 percent ownership in 1971 to 40.1 percent ownership in
1980), partly because foreign ownership declined but also because several
large firms did well. In addition to business strategies of diversification, these

---

[34] Jesudason, *Ethnicity and the Economy*, 128.

[35] Many see business groups and diversification as strategies to manage institutional deficits by
internalizing costs. See Nathaniel H. Leff, "Industrial Organization and Entrepreneurship in the
Developing Countries: The Economic Groups," *Economic Development and Cultural Change* 26, no. 4
(1978): 661–75; Tarun Khanna and Yishay Yafeh, "Business Groups in Emerging Markets: Paragons
or Parasites?," *Journal of Economic Literature* 45, no. 2 (2007): 331–72.

[36] See Jesudason, *Ethnicity and the Economy*, 150–51.

firms recruited UMNO political elites to take formal roles, for example as board members. (Figure 4.5 illustrates the continued importance of board personnel and interlocking directorships during the post-AFC period.) MUI, for example, recruited a member of parliament and the son of a former deputy prime minister; Genting recruited a former head of police and an UMNO elite, and Hong Leong enjoyed formal relationships with a suite of political elites.[37] In the early NEP period, the tight connections between the Chinese business elites and the UMNO political elites can be described as mutual alignment: the economy expanded during the 1970s (the average growth rate was 8.3 percent from 1971 to 1980), both because of commodity price booms and heavy state investment and because the fortunes of business elites grew concomitantly.[38] Tight state financial control through trustee shareholding meant that the state had oversight over most of the newly emerging Malay business elites, and Chinese elites were dependent on the state for approvals and expansion plans and, usually, subject to state oversight through shareholding and corporate governance mechanisms.

Asserting State Financial Control

The BN's political and social goals were enforced through substantial regime control over the financial sector during the NEP's first decade. The NEP architects sought to implement the NEP through control over equity markets, corporate governance, and the country's banking sector. To be clear, the government controlled more than just financial resources; the distribution of licenses, laws on employment, and affirmative action efforts, among other mechanisms, also facilitated state control of the economy and pursuit of the NEP. But the regime's goals were fundamentally about who owns wealth in Malaysia, making the financial sector the primary site of state control over the economy and over state-business relations. The extensive state control over the country's financial sector ensured alignment between business elites and the regime.

---

[37] Gomez and Jomo, *Malaysia's Political Economy*, 47. See also Heng Pek Koon, "The Chinese Business Elite of Malaysia," in Ruth McVey, ed., *Southeast Asian Capitalists* (Ithaca: Cornell University Press, 1992), 127–44; Sieh Lee Mei Ling, "The Transformation of Malaysian Business Groups," in McVey, ed., *Southeast Asian Capitalists*, 103–26.

[38] Growth rate from Bank Negara Malaysia. See *The Central Bank and the Financial System in Malaysia: A Decade of Change, 1989–1999* (Kuala Lumpur: Bank Negara Malaysia, 1999), 7.

State Shareholding

The first two decades or so of the NEP would see the government take an active role as a shareholder in the Malaysian economy; in the absence of Malay economic elites, the state would act as "trustee" in holding and developing national firms on behalf of the Malays. The government's expanded presence as shareholder came in the form of GLICs, whose assets expanded rapidly starting from the early 1970s. The GLICs were not invented with the NEP: as Table 4.4 shows, several were founded early during the regime-formation period and several also targeted Malay businesses and rural industry. The NEP, however, sought radical parity in every corner of Malay society, which would entail changing the urban/rural composition of the population and pushing *bumiputeras* "into business, even big business, very quickly."[39] Existing GLICs, like the Rural Industrial Development Authority and the MARA (Majlis Amanah Rakyat, or Council of Trust for the People), which focused respectively on rural enterprise and small-scale Malay business, were deemed insufficient. The Second Malaysia Five-Year Plan (FYP) (1971–75) proposed an injection of $4.3 billion in investment as part of the NEP, most of which would go through Pernas (Perbadanan Nasional Berhad, an agency owned by the Malaysian Ministry of Finance with a mandate to lead the development of the franchise industry), Malaysian Industrial Development Finance Berhad, a financial services provider, MARA, and the State Economic Development Corporations (SEDCs) to be established by Malaysia's state governments.[40]

The initial design of the NEP permitted *bumiputera* to access special shares in capital issuances, but early experiences gave rise to concerns that many were reaping quick gains by purchasing and then selling shares. By the late 1970s, policymakers had settled on a "trustee" model, by which the GLICs would hold shares on behalf of the country's Malay majority and would be entrusted with management of its wealth. By the mid-1970s, Permodalan Nasional Berhad (PNB), which had largely taken over the assets of Pernas, was the country's largest investor, and the GLICs were large and coordinated

---

[39] Mohamad bin Mahathir, *The Way Forward* (London: Weidenfeld & Nicholson, 1998), 11. On radical parity, Mahathir also states: "There had to be proportionally the same percentages of rich and poor *bumiputeras* as there were rich and poor non-*bumiputeras*," and the same in the realms of small and medium enterprises, professions, and so forth (17).

[40] Abdul, *Second Malaysia Plan*, 40.

Table 4.4 Government-Linked Investment Companies

GLIC	Date Established	Mission
Ministry of Finance, Inc (MOF, Inc)	1957	General holding company for state-owned assets
Employees Provident Fund (EPF)	1951 (preindependence)	General retirement/pension vehicle
Pilgrim's Savings Fund (LTH)	1969	Islamic financial services
Armed Forces Savings Fund (LTAT)	1972	Retirement fund for Malaysian Armed Forces members
Pernas	1969	Implement NEP (corporate restructuring, increase Malay corporate equity)
Permodalan Nasional Berhad (PNB)	1978	Implement NEP (corporate restructuring, increase Malay corporate equity)
Retirement Fund Incorporated (KWAP)	1991	Retirement fund for civil servants
Khazanah Nasional Berhad	1993	Sovereign Wealth Fund; Manage commercial assets; undertake strategic investments on the part of the nation

enough to move and concentrate wealth in "cartel-like networks."[41] The GLICs played a stabilizing role during the 1986 recession; in 1993, the Ministry of Finance and PNB were the top shareholders in the Kuala Lumpur Stock Exchange (KLSE), holding a quarter of all assets.[42] The GLICs would be a fixture in the Malaysian economy through changes in the NEP approach and enforcement. Though Malaysia experimented with privatization, which I discuss below, the scale of state shareholding afforded the government a critical tool, one it retained even as policy changed, to manage business elites.

The Banking System

The NEP's primary arena was corporate equity, but the country's banking system was also a tool for state-directed socioeconomic policy. Merchant

---

[41] Mehmet, *Development in Malaysia*; Edmund Terence Gomez, Thirshalar Padmanabhan, Norfaryanti Kamaruddin, Sunil Bhalla, and Fikri Fisal, *Minister of Finance Incorporated: Ownership and Control of Corporate Malaysia* (Singapore: Palgrave Macmillan, 2018), chap. 2.

[42] Gomez et al., *Minister of Finance Incorporated*, 39–40.

banks were established in the 1970s to assist "companies wishing to restructure their capital base in accordance with the need to provide opportunities for the indigenous population to own a significant proportion of the share capital in the corporate sector." Financial behemoths such as Malaysian International Merchant Bankers were established with shareholders linked to the GLICs and directly to the government.[43] But the government takeover of banks was rather slow. In 1970, just over one-half of the banking sector was owned by foreign firms, and most domestically owned banks were historically owned by Chinese business elites (e.g., Malayan Banking Bhd and United Malayan Banking Corporation Bhd). By the late 1970s, many of the Chinese-owned banks had passed to state ownership or Malayan control following runs and/or the pursuit of strategic assets by government companies. The pursuit of financial control was strategic, allowing the government to implement NEP objectives through credit controls and to "indirectly dominate" other sectors of the economy through oligopolistic financial control.[44]

Government policies toward the financial sector curtailed, but did not eliminate, private control over banks. A 1986 revision to the Banking Act of 1973, for example, limited individual equity ownership to 20 percent and family or corporation ownership to 10 percent, but existing owners were grandfathered in. This included the positions of elite Chinese families in banks, like the Oversea-Chinese Banking Corporation (OCBC) and United Malayan Banking. These banks enjoyed curious relationships with the country's major firms. As in Indonesia and China, most large conglomerate firms were either built on banks (e.g. OCBC) or expanded into finance from other industries. Unlike the other countries, however, privately owned banks held block shares of large firms alongside the government vehicles (GLICs), frequently exercising restraint in their levels of ownership and allowing the government's share to expand.[45] By 1990, only two of the top ten banks remained in Chinese hands: Southern Bank and Public Bank, owned by Teh Hong Piow. Teh Hong Piow's Public Bank is an illustration of the trust and mutual alignment between Chinese business elites and the state. Public Bank was founded in 1966 after Teh lobbied the finance minister and MCA president Tun Tan Siew Sin for a license; Prime Minister Tunku Abdul Rahman

[43] Bruce Gale, *1837: A 150-Year History of the Malaysian International Chamber of Commerce and Industry* (Kuala Lumpur: The Chamber, 1987), 120.

[44] Gomez and Jomo, *Malaysia's Political Economy*, 60–63.

[45] Lim, *Ownership and Control*, 87–93.

officially launched Public Bank in 1967, and many government ministers attended the ceremony. As other banks became targets for government take-over, Teh was close to government officials and knew that his bank would survive only if it supported government policies.[46] When Teh stepped down in 2018, he had been grandfathered in as one of three Malaysians allowed to own more than 10 percent of a financial institution.[47]

Stagnation and Liberalization

If elite Malaysians seemed aligned with the UMNO and the NEP, the same was not the case for Malaysia's non-*bumiputera* SMEs. Among Chinese middle-class Malaysians in particular, resentment toward the NEP festered, making unity within the Chinese ethnic community impossible and fragmenting the Chinese vote between elite, "establishment" parties (the MCA) and others that, directly or indirectly, were challenging the special status of Malays within the country. As one Malaysian Chinese political activist put it in 1980:

> We are, as Datuk Musa [Hitam] said "Little bubbles" which are easily man-ageable. . . . Why are we so divided? What must we do? We must rid our-selves of the myth of so-called Chinese economic power. A handful of individualistic millionaires and multi-millionaires amidst millions of other Chinese who are poor can hardly constitute an economic power. Even so, economic power and political power are inseparable but unequal. In the Malaysian context, politics is what determines the future of our people and our nation. Yet the vast majority of us continues to shy away from politics. Incidentally, real economic power lies not with us, never had been. It is now in the hands of the Government—in the SEDCs, in FELDA (Federal Land Development Authority), in PERNAS, in PETRONAS, etc.[48]

The festering division and dissent translated into a divided economic perfor-mance for the country.

[46] Vishal Jain and Dileep M. Kumar, "Story of 'Asia's Banking Grandmaster': Tan Sri Dato' Sri Dr. Teh Hong Piow: A Case Study," *Research Journal of Social Science & Management* 3, no. 9 (January 2014): 72–81.

[47] The cap was lowered from 20 percent to 10 percent by the 2013 Financial Services Act.

[48] Lim Fung Chee, "Seminar on Political Challenges of the Eighties for the Chinese Community," Kuala Lumpur, May 25, 1980, 4 (NUS Singapore-Malaysia Collection).

The Malaysian economy grew over the 1970s, buttressed by favorable terms of trade, high prices for natural resources, and heavy state investment. Yet the economy suffered from low investment in manufacturing, where 80 percent of output came from SMEs[49] and noncommodity export-oriented industries; private investment was less than 10 percent of GDP throughout the 1970s, while public investment from various government agencies averaged over 15 percent during the same period.[50] The gap between private investment and fiscal outlays for the NEP generated public deficits throughout the period, reaching over 20 percent of GDP by the early 1990s.

The Malaysian economy faced several challenges over the course of the 1980s. Beginning in 1983, the same global decline in commodity prices that catalyzed liberalization in Indonesia brought on a significant contraction of the Malaysian economy, particularly the revenues available to the government to invest in order to implement the NEP. The recession, the first to hit post-1969 NEP Malaysia, brought about an opportunity for political elites to rethink state control over the financial sector. The recession arrived as Mahathir Mohamad assumed the role of prime minister and UMNO head, bringing with him a different set of ideas about how to realize "Malay economic empowerment." Large-scale state shareholding on behalf of *bumiputeras* gave way to privatization efforts that sought to empower a new class of Malay business elites. Mahathir's different development philosophy and fiscal pressure on the state combined to justify a push for financial liberalization.

The liberalization drive also had a political logic. The 1986 elections presented serious challenges for the BN and its constituent parts. UMNO was rocked internally by the Spirit of '46 challenge, in which a faction of UMNO led by finance minister Razaleigh Hamzah broke with Mahathir to challenge him for party leadership. Mahathir bested his challenger, but the battle was expensive and involved a typical slate of election drama, including "dubious ballot counting, a mysterious black-out, and a notorious break for prayers (during which much last-minute lobbying took place)."[51] The MCA fared poorly in the 1986 elections, with the Democratic Action Party (DAP) gaining in opposition, leading to inept and divided political representation and almost no path for middle-class Chinese to shape NEP

[49] 关丹中华商会 (Kuantan Chinese Chamber of Commerce), Speech by Vice Minister of Industry and Commerce, February 1993, 89.

[50] *Laporan Ekonimi*, various issues. Cited in MCA, Seminar on Privatisation, Kuala Lumpur, May 12, 1991, 72–73.

[51] William Case, *Politics in Southeast Asia: Democracy or Less* (Richmond, UK: Curzon, 2002), 116.

implementation: "The Chinese began to feel trapped," leading many to fear for their children's chances for social advancement and to emigrate.[52] The BN would meet electoral challenges with classic tactics of "competitive authoritarianism": manipulating election timing, banning opposition rallies on the grounds of violence prevention, and constructing districts to assign extra weight to rural Malay votes.[53] The liberalization project was aimed at reigniting a stagnant economy and easing some elements of the NEP to ameliorate political dissatisfaction; as government ministers toured to sell liberalization plans, Chinese organizations, especially chambers of commerce, were sites where officials assured those groups that privatization and global opening would generate more opportunities for businesses of all kinds.[54]

As nonstate elites were given greater control over assets and greater leeway to use them, they were nonetheless still dependent on the state for resources. Privatization indeed created ethnic Malay corporate titans and large domestic firms that were putatively privately owned, but the business class still depended on the state for contracts, land and natural resources, and continued access to capital. The Malaysian financial sector experienced privatization and limited liberalization, but not the same level of opening experienced in neighboring Indonesia during the late 1980s and early 1990s. Moreover, both emerging Malay corporate elites and Chinese conglomerate firm owners enjoyed close and trusting relationships with the UMNO leadership. A loss of control over the financial sector yielded competitive clientelism rather than mutual endangerment.

Liberalization with Political Trust: The Emergence of Competitive Clientelism

The liberalization project would comprise a number of policies as well as privatization of state assets. The impulse to liberalize began as early as 1983,

---

[52] Michael Yeoh Oon Kheng, "The Chinese Political Dilemma," June 12, 1987, *The Chinese Community towards & beyond 1990 in Multiracial Malaysia* (NUS Singapore-Malaysia Collection), 12.

[53] See Brownlee, *Authoritarianism*, 96–99.

[54] For example, see 关丹中华商会 (Kuantan Chinese Chamber of Commerce), Speech by Vice Minister of Industry and Commerce, February 1993; 霹雳嘉应会馆九十五周年纪念特刊 (Perak Kaying Association) (July 1995); 华声 ：砂劳越华人社团联合总会会讯 (Newsletter of the Confederation of Chinese Association Sarawak), 1995; 美里诏安会馆五十一周年纪念特刊 (51st Anniversary Persatuan of Chawan Miri) (Sarawak, 2001).

and an early round of privatization in the late 1980s was followed by intensification in the 1990s.[55] The first privatization was of Telekom Malaysia in 1987; Mahathir himself articulated that the impetus was a lack of government revenues to modernize infrastructure for the expanding economy and the need to accelerate *bumiputera* ownership. In many ways, the success of connected non-*bumiputera* firms in the 1980s catalyzed political will to create Malay-owned firms to match them: "These conglomerates were growing bigger and bigger, and looked likely to become household names, even on a global scale. This posed a new challenge to the NEP."[56] In a sense, keeping compliant Chinese conglomerates around and allowing them to grow was useful for Mahathir and UMNO: they served as political foil to organize UMNO's appeal to its base and to structure its arguments about economic policy.

The privatization process directly transferred corporate assets from the state to Malay and non-Malay businessmen who enjoyed close connections with the major powerholders within the UMNO and the "selective distribution of government-created rents to a select group of businessmen."[57] Mahathir unapologetically pursued creating rich Malays "so that the number of Malays who are rich equal the number of Chinese who are rich . . . then you can say parity has been achieved."[58] These business elites were much more tightly tied to the UMNO as well as to individual powerbrokers within the party than ever before. Over the course of the two decades before the AFC, Malay and non-Malay businessmen received large state projects, investments, licenses, and sweetheart privatization deals thanks to their closeness to Mahathir himself, to his minister of finance (starting in 1984, Daim Zainuddin), or to Anwar Ibrahim. These links with political elites were relatively transparent in the sense that most observers of Malaysian politics and business could identify firms and business elites as clients of one or more political patrons.[59]

---

[55] The "1988 Privatisation Master Plan" study was released in 1991.

[56] Mahathir, *The Way Forward*, 25–26.

[57] Edmund Terence Gomez, "Malaysian Business Groups: The State and Capital Development in the Post-currency Crisis Period," in Sea Jin Chang, ed., *East Asian Business Groups: Financial Crisis, Restructuring, and New Growth* (New York: Oxford University Press, 2006), 120.

[58] Gomez et al., *Minister of Finance Incorporated*, 37.

[59] Indeed, Gomez and Jomo do this, and their identification forms the basis of Johnson and Mitton's (2003) seminal paper showing that crony firms suffered more during the 1997–98 crisis and that firms linked to Mahathir benefited more after the imposition of capital controls in September 1998. Gomez and Jomo, *Malaysia's Political Economy*; Simon Johnson and Todd Mitton, "Cronyism and Capital Controls: Evidence from Malaysia," *Journal of Financial Economics* 67, no. 2 (2003): 351–82.

UMNO and its political elites "took an active part in directing the development of firms that received state rents."[60] Politically appointed board members ensured that corporate maneuvers would benefit political patrons, fulfill state development targets (e.g., by channeling investments to certain sectors or regions), and sometimes benefit the business interests of political elites themselves. Unsurprisingly, meeting these objectives came at the expense of corporate profitability and efficient allocation of resources, but the regime was the dominant shareholder and corporate governance was organized to maximize political oversight. For example, one diversified conglomerate found itself pressured to make several overseas investments in countries and sectors well outside its core competence because the board was dominated by retired UMNO cadres pushing the regime's agenda regardless of the company's well-being.[61] Firms associated with Daim Zainuddin, who himself came from the private sector, seemed to be working narrowly for their patron's business interests directly rather than realizing regime goals, much less their own profitability.

This was the era of competitive clientelism, a form of state-business relations in which business elites compete to curry favor with political elites who, in turn, compete with one another to extract resources from business for political gain. Competitive clientelism differs from mutual alignment in that it features a "competitive rather than monopolistic market for state-supplied goods and services," but it differs from mutual endangerment in that the orientation of business remains centripetal rather than centrifugal.[62] In Malaysia, business elites of all ethnicities throughout the 1980s and 1990s continued to believe that, and behave as if, the fate of their firms depended on the BN remaining in power and that their cooperation with political elites would be returned.

Unlike the opacity and hedging relationships of mutual endangerment, competitive clientelism is relatively transparent and built on trust and reciprocity; relations among elites are based on expectations of mutual exchange and benefit, rather than threat, and they are fundamentally voluntary.[63] In

---

[60] Gomez, "Rise and Fall," 360.

[61] Interview, chief strategy officer of GLC, Boston, September 2018.

[62] Characterization from Doner and Ramsay, "Competitive Clientelism," 239.

[63] This does not mean clientelistic relationships are not contingent, but rather they are based on reciprocal exchange and volition. Allen Hicken, "Clientelism," *Annual Review of Political Science* 14, no. 1 (2001): 289–310, distills the following: "The delivery of a good or service on the part of both the patron and client is in direct response to a delivery of reciprocal benefit by the other party, or the credible promise of such a benefit" (291), and on volition, "Successful clientelist exchange is a mutually

Malaysia, it was abundantly clear to participants and observers what they should expect from clientelistic state-business relations: business elites received privileged access to state resources, and political elites received financial support from businesses for their own political advancement, typically through elections. Gomez and Jomo write that these arrangements were "reinforcing" for participants' "positions in the party and in business":

> Politicians who had exploited their political influence to help businessmen expand their corporate interests and those who had cultivated close ties with members of the business community found that they had an advantage over other aspiring politicians, especially during elections.[64]

Competitive clientelism does not produce efficient use of resources or eliminate corruption, to be sure, nor does it generate the deleterious spiral dynamics associated with mutual endangerment. Asset expatriation is unlikely because patrons and clients alike have incentives to keep resources local to maintain support networks.[65] The transparency of elite networks prevents weaponization of information, and business elites have no incentives to loot their own firms because they have long time horizons and every expectation that their political cooperation will be met with economic sources and reciprocal exchange maintained over time.

Aside from privatization, financial liberalization measures in Malaysia were more limited than those undertaken in Indonesia (or, decades later, in China). After losses in the banking sector associated with the 1986 recession, a 1989 law prohibited self-dealing (lending to companies with the bank's directors on their boards), required senior bankers to declare assets, and also required foreign banks to "Malaysianize" (incorporate locally). The latter regulation sought to both tame increasing flows of global capital and to generate competition for domestic banks.[66] Profits indeed increased in the late 1980s, but Bank Negara's prudential regulation and the lack of new entries into the sector (the last banking license was given in 1979) precluded

---

reinforcing equilibrium, with each side free to exit if they become dissatisfied with the nature of the relationship" (293).

[64] Gomez and Jomo, *Malaysia's Political Economy*, 81.

[65] Doner and Ramsay, "Competitive Clientelism," find this is the exact case with Sino-Thai business elites in Thailand (239).

[66] Gomez and Jomo, *Malaysia's Political Economy*, 64–66.

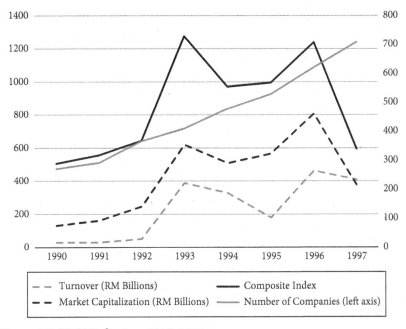

Figure 4.2 KLSE Indicators, 1990–1997

Source: Bursa Malaysia, World Stock Exchange Fact Book, Refinitiv Datastream

significant expansion.[67] In the manufacturing sector, the 1986 recession would prompt "less rigorous" enforcement of the NEP, including more ICA exemptions for manufacturing firms and investment promotion efforts for export-oriented firms. Foreign direct investment, especially regional capital, flowed in, prompting a surge in export growth.[68]

During the 1980s and 1990s, the KLSE would expand significantly. Mahathir's finance minister, Daim, was appointed in 1984, over the will of many other UMNO elites, with a mission to expand the capitalization of the KLSE and create large, Malay-owned business groups. Indeed, between 1989 and 1993 capitalization went from 105 percent to 324 percent of GDP, the highest ratio in Asia.[69] Figure 4.2 shows basic indicators of equity market growth over the 1990s.

---

[67] ASEAN Briefing, "Outlook on the Malaysian Economy 1990," Development Bank of Singapore, no. 13, 4.

[68] Mahathir, in *The Way Forward*, 20–21, claims the NEP was "less rigorously enforced." On ICA exemptions and export growth (8 percent annual growth from the late 1980s through 1997), see Gomez and Jomo, *Malaysia's Political Economy*, 79.

[69] Gomez, "Malaysian Business Groups," 125.

Privatization, and competitive clientelism, accelerated in the 1990s, and Malay and non-Malay elites benefited from its various forms as long as they were well connected. Vincent Tan Chee Yoin's Berjaya Group (as it eventually became known), for example, became private owner of Sports Toto, the state's lucrative gaming concern, and Ananda Krishnan benefited from other gaming privatizations and real estate deals because of his close-ness with Mahathir.[70] As the MCA declined in popular regard, and corre-spondingly in its access to state resources, non-*bumiputera* business elites pursued particularistic relationships with Malay political elites, but they did not abandon the regime. Political economy scholarship on Malaysia in the 1980s and 1990s, especially the work of Edmund Terrance Gomez and K. S. Jomo, painstakingly details corporate links between various economic elites and increasingly expensive and politically bitter fights among UMNO elites.[71]

Competitive clientelism may have generated unproductive rent-seeking and produced economic elites with a "subsidy mentality," but politically it facilitated power concentration in the hands of a narrow, if internally competitive, elite. Mahathir himself deinstitutionalized and personally concentrated power during the 1980s and 1990s, and the other dominant political elites (Anwar Ibrahim and Daim) were, prior to the AFC, loy-ally part of the central UMNO executive apparatus.[72] This centripetal ten-dency would serve the regime well during the same AFC that tore apart the New Order.

---

[70] Gomez and Jomo, *Malaysia's Political Economy*, 150–65.

[71] Ibid. Because my narrative about pre-AFC Malaysia does not challenge these understandings and because competitive clientelism is a form of state-business relations familiar to readers of this book, I do not attempt to replicate such work here. It bears much in common with "relationship capitalism," as described by Rajan and Zingales, or older concepts such as Mancur Olson's "distri-butional coalitions" or classic rent-seeking models. Raghuram Rajan and Luigi Zingales, *Saving Capitalism from the Capitalists: Unleashing the Power of Financial Markets to Create Wealth and Spread Opportunity* (New York: Crown Business, 2003); Mancur Olson, *The Rise and Decline of Nations: Economic Growth, Stagflation, and Social Rigidities* (New Haven: Yale University Press, 1982); Sylvia Maxfield and Ben Ross Schneider, eds., *Business and the State in Developing Countries* (Ithaca: Cornell University Press, 1997). See also Johnson and Mitton, "Cronyism and Capital Controls"; Edmund Terence Gomez, *Political Business: Corporate Involvement of Malaysian Political Parties* (Townsville, Queensland, Australia: Centre for South-East Asian Studies, James Cook University of North Queensland, 1994); Jesudason, *Ethnicity and the Economy*.

[72] Dan Slater, "Iron Cage in an Iron Fist: Authoritarian Institutions and the Personalization of Power in Malaysia," *Comparative Politics* 36, no. 1 (2003): 81–101. Gomez and Jomo, *Malaysia's Political Economy*, call this "executive dominance."

Crisis and Control

In addition to accelerated privatization, Malaysia in the 1990s undertook a renewal of its developmental and distributive goals and an opening to global capital. Three decades of the NEP had produced moderate economic success and, its architects claimed, a resounding political success. To be sure, the country had not experienced the kind of cataclysmic violence and threats to integrity symbolized by May 13. Economically, the average growth rate of 7 percent was below the 8 percent target of the NEP, but a reasonable achievement alongside the distributive goals, which were the priority. By 1990, *bumiputera* individuals and trust agencies owned a reported 19.2 percent of the country's wealth and Chinese owned 45.5 percent (an increase from 27.2 in 1970). (See Table 4.2.) The share for Malays was below the 30 percent target, but the country had come far and was in the midst of privatizing more assets into the hands of politically loyal, and ideally Malay, corporate titans.[73] Vision 2020, announced in 1991, renewed Malaysia's commitment to the goals of both the NEP and economic growth; Malaysia would become a fully industrialized, advanced economy by 2020.[74]

These ambitious goals would require the mobilization of capital, including both domestic investment and global capital. Policymakers, especially at Mahathir's and Daim's urging, sought to expand equity markets to furnish capital for private investment. Progressive measures liberalized Malaysia's markets to global capital flows during the 1990s, including developing offshore markets for the ringgit (in Labuan and in Singapore), facilitating unlimited portfolio inflows, and allowing banks to borrow abroad. Unlike Indonesia, Bank Negara limited portfolio outflows for corporations that had borrowed domestically and was not averse to experimenting with capital controls when it became concerned about external balances.[75] Clearly, Malaysian authorities, enabled by the dual distributive and growth goals, practiced greater macroprudential financial supervision than their

---

[73] Economic Planning Unit, "Seventh Malaysia Five Year Plan, 1996–2000" and Economic Planning Unit, "Eight Malaysia 2001–2005." See also Gomez, "Malaysian Business Groups"; Rawi Abdelal and Laura Alfaro, "Malaysia: Capital and Control," HBS Case 702-040 (2003), 6.

[74] See Koon Kew Yin, *Malaysia: Road Map for Achieving Vision 2020* (Petaling Jaya: Strategic Information and Research Development Centre, 2012); Ahmad Sarji Abdul Hamid, ed., *Malaysia's Vision 2020: Understanding the Concept, Implications, and Challenges* (Petaling Jaya, Selangor Darul Ehsan, Malaysia: Pelanduk Publications, 1993).

[75] Abdelal and Alfaro, "Malaysia," 6. See also Rawi Abdelal, *Capital Rules: The Construction of Global Finance* (Cambridge, MA: Harvard University Press, 2007), especially chap. 8.

counterparts in Indonesia or, eventually, China. But, nonetheless, financial liberalization could have enabled looting and fraud if economic participants had incentives to pursue it. As in China (as we see in Chapter 6), a "tripartite connection" between government, private capital, and the banking system allowed connected individuals to access loans and expand their assets, with the government controlling the banking sector in both countries.[76] But business actors in Malaysia expected reciprocity from the state, and therefore they had incentives to cooperate with long time horizons rather than to maximize current gains and expatriate assets.

In fact, Malaysia's experience with outward investment in the age of financial liberalization is an illustrative counterpoint to mutual endangerment in Indonesia and China. As policymakers looked for new sources of expansion in the 1990s and sought to reduce the income deficit in the balance of payments, they encouraged domestic firms to explore growth markets in Asia, such as Mainland China, so that Malaysia could "export its expertise to other nations, particularly developing countries, and invest in projects overseas."[77] This policy of "reverse investment," as it became known, would feature tight partnerships between corporate groups, including and especially non-*bumiputera*-owned groups, and the state. Reports from the time include details of "747s full of Malaysian businessmen looking for opportunities abroad" and especially trips to Mainland China by ethnic Chinese Malaysian capitalists, such as one in 1993 with three hundred such individuals accompanying Mahathir himself.[78] Larger firms, like Genting and YTL, stuck to their core businesses, but they expanded abroad with the blessing of UMNO elites. Smaller firms, including midsize Chinese-owned manufacturing operations, also received government support to expand abroad. Policymakers facilitated their pursuit of labor advantages in places such as China and saw advantages in having competitive non-*bumiputera*-owned firms repatriating profits and ceding domestic competitive space to Malay firms.[79] Firms did not engage in the sort of flight-to-safety pursuit of overseas assets the way that Chinese firms would decades later.

[76] Gomez et al., *Minister of Finance Incorporated*, 38–39.

[77] "Summary of Speech by Datuk Asmat Karamudin, Secretary General to the Minister for International Trade and Investment," *BERITA* (British Malaysian Industry and Trade Association) *Monthly Newsletter* (April–May 1997), 7.

[78] Gomez et al., *Minister of Finance Incorporated*, 45; quotation from *BERITA* (British Malaysian Industry and Trade Association) *Monthly Newsletter* (April–May 1997), 7.

[79] Interview, Ministry of Finance Office, Kuala Lumpur, October 2019; interview, Sunway executives, October 2018.

Financial liberalization efforts continued right up to the moment Malaysia's economy would plunge headlong into the AFC. Anwar's (October 1996) introduction of the 1997 budget proclaimed that "Malaysia is being developed as the premier capital market and services centre in Asia. We have begun a process of reform for this sector through the progressive liberalisation of banking and financial services."[80] Financial liberalization had been extensive in Malaysia, but the country's financial sector and largest firms were in far better condition than their counterparts in Indonesia and other countries affected by the AFC. Corporate leverage was significantly lower than that in these other countries, debt to GDP was but 45.6 percent, and the return on assets in the corporate sector was a reasonable 5.6 percent.[81]

After a decade and a half of liberalization, marked by privatization and more autonomous control of large corporate groups by a new class of Malay business elites, alongside an older and newer class of non-Malay elites, the Malaysian economy boomed. Driven by exports and investment, GDP grew at 10 percent. FDI and portfolio investment flowed in, fueling manufacturing growth in electronics as well as expansion of the KLSE and real estate growth. Yet the economy was showing signs of a bubble. As in the mid-1980s, a good deal of credit expansion went to the property sector and to the equity market, and asset prices were increasing relative to corporate revenues. Although FDI had increased in the late 1980s and early 1990s, by the mid-1990s portfolio flows had come to dominate.[82] Popular accounts from the time echo the sense of shared good times: "The Malays, like Malaysia's other ethnic groups, are enjoying their greatest period of prosperity since the days of the Malacca Sultanate!" reported one regional magazine.[83]

The Regime's Response

As in neighboring Indonesia, contagion quickly reached Malaysia after the devaluation of the Thai bhat and an initial attempt to defend the ringgit that

[80] "1997 Budget Speech by Anwar Ibrahim Introducing the Supply Bill," October 25, 1996 (NUS Singapore-Malaysia Collection).

[81] Corporate leverage ranged from 0.61 to 1.18 in the 1990s, compared to greater than 3 for Korea and an average of 2 for Thailand and Indonesia during the same period. Stephan Haggard, *The Political Economy of the Asian Financial Crisis* (Washington, DC: Institute for International Economics, 2000), 18, 59.

[82] Pepinsky, *Economic Crises*, 121–24.

[83] Quoted in Boo Teik Khoo, *Beyond Mahathir: Malaysian Politics and Its Discontents* (New York: Zed Books, 2003), 18.

ended within weeks, and Malaysia entered an unpleasant storm of capital outflows, asset price devaluations, and banking sector concerns. Elites within the UMNO, especially Mahathir and Daim on the one hand and Anwar Ibrahim on the other, fought among themselves for the remainder of 1997 and much of 1998 over how to respond to the crisis. Meanwhile, the ringgit was in free fall as Mahathir took an antagonistic stance toward global capital, blaming financiers and speculators for the crisis. Prominent accounts of the turbulence in Malaysia's response to the crisis point to elite political competition: Anwar was held in high esteem outside of Malaysia and, within the country, was regarded by many as the next prime minister and future head of party. Anwar and Mahathir maneuvered among political and business elites to recruit supporters and to grasp control of the country's overall response.

Anwar, who was minister of finance at the time, famously pursued implementation of what was known as an "IMF package without the IMF"; Malaysia was alone among the afflicted countries in not turning to the IMF, as the BN was unwilling to cede control of its decades-long redistributive project and to remove the state's hand from the economy. Anwar's initial package, promulgated in December 1997, would pursue government consolidation of financial institutions and some fiscal austerity measures to reassure investors and arrest capital outflows. Yet even Anwar himself would quickly roll back the austerity proposals to meet the expectations of connected business elites, including Chinese Malaysian elites. For example, a large dam project contracted to Ting Pek Khiing's Ekran Holdings was among the first announced to be deferred in an effort at fiscal austerity, but within months the government had instead taken over the concession and had bailed out Tiong.[84]

For his part, Mahathir sought to sideline Anwar; at the end of 1997, he formed the National Economic Advisory Council (NEAC) with Daim, the former minister of finance, as chair. The NEAC would serve as a competing locus of power and offer an alternative set of policy proposals, including cutting interest rates and offering a fiscal stimulus. Business groups seemed to prefer Daim and Mahathir, though again all UMNO elites, including Anwar, seemed persuaded by the demands that large firms had for lower interest rates and expansive government finance. By mid-1998, Anwar had ceded to Mahathir's position on several important fiscal and monetary matters,

[84] Pepinsky, *Economic Crises*, 124–25.

advocating releasing funds for contractors to revive business and, on the same grounds, justifying a reversal of tight monetary policy.[85]

Anwar and Mahathir disagreed substantively, to be sure, but their competition was political, and it was a clear manifestation of competitive clientelism. The contest was centripetal in that political and business elites were both oriented toward the central state, attempting to capture its resources and shape its response. In contrast to neighboring Indonesia, the expectation was that the political and business elites would return each other's cooperation rather than defect, and they did. After a year and a half of elite competition over the response and intense lobbying on the part of business interests, Mahathir imposed a suite of capital controls, essentially ending the offshore exchange of the ringgit, freezing portfolio outflows, and stabilizing the currency.[86] The day after imposing the controls, Anwar was ousted and eventually jailed on a variety of salacious and absurd charges, setting the stage for decades of contestation manifested in a *reformasi* movement that took Anwar as its progenitor.[87]

Scholars have written thoughtfully about the regime's crisis response, reception, and effects.[88] My focus is on how business elites behaved during the crisis, and the experience is notable for the purposes of my argument for what did not happen: while Indonesian tycoons accelerated looting and asset expatriation, their Malaysian counterparts were working with the regime to coordinate policy, rescue state and nonstate assets, and arrest the collapse in asset prices and the ringgit. They lobbied openly for favorable government interventions, including lower interest rates and an expansive fiscal policy as well as particularistic bailouts and capital injections. In 1997 and early 1998, the government intervened through the GLICs and GLCs (government-linked corporations) to recapitalize and rescue firms of "strategic importance," both those integral to the NEP agenda and those with significant government connections, helping to "insulate certain corporations

[85] Ibid., 127, 131.
[86] The controls, considered economic heresy at the time, are the subject of a large literature in economics and political science. For details on the controls themselves, see Stephan Haggard with Linda Low, "Appendix 2.1: The Political Economy of Malaysia's Capital Controls," in Haggard, *Political Economy*, 73–85.
[87] Weiss, *Protest and Possibilities*.
[88] Haggard, *Political Economy*; Andrew J. MacIntyre, *The Power of Institutions: Political Architecture and Governance* (Ithaca: Cornell University Press, 2003); Andrew J. MacIntyre, T. J. Pempel, and John Ravenhill, *Crisis as Catalyst: Asia's Dynamic Political Economy* (Ithaca: Cornell University Press, 2008); T. J. Pempel, *The Politics of the Asian Economic Crisis* (Ithaca: Cornell University Press, 2018).

and certain figures from suffering the adverse economic effects of the financial meltdown."[89] That UMNO rescued firms close to its elites is well established in journalistic and scholarly accounts.[90] While I will not rehash the
details of those corporate maneuvers here, Table 4.5 contains basic information about the regime's various modes of intervention to rescue, restructure,
and recapitalize firms and financial institutions.

The competition over the state's largesse—whether through particularistic bailouts, institutionalized restructuring vehicles like Danaharta and
Danamodal, or influencing macroeconomic policy—interacted intimately
with the political competition among UMNO elites. The political fortunes
of Mahathir, Daim, and Anwar were affected by their ability to recruit corporate supporters and credibly offer them state support. The political competition was one over power within the regime and, as in previous crises
(especially the Razaleigh Hamzah challenge of 1987), clientelistic relations
had consequences for both firms and politicians. Anwar's bid for power
within the UMNO was thwarted by business-elite opposition, and those
firms that did support Anwar found themselves on the outside of restructuring and state largesse following his ouster.[91]

In 2001, when Daim was also politically sidelined by Mahathir, his cronies
and their assets met a similar fate.[92] For example, Rashid Hussain, one of the
country's highest-profile financiers and an associate of Anwar and Daim, acquired the banking assets of Sime Darby, another major conglomerate, only
to be forced in 1998 to sell a large stake of his group (RHB) to Khazanah
in the face of a debt burden. Khazanah's stake was eventually passed to the
Employee's Provident Fund (EPF), which is now the bank's largest shareholder.[93] More generally, the regime engineered a major consolidation of the
country's financial sector—from fifty-eight financial institutions to ten an-
chor banks, five of which would be owned by the Malaysian government as
the largest shareholder (via GLICs). Daim initially sought to consolidate to

---

[89] Johan Saravanamuttu, "The Eve of the 1999 General Elections: From the NEP to *Reformasi*," in
Francis Loh Kok Wah and Johan Saravanamuttu, eds., *New Politics in Malaysia* (Singapore: Institute
of Southeast Asian Studies, 2003), 8.

[90] Pepinsky, *Economic Crises*; Gomez, and Jomo, *Malaysia's Political Economy*; Johnson and Mitton,
"Cronyism and Capital Controls."

[91] That Anwar's failure was ultimately due to elite business opposition is Pepinsky's main finding.

[92] Gomez, "Malaysian Business Groups," 126.

[93] See Leslie Lopez, "Malaysian Financier Rashid Hussain Is Forced to Sell Stake to Government,"
Wall Street Journal, November 30, 1998; interview KNB (Khazanah Nasional Berhad, Sovereign
Wealth Fund, Malaysia), November 2016; interview KL03, October 2018.

Table 4.5 Rescue and Restructuring in Malaysia, 1997–2000

Mode of Intervention	Financial Scope	Funding Sources	Target firm examples
Ad hoc intervention (particularistic corporate maneuvers to save connected firms)	Unknown	EPF Funds KWAP Khazanah (sovereign wealth fund) Petronas	UEM (engineering company)-Renong highway project and backward merger (fall 1997) RHB (bank) capital takeover Sime Bank Purchase of shares of Bank Bumiputera (August 1998) Purchases Konsortium Perkapalan Bhd (shipbuilder associated with Mahathir's son)
Danaharta (vehicle for restructuring distressed corporate assets and NPLs)	RM47.5 billion worth of NPLs by end of 2000	Initial attempt at issuing bonds failed Employee's Provident Fund (EPF) and Khazanah	Woo Hing Brothers Bescorp Industries Malaysia Electric Corporation Nine Timber Bundle Jupiter Securities
Danamodal (vehicle for recapitalization of troubled banks)			Sime Bank Bank Bumiputera Mbf Holdings Arab-Malaysia Group
Corporate Debt Reconstruction Committee (institutional support for restructuring debt and distressed assets)	n/a	Not explicitly funded; Corporate Debt Restructuring Committee had prerogative to impose conditions on restructuring and appoint new managers	Renong

Source: Thomas B. Pepinsky, *Economic Crises and the Breakdown of Authoritarian Regimes: Indonesia and Malaysia in Comparative Perspective* (New York: Cambridge University Press, 2009); Lee Kam Hing and Lee Poh Ping, "Malaysian Chinese Business: Who Survived the Crisis?," *Kyoto Review of Southeast Asia* (2003), https://kyotoreview.org/issue-4/malaysian-chinese-business-who-survived-the-crisis/; Stephan Haggard, *The Political Economy of the Asian Financial Crisis* (Washington, DC: Institute for International Economics, 2000).

six major banks, but Mahathir was persuaded, by the Chinese firms that had supported him during the crisis and whose support he needed, to expand that number and retain Chinese-owned financial institutions.[94]

Business elites called on political ties, but they engaged in none of the looting and asset expatriation that took place with Indonesia's efforts at re-capitalization and restructuring. On the contrary, firms sought help from the government in rescuing, and repatriating, their assets abroad. One non-Malay firm under a considerable debt burden asked the government to help it find a foreign buyer for assets in China and in turn, in part to curry favor, brought the ringgit back into the country at a critical time. The firm could have kept its assets outside of Malaysia, but it decided its long-term fate would be aided by cooperating with the government, with Mahathir specifi-cally, at the height of the crisis.[95] Ultimately, even at the moment of the crisis, "Elites had long displayed patterns of cohesive behavior, leaving them collec-tively amenable to the patronage that Mahathir could still dispense. Indeed, they continued to view him—quite unlike elites did Suharto in Indonesia—as the leader best able to preserve their positions and fortunes."[96]

Limits to Competitive Clientelism

To be sure, it is not my claim that every economic elite in Malaysia enjoyed trusting and cooperative relations with the BN regime. In general, my characterization of state-business relations is based on ideal types, and, in reality, political economies are diverse and complex. Some members of the Malaysian corporate elite, including Malaysians of Chinese descent, harbored deep anger at UMNO and felt betrayed by the NEP. Robert Kuok, Malaysia's richest man, famously fell out with the regime and diversified his empire into other parts of Asia. And Malaysia, like all economies, experi-enced fraud. My argument is not that there are no exceptions to trust and mutual alignment, but rather that mutual alignment and competitive clien-telism were the pervasive forms of state-business relations during the BN's tenure. My argument about trust and economic behavior is about general

[94] Gomez, "Malaysian Business Groups," 131. The ten would include Teh Hong Piow's Public Bank, Tan Teong Hean's Southern Bank, and Quek Leng Chan's Hong Leong Bank.

[95] Interview, Kuala Lumpur, 2016.

[96] Case, *Politics in Southeast Asia,*136.

norms, worldviews, and social expectations, and no characterization about social realities can apply to all social actors within a system.

That said, some elements of state-business relations in Malaysia are useful as "exceptions that prove the rule," or unexpected economic behaviors that illustrate the logic of how trust and financial control interact to affect state-business relations. First, Malaysia's most significant financial scandal before the AFC was the "cooperatives crisis" of 1985–86, during which the recession, driven by drops in commodity prices, reverberated through domestic credit institutions, generating bank runs and insolvency for a suite of deposit-taking cooperatives (DTCs), some of which were illegal. Initially, rumors of malfeasance at Setia Timor Credit and Leasing and a related company, Pan-Electric, caused a run on similar DTCs. Sporadic runs followed throughout 1986, and eventually twenty-four DTCs were found to be engaged in fraud, self-dealing, and "Ponzi scheme"-type lending. Several businessmen were arrested, others fled the country, and some half a million depositors—not an insignificant number in a country of sixteen million at the time—were left demanding rescue from the government. Importantly for my argument, all of the failed DTCs were run by regional Chinese firms serving regional Chinese markets, and the vast majority of depositors were working-class Chinese.[97] These were exactly the dissatisfied SMEs and marginalized Chinese business actors that distrusted the BN. And when the financial sector was expanding in the 1980s, they took advantage of the lack of regulatory oversight to engage in behaviors that seem like looting.[98]

A second series of events involved Mahathir and Anwar lobbing accusations of cronyism and corruption against one another at the height of the political competition during the AFC and during Anwar's trial in 1999. Anwar had been increasingly critical of Mahathir and other elites during the crisis for a lack of transparency in corporate governance, and Mahathir felt particularly threatened when an UMNO youth leader accused the UMNO leadership of the same *korupsi, kolsu, dan nepotisme* that was devastating

[97] One scholar estimates that one in three working-class Chinese families lost savings in the cooperatives crisis. Emile Kok-Kheng Yeoh, "Communal Economic Movement of Chinese Overseas: A Malaysian Case" (Kuala Lumpur: Institute of China Studies, ICS Working Paper Series no. 2008-16, University of Malaya, 2008), 31.

[98] Emile Kok-Kheng Yeoh, "Requiem for a Dream: The Rise and Fall of a Communal Economic Revival Movement," in Emile Kok-Kheng Yeoh and Joanne Hoi-Lee Loh, eds., *China in the World: Contemporary Issues and Perspectives* (Kuala Lumpur: Institute of China Studies, University of Malaya, 2008), 210–73; Andrew Sheng, "Bank Restructuring in Malaysia, 1985–88," in Dimitri Vittas, ed., *Financial Regulation: Changing the Rules of the Game* (Washington, DC: World Bank, EDI Development Studies, 1992), 124–48.

Indonesia; lists then circulated of connected elites, including political elites' family members, who had benefited from privatization deals and contracts. Mahathir circulated a list that included not only his own family members but also people close to Anwar.[99] Later, after Anwar's ousting, he used the trial to make allegations against Mahathir and others for corruption, while a former Anwar affiliate turned on him to allege that "slush funds" and "master accounts" were used by Anwar and others to steal state money.[100] To be sure, these episodes seem evidence of weaponized information, but they are notably different in that most of these relationships were widely known and the revelation of information was inconsequential; as the above sections note, firms and political officials shared open clientelistic relationships, and therefore the information was not easily weaponized. Moreover, these exchanges involved political elites alone; in the Malaysian case, we have no evidence that business elites enmeshed political elites in their activities to endanger them; instead, all the evidence shows that these relationships produced predictable exchanges of resources and rents.

The inability of UMNO elites to control the Malaysian businessmen whom they cultivated was relevant mostly to their economic and business activities rather than their political activities. Amid the challenges in the late 1980s and during the AFC in the late 1990s, business elites relied on the state for assurance and rescue, and they did not challenge the UMNO or Mahathir's leadership. Malaysia under the BN thus falls into the categories of both the democratic and the developmental paradoxes: the regime could not outmaneuver the elites it created to implement economic policy, and capitalist elites, "very subservient to the state," had little desire to push for political liberalization.[101]

Reconstituting Financial Discipline: The Resurgence of State Shareholding

In the immediate aftermath of the crisis, the government undertook measures to stabilize the economy and deal with restructuring in ways that ultimately amplified the power of the regime over the business elites. Capital controls facilitated lending to politically favored firms that were then more

[99] Gomez, "Malaysian Business Groups," 133.
[100] Khoo, *Beyond Mahathir*,112.
[101] Gomez, "Malaysian Business Groups," 134.

beholden to the political elites who had rescued them.[102] Mahathir had rejected the idea that cronyism caused the collapse of the ringgit, instead blaming "currency traders fiddling around with our currency."[103] As the Malaysian economy recovered and was even able to turn to global markets once again to borrow in 2000, Mahathir declared the victory of state intervention over neoliberal ideas of market discipline.

Public narratives aside, the regime learned that it could not entrust significant financial power to private businessmen because, simply, they could not be disciplined. This was held to be especially true in a climate of capital account openness, but the lesson was more general. As one senior UMNO official relayed: "The problem with the 1990s was that privatization and liberalization took control from [the party's] hands and put it in the hands of private businessmen. They thought that this was the goal of the regime—to create Malay businessmen. However, then the Malay businessmen waste the resources, so, okay, you give it to some non-Malays like Yeoh [Francis Yeoh, second-generation CEO of the YTL Group] who you know will be loyal but also know their business. But anyway, you can't trust most of these private guys to do the job. So then you get the crisis and they learn that the GLICs will have to do the disciplining."[104]

The post-AFC period saw a resurgence of the state's role as investor and participant in corporate governance and a relative decline in the independent power of connected businessmen. As we will see in the Chinese case, the initial impetus was to regain a footing amid the financial crisis as well as to reassert discipline and monitoring over a financial and corporate sector that was blamed for generating the instability. Related to GLIC shareholding, the post-AFC period witnessed a resurgence of interlocking directorships, by which a number of Malaysia's largest firms were connected through directors, many of whom had UMNO or government experience, serving on multiple boards.[105] Figures 4.3 and 4.4 illustrate the growth of government financial control over the top firms in the country, and Figure 4.5 shows how these same firms were connected through interlocking directorships. Both mechanisms bound together business and political elites in transparent relationships. As the GLICs reasserted financial control over the Malaysian

---

[102] Johnson and Mitton, "Cronyism and Capital Controls." On the developmental and democratic paradoxes, see Bellin, *Stalled Democracy*.

[103] Mahathir, quoted in Abdelal and Alfaro, "Malaysia," 1.

[104] Interview, senior UMNO official with a finance portfolio, Kuala Lumpur, November 2016.

[105] Gomez, "Malaysian Business Groups," 125–26.

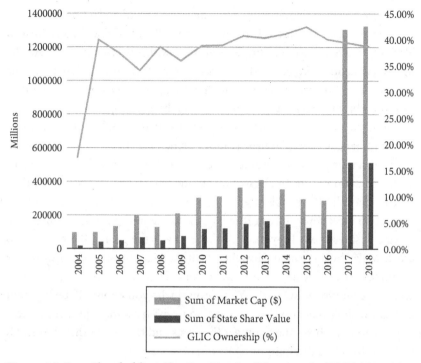

Figure 4.3 State Shareholding, Top One Hundred Firms on the KLSE, 2004–2018
Source: Data from Bursa Malaysia, via Bloomberg, Capital IQ, and Dataverse Refinitiv. See Appendix B for a list of state shareholding vehicles and a description of the data.

corporate sector, successive BN leaders tried to meet extensive state patronage and monitoring with incentives for managers and firms to perform
well and to generate profits. As one might expect, this proved to be a particularly difficult needle to thread.

For a good deal of the 2000s and 2010s, the GLICs adopted a paternal-
istic role in the economy, holding shares of much of the Malaysian corporate sector in trust but also acting as a transformative investor, pushing
management of firms to be more dynamic and innovative. In 2005, after
several years of weak performance in the country's largest firms after the
AFC, the Ministry of Finance and the five largest GLICs (EPF, Khazanah,
LTAT, LTH, and PNB) initiated the Government Linked Companies
Transformation Programme (GLCT).[106] The GLCT targeted the twenty

[106] Putrajaya Committee on GLC High Performance, *GLC Transformation Programme Graduation
Report*, August 2015, https://www.pcg.gov.my/media/1118/glctp-vol1-graduation-report.pdf.

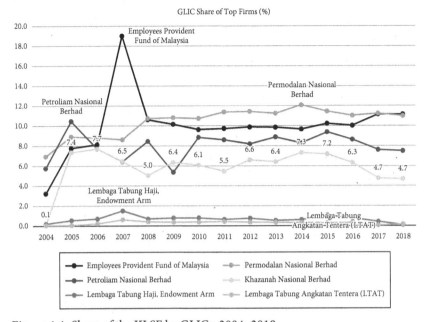

Figure 4.4 Share of the KLSE by GLICs, 2004–2018

Source: Data from Bursa Malaysia, via Bloomberg, Capital IQ, and Dataverse Refinitiv. See Appendix B for a list of state shareholding vehicles and a description of the data.

largest GLCs for professionalization and modernization in three areas: performance focus, nation-building and governance, and shareholder and stakeholder management. Ironically, these several bottom lines bear much in common with the government's own diagnosis of the causes of the poor GLC performance that served as the impetus for the GLCT.[107] These G20 firms (see Appendix B for details) and their leadership went through intense training and scrutiny regarding board and director effectiveness and efficient management of human resources and capital. They were encouraged to invest abroad to enhance competitiveness and innovation, but they were also pushed toward meeting "socially responsible" employment objectives. Interviews with executives from participating GLCs indicate that the program promoted professionalization of management and

---

[107] "GLCs were poor in managing costs and did not employ labour or capital as effectively as the competition. The underperformance was due to a host of factors including a lack of focus on the bottom line, ambiguous social responsibilities, ineffective boards and poor talent management among many others." Azman Mokhtar and Mohd Izani Ashari, Secretariat to the Putrajaya Committee on GLC High Performance, July 28, 2015, in ibid., 9.

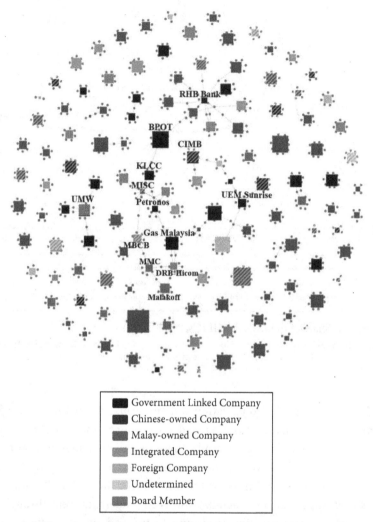

Figure 4.5 Firm Connections through Interlocking Directorships, 2018

Source: See Appendix B for a discussion of the firm data. Board member data from BoardEx and Capital IQ. Biographical data from company annual reports.

better corporate performance, especially through depoliticization and a focus on shareholder returns.[108]

At the same time, however, state shareholding and state involvement in corporate governance restricted the independence and maneuverability of

---

[108] Interviews with executives from Sime Darby, September 2017 and October 2018; TNB, September 2018; Maybank, October 2018; UEM, November 2016; and UMW, November 2016. Interview with PCG GLCT directors, November 2016, Kuala Lumpur.

management, and, according to many, the general security of state finance, has inhibited innovation in the country. As Figure 4.4 shows, GLIC ownership hovered around 40 percent of the market during the post-AFC period. Moreover, Malaysia's equity market is well developed relative to peer countries, a reflection of the regime's long-term focus on wealth sharing. As one investor remarked: "There is a savings glut and the savings keeps getting cycled into the KLSE, so company shareholder returns are good even when innovation is not great and performance is so-so, and there is not much aggression because of easy access to funds and little oversight."[109] Corporate sector leaders frequently complain of excessive state involvement, even bemoaning easy access to state capital because it comes with expectations of meeting political goals, whether in strategic investments that are loss-making or in enforcing what is commonly referred to as the "*bumi* agenda," or continued efforts at race-based redistribution.

The trajectory of Sime Darby, Malaysia's largest public firm by market capitalization for much of the 2000s and 2010s, is instructive. The company, famously nationalized in the 1970s by the so-called dawn raid, held a wide diversity of assets during the 1990s and 2000s—a merger of several plantation firms created a diversified conglomerate with holdings in plantations, trading and leasing, property management, and more. The merger, like any large corporate restructuring in the country, was at the urging of the EPF and PNB, which jointly held more than 60 percent of the firm after listing in 2007.[110] But performance was poor, and many observers blamed poor incentives for managerial and political interference. At the merger's outset, management guaranteed no job losses, which meant combining and overlaying management from various corporate infrastructures, and high commodity prices for palm oil made the plantation businesses profitable with few constraints for the other, less profitable, sections of the business, such as trading.

Government and shareholders aspired for Sime to become the "GE of Malaysia" and to have a "hand in every industry in the country," but quick moves into new sectors, such as energy services, resulted in losses. Moreover, government-to-government relations between Malaysia and other countries pushed international expansion activities, many of which were also loss-making. By the mid-2010s, poor corporate performance allowed the new leadership to push for a de-merger in concert with the PNB, and in 2017

---

[109] Interview, Kuala Lumpur, September 2018.
[110] Shareholding data calculated via data from Appendix B. Interview, Boston, September 2017.

the company would split into three separate firms—in plantations, property, and trading. Disconnecting the property and trading businesses from the lucrative palm plantations was meant to inject some discipline into the loss-making parts of the business, but there was some concern that access to government capital would inhibit a "culture of accountability": "There is this idea that 'Big Brother is taking care of me' and no one will stick it to a department that does poorly, and there is no good and accountable performance."[111]

The relationship between GLIC shareholding and labor was not unique to Sime Darby. Several GLCs complained that unions were powerful because they knew that firm leadership could not take strategic corporate decisions without the approval of GLIC shareholders, amplifying political concerns over business concerns.[112] Profit-oriented measures met with resistance from political imperatives manifest in labor concerns, subsidies for commodities such as gas or food, or government desires to pivot investments in specific areas or sectoral directions. The blurring of political and business goals inhibited focus, direction, and innovation, even to the frustration of some of the managers of the GLICs:

> I am not sure we know what we really want. There is a list of things that we want, and we don't know how to prioritize objectives. Do we want to escape the middle-income trap? Redistribute based only on race? Make money? Or undertake national strategic investments? If they want some of these things, they have to be willing to take it in the chin.[113]

It is impossible to ascertain whether corporate sluggishness in Malaysia is primarily the result of government influence or the result of a lack of management dynamism, but we see how the two are related. Corporate executives seem to blame the lack of dynamism on political demands, and politicians point to corporate ineptitude or demands for accommodation as reasons that policy changes do not succeed. What is quite clear is that the financial nexus between the regime and the country's corporate sector has muddied the objectives of each, yet they are inexorably bound together. The BN has enjoyed mutual alignment with the country's business elites, but this

---

[111] Interview, Boston, September 2017.

[112] At least two commercial banks with large GLIC holdings expressed reluctance to automate telling and business services because of a fear of union power based on political concerns of the government. Interviews, Kuala Lumpur, October 2018.

[113] Interview, high-ranking GLIC official, Kuala Lumpur, October 3, 2018.

Table 4.6 Election Results, 2008–2018

Year	Percentage of Seats Won (222 total)		Popular Vote	
	Barisan Nasional	Pakatan	Barisan Nasional	Pakatan
2008	(140) 63.1%	(82) 36.9%	51.1%	47.2%
2013	(133) 59.9%	(89) 40.0%	50.9%	47.4%
2018	(79) 35.6%	(113) 50.9%	33.8%	45.8%

Source: Compiled from Meredith L. Weiss, "Malaysia's 13th General Elections: Same Result, Different Outcome," *Asian Survey* 53, no. 6 (2013): 1135–58 and Ying Hooi Khoo, "Malaysia's 13th General Elections and the Rise of Electoral Reform Movement," *Asian Politics & Policy* 8, no. 3 (2016): 418–35, https://doi.org/10.1111/aspp.12273.

has occurred at the cost of economic dynamism and corporate risk-taking and performance, thus leaving the country with a political economy stuck between the particularistic needs of firms and the political imperatives of the regime. These stagnant economic issues would be laid bare in the explosive political dynamics of the Najib era.

Business and the Decline of UMNO Hegemony

We have been saved from corruption on the level of Zimbabwe.
—Malaysian CEO[114]

The post-AFC period ushered in political challenges in the electoral arena, which saw steady gains among parties that challenged the UMNO's political hegemony. Mahathir's conflict with Anwar resulted in the creation of the National Justice Party and demands for political reform (*reformasi*), which attracted defectors from the BN coalition and generated worsening results for the regime in every election after 2004.[115] Anxiety among UMNO leaders about the coalition's fate would find a combustible combination in its post-2008 leader, Najib Razak. Razak's personal background led him to meet UMNO's challenges by mobilizing financial resources to pay for election

[114] Interview, Port Klang, October 2, 2018.
[115] Weiss, *Protest and Possibilities*. See also Lynette H. Ong, *The Street and the Ballot Box: Interactions between Social Movements and Electoral Politics in Authoritarian Contexts* (New York: Cambridge University Press, 2022).

campaigns and the handouts they entailed. Ironically, the state's extension into corporate governance and emphasis on professionalism led to agents of the regime appearing on corporate boards everywhere (see Figure 4.5), but UMNO was nonetheless unable to tap into business resources for electoral funding. Najib would famously turn to another means of financing his politics in the formation of 1 Malaysia Development Berhad (1MDB), a new sovereign wealth vehicle that would become one of the largest financial frauds and corruption scandals in history, and in inviting Chinese investment in Malaysia as a flow of funds beyond the scrutiny of party and business elites. The state had substantial control over the financial sector, so much so that its own political elites could not manipulate it for narrow political purposes, and most business elites were unwilling to engage in the fraud and malfeasance for which Najib would eventually lose office.

Najib Razak became prime minister after the UMNO's victory but relatively poor showing in 2008, at that time the worst showing in BN history (see Table 4.6). Anwar Ibrahim's People's Justice Party had joined forces with the DAP and the Islamic Party of Malaysia to form an opposition coalition (Pakatan Rakyat, or the People's Pact). Anwar's coalition performed well in the 2008 elections, ending the BN's two-thirds majority in parliament for the first time since independence. The poor showing for the UMNO triggered the resignation of Badawi and the rise of Najib, a seasoned politician and the son of Abdul Razak Hussein, the second prime minister of Malaysia and the architect of the NEP. Razak's uncle, Hussein Onn, had been the third prime minister.

Najib seemed to begin as a reformer, promising to ease media control and implement pro-market reforms. His New Economic Model aimed to curtail NEP-type quotas, privatize GLCs, and shift the economy to higher-value goods and services.[116] This policy direction had both political and economic logics. Politically, it was a response to long-simmering frustrations with what was perceived as cronyism and corruption in the country. The BN's declining electoral advantages were mirrored by the ascendant *reformasi* movement that transcended the country's many social cleavages.[117] Economically, the Malaysian economy seemed stuck and the government feared a "middle-income trap." The Tenth Malaysia FYP in 2010 blamed "slowing momentum of growth" on "lackluster performance of private investments, which has

---

[116] Gomez, "Malaysian Business Groups," 58–63.
[117] Weiss, *Protest and Possibilities*.

fallen from an average of close to 25 percent of GDP through the 1990s to an average of about 10 percent of GDP" over the 2000s.[118]

Yet UMNO's apparent political weakness would cause Najib's reform program to sputter and stall. Party insiders resisted the prospect of reduced access to rents, and declining Malay loyalty led Najib and others to believe that disbursing patronage was critical to the party's survival.[119] Although Najib clung to the public image of reform, the state would tighten its economic grip through expanded control over the GLICs and GLCs, as evidenced in Figure 4.3.[120] After the 2013 elections, the worst in UMNO's history, Najib launched the Bumiputera Economic Empowerment program, committing to furthering affirmative action but with an emphasis on merit and market mechanisms.

All the while, Najib was searching for ways to fund the increasingly competitive and expensive elections. Malaysian election laws prohibited individual candidates from spending more than $47,000 during election periods, but parties were not subject to limits. The UMNO had long become a party of local businessmen, and election spending involved direct disbursements to "UMNO warlords" and vote-buying, especially in rural Malay areas.[121] Unlike in the 1980s and 1990s, UMNO could no longer rely on firms, even those the state funded, to generate the increasing amounts it took to compete in elections. One associate of a GLIC remarked in 2018: "1MDB was founded partly because we [and other GLICs] are too clean to do the sort of financial alchemy Najib and others wanted."[122] The blurred political and corporate imperatives pushed the GLICs and GLCs to pursue profits and strategic investments, but increased transparency in the corporate sector and shareholder demands for returns left little room for the sort of "political business"

---

[118] Economic Planning Unit, "Tenth Malaysia 10th MP," 4.

[119] Indeed, they might have been right. The BN's electoral machinery had long relied on patronage and dispersal of material goods to attract votes. Edward Aspinall, Meredith L. Weiss, Allen Hicken, and Paul D. Hutchcroft, *Mobilizing for Elections: Patronage and Political Machines in Southeast Asia* (New York: Cambridge University Press, 2022).

[120] Gomez, "Malaysian Business Groups," 59–60. Gomez also states that Najib's personal popularity improved (with job approval ratings going from 30 percent to 70 percent) with the announcement of the reforms, but the party's own apparatus constrained these programs.

[121] Poh Ping Lee, "Malaysia in 2015: A Denouement of Sorts for the Prime Minister," *Asian Survey* 56, no. 1 (2016): 101–7; William Case, "Stress Testing Leadership in Malaysia: The 1MDB Scandal and Najib Tun Razak," *Pacific Review* 30, no. 5 (2017): 633–54; Noree Siddiquee and Habib Zafarullah, "Absolute Power, Absolute Venality: The Politics of Corruption and Anti-corruption in Malaysia," *Public Integrity* 24, no. 1 (2022): 1–17.

[122] Interview, Kuala Lumpur, October 2018. See also Tom Wright, *Billion Dollar Whale: The Man Who Fooled Wall Street, Hollywood, and the World* (New York: Hachette, 2018), 38–41.

of funding elections via corporate shakedowns like those of the 1980s and 1990s.

1MDB would not be the only source of financial alchemy for Najib. His sense of electoral threat coincided with China's push for global connectivity in the form of the Belt and Road Initiative, which in 2013 was declared to be a campaign to impose political order on the already-underway efforts of Chinese firms to invest and compete abroad.[123] Chinese firms eager to undertake infrastructure projects in Malaysia would provide another source of opaque capital for UMNO's electoral efforts and, like 1MBD, they would be a source of dazzling corruption and creative accounting to which Malaysian citizens would come to object. Two signature projects are the East Coast Rail Link (ECRL) and Johor's Forest City, a large integrated development project across the Strait from Singapore. Both projects drew substantial public criticism, either because of the price of government contracts (ECRL), because of fears of upsetting Malaysia's delicate ethnic balance by selling real estate to buyers from Mainland China (Forest City), or because they generated fear of creeping Chinese power over the country.[124] Upon his election in 2018, Mahathir halted Chinese projects, especially those funded through debt and pending investigations, promised more details on the structure of the contracts and nature of the firms' relationships with Najib.[125] It is widely believed that, in the case of the ECRL, the ballooning of the project's costs had more to do with how much Najib and UMNO wanted for their election "war chest" than with any changing estimates of the costs themselves. The project was initially estimated at a RM27 billion cost by an independent feasibility study, but the contract with China was for a RM80 billion project, financed primarily by loans from the Export-Import Bank of China; even those close to the government were horrified by the inflation of the prices by which "sovereign debt that is the burden of Malaysian families was transmogrified into UMNO campaign funds with no accountability or public reckoning."[126]

---

[123] Generally, see Min Ye, *The Belt Road and Beyond: State Mobilized Globalization in China: 1998–2018* (New York: Cambridge University Press, 2020).

[124] Amrita Malhi, "Race, Debt, and Sovereignty: The 'China Factor' in Malaysia's GE14," *Round Table* 107, no. 6 (2018): 717–28.

[125] Guanie Lim, Chen Li, and Emirza Adi Syailendra, "Why Is It So Hard to Push Chinese Railway Projects in Southeast Asia? The Role of Domestic Politics in Malaysia and Indonesia," *World Development* 138 (2021): 105–272.

[126] Interview, finance official, Kuala Lumpur, September 2018. See also Hong Liu and Guanie Lim, "The Political Economy of a Rising China in Southeast Asia: Malaysia's Response to the Belt and Road Initiative," *Journal of Contemporary China* 28, no. 116 (2019): 216–31.

The attempt by the Malaysian corporate sector to professionalize and streamline in the 2010s led it to invest outside the country and to become more beholden to investors' bottom lines. Mutual alignment tied major firms to the regime's programmatic goals (redistribution, strategic investments) but removed business as a source of largesse for UMNO funds. Corporate leaders, before and after the 2018 election, prided themselves on becoming internationally competitive and "objective," or apolitical. One senior executive commented: "Yes, we still have political board members appointed by whoever, but we try to work around them. They don't understand the business and have no operational experience. We also don't rely on them for finance or contracts. It is about keeping the government out and staying objective."[127]

The fall of Najib was narrow and contingent; Najib nearly retained power despite the record of corruption. Business elites seemed, at least before the political turmoil that began in 2020, to welcome a new era embracing what was hoped to be a more "objective" ruling party under Mahathir, as the quotation at the beginning of this section suggests. A major financier summarized: "We will tolerate some corruption, but this was crossing a line and made us all look bad," and he explained that deals fell through with global partners who could not distinguish between the GLICs and 1MDB.[128] Mahathir's return to power heralded for many business leaders a restoration of trust between business and political elites. Even in the depths of the corruption and political crises of 2015–18, the looting remained confined to Jho Low and the state finance vehicle he created with Najib; firms, both those majority owned by the state and those with only minority state investment, retained longer time horizons and expectations that mutual alignment would hold.

Conclusion: The Costs of Discipline

> If no impediment at all is placed in the way of total Chinese domination of the economy of Malaysia, the country would certainly be prosperous. The Malay dilemma is whether they should stop trying to help themselves in order that they should be proud to be poor citizens of a prosperous country or whether they should try to get at

---

[127] Interview, division head of a large conglomerate, Kuala Lumpur, November 2016.
[128] Interview, Kuala Lumpur, October 3, 2018.

some of the riches that this country boasts of, even if it blurs the economic picture of Malaysia a little.

—Mahathir, "The Malay Economic Dilemma"[129]

Not unreasonably, most analyses of state intervention in the economy, especially those by economists and international financial institutions, focus on
the effects of those interventions on economic growth, competitiveness, and
human development. As the above quotation from Mahathir makes abundantly clear, political elites design state intervention with different goals in
mind, goals that often supersede that of economic growth. Throughout its
tenure, the BN danced between its ultimate goal of monopolizing political
power, which it viewed as dependent on a project of redistribution, and its
desire for economic growth and especially private investment. When the
state dominated the economy and exerted high levels of financial discipline,
economic stagnation eventually generated desires for liberalization. The next
chapters detail a similar dynamic in China whereby the state accommodated
private-sector actors to induce them to invest and innovate.

These dynamics are not especially surprising in light of thinking about
the "structural power" of business, by which business exerts implicit control over political elites who depend on their economic investment. But we
see during Malaysia's period of competitive clientelism how liberalization
and economic dynamism can nonetheless produce problematic politics for
regimes. Although business did not defect from the "elite cohesion" and
"protection pacts" that had structured Malaysian politics for decades (unlike their Indonesian neighbors), a lack of financial discipline did produce
waste, debt, and overinvestment that contributed to the onset of a financial crisis. This activity points to a form of power that business elites exercise over political elites beyond either structural or instrumental (lobbying)
power: the power to generate crisis and instability through reckless economic behavior.

In this book's conclusion, I return to this idea of "disruptive power." What
is interesting in the Malaysian case is that it is the only case in this study in
which political and business elites enjoyed trust and reciprocity and business elites were political insiders. And yet it is also the one in which business
elites showed the least power to shape regime policies and to gain independence from the state. The state's largesse, mostly in terms of distributing

---

[129] Mahathir, "The Malay Economic Dilemma," 83.

financial resources but also in terms of contracts and other resources, produced capitalists nurtured by the regime but also subject to the regime's ideas about how they ought to run their businesses. Malay capitalists owe their status to the state, if not to individual political elites, and so we may expect that these developmental and democratic paradoxes manifest in their case, but we also see Chinese Malaysian capitalists who have acceded to the regime's often punitive demands. I argue this adherence is a product of a legacy of communal violence that bound business and political elites together in lasting relationships of cooperation and trust. Chinese Malaysian elites ultimately accepted Mahathir's view of what a stable Malaysia required and ensured their own existential survival, even if it meant "betraying" their coethnics who occupied less fortunate territory in the socioeconomic pyramid.[130]

---

[130] The phrase "betray our brothers" was twice used in interviews with elite Chinese families.

5

China's Capitalists under Reform

The Life and Death of Mutual Alignment

Capitalism emerged in China in the ashes of the country's experience with state socialism. It is the consensus of a generation of research on just exactly how markets took hold in the People's Republic of China (PRC) that they did so from below. In the countryside, agricultural markets and household contract farming emerged, or re-emerged, in areas hardest hit by the famine that resulted from Mao's disastrous Great Leap Forward. To be sure, peasants did not act alone. Local leaders, from village-level cadres to provincial governors and party secretaries, supported grassroots decollectivization with actions ranging from benign neglect to shielding local practices to forming alliances with grassroots constituencies to pursue capitalist activities.[1] In urban and rural areas alike, local officials practiced a calculated forbearance, facilitating a kind of "institutional camouflage" by which the private sector found financial support and political tolerance well before formal institutions sanctioned its existence.[2]

These grassroots alliances—whether they are called "adaptive informal institutions," "special deals," or "profit sharing"—between emerging capitalists and the lowest levels of the party-state provide the answer to the puzzle of how China experienced capitalist growth in the absence of formal property rights protections.[3] The first few decades of China's reform era

---

[1] See Dali L. Yang, *Calamity and Reform in China: State, Rural Society, and Institutional Change since the Great Leap Famine* (Stanford: Stanford University Press, 1996); Qi Zhang and Mingxing Liu, *Revolutionary Legacy, Power Structure, and Grassroots Capitalism under the Red Flag in China* (New York: Cambridge University Press, 2019); David Zweig, *Freeing China's Farmers: Rural Restructuring in the Reform Era* (Armonk, NY: M.E. Sharpe, 1997).

[2] See Yasheng Huang, *Capitalism with Chinese Characteristics: Entrepreneurship and the State* (New York: Cambridge University Press, 2008); Kellee S. Tsai, *Back-Alley Banking: Private Entrepreneurs in China* (Ithaca: Cornell University Press, 2002); Kellee S. Tsai, "Adaptive Informal Institutions and Endogenous Institutional Change in China," *World Politics* 59, no. 1 (2006): 116–41; Meg Rithmire, *Land Bargains and Chinese Capitalism: The Politics of Property Rights under Reform* (New York: Cambridge University Press, 2015).

[3] These terms are from Tsai, "Adaptive Informal Institutions," 116–41; Chong-En Bai, Chang-Tai Hsieh, and Zheng Michael Song, "Special Deals with Chinese Characteristics" (Washington,

Precarious Ties. Meg Rithmire, Oxford University Press. © Oxford University Press 2023.
DOI: 10.1093/oso/9780197697528.003.0005

typify the mutual alignment pattern of state-business relations, in which an authoritarian regime organizes its institutions or informal practices—in this case both—to serve the productive interests of business, that is, to induce capitalists to invest in growth and development.

This chapter explains the rise and partial fall of mutual alignment. In many ways, I tell a story that will feel familiar to scholars of China's reform era: the private sector relied on informal relationships with political elites to solve problems, circumvent formal institutions, and seek security, and the party-state used public finance arrangements, its own internal hierarchy, and institutions that structured promotion to incentivize local officials to pursue growth and investment. In other ways, my focus differs from that of others, principally in asking why apparently cozy relations between state and business were growth-enhancing rather than collusive, wasteful, and corrupt. In short, where did the discipline come from?

The answer, I argue, can be found by examining the party-state's management of the system of capital allocation, meaning the organization of access to finance for both governments (public finance) and firms (banks, equity markets, and corporate finance). As scholars have widely acknowledged, the introduction of the tax-sharing system between central and local governments catalyzed local support for economic activity by entitling local governments to tax revenues generated by firms in their jurisdictions.[4] This organizing principle aligned the interests of officials and the business sector; whether local-government actors sought to maximize their chances for promotion, their access to resources, or their own personal enrichment, the path would be through facilitating business investment and growth. These incentives to generate local growth were coupled with access to resources, including power over local financial institutions, a combination that could—and, in many cases, did—generate substantial misallocation and waste without a source of coordination or discipline. That discipline, ironically, came from the financial system, which discriminated against the private sector, requiring investment to be sourced from retained earnings or from an informal financial sector that operated with a competitive logic.

[4] Jean Chun Oi, *Rural China Takes Off: Institutional Foundations of Economic Reform* (Berkeley: University of California Press, 1999); Susan Whiting, *Power and Wealth in Rural China: The Political Economy of Institutional Change* (New York: Cambridge University Press, 2001).

For the most part, political economy scholarship has viewed financial discrimination against the private sector as a source of arrested growth and misallocation of resources toward a bloated and undisciplined state sector.[5] I do not dispute these accounts. If the financial system had been open to private firms *and* structured to price risk appropriately, it stands to reason that growth would have been even faster and unaccompanied by the massive swelling of underperforming state-owned firms.[6] But, in the absence of macroeconomic financial controls in the form of competitive interest rates and competition among financial firms, discrimination against the private sector generated discipline and incentives for private firms to operate efficiently. Later in the 2000s, when credit access expanded but without accompanying financial liberalization, firms with privileged access to the state financial sector—whether private or state-owned—siphoned resources from that system in the absence of disciplinary restraints.

The second half of the chapter details this breakdown of mutual alignment. I focus on how two changes in the Chinese macroeconomy—the widespread growth of credit and dramatic changes in China's public finance system that led local governments to rely on land development for financial resources—disrupted the productive character of the codependence between business and local governments. Their own interests were still aligned, but the product of their collusion would no longer be mutualistic with society. Instead of working together to generate long-term investments that would produce growth and jobs, firms and local officials took advantage of their access to special resources, especially cheap credit and land, to enrich themselves. The discipline produced by financial constraints was removed at the same time that privatization and the creation of land markets created special access, facilitating widespread parasitic collusion between local governments and local firms and breaking the bonds that bound local governments and firms together in productive efforts. More generally, many firms exploited the partially liberalized financial system in collusion with political elites to engage in looting.

---

[5] For example, Chang-Tai Hsieh and Peter J. Klenow, "Misallocation and Manufacturing TFP in China and India," *Quarterly Journal of Economics* 124, no. 4 (2009): 1403–48, https://doi.org/10.1162/qjec.2009.124.4.1403; Yasheng Huang, *Inflation and Investment Controls in China: The Political Economy of Central-Local Relations during the Reform Era* (New York: Cambridge University Press, 1996); Huang, *Capitalism with Chinese Characteristics*.

[6] On nonperforming loans, see Victor C. Shih, *Factions and Finance in China: Elite Conflict and Inflation* (New York: Cambridge University Press, 2008).

The precariousness of capitalists within China's political system plays a consistent explanatory role across the reform era. Their sense of vulnerability casts a shadow on their interactions, leading them to pursue self-preservation in a variety of ways, including befriending officials and hiding or disguising their activities. The existential threat is manifest in short time horizons; capitalists operate expecting that policy environments can change anytime, and therefore they design business ventures to take advantage of short-term opportunities. When financial discipline constrains their resources, short time horizons produce a hypercompetitive market and frequent entrepreneurial failure as well as constantly morphing corporate forms to capitalize on shifting political safety zones. When financial discipline attenuates, short time horizons manifest in ways more threatening to political and economic stability, including financial fraud and mutually endangering political relationships.

Mutual Alignment: Public Finance and Private Firms

Two puzzles have motivated a generation of researchers on China's political economy, both of which underscore the ways in which the Chinese experience has challenged core tenets of social science. First, how has the CCP managed market-based economic reforms in the context of a Leninist political system, and, second, why have capitalists in China been willing to invest without legal protections for their property or persons? In general, the answer to both questions has been the same: the informal reorganization of the Chinese party-state has served the interests of business, and capitalists have accepted marginal incentives and "directionally liberal" reforms as sufficient guarantees to pursue investment and innovation.[7] Of all the regimes under study in this book, the Chinese Communist Party (CCP) has ironically been the most willing to embrace capitalists of all kinds in the pragmatic pursuit of economic growth while retaining a monopoly on political control. That embrace was fueled by corruption, and it imperfectly approximated institutions requisite for market activities, but it generated enough productive activity to lift hundreds of millions of people out of poverty and industrialize the world's largest country within a generation.[8]

[7] Huang, *Capitalism with Chinese Characteristics*; Justin Yifu Lin, "Rural Reforms and Agricultural Growth in China," *American Economic Review* 82, no. 1 (1992): 34–51.
[8] Ang, *How China Escaped*; Yuen Yuen Ang, *China's Gilded Age: The Paradox of Economic Boom and Vast Corruption* (New York: Cambridge University Press, 2020).

Broadly construed, this narrative is an accurate portrayal of state-business relations in China during the first two decades of the reform era, but it is also incomplete in important ways. First, as Chapter 1 argues, mutual alignment, like all relationships between business and political elites, is timebound. The CCP did not simply informally reorganize to accommodate business interests and thereby permanently ensure their loyalty. Scholars have examined how the CCP worked to maintain the loyalty of business elites over time, for example through corporatist style associations and by soliciting their participation in the formal institutions of the state.[9] Nevertheless, mutual alignment has led to a focus on "co-optation" and "cronyism" that often paints Chinese business elites as far more trustful and supportive of the regime than their behavior reveals them to be. In fact, China's early reform era is a case of mutual alignment with distrust: the CCP, in its own telling, pragmatically appealed to the efforts of private capitalists to generate economic growth, eventually allowing entrepreneurs to join the party itself, but the CCP never adopted formal institutions that would protect private property, leaving China's entrepreneurs in a long-term liminal state. Because of the history I describe in Chapter 2 and the nature of the CCP itself—a preference for campaigns and adaptive capacity over institutional constraints[10]—entrepreneurs in China pursued closeness to the regime out of distrust rather than trust.

Business and political elites can informally collude anywhere, but the result is not necessarily economic growth. In fact, collusion usually produces waste, instability, or stagnation rather than dynamic growth. When it does produce growth, as it has at times in all three countries under study here as well as in places such as Korea, Japan, Taiwan, Thailand, and beyond, there is usually some force imposing discipline on elites such that collusion is mutualistic for society (mutual alignment) rather than simply

[9] Bruce J. Dickson, *Wealth into Power: The Communist Party's Embrace of China's Private Sector* (New York: Cambridge University Press, 2008); Bruce J. Dickson, *Red Capitalists in China: The Party, Private Entrepreneurs, and Prospects for Political Change* (New York: Cambridge University Press, 2003); Scott Kennedy, *The Business of Lobbying in China* (Cambridge, MA: Harvard University Press, 2005); Kellee S. Tsai, *Capitalism without Democracy: The Private Sector in Contemporary China* (Ithaca: Cornell University Press, 2007). Scholars have also emphasized that participation in state institutions, especially in legislatures, is a strategy adopted by business elites to protect their property and to grow their revenues and profits. See Yue Hou, "The Private Sector: Challenges and Opportunities during Xi's Second Term," *China Leadership Monitor*, no. 59 (March 2019), https://prcleader.org/past-issues; Rory Truex, "The Returns to Office in a 'Rubber Stamp' Parliament," *American Political Science Review* 108, no. 2 (2014): 235–51.

[10] Sebastian Heilmann and Elizabeth J. Perry, eds., *Mao's Invisible Hand: The Political Foundations of Adaptive Governance in China* (Cambridge, MA: Harvard University Asia Center, 2011); Sebastian Heilmann, *Red Swan: How Unorthodox Policy-Making Facilitated China's Rise* (Hong Kong: Chinese University Press, 2018).

wasteful and corrupt. Scholars have offered several explanations for discipline in developmental states. Doner, Ritchie, and Slater argue that an external existential threat, such as that which China and North Korea posed for Taiwan and South Korea, motivated elites to collaborate in building prosperity and strength.[11] For those states and also for Japan, the focus on export-oriented growth and "picking winners" based on success in export markets also imposed discipline; firms could only expect to benefit from preferential credit and other state support if they competed effectively in global markets. These external forces of discipline worked through the financial system. Banks were typically centrally and hierarchically controlled, and they dispensed credit according to policy priorities set by those government ministries that coordinated industrialization efforts. Even so, developmental states and quasi-developmental states, especially Japan, South Korea, and Thailand, where growth was fueled by large conglomerate firms, were vulnerable to nonperforming assets in the financial sector, as financial crises and decades of financial stagnation have revealed.[12] Political control in the financial sector can produce discipline and productive growth, but it is difficult to maintain indefinitely, especially as privileged firms and their interests become entrenched and desires for new forms of growth motivate liberalization.

In China, the discipline for both political and business elites came primarily from the structure of the financial system—both the system of public finance (fiscal system) and the system of corporate finance. The incentives generated by both the public and corporate finance systems meant that, among nonstate firms, only productive firms could survive. To be clear, the financial system was not the sole source of discipline: Chinese firms famously integrated themselves into global supply chains, especially in the Pearl River Delta region, and, in this way, global markets also served to ensure that only efficient and productive firms survived. But the fiscal system also presented incentives for political officials to nurture those firms, and the system of corporate finance imposed financial constraints on those firms that ultimately generated efficiency.

[11] Richard F. Doner, Bryan K. Ritchie, and Dan Slater, "Systemic Vulnerability and the Origins of Developmental States: Northeast and Southeast Asia in Comparative Perspective," *International Organization* 59, no. 2 (2005): 327–61.

[12] Henry Laurence, *Money Rules: The New Politics of Finance in Britain and Japan* (Ithaca: Cornell University Press, 2001); T. J. Pempel, *A Region of Regimes: Prosperity and Plunder in the Asia-Pacific* (Ithaca: Cornell University Press, 2021).

Fiscal System

The city of Suzhou in Jiangsu province, a short hour's drive from Shanghai, sits in the middle of the Yangtze River Delta, one of the most economically dynamic and globally connected parts of China. The region has always been a source of ambitious officials, and Suzhou's mayors and party secretaries have often gone on to careers as central-level officials and executives at state-owned enterprises.[13] The city hosts a unique special economic zone: the Singapore-Suzhou Industrial Park (新加坡苏州工业园区, or SIP), which was established in the mid-1990s as an initiative of the Singapore government. As wages had risen substantially in Singapore and much of regional and global manufacturing was poised to move to China, the government wanted to promote Singaporean firms abroad to maintain their competitiveness, and it thus formed the SIP to "replicate Singapore rules and make it easier for Singaporean firms to invest abroad."[14] The SIP would not be the only zone in Suzhou. Firms wanted to take advantage of the tax benefits and other cheap inputs, especially land, that such zones offered, and by the early 2000s, the city, and even lower levels of government, had set up several other zones. By the mid-2000s, ownership of the SIP had been restructured in China's favor, and Suzhou had established itself as a hub of telecommunications, manufacturing, and other high-technology sectors. In 2012, at a presentation for visiting human capital researchers and experts, a high-level city official was asked why the Suzhou government had been so tireless in its efforts to recruit businesses to its jurisdiction. He had a one-word answer: "taxes."[15]

If Suzhou's officials had their eyes trained on Beijing, the same cannot be said for Plum County, a rural county relatively far from the urban powerhouses of the Pearl River Delta in China's South.[16] In the 1970s and early 1980s, Plum County's major economic activities included rice and tuber-crop farming, but villages in the county were beginning to benefit from resumed connections with overseas relatives, many of whom had resettled in Southeast Asia and Taiwan in the first half of the twentieth

---

[13] Ling Chen, *Manipulating Globalization: The Influence of Bureaucrats on Business in China* (Stanford: Stanford University Press, 2018).

[14] Interview, former Singapore government official, Singapore, October 2016.

[15] Presentation by Suzhou city officials, June 2012.

[16] Plum County is a pseudonym for a county (that eventually became an urban district) in Meizhou (梅州), Guangdong province. These insights are based on interviews conducted in Chaoyang and Shenzhen, June and July 2015.

century or earlier.[17] Over the course of the late 1980s and especially the 1990s, Plum County was transformed from an agricultural backwater to an industrialized hinterland. Overseas "relatives," however removed, mobilized connections to invest in the area, both genuine foreign direct investment (FDI) and apparent FDI round-tripped out of and back into China to obtain the tax benefits reserved for foreign investors.[18] Manufacturing, moving to Plum County from Hong Kong and elsewhere to take advantage of low wages, found local officials eager to attract businesses of all kinds, offering to facilitate finding land, recruiting labor, and "solving problems" that included establishing capitalist businesses in a Leninist legal and political environment. Unlike Suzhou, officials from Plum County were mostly locals and they harbored no ambitions of elite political careers. Nonetheless, like their counterparts in Suzhou, they assiduously pursued investment, foreign and local, partnering with entrepreneurs to facilitate round-tripping FDI and to mask private, nonstate firms as "town and village enterprises" (TVEs) as political cover in an era of uncertain legitimacy for capitalist activities. A former county official provided a slightly different answer from that of his counterpart in Suzhou when asked why he and his colleagues were willing to go to such lengths: "Generally, when local firms were successful, we also made money. We all got wealthy together."[19]

Taxes and personal and/or community enrichment seem to be very different motivations for fostering investment and protecting capitalists. Distinguishing between these motivations is important for some tasks, especially in debates about the party's internal management in which scholars have disagreed about the relative importance of factions and meritocracy and about whether Beijing optimizes for economic growth (GDP or output) or revenue (taxes) when it decides who rises within the ranks of

---

[17] The gazetteer for Plum County, which claims hundreds of thousands of overseas Chinese, is devoted to its emigrants and their contributions to their "ancestral home."

[18] Yasheng Huang, *Why Is There So Much Demand for Foreign Equity Capital in China? An Institutional and Policy Perspective* (Cambridge, MA: Weatherhead Center for International Affairs, Harvard University, 1999); Pempel, *A Region of Regimes.*

[19] Interview, former Plum County official, June 2015. My interviews in Plum County point in equal parts to self-enrichment and social esteem as motivations for "doing good for business." Several lineage groups were quite active in the county, and overseas "relatives" were active in sending funds for the renovation of ancestral halls and connecting with Plum County locals in transnational business networks. Lily Tsai finds that village-level officials were more effective at providing public goods when groups such as lineage organizations exercised moral accountability. Similarly, social solidarity seemed to facilitate political and business ties in Plum County and also to make "profit sharing" somewhat easier. Lily L. Tsai, *Accountability without Democracy: Solidary Groups and Public Goods Provision in Rural China* (New York: Cambridge University Press, 2007).

the party-state.[20] But, because of the structure of the fiscal system in the first decade and a half of the reform era, these different motivations produced a surprisingly similar political landscape for firms.

As Jean Oi and others have painstakingly shown, decentralization of fiscal revenues in the early 1980s gave local officials a "direct stake" in economic development.[21] China's fiscal system distinguishes between budgetary (预算内) and extrabudgetary (预算外) revenues. In the 1980s and early 1990s, budgetary revenues included categories of taxes (income and industrial-commercial taxes) that had to be shared with upper levels of government. By contrast, extrabudgetary revenues have historically included local tax and nontax revenue sources that accrue to local governments. Fiscal contracting systems stabilized expectations between different levels of government, and local governments enjoyed property rights over revenues they generated above that which they agreed to share upward, providing effective property rights incentives that turned local governments into effective entrepreneurs. Oi emphasizes that local officials' claim to revenues was both profession-ally and personally motivating; budgets were liberated with extra revenues, and ballooning residuals were distributed as bonuses.[22] Local government-owned firms, especially TVEs, grew under these conditions, but regional var-iation in industrial heritage generated different property rights arrangements in different places.

Scholars have understandably been motivated to explain TVEs, as their collective corporate form seems at odds with dominant accounts of work-able property rights institutions, but growth during the first decades of re-form was not all in TVEs. In rural areas without significant foundations of rural industry and public enterprises, local governments were likewise motivated to pursue economic growth, but they were more supportive of private enterprises.[23] In Zhejiang, as recent scholarship endeavors to show,

[20] Xiaobo Lü and Pierre F. Landry, "Show Me the Money: Interjurisdiction Political Competition and Fiscal Extraction in China," *American Political Science Review* 108, no. 3 (2014): 706–22; Victor Shih, Christopher Adolph, and Mingxing Liu, "Getting Ahead in the Communist Party: Explaining the Advancement of Central Committee Members in China," *American Political Science Review* 106, no. 1 (2012): 166–87; Pierre F. Landry, *Decentralized Authoritarianism in China: The Communist Party's Control of Local Elites in the Post-Mao Era* (New York: Cambridge University Press, 2008).

[21] Oi, *Rural China Takes Off*, 49.

[22] Ibid., especially chapter 2, pp. 38–49. See also Yi-min Lin, *Dancing with the Devil: The Political Economy of Privatization in China* (New York: Oxford University Press, 2017).

[23] Susan Whiting, *Power and Wealth*, shows that this was the case in places like Wenzhou, the fa-mously entrepreneurial city in Zhejiang, the province that led China in growth of the private sector. Rural industrial endowments came in the form of Commune and Brigade Enterprises, which devel-oped during the 1960s and 1970s. See also Zhang and Liu, *Revolutionary Legacy*, 196–203.

local officials were not desirous of promotion but rather relied on local bases of support, and they protected the private sector both before and after the onset of reforms.[24] And, while much is reasonably made about the TVE phenomenon, we now know that many "public" or "collective" firms were really private firms "wearing the red hat" for political protection, a phenomenon I discuss below.[25] Whether they supported local growth for political support, personal wealth, or professional development reasons and whether they accommodated private property forms or advanced market-oriented collective forms, fiscal arrangements meant that local officials benefited from the economic activity in their jurisdictions. In short, the fiscal system was a key node aligning interests between capitalists and the state at the local levels.

Fundamentally, China's public finance system ensured that local officials and local business communities were poised to do well together. Growing the local tax base required creating conditions that would allow local businesses to succeed, and officials themselves could get wealthy through bribes, kickbacks, and direct and indirect business stakes if the local environment was sufficiently dynamic. Yuen Yuen Ang presents these local officials' efforts at personal enrichment as a beneficial sort of corruption: access money that businesses paid to grease the wheels of commerce that act as a sort of "steroid" for economic growth.[26] Whether they are motivated by personal enrichment, ambition for promotion, a desire to improve their communities, or some combination thereof, local officials have had incentives and opportunities to collude extensively with business. Collusion, however, does not always produce economic growth. Access money, as Ang argues, can facilitate the right kinds of investment for productivity, but, in most places and at most times, it does not. Mutual alignment—which is mutualistic for society—obtains when political and business elites collude but are also constrained by disciplinary forces that push special resources toward productive, rather than just connected, firms. That discipline is provided by the financial system.

Financial System

I have argued that authoritarian regimes in pursuit of at least some market growth face a choice in how they manage the financial system: lax political

---

[24] Zhang and Liu, *Revolutionary Legacy*.
[25] Huang, *Capitalism with Chinese Characteristics*.
[26] Ang, *China's Gilded Age*.

control may facilitate the rise of economic elites beyond the regime's control, but political micromanagement of the financial sector may lead to capital misallocation and financial instability. During the early decades of market reforms in China, the CCP definitively chose the latter: politicized control over the financial sector, generally reserving credit access as the exclusive privilege of state firms and deliberately denying private businesses formal access to financial resources. Further, the financial system was built upon the party-state's organizational system, facilitating primarily political (rather than market) discipline and imperatives. The financial system's preference for state-owned enterprises (SOEs) contributed substantially to capital misallocation, arresting growth and constraining productivity.[27] The lack of financial support was but one of many obstacles that would frustrate, but not overwhelm, Chinese entrepreneurs during the early years of reforms. Their exclusion from the financial system lent discipline to the alignment of interests between the state and private-sector business in the early decades of reform.

Building a Financial System under Socialism with Market Characteristics

Like policymakers in early New Order Indonesia, China's reformists had to wrestle with how to generate capital for investment in the context of a state-dominated financial sector. In China's case, the financial system had played on the role of "cashier and accountancy" in the state socialist period, having had almost no hand in capital allocation, which was the purview of planners.[28] Reformers and technocrats in both countries were fearful of the macroeconomic instability inherent in a liberalized financial sector, and they initially pursued financial reforms that would leave political elites in control of credit allocation, primarily through interest-rate controls and credit quotas, and, of course, a state-owned financial system.

In the early years of reform and opening in Deng's China, debates surrounded the role of the financial sector in market reforms. In particular, different views emerged about how investment, especially public investment, should be funded: through fiscal or financial means (大财政, 小银行 versus 小财政, 大银行, literally "big finance, small bank" or "small

---

[27] Hsieh and Klenow, "Misallocation and Manufacturing TFP."

[28] Guofeng Sun, "Banking Institutions and Banking Regulations," in Marlene Amstad, Guofeng Sun, and Wei Xiong, eds., *The Handbook of China's Financial System* (Princeton, NJ: Princeton University Press, 2020), 9. See also 易纲 (Yi Gang), 中国金融改革思考录 (Thoughts on China's Financial Reform) (北京: 商务印书馆, 2019).

finance, big bank"). The question of using savings deposits, with banks as intermediaries, to fund public investment was thorny: Liu Hongrui, one of the architects of the early financial sector, recalls that savings deposits were imagined as a "caged tiger," and releasing them for fixed asset investment lending was considered dangerous at the time.[29] The question of extending credit to public enterprises was also thorny, and therefore private enterprises, which were beyond the political control of the party-state, were certain to be excluded from the formal banking system. This exclusion, as Liu's recollections highlight, was born as much from concern about the instabilities inherent in an expansive financial system as from an ideological bias against the private sector.

Financial Exclusion and Market Discipline

The private sector, then, turned to a range of informal options for financing growth, all of which provided disciplinary constraints and rewarded productive businesses. The sources of startup capital for nonstate firms in the 1980s and 1990s were limited and almost all were informal, a story told in Tables 5.1 and 5.2, based on data collected from surveys of private entrepreneurs over several decades.[30] As Table 5.1 shows, the top three sources of startup capital for business owners surveyed in 1988 were accumulated savings, loans from relatives and friends, and partner capital; only 5.5 percent of entrepreneurs listed "bank loans" as a principal source of initial capital, and only one-fifth of those surveyed relied on formal financial loans at all for startup capital. Table 5.2 shows that these trends persisted into the 1990s: retained earnings were the primary source of all kinds of capital for nonstate firms. Well into the mid-1990s, private firms relied on retained earnings to finance expansion and activities. In 1994, respondents indicated that 69 percent of profits were reinvested in production. The next greatest allocation for those profits was dividends to owners (7.7 percent) and "social engagements" (应酬) (5.5 percent), which can be read as leisure activities that likely involved both

[29] 刘鸿儒 (Liu Hongru), "回顾我国金融体制改革的历程" (Reviewing the History China's Financial System Reform), 百年潮, no. 5 (2009): 22–28.
    Liu Hongru played a role in the founding of the Agricultural Bank and served as deputy governor of the People's Bank of China (PBoC) in charge of financial system reform.
[30] The National Private Enterprise Sample Survey (中国私营企业抽样调查), commissioned as a joint project of the United Front Work Department, the All-China Federation of Commerce and Industry, and the Chinese Academy of Social Sciences, has been conducted roughly every other year since 1989.

Table 5.1 Sources of Startup Capital, 1988

	Principal Source	Secondary Source	Tertiary Source	Subtotal
Accumulated savings	45.3	16.6	6.5	68.4
Loans from relatives and friends	16.2	22.3	10.8	49.3
Partner capital	12.1	11.0	4.6	27.7
Bank loans	5.5	8.3	6.5	20.3
Credit cooperative	5.2	5.5	5.0	15.7
Personal borrowings	1.4	3.4	7.7	12.5
Inheritance	7.8	1.8	2.1	11.7
FDI	3.0	1.7	1.1	5.8
Collective loan	1.0	1.6	1.7	4.3
Other	1.0	0.8	0.8	2.6
No answer	1.6	27.0	53.2	

Source: "First National Survey of Private Enterprises" (conducted in April 1988), *China Private Economy Yearbook 1994* (中国私营经济年鉴1994) (Beijing: 中华工商联合出版社, 1994).

Table 5.2 Sources of Capital for Private Firms, 1992

	Founding Capital	Fixed-Asset Investment	Operating Capital
Retained earnings	55.9	66.6	68.3
Borrowings from friends and family	14.8	15.9	24.2
Bank, credit, and cooperative borrowings	18.2	16.4	38.5
Private savings	7.8	8.6	18.6
Other	1.4	1.3	2.1

Source: See Table 5.1.

employees and local officials, and were precisely the sort of things that mutual alignment and "profit sharing" entails.[31]

The reliance on retained earnings and informal finance, at least for what Yi-min Lin helpfully calls "genetic private enterprises" (as opposed to firms formed through privatization of state firms), imbued the system of corporate

---

[31] *China Private Economy Yearbook 1994* (中国私营经济年鉴1994) (Beijing: 中华工商联合出版社, 1994), 152.

finance with a kind of discipline.[32] In her study of variation in rural credit and rural industrialization in the first two decades of reform, Lynnette Ong finds that rural areas in which private enterprises led industrialization and faced financial constraints were able to prosper: "Private entrepreneurs were forced to use financial resources efficiently or risk going out of business and losing their life's savings."[33] Dependence on retained earnings for investment generated a hard budget constraint that compelled entrepreneurs to compete and generate revenue quickly in order to survive. Survey evidence confirms that capital constraints were indeed the cause of the demise of many firms: in the 1978–93 Survey of Entrepreneurs, the principal reason for business stoppage (39.6 percent) was capital shortages.[34] Similarly, 31.8 percent of respondents indicated that credit policy was the macroeconomic institution that most affected management; tax policy ranked third among 18.8 percent of respondents (after overall macroeconomic management).[35] Financial discrimination against private firms continued through the end of the 1990s, as firms reported in surveys that retained earnings remained their primary source of both liquid and investment capital, and credit requirements and guarantees were too strict for them to borrow from banks.[36]

To compete quickly in the 1980s and 1990s China required creativity and adaptation in both an uncertain and a constantly changing domestic market and, in some cases, insertion into unforgiving global and regional supply chains. Domestically, the market in early reform China famously grew "outside the plan"—a space for action independent of the state sector where firms met social needs with little regulation by government officials.[37] Space for independent action, again, did not mean security. On the contrary, ambiguity and uncertainty pervaded the status of the nonstate economy during the early reforms and shaped the worldviews and behaviors of China's early capitalists.[38] Early capitalists were quick to find a niche in local markets, and they pursued whatever business chances they could. Margins were tight and

---

[32] Lin, *Dancing with the Devil.*

[33] Lynnette H. Ong, *Prosper or Perish: Credit and Fiscal Systems in Rural China* (Ithaca: Cornell University Press, 2012), 13.

[34] 1978–1993 Survey of Entrepreneurs, *China Private Economy Yearbook 1994,* 142. The second largest category was "other" (28.7 percent), followed by "policy limits" (20.1 percent).

[35] Ibid., 164.

[36] *China Private Economy Yearbook 2001* (中国私营经济年鉴2001) (Beijing: 中华工商联合出版社, 2001), 357.

[37] Barry Naughton, "Chinese Institutional Innovation and Privatization from Below," *American Economic Review* 84, no. 2 (1994): 266–70.

[38] Dan Breznitz and Michael Murphree, *Run of the Red Queen: Government, Innovation, Globalization, and Economic Growth in China* (New Haven: Yale University Press, 2011), 12. I elaborate on "structured uncertainty" below.

time horizons relatively short, both because of financial pressures and because of chronic uncertainty.[39]

The experiences of entrepreneurs in both Suzhou and Plum County illustrate the role that extreme competition amid uncertainty and financial pressures played in shaping business practices. While Suzhou's institutionally unique zones appeared in the 1990s and favored foreign firms (because they could bring technological and managerial know-how), Suzhou's local genetic private capitalists were making markets in the absence of institutional help as early as the late 1970s. Suzhou entered the reform era with a firm foundation in rural industrialization, which helped launched the TVEs in the 1980s, but Suzhou was also home to a light industry base, especially in textiles, because of the region's famed silk production. Light industry eclipsed heavy industry at the outset of reforms; the 1985 ratio was 66:34, and by 1995 it had changed only marginally (62:38).[40] The 1980s saw the blossoming of both private (民营) firms and TVEs, as the industrial sector saw attrition and high levels of competition.

The city's textile firms had been nationalized in the 1950s, which included the merging of scores of private firms to form flagship brands and state factories. As state firms focused on revamping notable textile brands, smaller private firms and rural TVEs sought small niches in supply chains for different sectors, especially electronics. Entrepreneurs in the electronics sectors had little access to domestic banks. They self-financed or sought investors from Taiwan, where electronics manufacturers were increasingly turning to Suzhou for parts manufacturing and assembly. One entrepreneur connected with a Taiwanese contact to assemble cassette players as early as 1985. He secured some investment from the Taiwanese contact, the bulk of initial capital from family and friends, and partnered with a contact in the local government to register the firm (as a TVE, see "Shapeshifting" below) and to acquire the necessary workspace and permits. He remarked, "I could only take money from my friends and family because I had secured the distribution channel with [the Taiwanese contact]. Otherwise, it would have been too risky to establish such a business. We quickly found buyers within the

---

[39] Naughton, "Chinese Institutional Innovation," argues that product markets were established before property rights were established, contributing to innovation and experimentation on the part of local governments and business actors in accessing markets without markets for production factors and assets. TVEs, in Naughton's view, were part of the solution.

[40] *Suzhou Municipal Gazetteer: 1986–2005* (苏州市志: 1986–2005) (Nanjing: Jiangsu fenghuang kexue jishu chubanshe, 2014), 557.

province and expanded, but securing the initial market access was required for getting capital."[41]

In Plum County, emergent entrepreneurs relied on links with transnational supply chains and sources of finance at the outset of market reforms. Overseas networks facilitated connections with investors and business communities in Hong Kong, Taiwan, and farther afield in Southeast Asia. The local government courted diaspora communities as investors, based on the slogan, "To have a hometown is to invest in it, to have a family is to invest in it" (有家投家，有亲投亲). While two thousand individuals had "returned" from Malaysia, Indonesia, or Vietnam between 1950 and 1960, each county surrounding Plum County boasted ten thousand or more people who returned between 1979 and 1990.[42] Initially, local factories were established that relied on labor arbitrage—relatively lower wages in Guangdong province than in neighboring Hong Kong—for low value-added industries such as textiles and toys. One of the largest employers in one township in Plum County was actually a medium-sized facility for packaging textiles; clothing was manufactured in Hong Kong, but it was cheaper to ship it across the border to Guangdong for packaging and then re-export.[43]

As theoretical expectations about product cycles would predict, the region upgraded as it industrialized, first gaining the ability to manufacture low value-added goods and, eventually, to specialize in high value-added and even precision manufacturing. Entrepreneurs recall the early days of thin margins and low value-added activities as hypercompetitive. Small shops would pop up seemingly overnight, "like spring shoots after a rain"; if they did not insert themselves into supply chains by providing just-in-time delivery for orders that had to be scaled up or scaled down rapidly, they would disappear just as quickly. In accounts of private-market participants, officials solved many problems related to regulation and labor, but they offered few resources beyond official permits and political cover.[44]

Several prominent businesspeople were involved in many firms and sectors. One furniture upholsterer diversified into shoe manufacturing and eventually automotive interiors, but he cited at least five failed ventures along the way. In the case of the shoe market, the proprietor's first two ventures

[41] Interview, Suzhou, 2012.
[42] *Meizhou City Gazetteer* (1979–2000) (梅州市志) (Beijing: Fangzhi chubanshe, 2011), 1804–5.
[43] Interview, Hong Kong, June 2015.
[44] These insights are from a roundtable interview with members of an ethnic business association based in Plum County; interview, Shenzhen, June 2015.

were failures. After the second venture, he teamed up as an investor with a rival and poached several workers from yet another rival. The new firm gambled by bidding on a large project, and within a week it hired workers and organized production. It was able to meet the order and generate revenue quickly, or otherwise it would have failed just as rapidly.[45]

The hypercompetition, evident in many accounts of early reform-era industrialization, is evidence of discipline in the Chinese private and semiprivate sectors. Firms had to immediately prove themselves efficient because of hard budget constraints and constraints of transnational supply chains. A great deal of scholarship and popular commentary on China's private sector extols the creativity and clever ruthlessness of Chinese upstarts. Officials in Plum County, as I detail above, were effective at nurturing business in their jurisdictions, but, although they had incentives to privilege efficient firms whose success would further their own, they could not provide financial resources. As one former official recalled: "In the 1980s, we were learning which business owners were capable and which ones were not. We could only help solve problems, but they [the business owners] had to earn revenues on their own. We were lucky that buyers in Hong Kong could differentiate good and bad products, good and bad factories."[46]

Market orientations, regional connections, and leadership orientations differed profoundly between Suzhou and Plum County, as they did all over China. Yet in both places, and indeed across large swaths of China, the private sector blossomed and communities grew more prosperous. China experienced growth and prosperity, rather than crippling corruption and predation, because a combination of fiscal and financial discipline both aligned interests between business and local officials and disciplined their collaborations such that investments benefited society.

Of Bureaucrats and Business

The focus on financial discipline adds an important piece to the puzzles about China's growth, and one that dominant scholarly paradigms have ignored. Explanations of China's economic success, despite formal institutions that would seem to inhibit market growth, tend to emphasize bureaucratic

---

[45] Interview, Shenzhen, June 2015.
[46] Interview, Chaoyang, 2015.

incentives and the critical role of experimentation as the CCP's "work style." These explanations focus on the structure and style of the state, but they do not account for how and why business actors responded. Aligning the interests of business and bureaucrats was essential for igniting investment and growth, but ensuring that growth was productive required discipline. In short, political economy scholarship on China has overemphasized the role of incentives for state actors, but it has underappreciated the incentives, constraints, and worldviews of business actors.

A great deal of scholarship has looked to the Chinese party-state personnel management system as the primary explanation for how the CCP has been able to generate economic growth in the context of sclerotic Leninist institutions. The basic argument is that the CCP, a "decentralized authoritarian regime," built a meritocratic system for promotions within the party-state and "got the incentives right" for the rank and file by structuring contracts around the local officials' ability to deliver economic growth. The cadre responsibility system designated performance criteria for officials at all levels of the state and assigned special importance to outcomes related to economic growth, whether GDP growth in a particular locality or revenue collection.[47] Only officials who delivered on these growth-oriented mandates could earn promotions within the party-state and, especially for lower-level officials, could earn year-end bonuses.

Without a doubt, these institutionalized incentives have been incredibly important in generating economic growth in China. But recent scholarship—and the story of the rise and fall of mutual alignment as told in this book—shows that the focus on institutional incentives, while intellectually appealing, especially within neoinstitutionalist political economy, does not tell a complete story for a number of reasons. First, the vast majority of the Chinese bureaucracy comprises officials who do not have reasonable expectations for promotion, which is why the large body of scholarship that focuses on promotion and tenure patterns focuses only on the top 1 percent of political elites, usually municipal and provincial party secretaries and mayors or governors. The rest of the bureaucracy, and the local-level officials with whom most market participants and capitalists interact, are better described as "quasi-stationary vice leaders" or "stationary street-level bureaucrats."[48]

[47] Lü and Landry, "Show Me the Money"; Landry, *Decentralized Authoritarianism in China*.
[48] Ang, *How China Escaped*, 106. See also Genia Kostka and Xiaofan Yu, "Career Backgrounds of Municipal Party Secretaries in China: Why Do So Few Municipal Party Secretaries Rise from the

What motivates these bureaucrats? Many are motivated by financial gain. For a long time, the best way to do well for oneself financially was to meet or exceed contract targets. But, as Chinese society grew wealthier and (as I dis-cuss below) local governments no longer benefited from the tax revenue that they generated, it was quite easy to do well for oneself as a local official by taking kickbacks and using official connections to benefit family members, without worrying about earning bonuses by doing the less rewarding work of good governance. Graeme Smith finds that lower-level cadres pursued their work for its security ("iron rice bowl" position) and for the chance to access "gray income" and for the guaranteed pensions toward which they did not contribute.[49] Ben Hillman finds that local officials were engaged in "competi-tion for spoils organized around a relatively stable system of factionalism."[50]

In my own fieldwork in North China, I encountered relatively few urban or rural cadres who seemed to expect or to desire promotion within the party-state for reasons other than self-enrichment. Most of the district- and even municipal-level cadres at some distance from municipal party secretaries and mayors wanted to strike a balance between meeting basic standards for implementation and bettering themselves financially. As one land man-agement cadre remarked in 2008: "I want no attention from above, good or bad. I want to remain in my position, where I have good relationships with business and can help my family's situation improve."[51] This particular cadre appeared to be very corrupt, but my claim is not that every cadre was cor-rupt, but rather that socially beneficial state-business relations required an alignment of interests, broadly defined, rather than merely bureaucratic incentives.

Recall the officials of Plum County in Guangdong. In several hourlong discussions on why they promoted economic growth and worked to solve problems for emerging private-sector firms in the 1980s and 1990s, not a single member of a group of (eleven) officials whom I interviewed mentioned cadre responsibility contracts or promotion ambitions. Some were straight-forward about their own financial stakes, as many were helping members

County Level?," *Modern China* 41, no. 5 (2015): 467–505; Xueguang Zhou, "The Institutional Logic of Collusion among Local Governments in China," *Modern China* 36, no. 1 (2010): 47–78.

[49] Graeme Smith, "Getting Ahead in Rural China: The Elite-Cadre Divide and Its Implications for Rural Governance," *Journal of Contemporary China* 24, no. 94 (2015): 594–612.
[50] Ben Hillman, "Factions and Spoils: Examining Political Behavior within the Local State in China," *China Journal*, no. 64 (2010): 1–18.
[51] Interview, Liaoning, January 2008.

of their extended families establish viable businesses or receiving small kickbacks from profitable firms, and others wanted to see the local community prosper. Their motivations were more personal and community-bound; these local motivations were compatible with the party-state's larger project of generating growth by promoting business during the 1980s and 1990s, but one can easily understand how personal motivations could trump bureaucratic incentives under different conditions.[52]

Moreover, institutional arrangements and competition for promotion may incentivize economic growth, but they can do little to ensure that the growth is sustainable, good for society, or, in some cases, even genuine. Cadre responsibility contracts measure growth targets quantitatively, in terms of either GDP growth or, especially for very local officials, investment targets.[53] The political importance of these statistics has jeopardized their authenticity. Scholarship has uncovered how local officials "juke the stats" during leadership transition times; Premier Li Keqiang famously quipped that GDP statistics are "man-made, and therefore unreliable."[54] Even if the statistics are not false, local officials are nonetheless incentivized to produce economic growth in a way that prioritizes short-term GDP boosts rather than long-term, sustainable growth. As one local official stated in 2012, reflecting on efforts to demonstrate economic recovery following the global financial crisis: "Why would I ask the company about their business model [before leasing the

[52] Interview, Shenzhen, June 2015. These cadres had been retired for between seven and twenty-five years by the time I met them, and one can imagine that my interview sampling method, best described as opportunistic snowballing (I asked a contact to organize a group of locals for a discussion) selected only those in the area who had retired rather than those who had moved "up" to Guangzhou or Beijing. I did ask if they knew anyone who had been promoted in those days: they agreed that one official had become an official in a larger urban area in Guangdong. Furthermore, as noneconomic goals have figured more prominently in cadre responsibility contracts, scholars have found that the same institutional incentives have been less successful in getting local officials to do the work the center desires them to do when that work is not economically rewarding for them. A primary example is environmental protection, which more than a decade of a priority focus on lowering emissions and securing compliance with pollution regulations has failed to result in consistent and effective enforcement of standards. Instead, Beijing has resorted to "blunt force enforcement"—extreme measures such as drastic destruction of factories—to scare bureaucrats into compliance. Denise S. van der Kamp, "Blunt Force Regulation and Bureaucratic Control: Understanding China's War on Pollution," *Governance* 34, no. 1 (2021): 181–209. See also Sarah Eaton and Genia Kostka, "Central Protectionism in China: The 'Central SOE Problem' in Environmental Governance," *China Quarterly*, no. 231 (2017): 685–704; Denise van der Kamp, Peter Lorentzen, and Daniel Mattingly, "Racing to the Bottom or to the Top? Decentralization, Revenue Pressures, and Governance Reform in China," *World Development* 95 (2017): 164–76.

[53] Ang, *How China Escaped*, reproduces local contracts and investment targets. On the quantification of targets, see Jeremy Wallace, *Seeking Truth and Hiding Facts: Information, Ideology, and Authoritarianism in China* (New York: Oxford University Press, 2023).

[54] Jeremy L. Wallace, "Juking the Stats? Authoritarian Information Problems in China," *British Journal of Political Science* 46, no. 1 (2016): 11–29.

land]? They guarantee 300 million RMB in investment and I need invest‑
ment numbers right now. I can't worry about whether they make money in
five years."[55] The focus on GDP growth not only compromised statistical
accuracy but also produced an excessive focus on investment, generating
widespread debt and economic distortions. This was possible when the state
prioritized growth but no longer imposed sufficient discipline on either
public or private actors.

Last, a word is in order about theories of bureaucratic incentives and the
arguments I make in these chapters about the Chinese system. My argu‑
ment is that mutual alignment—socially beneficial growth and relative po‑
litical stability between capitalists and the state—was possible in China when
local officials pursued growth *and* the financial system imposed discipline
so that resources were used somewhat efficiently. Embedded in that argu‑
ment appears to be a conceptualization of bureaucrats as fundamentally self‑
serving, motivated by their own prosperity, whether through making money
by kickbacks, bettering themselves by making their extended communities—
and families—rich, or being promoted within the party‑state.

Cynical readers, and most economists, will not find this conceptualiza‑
tion problematic. Others, however, might think about the many local‑level
officials they have encountered in China and elsewhere who are motivated
to do well by the communities they govern for more professional or altru‑
istic reasons. I have also met these local officials, and the argument I make
does not purport to explain the behavior of all bureaucrats in China. In fact,
to return to the cases of Suzhou and Plum County, Suzhou's officials wanted
revenue for promotion, and Plum County officials wanted their extended
families and communities to do better than they had in the previous decades.
These motivations were self‑serving, but not entirely selfish. Ultimately, I do
not intend to advance a comprehensive theory of bureaucratic motivations
in China, nor does this argument require it. If some significant percentage
of any given jurisdiction's officials, especially those who interact with
businesspeople, are looking out for themselves and the formal institutions
permit them to do so, it is enough for the culture of state‑business relations
to be one of collaboration between these parties. And if there are few or no
disciplinary mechanisms to ensure that their collaboration benefits society,
rather than harms it, significant harm will ensue.[56]

[55] Interview, city in the Northeast, June 2012.
[56] I am grateful to William Hsiao and Roderick MacFarquhar for pushing me to clarify this.

Enduring Distrust: Capitalists as Tentative Political Partners

Before moving on to the second half of this chapter, in which I describe the breakdown in financial and fiscal discipline that characterizes China's political economy in the 2000s, it is worth returning briefly to the political status of capitalists. I argue in Chapter 2 that capitalists in China learned during the revolution and the early state-building period that the CCP would tolerate them to an extent as long as their actions furthered the goals of the regime itself, for instance in economic development and stability. During the cataclysms of the Cultural Revolution, which lasted a decade and immediately preceded the introduction of market reforms, capitalists learned the limits of the party's tolerance, and they learned that actions have long shadows. Even the capitalists, or suspected capitalists, who had most willingly sublimated their assets, skills, and futures into service of the PRC fell victim to political radicalism, losing their assets, statuses, family members, and lives.

As Deng's national-level reforms and other local efforts began to stimulate private risk-taking and market-making, capitalists, old and new, did not suddenly forget the regime's past treatment. The changes during the reform period were profound indeed. Businesspeople went from being social and political pariahs to being courted by local officials and placed at the center of an emerging national path to prosperity. But this did not make them safe, and it did not mean that they trusted the regime. From the late 1970s through the late 1990s, before the possibility of party membership was extended to private entrepreneurs in 2001, the budding private sector operated tenuously and without access to the formal resources of the state.

The liminal status of emergent capitalists—locally embraced for their contributions in generating wealth, jobs, and taxes but ideologically suspect and without formal protections from the country's institutions—led them to adopt creative strategies for survival. Economic actors drew on repertoires of behaviors learned during the revolutionary and Maoist periods, which I call collectively "adept dissimulation," to protect themselves and their interests in a political environment with endemic uncertainty and frequent political mobilization.[57] These behaviors, represented in Table 5.3, entail feigned loyalty combined with a general wariness of the regime, plans for self-protection, and

[57] I borrow this term from Gordon Bennett, *Yundong: Mass Campaigns in Chinese Communist Leadership* (Berkeley: Center for Chinese Studies, University of California, 1976), 87.

Table 5.3 Behavioral Manifestations of Distrust

Institutional	Firm-Level	Private
Join CCP Run for office/ hold a formal position	Disguise firm type Hide ownership Parrot official language and policies in firm reports and strategies Short time horizons in investment choices Asset expatriation/capital flight	Engage relevant actors in mutually incriminating behavior (vice) Offer (secretive) corporate stakes for political elites Personal wealth over and sometimes at the expense of firm health

short time horizons in expectation of policy changes or reversals. Business elites who did not face existential vulnerability would adopt behaviors in the first column and some from the second column, but generally they did not adopt those in the second and third columns. Precariousness is therefore manifest in private and firm behaviors designed to protect firms and businesspeople personally from state power.

Adept dissimulation, for obvious reasons, is difficult to disentangle from genuine loyalty to the regime. Convincing others that one's behavior is in service of the regime's goals is, after all, the point of the behavior and the means of self-preservation. How can we tell how capitalists during the reform era thought about their safety, legitimacy, and status?

Survey data are revealing, even under the constraints of authoritarian-opinion environments and preference falsification.[58] The state-conducted entrepreneur surveys I cite above ask about political status and interaction with the government. When asked to estimate their own political power, the average response of entrepreneurs in the early 1990s was 4.6 out of 10, with 1 being "relatively high" and 10 being "relatively low."[59] Through the decade, the data show that this estimation did not change, meaning that the entrepreneurs' estimation of their political status did not grow as market reforms deepened; the 1995 survey shows a 5.1 average ranking, lower than that in prior years, and the social prestige average is 4.2. This is especially

[58] Timur Kuran, *Private Truths, Public Lies: The Social Consequences of Preference Falsification* (Cambridge, MA: Harvard University Press, 1995); Kerry Ratigan and Leah Rabin, "Re-evaluating Political Trust: The Impact of Survey Nonresponse in Rural China," *China Quarterly*, no. 243 (2020): 823–38: Rory Truex and Daniel L. Tavana, "Implicit Attitudes toward an Authoritarian Regime," *Journal of Politics* 81, no. 3 (2019): 1014–27.

[59] *China Private Economy Yearbook 1996* (中国私营经济年鉴 1996) (Beijing: 中华工商联合出版社, 1996), 152.

Table 5.4 Survey Data on Entrepreneurs' Outlooks, 1995

Reasons for Positive Outlook	% Respondents	Reasons for Negative Outlook	% Respondents
Policy stability	42.9	Policy Discrimination	33.8
Political stability	32.0	Policy Instability	33.0
Impossible to roll back private sector	20.3	Extreme Competition	24.8
Building rule of law	4.8	Status of the Private Sector Unclear	8.3

Source: *China Private Economy Yearbook 1996* (中国私营经济年鉴 1996) (Beijing: 中华工商联合出版社, 1996), 165.

noteworthy after 1992, when Deng's Southern Tour solidified the path for market reforms following the post-1989 uncertainty, when we might expect that capitalists would express more confidence in a world in which "to get rich is glorious." Respondents gave other indications of unhappiness with government relations: 37.3 percent of respondents indicated that "collusion between power and money," the top answer given, was the most important social problem in 1995. The second most popular response was the "three chaotics" (三乱), referring to arbitrary demands for contributions, arbitrary fines, and arbitrary fees （乱摊派，乱罚款，乱收费）.[60] Answers to a 1995 survey question about entrepreneurs' reasons for pessimism or optimism are instructive (Table 5.4). "Policy stability" is the number one reason for those holding a positive outlook, and it is also the second most common reason cited for holding a negative outlook. The number one reason for pessimism is policy discrimination against the private sector. Entrepreneurs were apparently satisfied with some policy and political stability, but nonetheless they understood that their status remained precarious.

Shapeshifting: Changing Organizational Forms

Changes in business structure and designation over time provide another source of data on how capitalists thought of their own vulnerability. As has been widely documented, the private sector emerged prior to Chinese law granting such corporate forms and behaviors legal protections

[60] Ibid., 164.

and designations.[61] Non-state-run firms were designated as "people-run enterprises"

(民营企业), but this is not a legal designation; rather, it is a residual category of firms that are neither foreign-invested enterprises nor state-run firms.[62] A category of "private enterprises" (私营企业) appeared in 1988 and received formal legal protection in 1997, but various regions in China displayed vast differences in embracing and protecting private enterprises.[63] One solution to legal, and political, liminality has been to adopt corporate forms that appear safe, often described as "wearing the red hat" (戴红帽子).[64] Through 1988, private firms with more than eight employees were technically illegal; they were essentially forced to register as collective enterprises ("wearing the red hat") or to masquerade as parts of state enterprises or government organizations ("hang-on enterprises," 挂户企业).[65]

As the formal status of the private sector improved during the late 1990s and early 2000s, it would become marginally clearer how many enterprises had "worn the red hat." The 2000 Survey of Private Entrepreneurs found that one-fourth of respondents had done so, most in the 1980s (46.3 percent), but some even before 1979 (7.6 percent) or in the early 1990s.[66] Most had doffed their red hats between 1992 and 1996 (48.1 percent) or after 1997 (39.6 percent). Accounts of the practice vary: some estimate that 70 percent of the urban TVEs were in fact private firms. In some regions, more than 90 percent of TVEs were known to have been private firms.[67] Disguising private firms as more politically and legally acceptable TVEs is a kind of solution to a

---

[61] See Tsai, "Adaptive Informal Institutions"; Donald C. Clarke, "Economic Development and the Rights Hypothesis: The China Problem," *American Journal of Comparative Law* 51, no. 1 (2003): 89–111.

[62] On this, see Breznitz and Murphree, *Run of the Red Queen*, 77 and n. 60; Adam Segal, *Digital Dragon: High-Technology Enterprises in China* (Ithaca: Cornell University Press, 2003).

[63] Zhang and Liu, *Revolutionary Legacy*; Qi Zhang, Dong Zhang, Mingxing Liu, and Victor Shih, "Elite Cleavage and the Rise of Capitalism under Authoritarianism: A Tale of Two Provinces in China," *Journal of Politics* 83, no. 3 (2021): 1010–23; Whiting, *Power and Wealth*.

[64] Wenhong Chen, "Does the Colour of the Cat Matter? The Red Hat Strategy in China's Private Enterprises," *Management and Organization Review* 3, no. 1 (2007): 55–80. Tianli Feng and Guofeng Wang, "How Private Enterprises Establish Organizational Legitimacy in China's Transitional Economy," *Journal of Management Development* 29, no. 4 (2010): 377–93; Tsai, "Adaptive Informal Institutions," 116–41; Qi Zhang and Mingxing Liu, "The Political Economy of Private Sector Development in Communist China: Evidence from Zhejiang Province," *Studies in Comparative International Development* 48, no. 2 (2013): 196–216.

[65] Kellee Tsai points out that the eight-employee limit has roots in Marxist theory as the line over which a household producing unit becomes an exploitative enterprise. See Tsai, "Adaptive Informal Institutions," 128 n. 38.

[66] *China Private Economy Yearbook 1996*, 349.

[67] Kristin Parris, "Local Initiative and National Reform: The Wenzhou Model of Development," *China Quarterly*, no. 134 (1993): 242–63. See also Chen, "Colour of the Cat," 57.

lack of property rights protections as well as evidence that Chinese business actors are good at adapting to political uncertainty and taking advantage of opportunities. Other firm choices are more about adaptation, for example the rush to benefit from preferential policies designed to attract FDI and policies designed to facilitate development in high-tech sectors.

FDI has played a significant role in China's growth, catalyzing economic growth, providing sorely needed capital during the early reform era, and accelerating the country's transformation to the "world's factory" after World Trade Organization accession (in 2001). During each of these stages, evidence abounds that much of the "foreign" investment was round-tripped capital, exported by Chinese firms and then reinvested in China. Determining the volume of round-tripped capital is notoriously difficult for the obvious reason that it is meant to be disguised and, accordingly, frequently channeled through tax havens. But we know that the volume has been substantial: the World Bank estimates that round-tripped FDI could comprise one-quarter of China's FDI during the 1990s, and an Asian Development Bank estimate puts it higher, at 30–50 percent.[68] Chinese capital holders had significant business reasons for exporting and reinvesting capital as FDI, even in the early 1990s and 2000s. After Deng Xiaoping's Southern Tour of 1992, when most regions began to open in earnest to FDI, foreign capital was especially privileged in China. Governments sought FDI because of capital scarcity and a desire for foreign technology and managerial know-how as well as sources of politically useful competition for the public sector. Many areas offered a variety of preferential policies, including lower corporate and individual tax rates, special access to land and utilities, and the more informal benefits of government support, such as arranging labor recruitment and favorably interpreting environmental and labor laws to facilitate firms' goals.[69]

The other side of FDI round-tripping is capital flight, a key manifestation of distrust between capital holders and political elites, as I argue in Chapter 1

[68] World Bank, "Box 2.3, Round-Tripping of Capital Flows between China and Hong Kong," in Chapter 2, "Private Capital Flows to Emerging Markets," Global Development Finance: Financing the Poorest Countries (2002): 31; Geng Xiao, "People's Republic of China's Round-Tripping FDI: Causes and Implications," ADB Institute Discussion Paper no. 7 (July 2004); Terry Sicular, "Capital Flight and Foreign Investment: Two Tales from China and Russia," World Economy 21, no. 5 (1998): 589–602.

[69] Yasheng Huang, Selling China: Foreign Direct Investment during the Reform Era (New York: Cambridge University Press, 2003). Huang discusses FDI round-tripping on 37–41. Mary Elizabeth Gallagher, Contagious Capitalism: Globalization and the Politics of Labor in China (Princeton, NJ: Princeton University Press, 2005); Huang, Why So Much Demand; Margaret M. Pearson, Joint Ventures in the People's Republic of China: The Control of Foreign Direct Investment under Socialism (Princeton, NJ: Princeton University Press, 1991).

and demonstrate in the Indonesian case. Attempts to measure capital flight are somewhat more straightforward than measuring round-tripped FDI, but nonetheless they are complex and imprecise, again because capital exporters obscure their efforts to evade foreign-exchange restrictions, make use of opaque tax havens, and, as becomes increasingly important during a later period, disguise asset expatriation as commercially minded foreign investments.[70] Nonetheless, we know that capital flight from China during the reform era was quite high. Table 5.5 shows some estimates of the volume of capital flight from China in the early reform era. To be sure, much of this was reinvested as FDI, with a notable increase after 1992. Overall, most scholars view the high volume of capital flight and high volume of FDI in China as evidence of round-tripping and of what Terry Sicular helpfully summarizes as different incentives and different returns. Domestic savings, in particular, funded "both visible and hidden channels into offshore investments" because of insufficient domestic savings vehicles and also because the security offered to foreign investors exceeded that offered to domestic capital.

The corporate shapeshifting of Chinese firms became more intricate—and more destructive for the Chinese political economy—during the period of mutual endangerment that I describe in Chapter 6. Instead of adept dissimulation to protect productive efforts and get optimal deals and protection, shapeshifting took the form of manipulation of the financial system, even fraud, for personal enrichment rather than productive efforts. But I emphasize that behaviors related to distrust and vulnerability were present throughout China's reform era, and indeed before the reforms. Because of the presence of fiscal and financial discipline, the shapeshifting was productive. In the case of TVEs, it was even a solution to a problem of facilitating productive efforts in the absence of institutional structures, and in the case of round-tripping it enabled the repatriation of capital that had fled.

Three Represents and the Thinness of Co-optation
Before turning to the breakdown of mutual alignment with the disappearance of discipline, let me first anticipate an objection to designating private

[70] See Sarah Chan, "Assessing China's Recent Capital Outflows: Policy Challenges and Implications," *China Finance and Economic Review* 5, no. 1 (2017): 1–13; Yin-Wong Cheung and Xingwang Qian, "Capital Flight: China's Experience," *Review of Development Economics* 14, no. 2 (2010): 227–47; Frank R. Gunter, "Corruption, Costs, and Family: Chinese Capital Flight, 1984–2014," *China Economic Review* 43 (2017): 105–17.

Table 5.5 Estimates of Capital Flight from China, 1984–1994

	Sicular Estimate	Low Estimate (Balance of Payments)		High Estimate (Balance of Payments)	
	% GNP	$ millions	% GNP	$ millions	% GNP
1984		993	0.32	4,265	1.39
1985		2,140	0.67	5,368	1.69
1986		1,585	0.74	6,539	3.06
1987		1,722	0.56	10,165	3.35
1988	5.6	−985	−0.30	13,598	4.12
1989	6.1	427	0.10	20,554	4.99
1990	10.8	6,927	1.50	21,341	4.63
1991	10.9	−2,329	−0.58	29,691	7.45
1992	15.1	9,314	2.24	48,307	11.62
1993	13.0	−1,541	−0.31	44,646	9.01
1994	12.2	8,000	1.28	63,000	10.11

Source: "Sicular Estimate" uses capital flight data calculated by Frank R. Gunter, "Capital Flight from the People's Republic of China, 1984–1994," *China Economic Review* 7, no 1 (1996): 77–96, using a "residual method," which is the sum of the current account balance, net foreign investment, change in reserves, and change in foreign debt. The estimate adds in estimated misinvoicing between the PRC, but excluding Hong Kong and the rest of the world plus a bank debt adjustment to correct for gaps in Chinese foreign debt statistics. The "low" and "high" balance of payments estimates are also from Gunter, "Capital Flight." The balance-of-payments method is the sum of nonbank private short-term capital flows and net errors and omissions. The low estimate adds an estimate of misinvoicing between the PRC, including Hong Kong, and the rest of the world, and the high estimate adds estimated misinvoicing between the PRC, excluding Hong Kong, and the rest of the world. For the percentage of GNP in the balance-of-payments estimates, GNP figures come from the Economist Intelligence Unit. Terry Sicular, "Capital Flight and Foreign Investment: Two Tales from Russia and China," *World Economy* 21, no. 5 (1998): 593 and Gunter, "Capital Flight."

capitalists as politically vulnerable throughout the reform era: namely, that the CCP legalized private enterprise and even welcomed entrepreneurs into the party in 2001. The move, to be sure, was extraordinary: the party had formally banned recruiting entrepreneurs in 1989, but by 2001 the original enemy class of the regime was welcomed into its ranks. The legal status confirmed that private capitalists and private property were important. It is not reasonable, however, to imagine that the 2001 decision on party membership or the legal reforms, especially without an independent judiciary, reversed decades of distrust or eliminated the political vulnerability of the private sector.

For one, legal protection in Beijing can be meaningful only if its implementation by China's vast administrative machinery can be guaranteed,

which it could not. Second, the debate that followed the decision to embrace capitalists was vociferous. Party hardliners and critics openly accused
Jiang Zemin of betraying the revolution and of violating party discipline,
even comparing him to Mikhail Gorbachev and Lee Teng-Hui in public
newspapers and open letters. Jiang eventually suppressed the debate, for example by reorganizing newspaper editorial boards, but the opposition was
surely noted by private-sector actors who were adept at reading signals and
listening to official debates to gauge policy directions.[71]

More importantly, we know from copious research on the behavior of
the private sector, including elements within it that did join the party-state,
that those who joined did so to protect themselves amid a retained sense of
precariousness. Yue Hou's work on capitalists in public office demonstrates
this. She finds through surveys that businesses owned by members of local
congresses experienced less predation and expropriation, and she also finds,
through an online experiment, that businesspeople who identified as "loyal
to the party" or as formal officeholders received more responsiveness to their
concerns. Her qualitative fieldwork finds businesspeople engaging in extensive socializing with government officials as a means of self-protection. One
of her interviewees says, "I spend a quarter of my time socializing and it is ex-
hausting."[72] They exhaust themselves entertaining government officials and
engaging in expensive and time-consuming political campaigns for office because these formal and informal relationships are a means of self-protection
(even called "protective umbrellas," 保护伞) and information collection
amid existential threat.

Hou's private-sector elites in public office have sought a formal route to attain some political power in order to ward off any feeling of vulnerability. The
more informal routes, indeed the "socializing" routes, are known to nearly
anyone with a casual familiarity with the Chinese business environment.
Indeed, the popular and scholarly focus on guanxi (关系) elaborates how
social interactions between business and political elites (and indeed among
those groups) facilitate mutualistic relationships and capitalism. Some of this
work focuses on relationships as evidence of trust, but the more thoughtful
work focuses on relationships as a replacement for trust and a venue for in-
strumentalist exchange within acceptable social practices. David Wank

---

[71] Dickson's account of the debate is excellent. See Dickson, *Wealth into Power*, 70–79, esp. 78.
[72] Yue Hou, *The Private Sector in Public Office: Selective Property Rights in China* (New York:
Cambridge University Press, 2019), 113.

identifies a pattern of "symbiotic clientelism," by which entrepreneurs couch their financial relationships with party cadres ("backstage bosses," 后台老板) in the "popularly legitimated" idiom of guanxi.[73] The idea that the emergent business elite was intertwined with the political elites is foundational to a first generation of research on the emergence of markets in China.[74] But, although these relationships may have prevented businesspeople from organizing to fight for a liberal political system, we cannot conclude that the two parties enjoy either loyalty or trust. In short, their ties are precarious ones.

Informal relationships can threaten or protect in equal parts; vulnerable entrepreneurs subject to local officials' interpretations of policy and prioritizing pursue equality in the relationship by making their counterparts vulnerable. John Osburg's ethnography of business elites in Chengdu in the early years of the twenty-first century portrays them as "anxious," engaging in expensive rituals of socializing and vice, impressing one another with gendered behaviors of "brotherhood," including hiring sex workers and pursuing extramarital affairs to cultivate feelings（感情，or 人情）of intimacy and complicity that aide and protect them in business. Osburg's businessmen also complain about "endless social obligations" that preclude a business focus, much less their own leisure activities; some entrepreneurs even emigrate to find retreat from social networks they find oppressive.[75]

The clear analogy to these semi- or even nonvoluntary friendships built on vice activities is mafia organizations, and indeed Chapter 6 likens many large Chinese conglomerates to them. The point here is that, even during the period of mutual alignment, the fundamental vulnerability of the private sector profoundly structured behavior in China's reform era, even after private business was legalized and private property was protected. The formal acceptance of capitalists and private firms indeed affected expectations and behaviors, but, as Douglass North theorizes regarding institutional change, "While the formal rules may be changed overnight, the informal norms usually change

[73] David L. Wank, "The Institutional Process of Market Clientelism: *Guanxi* and Private Business in a South China City," *China Quarterly*, no. 147 (1996): 820–38.

[74] Dorothy J. Solinger, *China's Transition from Socialism: Statist Legacies and Market Reforms, 1980–1990* (Armonk, NY: M.E. Sharpe, 1993); Kevin J. O'Brien and Lianjiang Li, "Selective Policy Implementation in Rural China," *Comparative Politics* 32, no. 2 (1999): 167–86; Dickson, *Red Capitalists in China*; Dickson, *Wealth into Power*.

[75] John Osburg, *Anxious Wealth: Money and Morality among China's New Rich* (Stanford: Stanford University Press, 2013); John Osburg, "Making Business Personal: Corruption, Anti-corruption, and Elite Networks in Post–Mao China," *Current Anthropology* 59 (S18) (2018): S149–S159.

only gradually."[76] In the case of entrepreneurs and the party-state in China, organizations and actors were shaped by fifty years of formal and informal rules of capitalist vulnerability and inherent distrust of the party-state.

Campaigns and Uncertainty Post-Mao

Beyond this inherited distrust, the CCP's governance style relies on a level of uncertainty and even unpredictability that permeates state-business relations just as it permeates Chinese society at large. Campaigns have enjoyed enduring importance as a technology of governing in China, from the revolutionary period through the present (See Table 5.6).[77] While a few observers in the 2000s imagined a more technocratic, rather than mobilizational, politics in China, especially with regard to management of the economy, campaigns have featured prominently throughout and remain central to CCP rule. Table 5.4 provides a nonexhaustive list of national-level campaigns during the reform era; many other policy objectives are pursued through campaign-style activities without being officially named, and local governments engage in their own campaigns as well as implement those conceived from above. The cycles of campaigns, familiar to participants in China's market reforms, affected the behavior and expectations of capitalists as they emerged in China, specifically pushing them toward short time horizons and means of self-protection amid an uncertain and frequently threatening policy environment.

The reform era in China, like the Mao era that preceded it, is characterized by CCP "guerrilla policy style" that, according to Heilmann and Perry, involves embracing uncertainty and radical flexibility rather than routinization, institutionalization, or rule of law. The party's general approach is to resist standard operating procedures that can be "discerned by enemy forces" and embraces practical experience and inductive reasoning over abstractions; the top leaders' retain "strategic decisions," while implementation is the purview of local initiative and extreme opportunism with respect

---

[76] Douglass C. North, "Economic Performance through Time," *American Economic Review* 84, no. 3 (1994): 366.

[77] Kristen E. Looney, *Mobilizing for Development: The Modernization of Rural East Asia* (Ithaca: Cornell University Press, 2020); Heilmann and Perry, *Mao's Invisible Hand*; Tyrene White, *China's Longest Campaign: Birth Planning in the People's Republic, 1949–2005* (Ithaca: Cornell University Press, 2006).

Table 5.6 Selected National-Level Campaigns in Reform-Era China

Year	Campaigns
Deng Era (1978–92)	Anti–spiritual pollution, 1983 (清除精神污染) Strike Hard (anticrime), 1983 (严厉打击刑事犯罪) Anti–bourgeois liberalization, 1987 (反对资产阶自由化) One-child policy, 1976–2020 (计划生育)
Jiang Era (1992–2002)	Antipornography and Antipiracy Campaign (扫黄打非行动) Three stresses, 1998–2002 (三讲) Anti-Falungong, 1999–2005 Anticorruption (various) Develop the West, 2000 (西部大开发)
Hu Era (2002–12)	Combat SARS, 2003 Revive the Northeast, 2003 (振兴东北) Going Out (走出去) Central China Rising, 2004 (中部崛起) New Socialist Countryside, 2006– (总农村建设)
Xi Era (2012–)	Poverty Alleviation / Rural Revitalization, 2015–20 (精准扶贫) Anticorruption (various) Belt and Road Initiative, 2013– (一带一路) Made in China 2025, 2015– (中国制造) Strike Hard against Violent Terrorism, 2014– (严厉打击暴力恐怖) Anti-Covid-19, 2020–

to forging or breaking alliances.[78] Such an approach has allowed the regime to be tremendously adaptive, responding to challenges through experimentation and learning and resisting the sclerotic bureaucratization that imperiled other Leninist regimes' efforts to reform, modernize, or respond to crisis. This approach has its downsides in political volatility and a lack of political accountability and "procedural predictability."[79]

The experimentation and campaigns that comprise the CCP's "policy style" have a complex but adverse effect on business. In Chapter 2 I portray the Maoist era as a series of political campaigns during which all Chinese citizens learned to adjust and adapt to survive. For capitalists specifically, the first thirty years or so of the PRC featured a tepid embrace of capitalism followed by cycles of repression and political mobilization. The campaigns of the post-Mao era have been characterized as "managed," rather than mass, mobilization; the basic technology of propaganda, central goals, work teams,

---

[78] Heilmann and Perry, *Mao's Invisible Hand*, 13.
[79] Ibid., 14. Heilmann's later work also emphasizes the need for genuine policy feedback mechanisms.

and local targets has been deployed in pursuit of a variety of policy goals, from public health to social mores to regional development.[80] Moreover, Maoist-era campaigns tended to target various social groups—intellectuals, capitalists, party cadres—in ways that presented an existential threat. With the exception of the campaigns that target internal groups perceived to threaten the regime (e.g., in Table 5.4, the campaign against Falungong and what has become a genocidal campaign against Uyghurs in the "strike hard against violent terrorism") campaign, most post-Mao campaigns have not prominently featured violence or presented such an existential threat.[81] Capitalists as a class have certainly not been such targets, but nor have they been unaffected.

Campaigns, again whether as named policies like those in Table 5.4 or simply the kind of "campaign-style governance" that pervades policymaking and implementation at all levels in China, present both threats and inducements to social and economic actors. Threats are present when campaigns target specific actions. For example, antipiracy campaigns, both at the national level and in the "campaign-style enforcement" undertaken by local governments, turned a widely embraced business approach into a legal and political problem as officials suddenly enforced laws that had been on the books but for which forbearance had been the norm. What resulted from these campaign-style antipiracy efforts was a cat-and-mouse game for business and the state: "Counterfeiting operations are merely moved to the next village or the next town, and the fakes continue to be churned out until the next crisis, in a predictable cyclical pattern, results in the next campaign."[82]

Campaign-style enforcement is therefore the downside to the Chinese state's preference for ambiguity and experimentation over clarity of rules and boundaries. "Structured uncertainty" and "mixed signals" permit creative

---

[80] Elizabeth J. Perry, "From Mass Campaigns to Managed Campaigns: 'Constructing a New Socialist Countryside,'" in Sebastian Heilmann and Elizabeth J. Perry, eds., *Mao's Invisible Hand: The Political Foundations of Adaptive Governance in China* (Cambridge MA: Harvard University Asia Center, 2011), 30–61.

[81] It is worth clarifying that these two campaigns in particular are built on the idea that these groups threaten the regime, even though they did not in any actual way. It is impossible to ascertain whether the CCP and its leaders truly believe that the Falungong movement or the Uyghurs present an existential threat or whether such an idea is a pretense for crackdown and oppression. See James W. Tong, *Revenge of the Forbidden City: The Suppression of the Falungong in China, 1999–2005* (New York: Oxford University Press, 2009) and Sheena Chestnut Greitens, Myunghee Lee, and Emir Yazici, "Counterterrorism and Preventive Repression: China's Changing Strategy in Xinjiang," *International Security* 44, no. 3 (2020): 9–47.

[82] Martin K. Dimitrov, *Piracy and the State: The Politics of Intellectual Property Rights in China* (New York: Cambridge University Press, 2009), 5.

boundary pushing and adaptation, but this environment also ensures perpetual precariousness. The liminality enabled the Chinese state to experiment with policies and behaviors while retaining the ability to suppress those activities if they became problematic or inconvenient.[83] The antipiracy dynamics illustrate this logic well: parts of the Chinese state, including local-level officials, tolerate copying and IP infringement to allow local firms to develop, but then they punish those same firms when higher-level demands to stamp out IP theft seem to trump local incentives to foster growth. Local "brute force" antipollution enforcement follows a similar dynamic.[84]

Campaign politics also present inducements. Campaigns tend to pursue transformational goals, those that are beyond bureaucratic routines and annual targets; the list of campaigns in Table 5.4 suggests the kinds of goals, positive and negative, campaigns aim to achieve, all of which are beyond everyday political goals. In pursuit of these goals, campaigns are frequently accompanied by substantial resources. Campaigns to stop some sorts of behavior, for example piracy, are accompanied by resources available to parts of the bureaucracy that are newly empowered to execute them. Antipiracy efforts have been ineffective in part because so many parts of the Chinese bureaucracy involve themselves in the effort. Firms, foreign and domestic, pay fees (办案费) for government offices to act on their cases, and central campaigns offer more resources in the form of jobs and finances to monitor and enforce.[85] Campaigns for economic growth, whether they are geographic (e.g., targeting underdeveloped regions like the West, Center, or Northeast) or about upgrading or transforming an economic model (e.g., "Going Out," the Belt and Road Initiative, and Made in China 2025), all of which I discuss in Chapter 6), typically bring central investment and mobilize other kinds of resources, for example offering land resources or tax credits to firms that engage the campaign's major goals. It therefore behooves bureaucrats and business alike to emulate campaign propaganda and pursue one's own interests by engaging with the campaign's goals for both material gain and for political cover.

The status of capitalists and the style of politics in the PRC reveal continuities between the Maoist and reform eras that shape state-business

[83] Rachel E. Stern and Kevin J. O'Brien, "Politics at the Boundary: Mixed Signals and the Chinese State," *Modern China* 38, no. 2 (2012): 174–98; Breznitz and Murphree, *Run of the Red Queen*.

[84] Van der Kamp, "Blunt Force Regulation."

[85] Dimitrov, *Piracy and the State*; Andrew C. Mertha, "China's 'Soft' Centralization: Shifting *Tiao/ Kuai* Authority Relations," *China Quarterly*, no. 184 (2005): 791.

relations. Learned distrust of the CCP and the specific technology of CCP governance—mobilization campaigns—has produced a certain set of behaviors and attitudes for Chinese citizens who have become accustomed to seeking and assimilating information quickly, engaging in adept dissim-ulation, and appearing to align themselves with the political winds of the moment in order to survive. These learned behaviors served emergent (and re-emergent) capitalists well during the tenuous early decades of reform when their activities remained formally illegal but informally encouraged by various parts of the state.

In ways, the imperative for entrepreneurs to learn quickly and adapt has benefited the Chinese economy, generating the kind of competitive spirit and sensitivity to change that has enabled Chinese insertion into global supply chains and rapid scaling (in combination with low labor costs and other benefits, to be sure). But existential vulnerability produces behaviors that also are risky for the regime and the economy. These private, even surreptitious, behaviors that entrepreneurs pursue to protect themselves include engaging political elites in mutually incriminating behaviors, concealing assets, and preferring personal wealth accumulation over firm health, and even asset ex-patriation and theft. Some of these behaviors were evident in the early reform era, but many of them were constrained by the private sector's inability to access financial resources and therefore by the external discipline that was imposed on them by investors. But these behaviors do present challenges to the regime in the form of financial instability and the dynamics of corrup-tion and decay that hollow out the party's internal discipline and public le-gitimacy.[86] As mutual alignment broke down with fiscal reform and apparent financial liberalization, entrepreneurs did indeed begin to act in ways that challenge the regime's stability.

The Loss of Financial Discipline and the Breakdown of Mutual Alignment

In 2008 and 2009, the global financial crisis that began in the United States depressed global demand and provided an external shock to the

---

[86] Yuhua Wang and Bruce J. Dickson, "How Corruption Investigations Undermine Regime Support: Evidence from China," *Political Science Research and Methods* 10, no. 1 (2022): 3–48; Minxin Pei, *China's Crony Capitalism: The Dynamics of Regime Decay* (Cambridge, MA: Harvard University Press, 2016).

Chinese economy. The precipitous drop in external demand produced recession and unemployment, especially in areas of China, such as the southeast coast, that were manufacturing and export powerhouses. The Hu-Wen government responded with a massive stimulus: 4 trillion RMB for infrastructure and social welfare projects in 2009. Yet only 1.2 trillion RMB of that would come directly from Beijing; the rest came from local governments, state-owned firms, and banks.[87] In fact, 4 trillion RMB was a target, and political exhortations to lend, borrow, and invest were designed to convince economic actors to meet that target. They met and exceeded it. Investment comprised nearly one-half of GDP in the three years following the financial crisis, and in some places, including Chongqing and Tianjin, it exceeded 50 percent. The excess liquidity and ramped-up land development facilitated a construction-driven economic boom that saw China's urban land area expand by 35 percent between 2007 and 2013. The expansion in credit was just as massive. Loan volume in prefectural cities increased between 18 and 25 percent year on year from 2009 to 2011, and in some cities (especially interior cities like Chengdu) it nearly doubled.[88]

After the crisis and stimulus, international observers began to talk about China's "ghost cities" and "bridges to nowhere," and, domestically, concerns about land grabs and public and private debt began to build.[89] At the same time, debates aired in China, among elites and within the media and public sphere, about the direction of China's economic reforms. On the one hand, represented by Bo Xilai in Chongqing, some advocated an enhanced role for the state through financialization and infrastructure development, accompanied by anticorruption efforts and even Maoist nostalgia. On the other hand, there were advocates, represented by Wang Yang of Guangdong province, of a diminished role for the state and an enhanced role for markets

---

[87] Geoff Dyer, "Beijing Offers Just a Quarter of Stimulus Funds," *Financial Times*, November 14, 2008; Christine P. Wong, "The Fiscal Stimulus Programme and Public Governance Issues in China," *OECD Journal on Budgeting* 11, no. 3 (2011): 13; Barry Naughton, "Understanding the Chinese Stimulus Package," *China Leadership Monitor*, no. 28 (Spring 2009), https://www.hoover.org/sites/default/files/uploads/documents/CLM28BN.pdf.

[88] These data from CIEC Data measure monthly loan volume in prefectural and provincial cities.

[89] See Jiwon Baik and Jeremy Wallace, "Slums amidst Ghost Cities: Incentive and Information Problems in China's Urbanization," *Problems of Post-Communism* 70, no. 1 (2021): 11–26, https://doi.org/10.1080/10758216.2020.1860690; Christian Sorace and William Hurst, "China's Phantom Urbanisation and the Pathology of Ghost Cities," *Journal of Contemporary Asia* 46, no. 2 (2016): 304–22.

and even roles for nongovernmental organizations to review government budgets and to hold the state accountable.

The remarkable real estate and debt-driven investment appears to be a stepwise change in the macroeconomy, but in fact it represents an acceleration of trends that characterized China's political economy for years prior to the crisis. These include local government reliance on land sales to finance local government expenditures, reliance on investment to bump up GDP growth, and reliance on credit on the part of both firms and local governments. Broadly, these trends indicate a breakdown in party-state discipline over the economy, meaning its ability to ensure that both political officials and firms make economic decisions that are good for the regime and for society. By the mid-2000s, mutual alignment had broken down as the party-state lost control over the country's financial resources. In both the fiscal and the financial systems, this loss of control was the result of institutional changes we can track through the 1990s and early 2000s.

The Breakdown of Fiscal Discipline: Growing Reliance on Land and Debt

Though China grew quickly in the early reform era, growth was uneven throughout the country. Regions in the East benefited from geography, preferential policies, openness to global capital, and membership in overseas "China circle" networks, while interior and western regions, less fortunate in global connections or saddled with heavy socialist legacies, did not.[90] Moreover, the resources available to the central government were diminishing, precluding Beijing from making investments that might smooth these inequalities. Tellingly, the central government's share of revenues was declining both relative to local governments and relative to GDP, suggesting collusion between local governments and firms to evade taxes.[91] These widening disjunctures—interregional and central versus

---

[90] Meg Rithmire, "China's 'New Regionalism': Subnational Analysis in Chinese Political Economy," *World Politics* 66, no. 1 (2014): 165–94; Shaoguang Wang and Angang Hu, *The Political Economy of Uneven Development: The Case of China* (Armonk, NY: M.E. Sharpe, 1999); Whiting, *Power and Wealth.*

[91] Christine P. W. Wong, Christopher John Heady, Wing Thye Woo, and Asian Development Bank, *Fiscal Management and Economic Reform in the People's Republic of China* (Hong Kong: Oxford University Press for the Asian Development Bank, 1995), 48.

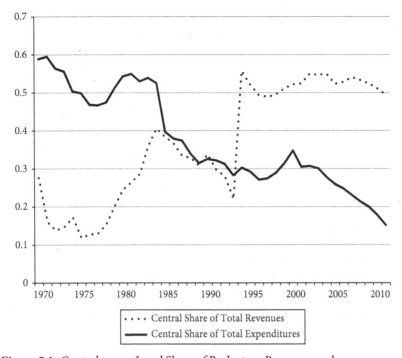

Figure 5.1 Central versus Local Share of Budgetary Revenues and
Expenditures, 1970–2010

Source: Ministry of Finance, via CEIC; National Bureau of Statistics, via China Data Center.

local—were a partial impetus for the 1994 recentralization of the country's
fiscal system. The 1994 reforms, conceived in the wake of a major inflationary
cycle, real estate boom, and acceleration of market reforms, reorganized
the tax collection system, recentralized the central government's share of
revenues, and left the lion's share of expenditures to local governments (see
Figure 5.1).

Local governments, essentially expected to raise revenues themselves
outside the formal tax system, were, in the words of one scholar, left "on a
shoestring."[92] Yet they were not bereft of resources. Public finance in China
is broken into "within plan" and "out of plan" (extrabudgetary) categories;

---

[92] Lily Tsai, quoted in Sebastian Heilmann and Elizabeth J. Perry, "Embracing Uncertainty:
Guerrilla Policy Style and Adaptive Governance in China," in Heilmann and Perry, eds., *Mao's
Invisible Hand: The Political Foundations of Adaptive Governance in China* (Cambridge, MA: Harvard
University Asia Center, 2011), 14 n. 42.

"within plan" (budgetary) includes revenues generated through regularly scheduled taxes and fees, while "extrabudgetary" indicates revenues generated through innovative or entrepreneurial local government activities. Over the course of the late 1990s and 2000s, the pursuit of extrabudgetary revenues came to dominate local government efforts. Most local governments replaced tax revenue with reliance on land sales and debt. Neither effect was entirely unintentional; by design, policymakers in Beijing devolved control over land and tacitly endorsed local government debt as a replacement for tax revenue.

The Land-Debt Nexus

China's policymakers were, beginning in the early reform era, interested in finding a means through which the country's land resources could generate much-needed capital, especially for urban growth in the context of a generation of underinvestment and unprecedented levels of rural-to-urban migration. Experiments with different models of pricing land in the 1980s led to a chaotic period in the early 1990s, during which the state encouraged the growth of a real estate sector and, tepidly, land markets, but land nonetheless remained owned by the "state" in urban areas and the collective in rural areas. An early 1990s real estate boom—real estate investment went from nothing in 1985 to 5 trillion RMB in 1992, or 20 percent of fixed asset investment—featured all sorts of "state" actors, including universities, hospitals, and various arms of local governments, participating in an "enclosures craze" (圈地热) to capitalize on their land resources.[93] After the bubble, policymakers wanted to unify the ownership of land—who benefits financially from land sales—with the power to draw urban plans, meaning municipal governments would be designated as owners of land and generate revenue from land leasing.[94]

The consequences of "land fiscalization" (土地财政) structured the Chinese political landscape over the following decades. Local governments were incentivized, even authorized, to expropriate rural

[93] See Meg Rithmire, "Land Institutions and Chinese Political Economy: Institutional Complementarities and Macroeconomic Management," *Politics & Society* 45, no. 1 (2017): 123–53.

[94] Legally, the state remains the owner of urban land, but land-lease markets enable local governments to lease land for commercial, industrial, and residential purposes and for varying durations.

landowners—peasants—to meet budgetary expenditures, transforming a countryside that had been racked by tax and fee protests in the 1990s into one aflame with land protests.[95] China urbanized rapidly over the 1990s and 2000s, a process driven more by land-hungry urban governments than by rural-to-urban labor migration or markets of any kind.[96] Central-local relations were also affected, as, beginning in the late 1990s, Beijing steadily strengthened hierarchical control over land supply. By the 2010s, China's land supply was controlled by a strict and hierarchical series of quotas, and the central Ministry of Land Resources manipulated the overall supply of land to manage China's macroeconomy and to facilitate specific regional development goals.[97] A key reason that the land supply could be a lever of macroeconomic control was its relationship to debt, another piece of the puzzle of the disintegration of fiscal discipline.

If land was one leg of the new fiscal system, debt was the other. As fiscal resources accrued in greater amounts to the central government, local governments pursued new means of borrowing to meet expenditure burdens. The inflationary episode in the 1990s alongside the Asian Financial Crisis (AFC), the regional effects of which alarmed policymakers in Beijing, prompted a recentralization of the major nodes in the financial system. The "Big Four" banks saw their personnel and credit decision-making systems removed from local branches and local party committees and reconcentrated in Beijing. Premier Zhu Rongji presided over the centralization to tamp the inflationary pressures of local government financial intervention and address the perennial problem of nonperforming loans (NPLs).[98] Indeed, inflation declined—the economy even experienced mild deflation in the late 1990s and early 2000s—as did overall lending. At the same time, however,

[95] Christopher Heurlin, *Responsive Authoritarianism in China: Land, Protests, and Policy Making* (New York: Cambridge University Press, 2016); You-tien Hsing, *The Great Urban Transformation: Politics of Land and Property in China* (New York: Oxford University Press, 2010); Rithmire, *Land Bargains*; Sally Sargeson, "The Politics of Land Development in Urbanizing China," *China Journal*, no. 66 (2011): 145–52; Susan Whiting, "Values in Land: Fiscal Pressures, Land Disputes and Justice Claims in Rural and Peri-urban China," *Urban Studies* 48, no. 3 (2011): 569–87; Daniel C. Mattingly, *The Art of Political Control in China* (New York: Cambridge University Press, 2020).

[96] Lynette H. Ong, "State-Led Urbanization in China: Skyscrapers, Land Revenue and 'Concentrated Villages,'" *China Quarterly*, no. 217 (2014): 162–79; Jeremy L. Wallace, *Cities and Stability: Urbanization, Redistribution, & Regime Survival in China* (New York: Oxford University Press, 2014).

[97] See Rithmire, "Land Institutions"; Yuan Xiao, "Making Land Fly: The Institutionalization of China's Land Quota Markets and ITS Implications for Urbanization, Property Rights, and Intergovernmental Politics," PhD dissertation, MIT, 2014.

[98] Shih, *Factions and Finance*, 167–78.

Zhu initiated an expansion of the financial system and the establishment and growth of local banks, an arrangement that Liu, Oi, and Zhang call the "grand bargain."[99] Local governments were barred from direct borrowing from banks, but they established "financial platform" (融资平台) companies, commonly called local government financing vehicles (LGFVs), as essentially state-owned firms that borrowed on their behalf. LGFVs are integrally linked to land, as most governments use land as collateral for loans from local banks.

The debt load of the LGFVs accelerated precipitously after the global financial crisis, when local governments were charged with spending on infrastructure and other programs to spur economic recovery. Beijing loosened the aggregate land supply to facilitate investment, and local governments used land as collateral to facilitate borrowing, creating a frenzy of real estate and infrastructure development and a massive accumulation of debt.[100] The total amount of this debt is disputed and opaque, but estimates range from 20 to 52 trillion RMB (in 2020), around half of GDP.[101] Over the course of the 2010s, authorities in Beijing engaged in complex regulatory and political maneuvers to put local government debt on the balance sheet, to manage shadow banking risks, and to facilitate continued growth without instability in the financial sector. I discuss these efforts as attempts to re-establish political discipline in Chapter 6. Clearly, the consequences of local dependence on land and debt for state-society relations, China's political geography and urban forms, financial stability, and central-local relations were substantial. But what did these reforms mean for state-business relations?

First, the replacement of taxes with land and debt (the two so related that one can group together land-driven debt accumulation and debt-driven land accumulation) drove a de-alignment of interests between the private sector and local governments that was nuanced but quite significant. Local governments still needed investment to drive economic growth (whether motivated by promotion, corruption, or esteem), but they had sources of investment that did not involve accommodating the interests of productive businesses. They could mobilize land resources and real estate–driven

[99] Adam Y. Liu, Jean C. Oi, and Yi Zhang, "China's Local Government Debt: The Grand Bargain," *China Journal*, no. 87 (2022): 40–71.
[100] See Rithmire, "Land Institutions"; Rithmire, *Land Bargains*, chap. 7; Victor C. Shih, "Local Government Debt: Big Rock-Candy Mountain," *China Economic Quarterly* 14, no. 2 (2010): 26–32.
[101] "China Hidden Local Government Debt Is Half of GDP, Goldman Says," *Bloomberg News*, September 29, 2021, https://www.bloomberg.com/news/articles/2021-09-29/china-hidden-local-government-debt-is-half-of-gdp-goldman-says.

investment to amplify GDP, give the appearance of an urban boom, and en-rich themselves, eliding the interests and participation of productive local firms. Second, because they stood to benefit less from the tax revenues generated by productive local firms, local officials had less to gain from their success. Instead, again whether to enrich themselves (corruption) or to swell local coffers, local officials had incentives to extort local firms, shaking them down for "extrabudgetary" fees or more traditional bribes.

Partial Financial Liberalization: The Loss of Party Control

In addition to the fiscal reforms and their effects, the period of the late 1990s through early 2000s was broadly one of apparent financial liberalization. The banking sector, equity markets, and corporate governance practices all un-derwent significant reforms that combined to form the edifice of a modern financial system. I describe these reforms as "apparent" and their results as an "edifice" because they appeared to establish competition and unleash market forces in capital allocation and to institutionalize corporate govern-ance procedures, but they did not, in fact, achieve these outcomes. Instead, the reforms loosened state control over the financial sector, inviting new participants and attenuating the role of political hierarchies and discipline over financial and nonfinancial firms, but they imbued neither markets nor regulators with the power to replace the state as a source of discipline. This partial liberalization interacted disastrously with the precariousness of the business class. As Chapter 6 documents, the short time horizons and oppor-tunistic outlook of many of the country's entrepreneurs enabled them to ma-nipulate an increasingly complex financial system, abetted by political elites at all levels of the state.

Financial Reforms: Contested Control and Ineffective Regulation

After the inflation cycle of the early 1990s that ended with fiscal recentralization, the reforms initiated in China's financial system were aimed at introducing market mechanisms and state regulatory authority to liberalize financial markets yet retain financial stability. Zhu Rongji presided over the most important policy changes, which included a recentralization of control over national banks, a liberalization of the regime for local banks, and a reconfiguration of the regulatory apparatus for the overall financial sector.

The recentralization efforts were twofold: first, concentrating the decision-making power for national banks—the "Big Four"—in party committees in Beijing rather than in committees at the local levels. The latter arrangement had, Zhu and others reasoned, resulted in too much politically directed lending at the behest of local officials, generating NPLs as well as the inflation cycles that appeared throughout the reform era. While this recentralization appeared to end the inflationary cycles, the NPLs did not disappear, and, in many ways, they became more intractable because of the other two reforms, which opened the financial sector to local banks and established a well-meaning but weak regulatory system.[102]

The means of regulatory reform and recentralization was a special commission—the Central Financial Work Commission (中央金融工作委员会, CFWC—created by central leaders, specifically Zhu Rongji, to establish "vertical management of cadres" and "shake off local and departmental influence" in financial supervision and management).[103] Rather than finding itself a permanent part of the party-state economic hierarchy, the CFWC was dissolved in 2003, when regulatory authority was placed in three different bodies to focus on securities (China Securities Regulatory Commission), banks (China Banking Regulatory Commission), and insurance (China Insurance Regulatory Commission).[104] This system in which monetary policy authority resides in the PBoC and regulatory authority is functionally divided among three sectoral agencies is known as "one bank and three commissions" (一行三会). This system was riddled with structural, personnel-related, and legal lacunae that, in combination, left China's financial system without hierarchies to impose discipline on the financial sector through regulation.

---

[102] Victor Shih, who sees the contests over the level of central control as factional conflict between technocrats and "generalists," calls the post-recentralization phase a "long cycle." There is, perhaps, a case to be made that this long cycle ended in the aftermath of the 2008 AFC and the CCP's very large stimulus package as well as the rise of Xi Jinping, but I think the better interpretation is that the forces pushing against financial discipline changed from local governments to crony firms, and the CCP took time to learn how to discipline agents outside the party-state. In other words, in the period of Shih's study, the relevant conflict could have indeed been between central technocrats and more local political officials, but the source of indiscipline and risk in the period I study here, after the late 1990s, is also the private sector.

[103] Sebastian Heilmann, "Regulatory Innovation by Leninist Means: Communist Party Supervision in China's Financial Industry," *China Quarterly*, no. 181 (2005): 1–21.

[104] In addition to Heilmann's piece, see Margaret M. Pearson, "The Business of Governing Business in China: Institutions and Norms of the Emerging Regulatory State," *World Politics* 57, no. 2 (2005): 296–322.

Structurally, the one bank, three commissions model divides authority over financial regulation functionally across sectoral agencies. Such a system was perceived as appropriate for China's stage of financial development at the time. Prior to 2003, the PBoC was both the macroeconomic regulator and the sole financial regulator, and therefore a functional division was seen as a solution to financial market development in various sectors and a necessary step toward an advanced financial system.[105] Yet the sectoral division of labor was mismatched with a model of "mixed financial operations" (混业经营模式) developing in China at the time, by which firms or conglomerates participate in various sectors of China's financial system simultaneously. Many firms held shares in banks as well as nonbank financial institutions (such as insurers or trusts), a practice that would come to facilitate self-dealing. Moreover, while regulatory bodies were tasked with managing risks specific to the respective sectors, there was no regulatory body charged with managing overall financial risk and no coordination mechanism among the three equally ranked regulatory bodies, each of which was administratively separate from the PBoC.[106]

Further, the national regulatory bodies did not coordinate effectively with local regulatory bodies; even the names of the local bodies deviated from those in the national system, and oversight power over regional financial supervisors was weak.[107] National bodies were perceived as being quite disconnected from local practices and fixated on central-state-level institutions (such as large national banks or holding companies), enabling a variety of "grassroots" private financial-innovation practices to emerge in spaces

[105] 崔鸿雁 (Cui Hongyan), "建国以来我国金融监管制度思想演进研究" (Research on the Evolution of China's Financial Supervision System since the Founding of the State), 复旦大学经济学院博士学位论文, 2012年, 5月; 崔琳 (Cui Lin), "统一监管还是分业监管: 基于不完全契约的视角" (Integrated Regulation or Separated Regulation: An Anarchy from the Perspective of Incomplete Contract Theory), 金融评论, 2019年, 第6期: 68–85, 122何德旭 (He Dexu), "金融监管: 世界趋势与中国的选择: 兼论中国银监会的设立" (Regulatory Supervision–Global Trends, and China's Choices: Also on the Establishment of China's Banking Regulatory Commission), 管理世界, 2003年,第9期: 52–61.
[106] 于永宁 (Yu Yongning), "'一行三会'监管协调机制的有效性问题" (On the Effectiveness of the Coordinating Mechanisms for Financial Supervision in China), 山东大学学报 (哲学社会科学版) , 2012年, 第4期: 54–58; 王立锋 (Wang Lifeng), "我国金融监管框架优化路径研究" (Research on the Path to Optimize China's Financial Regulatory Framework), 中央党校博士学位论文, 2018年, 7月. Wang Lifeng notes that it not until 2013 that the Joint Conference on Financial Supervision (金融监管协调部际联席会议) was established.
[107] 周逢民 (Zhou Fengmin), "中央与地方政府金融监管模式选择" (The Choice of China's Model of Central and Local Financial Supervision), 金融发展评论 , 2012年, 第5期: 70–75.

unregulated and ill-understood by those in Beijing.[108] For example, the
2015 financial crisis, the rise of peer-to-peer lending, the sheer scale of mobile payments and financial firms, such as Ant Financial and the rise of "gray
rhinos" (large, indebted conglomerates) all took regulators somewhat by surprise. I detail each of these phenomena in Chapter 6.

Personnel management of the three commissions, especially in combination with a lack of clear legal authority, as described below, left the commissions
ripe for collusion with the firms that they were tasked with regulating. For a
variety of reasons, these regulatory bodies found themselves in a sort of pur-
gatory within the Chinese political system, neither imbued with professional
regulatory power nor in a position of prestige with the CCP. Only the CSRC
did not have to share its regulatory tasks (i.e., oversight of the Shenzhen and
Shanghai Stock Exchanges) with other bureaucracies, but the CCP's own goals
of financial stability eventually overrode the professional regulatory focus of
even that body.[109] The staff were governed by the cadre management system,
but a lack of formal restraints on their power or prohibition on "revolving
door" movement between regulatory agencies and the private sector, especially for the rank and file, made it relatively easy and enormously beneficial
to abuse their positions. For all three sectors, regulators had power to grant
market entry by issuing licenses, which was easy to monetize. They also had
privileged access to information about changes in the financial system and
firm activities, which they used quite frequently for private gain.[110]

As I detail in Chapter 6, corruption and collusion between regulators and
financial system participants was rampant. Large numbers of regulators
"jumped into the sea" (下海) to run financial firms just as participants in
the industry "came ashore" (上岸) to supervise the firms that once had em-
ployed them and might employ them again in the future. Scholars of financial regulation in China have criticized this "relationship network" whereby
regulators and the regulated constitute "one large family" that participates

段志国 (Duan Zhiguo), "分权背景下的地方金融监管权研究" (Research on Local Financial
Supervision against the Backdrop of Decentralization), 中央财经大学院博士学位论文,
2016年, 5月.
    See John K. Yasuda, *On Feeding the Masses: An Anatomy of Regulatory Failure in China*
(New York: Cambridge University Press, 2018).

[108] 张承惠 (Zhang Chengwei), "关于我国金融监管框架重构的思考与建议" (Thoughts and
Suggestions on the Reconstruction of China's Financial Supervisory Framework), 重庆理工大学学
报, 2016年, 第30卷, 第9期.
[109] Pearson, "Business of Governing Business."
[110] 陈银峰 (Chen Yinfeng), "论中国的金融监管与金融反腐败" (On Chinese Financial
Regulation and Financial Anti-corruption), 商场现代化(学术版), 2009年, 第9期: 52–53.

in "black box operations" to reap enormous profits.[111] Officials within the three regulatory agencies have prided themselves on their professionalism, but they recognize that reforms of financial institutions can only go so far in a one-party state where securities laws are difficult to enforce vis-à-vis those with political connections. This is especially true when capital markets are dominated by state-owned players with political ranks much higher than those of the regulators who oversee them.[112] Legally, the scope of financial regulatory authority was never clearly defined, leaving regulators too powerless to take on some activities but also, at the individual level, insufficiently restrained and able to waive or wield power at will.[113]

Ironically, the move to imbue regulatory power over the financial sector in state agencies attenuated the power of the party but then left a vacuum since neither markets nor legal structures replaced the party hierarchies. In combination with the failure to establish a market-driven incentive structure for financial executives and dispersed regulatory authority in three disconnected commissions, these reforms created new sources of a "hierarchical breakdown" that facilitated widespread corruption and predatory behavior, in particular on the part of large conglomerates.[114]

Expanding the Financial Sector

These unsuccessful efforts to establish an effective regulatory structure were accompanied by a wider opening of the financial sector to nonstate participants. Unlike in Indonesia, where private entry into the banking sector was fully opened, China's financial sector remained dominated by state institutions but private access to capital was possible through an increasingly dispersed banking sector. Critically, access to the banking sector was neither closed to the private sector, as it had been during the 1980s and 1990s, nor open and subject to market competition, for example, in terms of dispensing credit based on market interest rates. Instead, the Chinese financial sector was partially liberalized, privileging politically connected firms

---

[111] Ibid.; interview, former China Banking Regulatory Commission official, Shanghai, April 2017.

[112] These sentiments were conveyed during an interview with CSRC officials, Shanghai, May 2017.

[113] 段志国 (Duan Zhiguo), "分权背景下的地方金融监管权研究" (Research on Local Financial Supervision against the Backdrop of Decentralization); 曾筱清 (Zeng Xiaoqing), 李萍 (Li Ping), and 吕婷婷 (Lu Tingting), "金融改革与金融监管的互动分析及其立法建议" (Analysis of the Reciprocal Relationship between Financial Reform and Financial Regulatory Control: Some Related Legislative Issues), 中央财经大学学报, 2003年, 第3期.

[114] Heilmann predicts this would be the case, drawing on Steven Lee Solnick, *Stealing the State: Control and Collapse in Soviet Institutions* (Cambridge, MA: Harvard University Press, 1998).

while also shielding them from market discipline. What was new with the
financial expansion was that the politically connected firms included nonstate or private firms; generations of scholarship on authoritarian and especially state socialist financial systems, including that in China, has fixated on
the inherent problems of credit access for state firms, but nonstate access to
credit is not automatically efficient or productive.[115] A vulnerable and distrustful private sector can engage the financial system in ways even more destructive than can state firms without hard budget constraints.

The period following the recentralization of fiscal revenues and of personnel appointments in the Big Four banks was also one of expanding participation in the financial sector, specifically the entry of local banks. Local
banks remained state-owned but by local levels of the state, typically provincial and municipal governments, and their number rose rapidly in the latter
half of the 1990s and the early 2000s. There were fewer than ten major banks
in the early 1990s, more than sixty by 1997, and eighty by 2005. During the
late 1990s and 2000s their assets grew as well; the share of banking assets
owned by the Big Four declined from 95 percent in 1994 to 60 percent in
2002 and to less than 40 percent in 2014.[116] While the lending practices of
the Big Four would remain the purview of the central government (through
hierarchical personnel control), local banks were more exposed to the influence of local governments. Indeed, the assets (i.e., loans) and liabilities (i.e.,
deposits) increased in step with the overall expansion of the sector and, importantly, local banks facilitated the expansion of local government debt.[117]

The expansion of the financial sector to new financial institutions brought
expanded lending, in particular to the nonstate sector. Indeed, in keeping
with the argument presented in Chapter 1, reformers in China pursed financial liberalization precisely to facilitate resource allocations to the private
sector as well as a source of discipline for state firms. As Figure 5.2 shows,

---

[115] János Kornai, *The Socialist System: The Political Economy of Communism* (Princeton, NJ:
Princeton University Press, 1992); Charles W. Calomiris and Stephen H. Haber, *Fragile by Design:
The Political Origins of Banking Crises and Scarce Credit* (Princeton, NJ: Princeton University Press,
2014); Adam Yao Liu, "Building Markets within Authoritarian Institutions: The Political Economy of
Banking Development in China," PhD dissertation, Stanford University, 2018; Edward S. Steinfeld,
Forging Reform in China: The Fate of State-Owned Industry (New York: Cambridge University Press,
1998).

[116] These data are from Liu, "Building Markets," 64.

[117] Bank balance sheet data indicate that the assets of banks of varying size grew at comparable
rates over the course of the late 2000s. The average three-month growth rate from 2009 to 2021
was 3.60 percent for large banks, 2.54 percent for medium banks, and 5.19 percent for small banks.
People's Bank of China data, via CEIC.

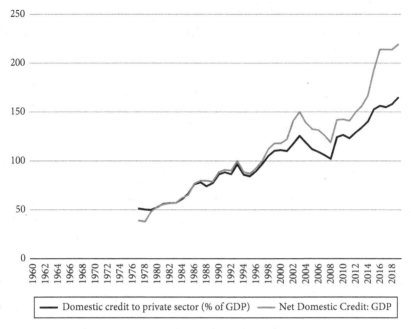

Figure 5.2 Credit Expansion in China during the Reform Era
Source: Data from World Bank and BIS; GDP data from World Bank.

overall lending increased dramatically in China after the late 1990s, and, especially before 2015, most of the new lending went to the private sector.

Shadow Banking

Yet, despite this overall increase in credit to the private sector, after the partial liberalization the private sector faces continued barriers to access in the financial system. Banks remain tightly regulated; in addition to reserve requirements and capital adequacy regulations, Chinese banks face strict rules on the risk-weighting of loan portfolios and on capital consumption, and caps on lending in specific sectors (e.g., real estate) constrain the expansion of bank assets (loans) and their operating profits.[118] The formal supply of credit—loans that fall within the regulations—has long been insufficient to meet both the demand for credit in the Chinese economy and the desire for financial institutions to expand revenues and profits. The gap is filled by

---

[118] Guofeng Sun, "China's Shadow Banking: Bank's Shadow and Traditional Shadow Banking" (BIS Working Paper no. 822, November 2019), 5; Sun, "Banking Institutions and Banking Regulations."

shadow banking, a collection of activities that expand credit but do not appear on the balance sheets of Chinese banks. In general, policymakers and scholars identify two categories of activity that are described as shadow banking: first, credit intermediation by nonbank financial institutions, which is a form of shadow banking present in many economies, including economies with developed financial sectors (such as the United States) and, second, "banks' shadow," credit created through the expansion of banks' liabilities by hidden balance-sheet items. This latter form of credit expansion has been uniquely significant in China, as banks collude with one another and with firms to extend loans to firms by disguising them as interbank assets or other forms of investments so as to circumvent strict regulations.[119]

The entrance of nonbank financial institutions has also been significant. These institutions include everything from securities brokers, insurance firms, and investment banks to person-to-person lending platforms, leasing companies, and pawn shops. Some such institutions clearly enjoy more assets than others, but they all have played roles in the growth of debt in the Chinese economy since the 1990s. Comprehensive data on the growth of these institutions are difficult to come by, but Table 5.7 shows the increase in overall nonbank financial institutions according to official CBRC data during the 2000s. Importantly, the divided regulatory system left the government with little oversight into the connections between nonbank financial institutions and banks and few tools to manage the overall expansion of credit and the risks it entails in both size and distribution.[120]

Chapter 6 discusses the rise of firms with multiple financial vehicles, which facilitated extensive self-dealing, "financial innovations" such as peer-to-peer lending, and the rapid expansion of equity markets in 2012–16. All of these phenomena entailed the development of substantial, even systemic, financial risks, some of which are evidence of the looting and

---

[119] Kinda Hachem, "Shadow Banking in China," *Annual Review of Financial Economics* 10, no. 1 (2018): 287–308, https://doi.org/10.1146/annurev-financial-110217-023025\; Sun, "China's Shadow Banking."

[120] The lack of coordination in the regulatory system was cause for criticism within Chinese academic and policy circles early during this period. See 中国人民银行济南分行课题组 (People's Bank, Ji'nan Branch, Research Group), "'一行三会'体制下的金融宏观调控与监管协调的综合效能研究" (Research on the Comprehensive Effectiveness of Financial Macro-control and Regulatory Coordination under the System of One Bank and Three Commissions); 金融研究. 2005 增刊; 何德旭 (He Dexu), "金融监管: 世界趋势与中国的选择: 兼论中国银监会的设立" (Regulatory Supervision, Global Trends, and China's Choices: Also on the Establishment of China's Banking Regulatory Commission); 邢桂君 (Xing Guijun), "我国金融控股公司监管研究" (Research the Supervision of Chinese Financial Holding Companies), 金融与经济, 2008年, 第6期.

Table 5.7 Growth of Bank and Nonbank Financial Institutions, 2004–2019

	Banking Institutions*	Policy Banks	Large Commercial Banks	Shareholding Commercial Banks	City Commercial Banks	Nonbank Financial Institutions	Asset Management Companies
2004	33,862	3	4	12	112	148	
2005	28,067	3	4	13	113	150	
2006	19,797	3	5	12	113	130	
2007	8,877	3	5	12	124	148	4
2008	5,634	3	5	12	136	162	4
2009	3,857	3	5	12	143	174	4
2010	3,769	3	5	12	147	208	4
2011	3,800	3	5	12	144	243	4
2012	3,747	3	5	12	144	262	4
2013	3,949	3	5	12	145	307	4
2014	4,089	3	5	12	133	323	4
2015	4,261	3	5	12	133	385	4
2016	4,398	3	5	12	134	412	4
2017	4,532	3	5	12	134	437	4
2018	4,571	3	6	12	134	444	4
2019	4,595	3	6	12	134	451	4

Source: CBRC, via CEIC.

* The total number of banking institutions includes urban credit cooperatives before 2009, after which they disappear, as well as rural financial institutions, which number more than 30,000 in 2004 but fewer than 4,000 in 2019. These institutions do not hold significant assets, nor do they play major roles in credit creation for either the private or the public sector.

financial manipulation that are characteristic of mutual endangerment. There is a large literature, in both English and Chinese, that examines the evolution of China's financial system and, in particular, the phenomenon of shadow banking.[121] I do not intend to intervene in either financial economics investigations of how resources have been allocated or policy debates about how China's regulatory system ought to be structured. Rather, my goal is to show that China's process of partial financial liberalization attenuated state control but failed to produce the sort of transparency and regularized rule enforcement that would produce effective market discipline. In all three cases, partial financial liberalization generated resource misallocation and corruption, outcomes decidedly unsurprising based on generations of thinking about economic incentives. But in China, as in Indonesia, the standard effects of partial liberalization met the decidedly unusual politics of a vulnerable business class that had informal relationships with political elites.

Conclusion: The End of Alignment

What happened in the 2000s is that all the central SOEs pretended to be real firms with a modern corporate organization, but they were not. They were just empty houses for whatever the government

---

[121] Kaiji Chen, Jue Ren, and Tao Zha, "The Nexus of Monetary Policy and Shadow Banking in China," *American Economic Review* 108, no. 12 (2018): 3891–936; Franklin Allen, Yiming Qian, Guoqian Tu, and Frank Yu, "Entrusted Loans: A Close Look at China's Shadow Banking System," *Journal of Financial Economics* 133, no. 1 (2019): 18–41; Kinda Hachem and Zheng Song, "Liquidity Rules and Credit Booms," *Journal of Political Economy* 129, no. 10 (2021): 2721–65, https://doi.org/10.1086/715074; 孙国峰 (Sun Guofeng), 第一排: 中国金融改革的近距离思考 (China's Financial Reforms: Through the Eyes of a Front-Bencher) (北京: 中国经济出版社, 2012); 王浩 (Wang Hao), 王红林 (Wang Honglin), 王立升 (Wang Lisheng), and 周皓 (Zhou Hao), "影子银行：中国利率市场化双轨改革机制" (Shadow Banking: China's Dual-Track Reform Mechanism to Liberalize Interest Rates), 清华五道口金融学院, January 5, 2008, http://www.pbcsf.tsinghua.edu.cn/portal/article/index/id/2188.html; 朱民 (Zhu Min), "功能监管是未来方向，金融委发挥协调作用" (Functional Supervision Is the Future Direction, and the Financial Commission Will Play a Coordinating Role), 清华五道口金融学院, November 24, 2017, http://www.pbcsf.tsinghua.edu.cn/portal/article/index/id/1317.html; 吴晓灵 (Wu Xiaoling), "防控金融风险 注重金融安全" (Preventing and Controlling Financial Risks with a Focus on Financial Security), 清华五道口全球金融论坛上的讲话, June 3, 2017, http://www.pbcsf.tsinghua.edu.cn/portal/article/index/id/1187.html; Zhuo Chen, Zhiguo He, and Chun Liu, "The Financing of Local Government in China: Stimulus Loan Wanes and Shadow Banking Waxes," *Journal of Financial Economics* 137 (2020): 42–71; Carl Walter, "Convergence and Reversion: China's Banking System at 70," *Journal of Applied Corporate Finance* 32, no. 4 (2020): 34–43; Carl E. Walter and Fraser J. T. Howie, *Red Capitalism: The Fragile Financial Foundation of China's Extraordinary Rise* (Hoboken, NJ: Wiley, 2011).

wanted to do. I think many in the non-state sector thought we could do the same.[122]

In the years since the AFC of the late 1990s, the financial system witnessed two transformations: corporate governance reform and restructuring and partial liberalization of the financial sector. In combination, these reforms attenuated the party-state's control over the financial sector but without replacing strict party control with rule of law or market discipline. In the fiscal sector, China's economic policymakers centralized the bulk of tax resources but left the lion's share of the expenditure burden to local governments. At the same time, land "markets" grew as a source of revenue for local governments, as did debt instruments.

Each of these reforms bears some resemblance to liberalizing reforms as they appeared to push institutions in China's political economy away from state socialism and toward what might appear to be a market economy. Yet, clearly, in each arena, the reforms were "partial" in that they were directionally liberal but with retained state control or lack of true market oversight. For example, corporate governance reform was initiated in the SOEs themselves progressively over the course of the first decade of the century to remove firm control from the ministries and to introduce a shareholder model. As is widely documented, the establishment of the State-Owned Assets Supervision and Administration Commission (SASAC) put the state in the position of dominant shareholder and pushed SOEs to adopt modern corporate forms and eventually list on various public exchanges. Yet clearly the state would retain control, and minority shareholders would have little power if their wishes ran counter to those of the SASAC, even when SOEs were charged with pursuing political objectives that would generate few or negative returns for shareholders. The superficiality of corporate governance mechanisms and market discipline for the state sector was not lost on non-state economic participants, who deftly adopted the same superficialities in service of their own efforts.

In introducing corporate governance reforms, the development of equity markets, and the liberalization of banking, the CCP pursued market mechanisms without market discipline. Market mechanisms were to aid the party-state in achieving its objectives of economic growth but without relinquishing control over major factors of production or introducing

---

[122] Quotation from Shanghai-based accountant, personal communication, 2017.

instability. These practices are a kind of "rule by market," analogous to the role of law in contemporary China, whereby the regime pursues "rule by law" to buttress its own power but resists "rule of law" by which the state itself is constrained.[123] Rule by market can work to generate productive economic behaviors and to constrain damaging behaviors only if market mechanisms are really allowed to function. By contrast, when many within an economy are immune from market discipline and the state is intolerant of transparency of information and firm failure, both of which are necessary for discipline, partial markets are easy arenas in which politically connected actors enrich themselves at society's expense.

As disciplinary mechanisms faded from both the financial and fiscal systems, political and business elites were enabled, even incentivized, to collude with one another to enrich themselves on short time horizons. As I argue in Chapter 2 and here, the incentives, indeed the worldviews, of the political and business elites were shaped by the existential vulnerability inherent to their political status and China's policymaking style. Not all firms desired to engage in corrupt misallocation of resources and looting; some were deeply embedded in global supply chains that exerted significant discipline, some were too small to capture resources in this way, and still others were helmed by entrepreneurs with genuine desires to build competitive and productive firms. The argument I present about the shift from mutual alignment to mutual endangerment describes both the meso and the macro environments of state-business relations rather than predicts individual behavior under most circumstances. The patterns of political-business elite interactions that emerged in the context of vulnerability and partial financial liberalization are metastatic, expanding through the political economy as participants fold ever greater numbers of their counterparts into mutual endangerment.

---

[123] Ching Kwan Lee, *Against the Law: Labor Protests in China's Rustbelt and Sunbelt* (Berkeley: University of California Press, 2007).

6

Elite Disintegration

The Moral Economy of Mutual Endangerment in China

On 1 March 2017, in the fifth year of Xi Jinping's sweeping anticorruption campaign, Chen Xu of the Shanghai People's Procuratorate, the provincial municipality's highest legal authority and the office in charge of corruption prosecutions, was detained by authorities and charged with corruption. Specifically, Chen was alleged to have "manipulated legal trials for personal ends," receiving bribes via his relatives and violating the Chinese Communist Party (CCP) ban on participating in commercial activities. The Central Commission on Discipline Inspection (CCDI) used quite harsh language in Chen's case, branding him as a "notable example of an official with no scruples about continuing corruption activities even after the Eighteenth Party Congress" (at which Xi Jinping assumed power and announced his anticorruption efforts).[1]

After Chen's arrest, rumors about the misdeeds of Chen and his family swirled in the unofficial media. Chen was alleged to have been involved in a notorious real estate auction fraud in which a prominent piece of land was sold at an unreasonably cheap price to a firm controlled by people closely linked to Shanghai's legal officials. Further, during the Procuratorate's own investigation of the fraud, it was rumored that two local investigators and two local witnesses (the general manager of a local auction company and his wife) were murdered. These rumors were widespread online, but they never appeared in formal charges or reputable sources.[2] Chen was never accused of homicide but was sentenced to life in prison for corruption

---

[1] These details are from the CCDI website on examinations and investigations (审查调查) where official details of corruption cases have been posted since 2013, https://www.ccdi.gov.cn/scdcn/. I collected details about corruption cases of senior state officials between 2012 and 2017, details in Table 6.3.

[2] For example, see http://www.scyjlaw.com/article-3170-1.html (accessed June 19, 2018) and http://finance.ifeng.com/a/20170526/15410828_0.shtml (accessed June 19, 2018). These and similar posts were available in 2017 but have since been removed from the web.

Precarious Ties. Meg Rithmire, Oxford University Press. © Oxford University Press 2023.
DOI: 10.1093/oso/9780197697528.003.0006

charges, and he publicly confessed to having preferences for a luxurious lifestyle.[3]

The month before Chen's arrest, in an unrelated incident, one of China's most prominent tycoons, Xiao Jianhua of the Tomorrow Group, was forcibly removed from his luxury apartment in Hong Kong and transported across the border to the Mainland. Unlike when party and/or state officials are taken into custody, no formal charges were announced, and Xiao remained in detention for five years before his trial began in 2022. Until then, Xiao had been touted as a "banker to the ruling class," one of contemporary China's most politically favored business elites, having taken the side of the regime as a college student in 1989 and endearing himself to CCP elites in the decades since. At the time of his downfall, Xiao presided over a sprawling business empire, much of which was hidden. Starting in 2004, Xiao and his wife resigned from formal positions in businesses they controlled, anywhere between two and three thousand companies worth as much as $100 billion according to press reports and other investigations, though official corporate filings indicate only twenty-six formal subsidiaries and an additional six reported in bond prospectuses.[4] Xiao's empire was built on control of financial firms, holding licenses in securities, insurance, and banking firms, many of which were obscurely connected with other companies in the group. By 2020, the state had seized almost all of the assets connected to the Tomorrow Group and had accused its various firms of corporate governance violations and obfuscation of the ultimate owners. For its part, the Tomorrow Group, even with Xiao Jianhua in custody, accused the government of defamation and denied it had taken excessive risks or illegal actions.[5] At the time of his abduction, Xiao was a Canadian citizen

---

[3] Chen Xu's written confession was featured in a 2017 exhibit, held at the Beijing Exhibition Hall, "Five Years of Hard Work" about the anticorruption campaign. A photograph of the confession is available at https://www.oeeee.com/mp/a/BAAFRD00002017092954085.html (accessed June 19, 2019).

[4] This chapter draws on data collected on large Chinese firms using corporate filings. A research team under my supervision used China's Bureau of Industry and Commerce (工商局), WIND database, and various databases containing corporate financial information to collect filings and prospectuses for a selection of large Chinese firms. Appendix C details the data collection, and the sections below describe the findings. For press reports on Xiao's empire, see 苏龙飞 (Su Longfei), "明天帝国：影子金融大亨肖建华的资产版" (Tomorrow Empire: Asset Map of Xiao Jianhua), 新财富 (New Fortune), April 5, 2013, 38–73, at http://www.xcf.cn/newfortune/fmgs/201304/t20130407_426444.htm.

[5] David Barboza, "China Seizes Tycoon's Assets," Wire China, July 17, 2020. The Wire obtained a copy of the company's statement before it was removed from the web, https://www.thewirechina.com/2020/07/17/china-seizes-tycoons-assets/.

with passports from Antigua and Bermuda, and he had donated $10 million to Harvard University.[6]

These cases entail many elements of state-business relations and corruption that are typical of China in the twenty-first century, during which time state-business times became precarious for both sides. I detail more systematic data below to show that many of China's high- and low-profile corruption cases not only involved bribery for business advantage but also elements of fraud (looting of state assets and wealth), the use of unofficial media sources to reveal details, whether rumors or facts, of the activities of political and business elites, the use of families to obscure connections, and even the use of violence to eliminate personal threats. Many of these elements are features of mutual endangerment and appear similar to patterns of state-business relations that I detail in late New Order Indonesia. Corruption, to be sure, was plenty evident throughout China's reform era, but these patterns are a far cry from the "special deals" and "steroid for growth" style of state-business coziness that facilitated economic growth amid imperfect formal institutions.[7] By contrast, mutual endangerment entails fraud and malfeasance, a massive leakage of wealth and resources from China abroad, a growing legitimacy deficit with public perceptions that the CCP has become corrupt and undisciplined, and deep financial risk imperiling China's economic stability.

This chapter details what I call "elite disintegration," the process by which mutual alignment between state and business devolved into mutual endangerment and produced dual political and economic crises for the regime. The process is a disintegration rather than an abrupt rupture; as I argue in Chapters 2 and 5, mutual alignment is built atop distrust, with financial discipline preventing distrust from becoming short-termism and fraud. In China, the source of that distrust was the fundamental political insecurity of capitalists. Capitalists' precariousness extended beyond the time of Mao's death and the onset of reforms. Ironically, political insecurity was a motive for informal collusion between private-sector elites. In a world where formal laws and national political institutions could not and did not protect

[6] Benjamin Haas, "Chinese Billionaire Xiao Jianhua 'Abducted' from Hong Kong Hotel," *The Guardian*, February 1, 2017, https://www.theguardian.com/world/2017/feb/01/chinese-billionaire-xiao-jianhua-abducted-from-hong-kong-hotel-reports; James Areddy, "Missing Billionaire Has Ties to China's Military," *Wall Street Journal*, April 18, 2017, https://www.wsj.com/articles/missing-billionaire-has-ties-to-chinas-military-1492536233.

[7] These terms are from Chong-En Bai, Chang-Tai Hsieh, and Zheng Michael Song, "Special Deals with Chinese Characteristics" (Washington, DC: NBER Working Paper no. 25839, 2019) and Yuen Yuen Ang, *China's Gilded Age: The Paradox of Economic Boom and Vast Corruption* (New York: Cambridge University Press, 2020).

risk-taking entrepreneurs, they sought local protection, or unwritten rules (潜规则).[8] As I have argued, local protection was based on mutual economic interests (bribes, kickbacks, and incentives to spur local growth), but the relationships are social as well, famously so.

Nearly every memoir of doing business in China, from the early reform era through the onset of Xi Jinping's anticorruption campaign in 2012, is filled with salacious tales of cultivating relationships, or guanxi (培养关系). Sociologists and anthropologists have characterized guanxi as reciprocal, iterated interactions, with both parties expected to contribute *and* benefit at different times.[9] The content of these relationships is revealing; informal relationships frequently involve illegal activity (such as gambling and prostitution) and elaborate banqueting to tie parties together inexorably. Mutual enmeshment in illicit activities ensures that, should business relationships become complex, one party cannot easily betray or abandon the other. John Osburg, describing the "inflationary dynamic of business entertainment," quotes a popular internet saying: "Doing a hundred good things for the leader is not as good as doing one bad thing with the leader. If the leader takes you to do a bad thing together, that means there will be a hundred good things waiting for you!"[10] These sentiments, widely reflected in my own field-work, are expressions of precarious ties. Capitalists have pursued ever-more intimate relationships with political elites not out of love for the party but out of fear.

As discipline attenuated with the fiscal shift to land finance and partial liberalization in the financial sector, a process I described in Chapter 5, state-business relations moved toward mutual endangerment. Financial systems became open to predation of political and business actors with short time horizons, and the incentives of many rank-and-file political officials, and even political elites, departed from the regime's overall goals. The three manifestations of mutual endangerment—weaponized information, asset expatriation, and looting—became readily evident in China's political economy by the early 2010s and especially during the first few years of Xi

---

[8] John Osburg, *Anxious Wealth: Money and Morality among China's New Rich* (Stanford: Stanford University Press, 2013), 32.

[9] Thomas Gold, Doug Guthrie, and David L. Wank, eds., *Social Connections in China: Institutions, Culture, and the Changing Nature of Guanxi* (New York: Cambridge University Press, 2002); Osburg, *Anxious Wealth*; David L. Wank, *Commodifying Communism: Business, Trust, and Politics in a Chinese City* (New York: Cambridge University Press, 1999).

[10] Osburg, *Anxious Wealth*, 37. See also Yue Hou, *The Private Sector in Public Office: Selective Property Rights in China* (New York: Cambridge University Press, 2019).

Jinping's administration, during which looting and asset expatriation accelerated precisely as Xi threatened to crack down.

Mutual Endangerment in Contemporary China

> I came to believe that in China a long-term business model wouldn't work. I began to understand what some of my entrepreneur friends had been telling me all along: the smart way to do business in China was to build something, sell it, take money off the table, and go back in. If you invest $1 and you make $10, you take $7 out and reinvest $3. But if you keep $10 in, chances are you'll lose it all.
>
> —Desmond Shum[11]

This section examines evidence for the manifestation of mutual endangerment in China: weaponized information, asset expatriation, and looting. Before this presentation of evidence, however, I express the same caveat about mutual endangerment and state-business relations generally that I state in the Indonesian and Malaysian cases: no single pattern of relationships can be realistically expected to characterize state-business relations in all sectors of a political economy. At the same time that China's economic expansion was driven by credit and looting, China was becoming the "world's factory," the world's largest exporter (accounting for 10 percent of global exports by 2011), and the largest destination for foreign direct investment (FDI) in the developing world.[12] That a dynamic and competitive export-driven economy flourished alongside a deeply corrupt and distorted economy supports rather than challenges the theory I have developed: where Chinese firms were subject to market discipline, they were productive, and where they were not, and especially in domestic sectors where resources were closely linked to political power (e.g., real estate and finance), they looted. Even so, my contention is not that mutual endangerment obtains in a mechanistic or deterministic way, even in the above sectors. Rather, the pattern of state-business relations emerges and expands gradually and snowballs; as greater numbers of firms and individuals, whether business or

---

[11] Desmond Shum, *Red Roulette: An Insider's Story of Wealth, Power, Corruption and Vengeance in Today's China* (New York: Scribner, 2021), 194.
[12] Data from IMF Balance of Payments.

political elites or both, engage in mutual endangerment, the incentives for others to do so expand as well.

Asset Expatriation

Over the course of the 2000s, the People's Republic of China (PRC) became both the developing world's largest destination for FDI and then, in 2015 for the first time, a net capital exporter. In 2017, China's outward foreign direct investment (OFDI) stock hit $1.8 trillion, sixty-two times the 2002 amount.[13] China's shift to global economic power has generated an appropriately large literature on its role in the world and its behavior as financier, lender, and investor. The vast majority of this literature focuses on the strategic aspects of China's outward investment and/or its effects on the host countries.[14] Lost in loud discussions about whether China is "buying the world" is the fact that much of the capital expatriated from China, the purpose of which is to pursue safety by investing abroad, is less strategic and more crony. Figure 6.1 shows aggregate data on capital flows from China between 2000 and 2022. Clearly, over the same period during which China was pursuing the Belt and Road Initiative (BRI) as well as strategic acquisitions in worldwide technology sectors (2013–18), the amount of capital leaving China via direct investments was equal to or less than the volume of capital secreted out of the country (measured in errors and omissions). Capital flight generally indicates outflows of resident capital and frequently indicates expectations of economic or political crisis, or at least insecurity. That flight, through both legal and illegal channels, accelerated as China's financial system opened up after 2005 and even more so under Xi Jinping.

Asset expatriation and capital flight are basic manifestations of distrust between business actors and political elites. In the Indonesian case, the

---

[13] This section draws on Meg Rithmire, "Going Out or Opting Out? Capital, Political Vulnerability, and the State in China's Outward Investment," *Comparative Politics* 54, no. 3 (2022): 477–99, https://doi.org/10.5129/001041522X16244682037327. Material reproduced here with permission from *Comparative Politics*.

[14] See Ching Kwan Lee, *The Specter of Global China: Politics, Labor, and Foreign Investment in Africa* (Chicago: University of Chicago Press, 2017); Peter Nolan, *Is China Buying the World?* (Cambridge: Polity, 2012); Maria Repnikova, *Chinese Soft Power* (New York: Cambridge University Press, 2022); Kai Guo, Ningxin Jiang, Fan Qi, and Yue Zhao, "RMB Internationalization: Past, Present, and Prospect," in Marlene Amstad, Guofeng Sun, and Wei Xiong, eds., *The Handbook of China's Financial System* (Princeton, NJ: Princeton University Press, 2020), 229–51.

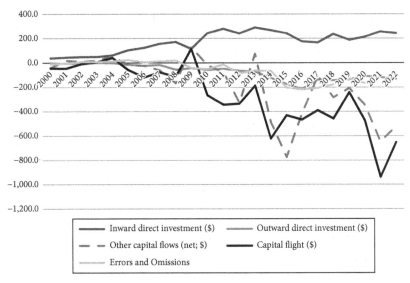

Figure 6.1 Capital Flows, China 2000–2022 ($ billions)

Note: "Capital flight" is the current-account balance with the sign reversed plus the change in international reserves, minus the change in total external debt stock (not adjusted for the effects of cross-currency valuation changes), minus net direct investments.

Source: IMF Balance of Payments data, via Economist Intelligence Unit.

arrangement between Suharto and the Chinese business elites was premised on an open capital account that allowed business elites an exit path for the duration of the regime. In China, however, capital controls have been a fundamental feature of the PRC's tepid embrace of global capital. Over the course of the 2010s, capital controls were liberalized, both formally and informally. Formally, the rules governing the convertibility of the RMB were relaxed progressively and significantly between 2008 and 2015, culminating in the currency's inclusion in the IMF Special Drawing Rights (SDR) basket in 2015.[15] Informally, various government initiatives, including campaigns such as "Going Out" and the BRI, to push Chinese firms abroad seemed to welcome capital outflows and exert political pressure on the Ministry of Commerce and the State Administration of Foreign Exchange to facilitate conversion and outward investment.[16]

[15] Ibid.

[16] Min Ye, "China Invests Overseas: Regulation and Representation," *Modern China Studies* 21, no. 1 (2014): 173–204.

Chapter 5 details how illicit flows of RMB, for example through FDI "round-tripping," represented distrust and dissimulation on the part of domestic capital-holders. As the errors and omissions trends show, illicit outward flows continued during the period of financial liberalization in the twenty-first century, but, for the first time, Chinese firms had a politically acceptable and legally clear path abroad. Academic and popular treatments of China's transition to capital exporter have focused primarily on the role of SOEs and Beijing's strategic interests in pursuing natural resources, infrastructure development, and more advanced technological resources. Those pursuits are real, of course, but they have unfolded alongside an exodus of what is best termed "crony capital" seeking to turn domestic access to the financial system into global assets beyond the reach of the PRC state.[17]

It is not straightforward to disentangle asset expatriation from commercially minded outward investment, nor is it simple to track capital flight and to discern its logic. After all, these actions are designed to obscure and disguise, and "crony capital" is characterized by its political logic rather than the form of investment per se. Yet we can see the progress of capital flight in a number of ways. First, contrary to the narrative that Chinese OFDI pursues institutionally weak environments and natural resources, much of the post-2010 OFDI went to the developed world, and it was in sectors, such as real estate, finance, tourism, and hospitality, perceived as safe assets. Figure 6.2 shows aggregate China's OFDI from 2005 to 2018. It is readily apparent that the massive expansion of OFDI under Xi Jinping is mostly attributable to capital flows to Europe and the United States.

Second, the logic of asset expatriation is visible when examining the activities of large conglomerate firms, particularly those with close relationships with political elites. In a system with political trust, we would not expect the most connected firms to be the ones that expatriate assets, but in fact political closeness with distrust produces exactly this pattern. Here the activities of a set of firms designated by Xi Jinping as "gray rhinos," posing systemic risks to China's financial stability, are particularly instructive. Table 6.1 displays basic descriptive data on the overseas activities of HNA, Dalian Wanda, Fosun, and Anbang, four firms that came under investigation in 2016–17 as a result of their financial and global activities.[18] I discuss these firms and their

[17] Rithmire, "Going Out."

[18] Hongyuran Wu, Nan Guo, and Cheng Leng, "China Asks Banks to Assess Credit Risks Linked to Firms Active in Overseas Deals," *Caixin Global*, June 22, 2017, https://www.caixinglobal.com/2017-06-22/china-asks-banks-to-assess-credit-risks-linked-to-firms-active-in-overseas-deals-101104621.html.

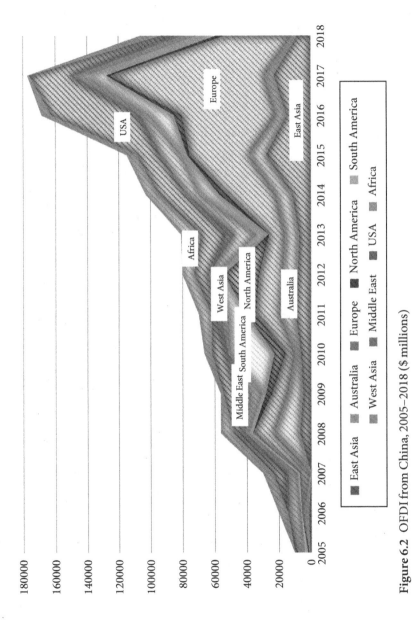

Figure 6.2 OFDI from China, 2005–2018 ($ millions)

Source: China Investment Tracker, American Enterprise Institute.

Table 6.1 Overseas M&A Activity of Four "Gray Rhino" Firms, 2001–2017

	HNA	Dalian Wanda	Fosun	Anbang
Number of deals	60	19	37	12
Disclosed value ($ billions)	$16.08	$13.96	$11.18	$14.40
% Western Europe, Oceania, North America	68	89.50	86	83
% Hong Kong	27	10.50	0	0
% tax havens	7	0	5	0
Number of deals after 2013 (onset of anticorruption campaign)	46	17	36	12
ICIJ appearances	3	2	3	0
Top industries	1. Air Transport (14) 2. Transportation Services (7) 3. Hotels and lodging (6) 4. Holding and Other Investments (5) 5. Securities and Commodity Trading (5)	1. Amusement and Recreation (8) 2. Motion Pictures (5) 3. Real Estate (2) 4. Engineering, Accounting, Research, Management Services (2)	1. Insurance (8) 2. Holding and Other Investment (7) 3. Mining / Oil & Gas (4) 4. Wholesale Trade (3) 5. Real Estate (3) 6. Apparel (3)	1. Insurance (5) 2. Hotels and Lodging (3) 3. Holding and Other Investments (2)

Source: Company filings accessed via State Administration of Industry and Commerce; WIND database; FactSet database; and ICIJ data. See Appendix C.

conflict with the CCP in greater depth later in this chapter: by 2020, HNA and Anbang had been nationalized and their founders jailed, and Dalian Wanda and Fosun had been forced to "unwind" many of their global and financial endeavors. Collectively, these four firms deployed more than $50 billion in outward mergers and acquisitions (M&As) between 2001 and 2017. Acquisition of firms is preferable to "greenfield" FDI because Chinese investors can then acquire performing assets and even overpay. In addition to looking at their formal and public M&A deals, I use data from the International Consortium of Investigative Journalists (ICIJ) "Offshore Leaks" database, which contains information on offshore firms and intermediaries leaked from a variety of sources. Offshore firms are typically constructed to obscure ownership, and the ICIJ data are not, to be sure, exhaustive of all offshore activities, but rather they are convenient samples of data from various investigations or leaks. Firm names in offshore data differ from formal firm names in domestic registrations, and therefore in Table 6.1 I use the addresses of the registered firms, checking all ICIJ data and all addresses of registered firms that appear as subsidiaries of the four companies (see Appendix C and the below section on "Looting" on how I obtained subsidiary information).[19]

As the PRC encouraged global investments through the BRI and other campaigns, distrustful but adept business elites turned their privileged access to China's undisciplined financial system into secured globalized wealth. For example, take (now defunct) CEFC (China Energy Company, Ltd.), a privately owned company headed by tycoon Ye Jianming that invested billions across Eastern Europe, Africa, and the Middle East. The company cultivated relationships with political and business elites abroad by implying it had deep ties with Chinese leaders and associating itself with China's promises to bring growth and connectivity to the world. The company's outright use of bribery attracted the ire of Western officials, and its involvement in high-level politics in countries such as the Czech Republic contributed to backlash against China's influence. Ye was detained by Chinese authorities in March 2018 after one of his employees was arrested in New York on bribery charges. When CEFC and its chairman fell in 2017–18, the company held more than $15 billion in debt and owned luxury properties from New York to Hong

---

[19] See ICIJ, https://offshoreleaks.icij.org/. ICIJ notes, and so should I, that an appearance in the offshore leaks data is not evidence of wrongdoing, only that a person or company or, in this case, address was involved in the setup of offshore companies. The ICIJ data are rendered in pinyin, making it difficult to connect the names of individuals listed in the ICIJ data to known Chinese firms because of the commonness of most Chinese names. Appendix C presents in more detail how I used the data.

Kong.[20] Representatives of another firm, one that came under investigation in spring 2017 for amassing excess risk and suspicious financing of overseas expansions, explained its strategy was to "ride alongside the BRI," pursuing deals especially in European countries where bilateral diplomacy in the BRI context created a favorable environment for Chinese firms. This firm's investments were not in infrastructure (as would be directed by the BRI) but rather in real estate and entertainment. One representative reported that its executive team tried to plan its trips to coincide with BRI-related events to "benefit from the relationship" between China and BRI countries.[21]

The flood of assets overseas has been a source of frustration for the CCP in the context of the anticorruption campaign and efforts to manage the value of the RMB. In 2015, as I detail below in the discussion of China's 2015–16 financial crisis, when the RMB was included in the IMF's SDR basket and its value permitted to float slightly, its value dropped, a surprise to some monetary authorities in China and many observers abroad. As capital flowed out of China, policymakers became concerned about conserving foreign exchange and protecting the value of the RMB. In 2016, after just a few years of a permissive capital environment, the CCP adopted targeted controls on "irrational investments," meaning property, entertainment, vice, gaming, and sports—exactly the sectors attractive to business elites seeking safety and prestige purchases.[22] Zhou Xiaochuan, PBoC governor until 2018, said in 2016: "Of course, as we have noticed, some people are pursuing emigration and investing in overseas real estate due to concerns with confidence, property protection and original sins; some businessmen are investing overseas through acquisitions, not due to comparative advantages or to expand into new markets, but to keep a way open for exit in the context of incomplete bankruptcy law in China."[23] Domestic regulation since 2016 has focused on limiting "systemic risks," principally meaning heavily indebted firms with significant overseas risks. In late 2017, the National Development and Reform Commission, which saw its own power grow with greater government influence, announced a new system to monitor Chinese firms abroad,

---

[20] David Barboza and Michael Forsythe, "Behind the Rise of China's HNA: The Chairman's Brother," *New York Times*, March 27, 2018, https://www.nytimes.com/2018/03/27/business/hna-group-deals-china.html; Alexandra Stevenson et al., "A Chinese Tycoon Sought Power and Influence. Washington Responded," *New York Times*, December 12, 2018.

[21] Interview, Beijing, June 2017.

[22] "State Council Issues Guideline on Overseas Investment," August 18, 2017, http://english.gov.cn/policies/latest_releases/2017/08/18/content_281475798846134.htm.

[23] People's Bank of China, "Transcript of Governor Zhou Xiaochuan's Exclusive Interview with Caixin Weekly," February 14, 2016, http://www.pbc.gov.cn/english/130721/3017134/index.html.

Table 6.2 CCP Efforts at International Asset Recovery, 2008–2021

	Time Frame	Individuals Apprehended	Assets Recovered
"Operation Foxhunt"	2008–	2008–14: 730 2015: 857 2016: 951 2019 (by November): 1841	4.091 billion RMB (in 2019)
"Operation Skynet"	2014–	7,831 (as of June 2020)	19.654 billion RMB (June 2020)

"Red 100 Notice"	2022	Individuals apprehended: 60
		Work units of targets
		  State firms: 33
		  State banks or financial firms: 14
		  Private firms: 31
		  Government offices: 25
		  Other (e.g., universities): 2
		  Firms with unclear ownership: 9	

Source: Official data released by Public Security Bureau accessed via media reports and press releases, e.g., https://www.ccdi.gov.cn/toutiao/201901/t20190109_186614.html (accessed May 18, 2022). Firm ownership (state versus private) was determined via WireScreen; I designate any firm with more than 50 percent state ownership as state. Numbers for "Operations Foxhunt" and "Skynet" via media reports.

by recording and tallying illegal activities as well as actions that "disrupt foreign economic cooperation, adversely impact the Belt and Road Initiative, or harm China's reputation."[24]

The dynamics of asset expatriation are on display as well in the CCP's efforts to repatriate from abroad "economic criminals" as well as their assets. "Operation Foxhunt" (猎狐) (2008–) and "Operation Skynet" (天网行动) (2014–) are two related campaigns to recover people and assets from abroad. Both involve actions at the central and provincial/municipal levels. Official statistics indicate that thousands of "economic criminals," including party members and government officials, have been apprehended or "persuaded to return" over the course of the campaigns (see Table 6.2). Relatedly, the so-called "100 Red Notice" (百名红通) publicizes details of fugitives whom the Chinese government seeks to pursue through Interpol. Many of these fugitives were apprehended during the above two campaigns; these criminals and former officials are pursued by the Office of International Pursuit of

---

[24] Lusha Zhang and Elias Glenn, "China to Set Up System to Monitor Its Firms Overseas," Reuters, November 28, 2017, https://www.reuters.com/article/us-china-investment-overseas/china-to-set-up-system-to-monitor-its-firms-overseas-idUSKBN1DS0NR.

Fugitives, Assets, and Asset Recovery (中央反腐协调小组国际追逃追赃工作办公室) within the CCDI. To be sure, most of these targets are officials charged with embezzlement from state offices and firms, but, as Table 6.2 shows, nearly one-third had helmed private firms.

Weaponized Information

Of the three cases examined in this book, relations between political and business elites have been the most secretive in China. Malaysian firms formally seated political officials on boards, and patron-client relations were transparent enough to enable outsiders to bet on firms based on their patron's political fortunes and academics to measure how ties translate into resources. Indonesian firms were essentially all linked to Suharto and his family. In China, however, connections between CCP elites and the businesses they support are rumored, informal, and designed to obscure. Research on the "returns to office" and the returns to connections in China has concluded that firms benefit materially from their connections to political elites and political institutions, a finding that accords with expectations of nearly any theoretical approach to state-business relations.[25]

Mutual endangerment, however, is theoretically and empirically distinct from "relationship-based capitalism" in at least two ways. First and most obviously, elites are enmeshed in relationships not only to further one another's material or power accumulation but also to tie fates such that demise for one side threatens the demise of the other. Second, under mutual endangerment, business elites pursue dispersed relationships with a variety of political elites so as to widen their protective umbrella and diversify their investments in political security. These weblike patterns of relationships, unlike clear, hierarchical, patronage relations, are more difficult to identify or measure because they are designed to obscure and to lend resiliency to elite fortunes. The secrecy of these relationships also imbues the parties with inherent power: the implicit threat of revelation of illicit relationships binds the parties together, even when the relationship no longer yields material benefits.

---

[25] Hou, *Private Sector in Public Office*; Rory Truex, "The Returns to Office in a 'Rubber Stamp' Parliament," *American Political Science Review* 108, no. 2 (2014): 235–51; Yuhua Wang, "Betting on a Princeling," *Studies in Comparative and International Development* 52, no. 4 (2017): 395–415.

Like the other manifestations of mutual endangerment, information weaponization is difficult to observe systematically but is simple to observe anecdotally and with clearly observable effects on the political economy. The best, if most extreme, example of the logic of weaponized information comes from China's most colorful fugitive "dissident," Guo Wengui, who became involved in US politics following his defection from China in 2014 and his connection to political figures on the US right. In China, Guo rushed to join the business elite through real estate development and diversified investments in the mid-2000s, winning a bid to develop a major commercial project in Beijing only after turning over a sex tape featuring an official who opposed the deal.[26] Guo continued to adeptly weaponize information, famously summoning high-level officials at a whim and embedding himself in elite circles for protection.

Guo fled China in 2014, eventually exiling himself in a penthouse apartment in New York City, from which, by 2017, he had launched a media career in making accusations against high-level CCP officials from a place of relative safety. His assets in China, which he claimed to be worth $17 billion, had been seized by the government, which also sought his extradition from the United States. Yet Guo logged hundreds of hours of live-streaming and recorded videos and interviews in which he told salacious stories of business deals and corruption of behind-the-scenes political backers. Some of the accused, such as Xi's anticorruption czar, Wang Qishan, remained in the top echelons of leadership, while Guo's major patron had earlier been felled by the campaign.

My point is not that Guo's accusations were true, but rather that they were powerful. In fact, as one interlocutor in Shanghai during the height of Guo's storytelling explained, many business and political elites in China assumed or knew that he was telling truths and half-truths along with lies and he was mixing up which events and actions connect to which proper nouns: "He is wielding a sort of threat: I can connect these dots at any moment and take down some powerful people. Many people do this sort of thing implicitly, but he is being very direct."[27]

---

[26] The commercial project is Beijing's Pangu Plaza, named after one of Guo's firms, near the 2008 Olympic site. These details are from Michael Forsythe, "As Trump Meets Xi at Mar-a-Lago, There's a Wild Card," *New York Times*, April 4, 2017, https://www.nytimes.com/2017/04/04/world/asia/china-mar-a-lago-guo-wengui.html.

[27] Interview, business elite, Shanghai, 2017.

The Guo saga illustrates the logic of the weaponization of information. Chapter 5 details how social relations between entrepreneurs and political officials facilitated business in a context of inhospitable institutions but also guaranteed reciprocity in the absence of trust. At restaurants and bathhouses and KTV clubs, aspiring or accomplished businesspeople impress political patrons into compromising activities not because they feel close to power but because they feel vulnerable. As the financial sector became less disciplined and more open to new participants, political officials and their family members held hidden stakes in firms, and compromising information centered on the financial activities of political elites. Exposés on the wealth of various political elites that appeared in major Western media outlets, including the *New York Times* and *Bloomberg*, resulted in visa denials for some reporters, revealing both the extent of elite capture of resources and the regime's sensitivity about it.[28]

I narrated how weblike relations among Indonesia's business elites and between those elites and members of the political establishment constrained the state's ability to discipline business and rein in its more problematic behaviors. This is, after all, the purpose of keeping one's enemies close, as the adage goes. The same logic is at work in China, even in the context of Xi Jinping's sweeping anticorruption campaign. The campaign has provided a remarkable source of data about how corruption works in China and its effects on the economy and society; I say more about this below. But the targeting of some officials and some businesses and the apparent immunity of others has given rise to suspicions that some individuals are protected by those in power who stand to lose from someone's downfall. Here we see implicit weaponization of information, although it is impossible to observe from the outside exactly what is known and why the powerful protect some and not others. We also observe a different form of weaponization: leaks to the press to challenge the apparent impunity of some firms.

The story of the Wangxin Group (网信集团) is instructive. In July 2019, *Caixin*, China's most reputable and most independent media outlet

---

[28] David Barboza, "Billions in Hidden Riches for Family of Chinese Leader," *New York Times*, October 25, 2012, https://www.nytimes.com/2012/10/26/business/global/family-of-wen-jiabao-holds-a-hidden-fortune-in-china.html. David Barboza and his team won a Pulitzer in 2013 for the Wen Jiabao report. Michael Forsythe was part of a team that won the George Polk award in 2013 for reporting on China's political elite. Michael Forsythe, "Xi Jinping Millionaire Relations Reveal Elite Chinese Fortune," *Bloomberg*, June 29, 2012, https://www.bloomberg.com/news/articles/2012-06-29/xi-jinping-millionaire-relations-reveal-fortunes-of-elite?leadSource=uverify%20wall.

reporting on official corruption and the business world, broke an exclusive story about a scandal within a group including a Hong Kong–listed subsidiary, a Mainland-based related party, and Wangxin, all three part of the "Pioneer System" of firms.[29] *Caixin*'s report cites "sources close to regulators" and undisclosed sources that Pioneer Payments, a Mainland-based peer-to-peer (P2P) financial business, had misappropriated funds.[30] The ultimate owner of the system, Zhang Zhenxin, allegedly died in London in September 2019, though many former employees and others consider the death uncertain and a possible fake.[31] In June 2020, *Caixin* published another exclusive reporting that Wangxin Wealth had admitted to misappropriating funds and that one of its firms had repeatedly requested government inspection but that regulators seemed to be protecting the firm: "Since Wangxin's July 2019 financial difficulties, due to false self-financing, poor business, virtual currency investment losses, transfer of overseas assets, etc. the 'Pioneer System' has amassed a 70 billion [RMB] debt that it has not been able to fill, involving nearly 200,000 investors. . . . A former employee of Pioneer expressed doubts to the *Caixin* reporter: 'Pioneer stabbed such a big hole in itself, but it was able to return in one piece, so far no one in senior management was investigated. Why is this?' "[32]

Looting

Looting involves behaviors that, beyond simple "corruption," seek to maximize the current extractable value of a firm at the expense of long-term viability and at cost to society. Instead of simply rent-seeking or bribery, which secure business gains for a firm even if they are costly for society, looting involves a "topsy-turvy world" in which firms and managers have incentives

---

[29] "System" (系) is a term widely used to describe loose corporate groups in China, comprising both formal subsidiaries and informally affiliated firms. I say more below about these systems.

[30] "独家|"先锋系"旗下先锋支付挪用银行T+0资金未还　涉网信P2P" (Exclusive|: "Pioneer Department" Embezzles Bank T+0 Funds and Has Not Yet Repaid P2P), *Caixin*, July 8, 2019, https://finance.caixin.com/2019-07-08/101436880.html.

[31] "独家张振新死亡证明来了价值5000万豪宅距病逝医院一英里" (Exclusive: Zhang Zhenxing's Death Certificate Arrives; His Mansion Worth 50 Million Yuan Is One Mile Away from the Hospital Where He Died), *Caixin*, October 8, 2019, https://finance.caixin.com/2019-10-08/101468915.html?sourceEntityId=101570219.

[32] "独家|网信理财承认曾挪用先锋支付14.95亿元" (Exclusive: Wangxin Wealth Management Admits to Misappropriating 1.495 Billion Yuan from Pioneer), *Caixin*, June 20, 2020, https://finance.caixin.com/2020-06-20/101570219.html.

to destroy their businesses to maximize their gains.[33] In the classic description, Akerlof and Romer focus on expectation of bailout as an explanatory
mechanism, but expectations of political demise work in the same direction.
Economic actors who have short time horizons and face existential uncertainty may rationally maximize their current access to resources through
fraud and bankruptcy for profit. They may expect political connections to
facilitate bailouts and impunity or that the winds will change and they will
find themselves excluded from the possibility of economic gains. Looting,
weaponized information, and asset expatriation work in tandem: vulnerable
elites foster close but mutually endangering relationships with elites and use
their closeness to loot and funnel assets abroad to safety.

Looting can happen anywhere, of course, but the moral economy of contemporary China, like that of late New Order Indonesia, features widespread
fraud, indebtedness, and theft of state and social assets through elite collusion.
By almost any account, including the CCP's own, China's financial markets
were riddled with fraud during the 2000s and 2010s as they expanded (see
Figure 6.3 for data on the number and volume of IPOs in the Shenzhen and
Shanghai exchanges). Looting preceded the opening of the financial system
(as I show in the case of the Delong Group, below), but liberalization in the
2000s allowed the practice to accelerate, even metastasize, throughout the
system. As some financial participants and regulators made use of expanded
financial market access to enrich themselves through obfuscated corporate
forms, plunder of resources, related party transactions, and even outright financial fraud such as falsifying financial data, many others found themselves
pressed into such activities. My fieldwork interviews with firms, regulators,
and observers in China (see Appendix D) features repeated expressions of
unintentional engagement in these activities; not all individuals set out, necessarily, to loot their own firms, nor did regulators intend to abet them, but
collective ideas about short time horizons and the futility of long-term planning shaped behaviors that emerged gradually with the cumulative choices
that individuals made.[34]

As the Chinese financial system has expanded to include more nonstate
firms in both equity (stock exchanges) and debt markets (bank borrowings
and corporate bonds), looting has become manifest in financial schemes that

[33] George A. Akerlof and Paul M. Romer, "Looting: The Economic Underworld of Bankruptcy for
Profit," *Brookings Papers on Economic Activity*, no. 2 (1993): 1–73, https://doi.org/10.2307/2534564.
[34] Barbara Levitt and James G. March, "Organizational Learning," *Annual Review of Sociology* 14,
no. 1 (1988): 319–40, https://doi.org/10.1146/annurev.so.14.080188.001535.

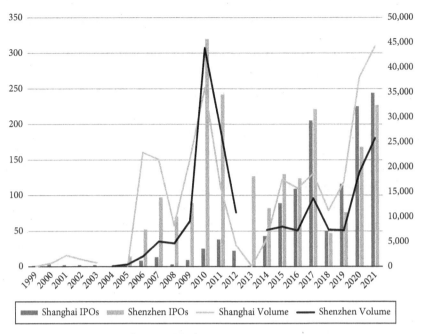

Figure 6.3 Expansion of Equity Markets, 1999–2021

Note: Right side is number of IPOs (bar), and left side is capital volume of IPOs (millions USD, at historical exchange rate). The China Securities Regulatory Commission restricted IPOs from late 2012 through 2013 following declining share prices and concerns about excessive listings and capital misallocations.

Source: Capital IQ.

have shaken the stability of China's economy and public trust in firms and markets. And as Chinese firms have gone global in the last decade or so, so have schemes of mafia-like firms. Take the case of China's supposed answer to Starbucks, Luckin Coffee, which is part of Lu Zhengyao (Charles Lu, 陆正耀)'s Shenzhou system (神州系), which started in the 1990s as many government officials were "jumping into the sea" of business and state-owned firms were undergoing ownership reforms.[35] Lu was aided by a senior official in Beijing to acquire the majority of China Telecom's Beijing business and to be introduced to domestic and foreign financiers. Luckin Coffee was headed by Jenny Qian (钱治亚), who started out as Lu's assistant and worked in the Shenzhou system for thirteen years. The Shenzhou system seemed perennially close to the edge of financial ruin, requiring rescue by investors, and it

[35] Bruce J. Dickson, *Red Capitalists in China: The Party, Private Entrepreneurs, and Prospects for Political Change* (New York: Cambridge University Press, 2003).

relied on a method of price cutting and rapid expansion in nearly every business it entered.

Luckin Coffee refreshed a record for speed of its IPO, listing on the NASDAQ within eighteen months of its founding in 2017. By early January 2020, Luckin was valued at $10.6 billion. At the end of that same month, however, a famed American short-seller tanked the company's stock by announcing it had received an anonymous report about the company's fraudulent revenue reporting and declaring it a "fundamentally broken business."[36] Luckin eventually announced it had discovered an extensive fraud, blaming its chief operating officer for fabricating and inflating sales. Behind the scenes, however, Jenny Qian, Charles Lu, and others seemed prepared for the company's fall. Luckin's directors, executive officers, and major shareholders, including Jenny Qian and Charles Lu, pledged 47 percent and 30 percent respectively of their shares for cash for an estimated total of $2.5 billion among them. International investors will likely fail to recover funds from Luckin and its principals because of the company's complex ownership structure that leaves ownership of its assets in a Chinese firm even as it raises capital in foreign markets.[37]

Other firms have taken advantage of regulatory lacunae to acquire financial firms or to exploit financial markets for self-dealing. Anbang, for example, funded its aggressive domestic and international expansion efforts by selling investment products to Chinese savers. The products offered higher returns than low domestic bank deposit rates, but they posed questionable risk coverage, and Anbang regularly exceeded quotas and skirted regulations thanks to its high-level political connections.[38] Anbang had financial relationships with hundreds of investment companies, taking large or small positions in firms that, in turn, would then reinvest in Anbang's own firms through several layers of partnerships.[39]

[36] Joshua Fineman and Yueqi Yang, "Citron, Muddy Waters Clash on Twitter over Chinese Coffee Chain," *Bloomberg*, January 31, 2020, https://www.bloomberg.com/news/articles/2020-01-31/short-sellers-take-to-twitter-for-spat-over-chinese-coffee-chain. Much of the material here reproduced with permission from Meg Rithmire and Hao Chen, "The Emergence of Mafia-Like Business Systems in China," *China Quarterly*, no. 248 (2021): 1037–58, https://doi.org/10.1017/S0305741021000576.

[37] Steven Davidoff Solomon, "Luckin Scandal Exposes Risks in U.S.-China Rift," *The Wire*, May 10, 2020, https://www.thewirechina.com/2020/05/10/luckin-scandal-exposes-risks-in-us-china-rift/.

[38] One insurance regulator remarked that some companies, including Anbang, were beyond the purview of regulators because they were politically protected and secure. This did not change until 2016–17, when officials in Beijing began talking about systemic financial risks. Interview, Shanghai, May 2017.

[39] Tingbing Guo, "In Depth: A Maze of Capital Leads to Anbang's Aggressive Expansion," *Caixin*, April 30, 2017, https://www.caixinglobal.com/2017-04-30/a-maze-of-capital-leads-to-anbangs-aggressive-expansion-101084940.html.

Many of China's largest conglomerate firms, about which I say more below, have a few listed firms. These firms are, in reality, controlled in such a way as to obscure a concentration of shareholder power to reassure minority investors. A common strategy is to use shadow firms to gain obscured control of financial firms, which are then used to finance more self-dealing and expansion. This was the case with Tomorrow Group's Baoshang Bank, which was 89.27 percent owned by Tomorrow Group through combined holdings of dozens of shareholders. The bank then loaned over 150 billion RMB to over two hundred shell companies registered by the Tomorrow Group, all of which were nonperforming when the state seized Tomorrow's assets.[40]

Falsifying revenues and manipulating stock prices appear to be a relatively common practice in China in the 2010s. As in any economy, estimating the universe of fraudulent practices is difficult, or impossible, and this is the case especially in China, where press controls limit inquiries into business practices and political protection precludes many revelations. Still, financial malfeasance has been widespread enough to be considered "the norm, not the exception" by many, including market participants, regulators, and journalists who cover China's financial markets.[41]

A spate of IPO frauds in the 2000s reveals a pattern of falsifying firms' financial data and/or disguising ownership, typically abetted by a highly ranked local or national official as well as by law and accounting firms, and with the goal of appropriating investors' funds for personal enrichment. Jiangsu Sanyou, a textile company, listed in 2005 with a corporate structure that showed two state-owned firms as the controlling shareholders. But it was later revealed that the two state firms (owned by the Nantong Municipal Government) had transferred control to nine individuals, including the chairman of Jiangsu Sanyou. In addition to the concealed transfer—an act of stealth privatization while retaining the appearance of state control to assure shareholders—the nine shareholders borrowed illegally from local banks to

[40] Qinqin Peng and Wei Han, "China Allows Baoshang Bank to Go Bankrupt in Final Cleanup," *Nikkei Asia*, August 7, 2020, https://asia.nikkei.com/Spotlight/Caixin/China-allows-Baoshang-Bank-to-go-bankrupt-in-final-cleanup; 周学东 (Zhou Xuedong) , "中小银行金融风险主要源于公司治理失灵: 从接管包商银行看中小银行公司治理的关键" (The Financial Risks of Small and Medium Banks Mainly Stem from the Failure of Corporate Governance: The Baoshang Bank), 中国金融, 2020年, 第15期: 19–21, http://www.cqvip.com/qk/96434x/202015/7102558 854.html. (accessed February 21, 2021)

[41] The quote "正常行为，不是特别的" (the norm, not the exception) is from an interview with a former accounting firm executive, Boston, November 2019. Similar sentiments were expressed by other interviewees. On the difficulty of measuring the incidence of corporate malfeasance, see Eugene Soltes, "The Frequency of Corporate Misconduct: Public Enforcement versus Private Reality," *Journal of Financial Crime* 26, no. 4 (2019): 923–37, https://doi.org/10.1108/JFC-10-2018-0107.

acquire their equity in the firm. Several directors were fined and temporarily barred from participating in listed companies, and local officials were disciplined for abetting the concealed ownership.[42]

As financial liberalization measures met technology and the consumer finance sector, fraud immediately became widespread and politically consequential, especially in the P2P lending sector, in which Chinese household savers invested in technology-enabled lending platforms. The P2P sector, which started in the early 2010s in China, occupied a regulatory blank space: the China Banking Regulatory Commission (CBRC) claimed jurisdiction over lending, while the CSRC was to regulate equity crowdfunding and the PBoC was generally charged with regulating "internet finance." Not until 2016 did regulations firmly put the CBRC in control of online finance, but by that time there were an estimated 1,778 "problematic platforms," 43.1 percent of the total number, and most of those were dubbed "runaways" (跑路), with platform owners absconding with funds.[43] By 2018, fraud and misconduct in the sector had become a social stability issue, with protests late that summer prompting hundreds of police to block access to financial centers in Beijing and Shanghai.

The saga of Lu Zhijian (卢智建) and Investment House (投之家) exemplifies the logic of looting a partially liberalized financial sector. Investment House was established in 2014 by a well-known financial entrepreneur who sold his stake in 2017 as many of the P2P platforms were beginning to collapse under new regulations and general financial tightening. Between late 2017 and mid-2018, two investment holding companies acquired controlling shares in the platform, and, in time, it was revealed that these companies were held by Lu Zhijian, associated with a Wenzhou family that had strategically acquired equity in various listed companies and state-affiliated firms and had used those vehicles to invest in P2P platforms. The platforms, in turn, loaned money as "investments" in shell companies controlled by the Lu family. When several platforms began to crash in 2017–18, the Lu family "ran away" with investors' funds.[44]

---

[42] 中国证券监督管理委员会 (China Securities Regulatory Commission), "证监会查处江苏三友信息披露违法行为" (CSRC Investigates and Punishes Jiangsu Sanyou's Illegal Information Disclosure Behavior), December 9, 2011, http://www.csrc.gov.cn/csrc/c100200/c1000600/content.shtml.

[43] Robin Hui Huang, "Online P2P Lending and Regulatory Responses in China: Opportunities and Challenge," *European Business Organization Law Review* 19, no. 1 (March 2018): 63–92, https://doi,org/10.1007/s40804-018-0100-z.

[44] "投之家幕后嫌犯卢智建被警方抓获" (Lu Zhijian, Suspect behind Investment House, Is Arrested by Police), 新浪财, September 13, 2018, http://finance.sina.com.cn/money/bank/dsfzf/2018-09-13/doc-ihkahyhw6442228.shtml.

The Moral Economy of China's Late Reform Era: Official Theft and Mafia Systems

That corruption has been widespread in China's economy for several decades is not at all surprising to either China scholars or students of corruption more generally, but scholars have addressed productively the puzzle of both the widespread corruption and the rapid economic growth. Explanations have mostly focused on the incentives, behaviors, and political management of political officials; the story is that corruption has not cannibalized economic growth in China because the corruption has been of a type that facilitates economic growth (in Ang's terms, "access money" rather than theft), and it emerged after, rather than before, competitive markets exploded, and because the CCP has imperfect but sufficient means of disciplining itself (meritocracy combined with anticorruption campaigns).[45] While I do not disagree with this characterization of the early reform era, what we see in the late reform era—after the early 2000s, as I discuss in Chapter 5—is the emergence of new sets of business actors, new forms of state-business relations, and, indeed, a more pernicious class of corruption. I submit that analysis of corruption in China has focused primarily on political officials and their behaviors to the neglect of attention to business actors. If business actors seeking long-term revenues and profitability predominate, then perhaps the widespread "access money" activity facilitates economic dynamism in an inhospitable institutional environment. But if business seeks short-term gain and distrusts the regime, economic actors will collude with political officials to engage in what appears to be more like theft, even grand theft, at extreme cost to society.

Most of the evidence presented here will focus on the business side—on the emergence of behemoth conglomerate firms more akin to "mafia systems" than traditional firms, on the explosion of financial fraud, and on the dramatic increase of corporate debt that accompanied the loosening of financial discipline. But the evidence of official corruption that has accompanied Xi Jinping's sweeping anticorruption campaign also reveals the shift away from access money to theft and, generally, to a moral economy consistent with mutual endangerment. I began this chapter with examples of this behavior,

---

[45] Ang, *China's Gilded Age*; Andrew Hall Wedeman, *From Mao to Market: Rent Seeking, Local Protectionism, and Marketization in China* (New York: Cambridge University Press, 2003); Andrew Hall Wedeman, *Double Paradox: Rapid Growth and Rising Corruption in China* (Ithaca: Cornell University Press, 2012).

Table 6.3 Corruption Cases, 2012–2017

	Total	Business Links	Family Business	Looting	Finance	Land
Central	117	113	69	53	34	64
Shandong	30	30	7	6	3	7
Shanghai	19	19		2	3	3
Chongqing	21	18	4	6	3	3
Tianjin	6	6	3	0	1	2
Total	193	186 (96%)	83 (43%)	67 (35%)	47 (24%)	79 (41%)

Source: Names and basic charges are from the CCDI. I obtained more information on the political and business activities of each official via the top three press hits on each official.

but we can find it more systematically as well. Table 6.2 displays descriptive data on each of the officials brought under formal investigation (双规) by the CCDI at the central or national level between 2012 and 2017 as well as all of those at the provincial level in Shandong, Chongqing, Tianjin, and Shanghai. The data show how the expansion of financial access, the rising importance of land assets and land fiscalization, and business links interacted to facilitate looting. Unsurprisingly, nearly all (96 percent) of the corruption cases involved links to business, 43 percent involved officials diverting opportunities and resources to family-member firms, 41 percent of cases involved land deals, 24 percent involved financial firms, and 35 percent involved activities I code as "looting," meaning the theft of resources for no clear business gain.

There are clear limits to the inferences we can draw from these data. Corruption cases brought by the CCDI are not representative of all corruption in China, but rather are representative of the CCDI's priorities, which may focus on eliminating particular kinds of corruption, more political objectives, or both.[46] My argument is not about the incidence of looting or mutual endangerment, but rather to show how the emergence of looting or mutual endangerment is linked to financial liberalization and distrust and to describe their political effects. That the CCDI has targeted these forms of corruption indeed shows the political importance of the phenomena.

[46] Xi Lu and Peter Lorentzen, "Rescuing Autocracy from Itself: China's Anti-corruption Campaign" (Working Paper, University of San Francisco, 2016).

Delong

The many large conglomerate firms that would emerge in the 2000s had a precursor. In the late 1990s, the largest private firm in China was a diversified conglomerate called the Xinjiang Delong Group (Delong). The firm emerged in Xinjiang province in the early 1990s, founded by Tang Wanxin (唐万新), a serial entrepreneur who got his start mismanaging a state farm connected with the Xinjiang Institute of Petroleum, where Tang had been a student. After the farm failed, Tang, his older brother, and several close business partners founded a few companies in the late 1980s, including a color film processing venture that finally met success. Tang and the partners took the initial earnings and expanded rapidly, acquiring management talent and diversifying into satellite receivers, hotel and club management, and consulting firms for Chinese students seeking to go abroad.[47]

The opening of China's stock market in the early 1990s, however, accelerated the growth of Delong. Starting in 1992, Tang and his brother started investing in a wide variety of stocks, and they used their early earnings to establish the Delong Industrial Corporation of Urumqi (乌鲁木齐德隆实业公司) with 2 million RMB in registered capital, followed by the Delong Real Estate Corporation with 5 million RMB. Tang relied on local connections with officials to secure construction projects and expand into industrial farming once again in the early and mid-1990s.[48] But Tang's ambitions were primarily in the financial sector.

Starting early in the 1990s, Tang and his partners navigated the murky and uncertain world of China's incipient financial markets. They first established Xinjiang Financial Leasing Ltd., a nonbank financial institution, and used its seat on a regional bond market to borrow 300 million RMB from trust companies.[49] The leasing firm was restructured under a debt burden, and when the PBoC cracked down on financial organizations in 1994, Delong's management was committed to growing through financial transactions in China's ever-changing markets. In the late 1990s, the firm relocated its

---

[47] 唐立久 (Tang Lijiu) and 张旭 (Zhang Xu), 解构德隆 (Deconstructing Delong) (杭州: 浙江人民出版社, 2005), 5–7.

[48] Ibid., 14–15, 17–19.

[49] Ibid., 15. In the early 1990s, China's bond markets were "physical" and located in a few regional centers, including Wuhan, where Delong's firm held a seat. See Marlene Amstad and Zhiguo He, "Chinese Bond Markets and Interbank Market," in Marlene Amstad, Guofeng Sun, and Wei Xiong, eds., *The Handbook of China's Financial System* (Princeton, NJ: Princeton University Press, 2020), 105–50.

headquarters to Beijing and then to Shanghai, and it established a number of financial firms, including asset management and investment holding firms, as well as an international arm with a liaison office in North America (through which Tang invested in several projects in Canada).[50] By August 2000, Delong Strategic Investment Ltd. had 500 million RMB in registered capital and thirty-three shareholders, and it had grown quickly through bank loans and commissions from its financial firms, many of which it owned indirectly.[51]

Trouble started for Delong in the early 2000s, beginning with a run on a trust (Jinxin Trust, 金信信托) it owned indirectly. Jinxin, like many of the financial firms affiliated with Delong, seemed to operate on thin margins and was accumulating deficits even as assets under management grew. The run spread to other Delong affiliates, bringing sometimes violent confrontations with investors and clients.[52] Several press reports appeared, including one written by a well-known economist and public intellectual, accusing Delong of financial malfeasance and fund-raising practices resembling a Ponzi scheme.[53] Though the company's financial problems began in 2001, 2002–3 saw great growth and diversification as the company expanded into agricultural markets, animal husbandry, heavy-duty vehicles, tourism, and more. These investments, pursued on top of a financial crisis within the company, exhausted the company's resources and accelerated its collapse. By spring 2004, the company had laid off much of its workforce, share prices of its three original public vehicles had bottomed out, and banks cut the firm off from new financing. Local governments in various parts of China began to seize the firm's remaining physical assets, and by December 2004, Tang Wanxin, after attempting to flee to Burma, was under arrest for illegal fund-raising and stock price manipulation.

The trajectory of Delong surfaced repeatedly during my fieldwork in the late 2010s as a sort of parable of financial market participation in China. But instead of a cautionary tale or a reference to extreme behavior, many interlocuters saw Delong as a larger-scale version of patterns of behavior regularly visible in China's political economy. The managing director of a midsize investment fund remarked:

[50] Tang Lijiu (唐立久) and Zhang Xu (张旭), 解构德隆 (Deconstructing Delong), 20–24.
[51] Ibid., 26.
[52] Ibid., 29–30.
[53] 郎咸平 (Lang Xianping), 新财富 (New Wealth Magazine), April 2001; 成都商报 (Chengdu Commercial Newspaper), July 2003.

Actually, Delong is not so surprising to me at all. The basic transactions and organization are actually quite familiar even now. Maybe they were just the first to do it, and their political connections were not as good as the firms that do the same things now.[54]

Delong may not have been organized expressly to loot and explode, but the firm's organization and management actions facilitated and accelerated the explosion. The firm was notable in the 1990s as one of the first Chinese private firms to grow by navigating equity and bond investments and even minority investments in banks as well as other financial firms. But as the financial system liberalized, many private firms grew large through financial market participation, and many found themselves indebted, pursuing overseas investments and meeting legal troubles, much like those of Delong's founders.

The Emergence of "Mafia Systems"

To understand the moral economy of late reform China, we might first ask how the actual economy is structured.[55] Over the course of the twenty-first century, the Chinese economy came to be dominated by incredibly large business systems.[56] A large literature examines one type of these behemoth firms—state-owned enterprises (SOEs), especially the hundred or so firms at the "commanding heights" of the Chinese economy owned by the central government.[57] The restructuring, public listing, and expansion of these firms are relevant to the development of nonstate business systems, but SOEs have

[54] Interview, Shanghai, March 2017.

[55] These sections draw on Rithmire and Chen, "Emergence," with permission from the *China Quarterly*.

[56] I prefer the term "system" because these business groups are described in China as systems (系), as in the "Tomorrow System" 明天系. I do use it interchangeably with business groups or conglomerates, although I acknowledge that some scholars distinguish these corporate forms. Tarun Khanna and Yishay Yafeh, "Business Groups in Emerging Markets: Paragons or Parasites?," *Journal of Economic Literature* 45, no. 2 (2007): 331–72, https://doi.org/10.1257/jel.45.2.331.

[57] Wendy Leutert, "State-Owned Enterprise Mergers: Will Less Be More?," *China Analysis* (European Council on Foreign Relations), no. 197 (2016), https://ecfr.eu/wp-content/uploads/China_Analysis_%E2%80%93_Big_is_Beautiful.pdf; Chen Li, "Holding 'China Inc.' Together: The CCP and the Rise of China's Yangqi," *China Quarterly*, no. 228 (2016): 927–49, https://doi.org/10.1017/S0305741016001466; Barry M. Naughton and Kellee S. Tsai, eds., *State Capitalism, Institutional Adaptation, and the Chinese Miracle* (New York: Cambridge University Press, 2015); Yingyao Wang, "The Rise of the 'Shareholding State': Financialization of Economic Management in China," *Socioeconomic Review* 13, no. 3 (2015): 603–25, https://doi.org/10.1093/ser/mwv016.

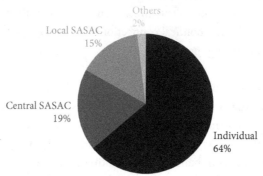

Figure 6.4 Actual Controller of Firms

received tremendous attention relative to the other corporate form at the apex of the Chinese economy—the large nonstate business group.

How large are Chinese business groups and how are they organized? Figure 6.4 and Tables 6.3 and 6.4 show data from a sample of four hundred firms on a list of Chinese firms that pursued either a transnational merger or an acquisition between 2001 and 2018. I collected corporate filing data on the four hundred sampled firms, including ownership structure, actual controller, legal representative, subsidiaries, investments, and so forth.[58] Figure 6.4 shows the distribution of actual controllers, once one follows the ownership structure and layers to find a final controller. The majority of firms (64 percent) are owned by individuals, and 34 percent are owned by the central or local State-owned Assets Supervision and Administration Commission (SASAC). We found that 88 percent of firms in the sample have more than one parent company or layer of ownership. The mean number of layers—how many parent companies we had to look through to find an actual controller—is 3.51, with a very high standard deviation—7.09. The maximum number of parent companies is sixty-three (for China Minsheng Investment Group, 中国民生

---

[58] "Actual controller" (实际控制人) refers to the ultimate parent of the company (it can be an individual, a local government, or the central SASAC), which can be discovered by following all layers of the ownership structure; "legal representative" (法人代表) is a natural person who acts on the company's behalf and bears civil, administrative, and even criminal liability for the company. We collected the transaction data from FactSet Merger and used WIND to find the corporate filing information. Clearly, a random sample of firms with a transnational reach is not a random sample of all firms in China, but it qualifies as a convenience sample. A convenience sample is appropriate for our purposes because this chapter's purpose is to describe a specific mode of business actors in China's political economy rather than to make arguments about how representative these firms are.

Table 6.4 Business Activities of Legal Representatives (for nonstate firms)

	Median	Mean	75%	Std. Dev.	Max
Companies for which a person is the legal representative	14	41.97	45	90.15	858
Of those: holding companies	5	11.31	10	35.57	411
Number of companies in which invested	2	3.63	5	5.32	50

Note: $N = 159$.

投资集团, discussed below), and the highest number of layers in our sample is eleven. For privately owned firms in our sample, 69 percent of the firms' legal representatives and actual controllers are not the same person.

We then took the legal representatives as a population group and collected data on their activities, including the number of companies they represented and, of those, how many were classified as "holding companies" and in how many companies they held investments (either minority or majority stakes). These data are displayed in Table 6.3. Though the median number of firms owned by an individual is fourteen, a high mean and the standard deviation indicate a long tail, meaning quite a few individuals appear to be linked to extensive networks of companies. Table 6.4 displays data on the number of subsidiaries (a controlling stake) and invested companies (any stake) by firms actually controlled by individuals. Here we see the median numbers of subsidiaries and invested companies are 14.5 and 23, respectively, with a high standard deviation of 46 and 68, respectively, and the maximum up to 337 and 613, meaning that many firms in China are clearly part of large, sprawling networks of firms connected through layers of ownership. Note that these data require tracing ultimate parents through corporate filings, but these data do not—and one cannot, without detailed work and close knowledge of the people and their families—show networks designed to be opaque and connected through obscure family and friend relationships.

Delong was unique in the 1990s for its size, diversification, and financial engagement, but, as the data from the convenience sample show, the 2000s saw the emergence of a number of large firms similar to Delong in terms of organization and internal logic (see Tables 6.4 and 6.5). Many of these firms are more akin to mafia systems, or organized crime, than they are to other conceptualizations of firms (i.e., entrepreneurs, small and medium enterprises, state-owned enterprises, national champions, and so forth) or

Table 6.5 Investments by Firms with Nonstate
Individuals as Actual Controllers (# firms)

	Median	Mean	75%	Std. Dev.	Max
Subsidiaries	14.5	29.87	34	46.04	337
Investments	23	41.01	45	68.35	613

Note: Number of firms with individual as actual controller = 162.

even business groups. Rather than pursuing the objective of maximizing long-run profits, these systems are organized to plunder state and social resources and to obfuscate their political connections and their own corporate governance. Some seem to have been designed to accomplish these goals, while others veered toward these behaviors as they interacted with other participants in the Chinese political economy, including firms and political actors, over time. A rich literature in sociology and political science understands firms as "socio-political conflict systems subject to economic constraints."[59] Firms as conflict systems are, however, also subject to political constraints; in China, political vulnerability and inherent uncertainty are the most important of these constraints. Mafia systems grew large and complex to respond to these constraints, and they developed internal logics and relationships with the state and society that accord with mutual endangerment.

In characterizing certain large conglomerate firms as "mafia-like business systems," I do not mean that they are the actual Mafia in the sense of organized groups that use violence to sell protection or subnational groups whose control of force either challenges or substitutes for the state.[60] Mafia-like business systems do not primarily wield violence as a tool of power, though neither is it unheard of. Violence manifests in a few ways: suicides of system affiliates, suspicious "accidental" deaths and occasional murders, and, most frequently, the use of state violence—arrests, imprisonment, even

[59] James G. March, "The Business Firm as a Political Coalition," *Journal of Politics* 24, no. 4 (1962): 662, https://doi.org/10.2307/2128040.

[60] Diego Gambetta, *The Sicilian Mafia: The Business of Private Protection* (Cambridge, MA: Harvard University Press, 1993); Charles Tilly, *Coercion, Capital, and European States, AD 990–1990* (Cambridge, MA: Basil Blackwell, 1990). On actual organized crime groups in China, see Osburg, *Anxious Wealth*; Lynette H. Ong, *Outsourcing Repression: Everyday State Power in Contemporary China* (New York: Oxford University Press, 2022); Minxin Pei, *China's Trapped Transition: The Limits of Developmental Autocracy* (Cambridge, MA: Harvard University Press, 2006).

kidnapping—to settle scores among system participants.[61] Further, mafia-like business systems, unlike the real Mafia, use extortion and clandestine activities to pursue legal businesses—for example, finance, real estate, entertainment—rather than illegal businesses, such as gambling, prostitution, or drug trafficking.

These firms are more akin to mafia because of the centrality of extortion: they obtain business resources, such as state assets, land, credit, or prestige, through threat and unfair means, but the threat is not one of violence executed by the firm itself but rather exposure, incrimination, and, by extension, the coercive power of the party-state.[62] Research on political economies with emergent markets, for example post-Soviet Russia, has identified organized crime as a particular solution to the problem of lack of rule of law or trust in markets, providing protection when the law and social norms do not.[63] Mafia-like business systems in China emerged in a similar context of limited formal property rights protection and pervasive distrust and uncertainty, but instead of using thugs and violence to extort resources from the state and society, they manipulate a combination of political relationships, corporate governance institutions, and the tools of financial capitalism. In this sense, if postcommunist Russia features "violent competition for the spoils of Communism," China's mafia-like business systems are manifestations of clandestine competition for the spoils of Chinese capitalism.[64]

One example can be seen in the fall of Xiang Junbo (项俊波), former chairman of the China Insurance Regulatory Commission, who was sentenced to eleven years in prison in 2020 after being dismissed from public office and expelled from the party in 2017. Xiang had presided over a tremendous expansion of the insurance sector between 2011 and 2017, in particular expanding the number of licenses issued to firms to deal in financial insurance products. Looser regulations and political connections encouraged many firms to use insurance-sector companies to raise funds that were used

---

[61] Research by economists on the relationship among organized crime, violence, and politics suggests that violence is evidence of instability in the arrangements between political elites and mafia groups. Alberto Alesina, Salvatore Piccolo, and Paolo Pinotti, "Organized Crime, Violence, and Politics," *Review of Economic Studies* 86, no. 2 (2019): 457–99, https://doi.org/10.1093/restud/rdy036.

[62] Many argue, following Schelling, that extortion is the core activity of organized crime. Thomas C. Schelling, *Choice and Consequence* (Cambridge, MA: Harvard University Press, 1984).

[63] Stanislav Markus, *Property, Predation, and Protection: Piranha Capitalism in Russia and Ukraine* (New York: Cambridge University Press, 2015); Gambetta, *The Sicilian Mafia*; Vadim Volkov, *Violent Entrepreneurs: The Use of Force in the Making of Russian Capitalism* (Ithaca: Cornell University Press, 2002); Stephen Handelman, *Comrade Criminal: The Theft of the Second Russian Revolution* (London: Michael Joseph, 1995).

[64] Handelman, *Comrade Criminal*, 10.

in complex financial maneuvers that ultimately generated risks for savers and investors. Xiang was accused of "colluding with financial predators," who "hunted" Xiang and other officials in the financial sector.[65] Xiang was linked especially to Anbang, which became the third largest insurance company within two years (2014 to 2016) and whose chairman, who was arrested a few months after Xiang's fall, bragged about his access to Xiang.

Mafia business systems are characterized by predation, threat, and mutual endangerment in their internal relations and their relationships with the state. Tania Murray Li, in a discussion of Indonesian plantations, describes a mafia system as "an extended, densely networked predatory system in which everyone . . . must participate in order to get somewhere, or simply to survive. Predation means plunder; it also means consuming weaker animals. Hence anyone who does not become mafia—both defensive and predatory—is simply prey."[66] To interact with systems that are designed to plunder and that both threaten and protect is to be pressed into the system, voluntarily or not. The presence of large mafia-like systems has become a feature of China's political economy more broadly, a phenomenon all political economy players must navigate rather than isolated practices cordoned off from the "legal" or mainstream economy.

Looting in Large Business Systems

Business groups in many places pursue the capture of rents, for example monopolies on licenses, pet projects, and favorable access to financial capital, but the activities of mafia-like systems move beyond rent-seeking because they involve theft. Mafia-like systems do not only pursue rents as a sort of "nonmarket strategy" to enhance corporate performance; rather, they are organized to facilitate the flow of public resources into private coffers, mostly with any productive activity as epiphenomena. Looting practices are replicated within the organizational hierarchy. Employees and managers who do not take advantage of and exploit their positions, for example by

---

[65] 杨巧伶 (Yang Qiaoling), "特稿: 项俊波保监会五年落幕有看点." (Special: What to Watch for at the End of Xiang Junbo's Five Years at the Insurance Regulatory Commission), *Caixin*, April 10, 2017, https://finance.caixin.com/2017-04-10/101076536.html.

[66] Tania Murray Li, "After the Land Grab: Infrastructural Violence and the 'Mafia System' in Indonesia's Oil Palm Plantation Zones," *Geoforum* 96 (2018): 329, https://doi.org/10.1016/j.geoforum.2017.10.012.

taking cuts of transactions or wielding information against others to extract personal benefits, find themselves exploited, weakened, and nonetheless compromised by the system such that they come to defend and perpetuate it in order to survive. In short, mutual endangerment with large firms is a form of large-scale plunder.

Plunder was present at the inception of many of the private business systems that rose to the apex of the Chinese economy between 2004 and 2014. During the period between the late 1980s and the late 1990s, many local governments were under pressure to improve the bottom lines of their state-owned enterprises or to privatize them.[67] In practice, many sought private partners to provide capital and to manage these enterprises. For example, a firm that dominates a large inland province in China began when the provincial authorities invited a private entrepreneur to take a large stake (between 40 and 49 percent) in a provincially owned pharmaceutical company. That company then borrowed heavily from state banks in the middle to late 1990s to buy, at deeply depressed prices, other, smaller provincial and municipal enterprises in related or unrelated industries. The larger parent company then borrowed more extensively, using the assets of subsumed companies (especially land) as collateral, right up until the moment of privatization, which also occurred stealthily. Rather than buying a majority stake in the company outright, several of the entrepreneur's family members bought small stakes through holding companies, allowing the central owner control rights.[68] This kind of "stealth privatization"—taking control of state assets, accessing preferential state loans, and then privatizing these assets without public notice but with informal political support—was widespread.

A pervasive uncertainty affected the evolution of what would become large business systems. Insecurity generated short time horizons for owners and managers, and those short time horizons are reproduced within the organization's hierarchy. One person close to the managing family of a system put it this way:

> In the early days, they didn't know what would happen to their investments, so they took every opportunity they could. If a friend was in a high position at a bank, they would borrow because who knows what would happen

[67] Yi-min Lin, *Dancing with the Devil: The Political Economy of Privatization in China* (New York: Oxford University Press, 2017).

[68] Interviews with provincial and municipal officials, northern China, 2007–12.

tomorrow. For me, I could also lose my job anytime! So I took every opportunity to get rich. Get rich today because tomorrow you don't know.[69]

This participant went on to describe his strategies for "getting rich today,"
which included bringing his own extended family members into investments
and purchases, steering contracts toward friendly firms for clandestine
kickbacks, and inflating the prices of subcontracts within the organization
and outside of it to pocket the money for himself.

The internal replication of the plunder principle creates an organization in
which every participant expects to get a "cut" along the way. Indeed, a typical
deal proceeds in this way. When crony firms borrow from banks, they do so
through an "introductory contact" (介绍人), who then takes a small fee, usually a percentage of the loan volume. All parties, then, have incentives to in-
flate deal prices—loan officers and introducers, who get a cut, and borrowers,
who enjoy access to cheap credit.

The rapid rise and fall of the China Minsheng Investment Group (CMIG)
illustrates the logic of looting as it applies to relations within mafia-like business systems and between them and the state. CMIG nominally is a privately
owned and managed firm with significant state backing and formal approval
from the State Council to become the "J.P. Morgan" of China by investing in
industrial upgrading.[70] In 2019, CMIG had sixty-two shareholders, of which
held 2 percent or less and only one held more than 4 percent. That one shareholder, which held 16.91 percent of CMIG in March 2019, was a shell company owned and controlled by CMIG's management team. The idea behind
the dispersion of the shareholders was to preserve the independence of the
company's management, a model borrowed from China Minsheng Bank,
a major privately owned bank where CMIG's founding chairman, Dong
Wenbiao (董文标) had spent most of his career. Within five years of its establishment in 2014, CMIG had accrued over 300 billion RMB in debt, mostly
financed by state banks, and it entered into state receivership.[71]

[69] Interview, Hong Kong, June 2015.
[70] CMIG (China Minsheng Investment Group), "中民投于中国长城开展全民合作" (CMIG and
China Great Wall Begin Collaboration on All Fronts), March 1, 2019, https://www.cm-inv.com/cn/
companyNews/2299.htm; CMIG, "中民投的远景和第一步, 对话董文标" (The Background and
the First Steps of CMIG: A Conversation with Dong Wenbiao), November 12, 2015, https://www.
cm-inv.com/cn/ourtalk/1012.htm (accessed May 2019).
[71] Yanrong Chen (陈彦蓉), "中民投新管理架构浮出水面" (A New Management Structure for
CMIG Has Surfaced), China Financial News, August 27, 2019, http://www.financialnews.com.cn/
jigou/rzzl/201908/t20190827_166818.html (accessed November 2019).

Pathologies in the management and organization of CMIG, explained by the plunder principle, contributed to the company's debt burden and failure. CMIG was characterized by a culture of risk-taking and informal relationships. According to interviews, the company's operational mode was "Do it first and ask later" (先弄了再说) and literally "Eat meat together" (一起吃肉), rather than careful assessment of investment opportunities and professional management of capital. The company culture was also described as "fly-by-night family culture" (江湖大哥文化), connoting a kind of familial relationship among grifters.[72] Almost all of the shareholders in CMIG and the executive team are personally connected to Dong Wenbiao. Dong and his inner circle served the function that a central family usually does in most mafia systems. As one analyst put it, "The shares of CMIG are too scattered. No one really cares about the company's money, nor do they care whether a project is really making money."[73]

In its five short years, CMIG's principals practiced organized plunder with state resources, likely applying practices honed through years of participation in other mafia-like systems. Almost all of the group's activities were either related-party transactions or high-profile wastes of state resources in feigned efforts to invest in strategic sectors. For example, some private firms first invested a few billion RMB to become CMIG shareholders. Then subsidiaries of CMIG awarded projects and contracts at inflated prices to firms affiliated with those shareholders, including transactions that appear to only provide use of CMIG assets for individual executives associated with the shareholding firms.[74] Many more of CMIG's individual shareholders pledged their shares to banks to acquire more loans, including in foreign currencies.[75]

How did CMIG devolve into organized plunder and self-dealing essentially at its inception, especially as the company was vested with political importance at a time of conflictual state-business relations in China, and during which, one might imagine, this kind of risk-taking would be especially costly? The company's principals combined a learned culture of organized plunder with access to tremendous state resources. Once it became clear that

[72] The Chinese literally translates to "people wandering from place to place and living by their wits in a big-brother culture," and the connotation is similar to itinerant con men. Personal communication, July 2019. I am grateful to Hao Chen for sharing these insights.
[73] 吴红毓然 (Wuhong Weiran), "断臂求生中民投" (CMIG Seeks to Survive by Breaking Its Own Arm), *Caixin*, February 18, 2019, https://weekly.caixin.com/2019-02-16/101380357.html.
[74] Interview, Shanghai, July 2019.
[75] 凌华薇 (Ling Huawei) and 吴红毓然 (Wuhong Weiran), "董文标转身" (Dong Wenbiao's Turnaround), *Caixin*, August 18, 2014, https://weekly.caixin.com/2014-08-15/100717205.html?p1.

some of CMIG's shareholders were self-dealing and many of its executives engaged in self-enrichment at the expense of the firm's future, no one had any incentive to defect from the arrangement. Instead, the plunder accelerated while state resources—credit, prestige of the company's name, political untouchability—were still accessible.

Secrecy and Obfuscation

Whereas most Malaysian firms have formal and transparent relationships with political elites and the regime, secrecy and obfuscation underlie the organization of elite state-business relations in China, and this is the case to a far greater degree than it was in Suharto's Indonesia. As the above data show, many large systems have sprawling connections among firms and are tied to shareholders whose identities are obscured by design. We know from widespread forensic reporting that political elites are connected to business empires through hidden relationships that are nearly impossible to uncover or track systematically. Mafia-like systems feature in particular tortuous paths of connection within firms, between firm assets and their actual controllers, and between firms and their political patrons.

In addition to layers of corporate organization (see Table 6.6), many mafia-like systems are controlled by a person or a family that operates behind the scenes. Take Xiao Jianhua's Tomorrow System as an example. A major strategy of the Tomorrow System was to "hide and disperse" (隐蔽+分散), which means that major personnel, assets, subsidiaries, and social networks were managed to be obfuscated, even to its internal employees. As early as 2004, Xiao and his wife systematically hid all of their positions within the system, resigning from affiliated firms as supervisors and not listing as direct shareholders. To control his empire, Xiao built and controlled a large management team, and he cultivated dependence on himself. Xiao's team had over a hundred people who were capable and loyal to Xiao, many of whom started following Xiao in the 1990s. To ensure Xiao's own authority, directors were ordered to rotate among Tomorrow's subsystems (e.g., listed firms, banks, securities, insurance) to prevent the formation of factions within the Tomorrow System.[76]

---

[76] 苏龙飞 (Su Longfei), "明天帝国: 影子金融大亨肖建华的资产版" (Tomorrow Empire: Asset Map of Xiao Jianhua).

Table 6.6 Corporate Organization, Select Conglomerates, 2018

Name	Total Subsidiaries	Inexplicit Subsidiaries*	Listed Firms	Financial Firms	Business Services	ICIJ Appearance	Personnel Formally Accused/Convicted of Corruption or Malfeasance
Dalian Wanda	1,188 7 levels		1	36	98	2	VP of Commercial Management Group (Zhu Zhanbei) colluded with supplier to inflate contract amounts and embezzle. Four regional executives demanded bribes from suppliers, merchants, and employees. 2017 investigation into irregular financing of overseas acquisitions; unwinding of positions.
Fosun	624 9 levels	39	7	57	183	3	Chairman (Guo Guangchang) detained several times since 2015; in 2020 accused of colluding with the deputy mayor of Shanghai for stock manipulation. 2017 investigation into irregular financing of overseas acquisitions; unwinding of positions
New Hope	1,002 9 levels	886	1	36	92	0	CSRC action for delayed financial report of related-party stock purchase
Evergrande	2,934 11 levels	n/a	3	44	643	3	VP (Jiang Mingli) investigated for excessive borrowing and default in 2022. Real estate executive (Zuo Ying) colluded with rival firm to inflate bid for land and cause losses to company for personal gain.

(continued)

Table 6.6 Continued

Name	Total Subsidiaries	Inexplicit Subsidiaries*	Listed Firms	Financial Firms	Business Services	ICIJ Appearance	Personnel Formally Accused/Convicted of Corruption or Malfeasance
Zhongzhi	817 9 levels	169	0	102	258	3	3 subsidiaries convicted of financial crimes: China Hi-Tech chairman of illegal financing and transfer of monetary interest; Grand Image of exaggerating income and concealing debt to acquire financing; Medium-Range Rental fined for insider trading and causing firm stock prices to drop
CEFC	90 8 levels	n/a	0	19	19	0	Deputy general manager in Shanghai confessed to fake contracts, illegal loans, and embezzlement Founder (Ye Jianming) investigated for bribing officials in Chad and Uganda in concert with state officials and colluding with Guangdong officials and the Bank of Communications in illegal acquisition of bank shares
HNA	1,051 11 levels	208	13	139	400	3	Chairman (Chen Feng) and CEO (Tan Xiangdong) accused of illegally absorbing public deposits and fund-raising fraud during HNA restructuring; also accused of related-party transactions and embezzlement for family and friends. CFO accused of contract fraud, embezzlement.
Oceanwide	292 (9 levels)	2	1	55	93	0	Several domestic bond defaults; CSRC actions for failing to disclose major litigation between bank and subsidiary; 2 billion RMB lawsuit for disclosure failures
Golden Dragon	148 4 levels	5	26	20	10	0	Chairman sentenced to two years in prison for bribing former Guangdong province governor (Liu Zhigeng) for bank loan facilitation

Baoneng	837 6 levels	5	2	37	276	1	Executives colluded with Shanghai Bank to inflate asset prices and loans and to embezzle; illegal loan activities; embezzlement of depositor assets. 2022 debt crisis; default on financial products and loans.
Tomorrow	20 (3 levels)	7	3	4	3	0	CEO founder (Xiao Jianhua) under custody in 2017; trial began 2022 on unspecified charges; group broken up and assets seized
Anbang	91 8 levels	5	7	17	23	0	Founder and CEO (Wu Xiaohui) sentenced 18 years for fund-raising fraud and embezzlement; firm nationalized
Wanxiang	70 5 levels	1	2	2	7	1	Wanxiang Finance fined for providing loans to nonmember entities (P2P fraud) and failure to disclose lending risks and imprudent lending

Source: Corporate form information from WIND database, China Bureau of Industry and Commerce (工商局), and WireScreen. Corporate malfeasance information from media reports and court filings; I include only formal accusations from the CCDI, the Chinese judicial system, or regulatory agencies. See Appendix C.

* Figures come from bond prospectus filings rather than from information on the formal corporate ownership structure.

Obfuscation further facilitates looting, for example through hidden related-party transactions. These transactions facilitate both "tunneling" (transferring assets and profits out of firms to benefit the controlling shareholders and to expropriate minority shareholders) and inflating the balance sheets of firms to borrow from financial institutions.[77] The Tomorrow System, for example, adopted a strategy of "distancing related-party transactions" (关联交易非关联化) through shadow firms and labyrinthine corporate structures. In 2008, Tomorrow's two listed firms, Shanghai Ace (爱使股份) and Tomorrow Tech (明天科技), bought Ronglian (荣联), a nonlisted, Inner Mongolian local company with net assets of 14.8 million RMB. At the time, Ronglian had only one doomed project with no future prospects. However, Tomorrow's two listed firms invested 810 million RMB in that company, an amount that was fifty-four times Ronglian's net assets. It was reported that the Inner Mongolian company was highly likely to become a firm within the Tomorrow System, though its parent companies (also nonlisted) had no shareholding connections with the Tomorrow System.[78] In this way, Tomorrow Group was able to raise funds from investors on China's stock markets and then transfer that money to unlisted firms, essentially expropriating the minority investors.

Conclusion

This chapter has described mutual endangerment in China and its connection to distrust and how partial financial liberalization facilitated a metastasis of destructive corporate behaviors during the first two decades of this century. Much of this activity, as the theory presented in Chapter 1 predicts and as experienced in Indonesia, culminated in a series of financial crises in China, beginning in 2015 and churning slowly through a debt crisis for several years following.

Putting China's reform era into this larger narrative of mutual alignment to mutual endangerment helps make sense of a number of puzzles about

---

[77] Simon Johnson, Rafael LaPorta, Florencio Lopez-de-Silanes, and Andrei Schleifer, "Tunnelling," *American Economic Review* 90, no. 2 (2000): 22–27. Most work on propping, tunneling, and related-party transactions relies on announcements made by listed firms in markets where related-party transactions are mostly legal. In the Chinese context, many of the transactions are much more difficult to trace. See Winnie Qian Peng, K. C. John Wei, and Zhishu Yang, "Tunneling or Propping: Evidence from Connected Transactions in China," *Journal of Corporate Finance* 17, no. 2 (2011): 306.

[78] 苏龙飞 (Su Longfei), "明天帝国：影子金融大亨肖建华的资产版" (Tomorrow Empire: Asset Map of Xiao Jianhua).

China's political economy. Namely, why did the CCP apparently embrace capitalists and then turn on them just as the regime was seeking to push China from a middle-income to an advanced economy? Why did capitalists appear to embrace the regime after its history of punishing them? Why did China's political economy, especially under Xi Jinping but also before his assumption of power, appear to veer rather dramatically from reforms to a heavy-handed role for the state? Why have large, nonstate firms in China assumed debt burdens that appear to be existential threats for the firms themselves? Chapter 7 will focus on the sense of threat that mutual endangerment generated for the regime and the CCP's efforts to address it.

7

Crisis and Reconfiguration

The Chinese Communist Party versus Business

Specifying forms of state-business relations helps us better understand the politics they generate. Mutual alignment produces stagnation, while mutual endangerment manifests in economic behaviors that can generate crisis. Ties were precarious in both Indonesia and China, but the powers of those states to intervene in economies differ markedly. The Chinese Communist Party (CCP) enjoys broad controls over cross-border capital flows as well as an ability to essentially set prices (to control supply and demand) in markets for labor, land, and capital.[1] No crisis similar to the Asian Financial Crisis that felled the New Order has befallen China, but we can nonetheless observe the ways in which mutual endangerment generates economic instability at two sites of crisis in contemporary China: an equities market crisis that began in 2015 and a debt crisis that simmers threateningly beneath the regime's efforts to reconfigure economic growth.

China presents an interesting case of a regime attempting to address the problems of mutual endangerment. The CCP has reacted with force to the pathologies of mutual endangerment, deploying and reinvigorating the party-state in an attempt to restore discipline in the political economy and to address domestic and transnational threats.[2] The broad resurgence of the state involves a reassertion of state financial control in China through corporate governance and shareholding combined with deployment of the regime's coercive apparatus. These actions amount to an attempt by the party-state to return to mutual alignment, albeit a different form than the kind that obtained in the 1980s and 1990s, through state, rather than market, discipline. The final section of this chapter will examine the consequences of

---

[1] Kristen Looney and Meg Rithmire, "China Gambles on Modernizing through Urbanization," *Current History* 116, no. 791 (2017): 203–9, https://doi.org/10.1525/curh.2017.116.791.203.

[2] This insight owes much to my collaborative work with Margaret Pearson and Kellee Tsai on "party-state capitalism." See Margaret Pearson, Meg Rithmire, and Kellee S. Tsai, "Party-State Capitalism in China," *Current History* 120, no. 827 (2021): 207–13, https://doi.org/10.1525/curh.2021.120.827.207.

Precarious Ties. Meg Rithmire, Oxford University Press. © Oxford University Press 2023.
DOI: 10.1093/oso/9780197697528.003.0007

a potential return to forced mutual alignment through extreme state discipline of the financial sector.

Crises of Mutual Endangerment

In Suharto's Indonesia, a decade and a half of financial liberalization culminated in a historic financial crisis that eventually ended the regime. I argue in Chapter 4 that the dynamics during the crisis—not only the causes of the crisis—both demonstrate mutual endangerment and help explain why the crisis was so deadly for the regime: business elites turned away from Suharto, accelerating looting and asset expatriation. They could do so because of the New Order's open capital account. In China, a few years into the administration of Xi Jinping and at the high tide of his anticorruption efforts, a financial crisis, or really a series of small financial crises, laid bare the extent of mutual endangerment in China. Similar to Indonesia, the dynamics during these crises include accelerated looting and asset expatriation as well as general abuse of state resources with the expectation of either impunity or demise.

To state the obvious: the CCP did not collapse as a result. My argument is not that mutual endangerment causes regimes to fall (or that mutual alignment prevents them from doing so). Unlike Suharto, the CCP enjoyed access to a number of policy and monetary resources and deployed its own coercive apparatus to stem the negative effects of mutual endangerment and attempt to stamp it out. The core argument in this book is that distrust combined with financial liberalization creates mutual endangerment, and a key pathology of this pattern in state-business relations is financial instability associated with fraud, excessive debt, and capital outflows. These are exactly what we observe in mid-2010s China after years of financial liberalization.

"Irrational Selling" and "Malicious Activity": The Stock Market Crisis of 2015

The cycle by which a regime liberalizes the financial to generate growth only to find excessive risk-taking and instability is on display in the experience of China's stock market crisis of 2015–2016.[3] Toward the end of 2014,

---

[3] As for the title of this section, the China Securities Regulatory Commission (CSRC) accused market participants of both of these activities: Ben Moshinsky, "China's 'National Team' Is Doing

China's economic growth was slowing for the first time since the AFC. With a 7.3 percent growth rate in the third quarter of 2014, its slowest pace in almost five years, economists predicted that China might not meet its annual growth target for the first time since 1998.[4] Faced with a slumping economy, the Chinese government initiated several unusually broad reforms to increase bank lending.[5] The government also encouraged public investment in the stock market through other means. In an editorial published on April 21, 2015, that quickly went viral, state-run news outlet *People's Daily* urged the public to place its trust in the stock market and continue to invest.[6] The article claimed that the recent stock market rise marked only the beginning of a bull market, dismissing fears of a bubble—"What's a bubble? Tulips and Bitcoins are bubbles," the author taunted—while claiming that continued investment would enjoy "support from China's grand development strategy and economic reforms."[7]

The government's efforts, both direct and indirect, saw results. In December 2014, investors in Shanghai and Shenzhen opened almost nine hundred thousand new stock trading accounts in the span of one week, the most in seven years.[8] Stocks climbed to unprecedented highs in the first half of 2015: the Shanghai and Shenzhen stock markets doubled and even tripled over the course of a year, with some companies trading at three hundred times earnings by the stock market's peak on June 12, 2015.[9] The rapid growth raised concerns for multiple reasons, however. First, stocks rose, but the economy was still slowing. The International Monetary Fund (IMF)

Everything in Its Power to Stop Stocks Crashing: Here's the Playbook," *Business Insider*, January 5, 2016; Keith Bradsher, "Guide to China's Market Turmoil," *New York Times*, August 24, 2015.

[4] Lingling Wei, "China Central Bank Cuts Interest Rates," *Wall Street Journal*, August 25, 2015.

[5] In September and October 2014, the People's Bank of China (PBoC), China's central bank, injected more than $126 billion into Chinese banks. In another effort to increase the volume of loans, the PBoC cut interest rates for the first time in two years on November 23, 2014, lowering the benchmark one-year loan rate by 0.4 percentage point to 5.6 percent. On February 4, 2015, the PBoC relaxed the reserve ratio by half a percentage point, in effect freeing up about 500 billion yuan, or $81 billion, in funds for banks to lend. On April 16, 2015, the PBoC offered commercial lenders 10 billion yuan of reverse repurchase agreements, or reverse repos, also to facilitate lending. See Wei, "China Central Bank"; Shen Hong, "PBOC Cash Injection May Dim Hopes for Stronger Easing," *Wall Street Journal*, June 25, 2015.

[6] Evan Osnos, "The Real Risk behind China's Stock Market Drama," *New Yorker*, July 15, 2015.

[7] 王若宇（Wang Ruoyu), "4000点才是A股牛市的开端" (4000 is the Beginning of an A-Share Bull Market," *People's Daily*, April 21, 2015.

[8] Neil Gough and Cao Li, "Seeking to Ride on China's Stock Market Highs," *New York Times*, December 29, 2014.

[9] David Barboza, "Chinese Investors Who Borrowed Are Hit Hard by Market Turn," *New York Times*, July 6, 2015.

predicted that the Chinese economy would grow at only 6.8 percent in 2015, well below the 7.4 percent growth seen in 2014. Second, it appeared that much of the growth coincided with an explosion of margin lending or using borrowed money to buy securities. On May 27, 2015, total margin debt outstanding grew five times in just one year, reaching 2 trillion yuan, or $322 billion.[10] Margin debt accounted for 8.7 percent of the free float on Chinese stocks, compared to only 2.8 percent in the United States. Margin lending created extra volatility in markets because if the markets headed south, brokers could call in margin loans and force investors to repay borrowings, often by selling stocks. Moreover, individual investors often traded stocks bought quickly with borrowed money, amplifying volatility. In May 2015, stocks with margin debt changed hands an average of twenty-three times, while stocks without traded five times.[11]

The government recognized the threat that widespread margin lending posed and took measures to curb its growth. The China Securities Regulatory Commission (CSRC) conducted an inspection of forty-five securities companies in December 2014 and found three of the largest companies— CITIC Securities, Haitong Securities, and Guotai Junan Securities—were violating regulations, including illegally extending margin contracts past the six-month limit set by the CSRC.[12] The imposed limit was intended to force investors to recognize losses and close out accounts instead of using credit to extend trades indefinitely. As punishment, the CSRC banned the three brokerages from opening new accounts for three months. Nine other brokerages were also found to have been serving unqualified clients, and following further investigations, the CSRC punished six for related violations, also banning new accounts.[13] Great Wall Securities Co., Ltd., Huatai Securities, and Guosen Securities, three of the top brokerages, were included in the sanctions.[14]

Markets unraveled quickly in response to fears that the government was cracking down on margin trading. Even as China's four securities newspapers published editorials claiming that the bull market remained

[10] Editorial Board, "China's Unsettling Stock Market Boom," *New York Times*, June 15, 2015.

[11] Jack Wong and Chao Deng, "Chinese Firms Discover Margin Lending's Downside," *Wall Street Journal*, June 30, 2015.

[12] Gabriel Wildau, "Explainer: Margin Finance in China," *Financial Times*, January 19, 2015.

[13] Adam Jourdan, "China Punishes Six Brokerages for Margin Trading Violations-Regulator," Reuters, April 4, 2015.

[14] The three other sanctioned brokerages were Minmetal Securities Co., Ltd., Huaxi Securities, and China International Capital Corp.

alive, the Shanghai Composite Index lost more than one-third its value during the second half of June 2015. After first embracing a "normal self-correction," the CSRC said in late June that an "excessively fast correction" would be unhealthy and the risks of margin lending and short-selling would be manageable. By early July, the CSRC had reversed the exact limits on margin lending it had imposed less than a month earlier to boost markets, and it also announced a probe into potential illegal stock manipulation and sources of the stock market rout.[15]

Early July brought two heavy-handed moves on the part of the CSRC and the PBoC to stabilize markets: IPOs were suspended on July 4, affecting an estimated 4 trillion RMB in planned issuances, and the government announced it would establish a market-stabilization fund comprising a "national team" (国家队) of brokerages to purchase shares of blue-chip exchange traded funds (ETFs).[16] The Central Huijin Investment Company, which traditionally held banking assets, assured the public it would continue to purchase ETFs, and the China Securities Finance Corporation quickly followed. Various measures to ease investment accompanied the massive deployment of state capital by the "national team," and government-owned news media projected confidence. Tsinghua University graduates were instructed to shout, "Revive the A-shares, benefit the people!" at their commencement ceremony.[17]

The capital injections seemed to arrest the market decline in July, but August brought troubles anew. First, the PBoC loosened convertibility of the RMB and immediately devalued the currency by 2 percent against the dollar, the largest devaluation since the modern exchange-rate system was introduced in 1994. The devaluation was part of the PBoC's efforts to comply with IMF expectations for the RMB's inclusion in the "Special Drawing

---

[15] The decisions were to relax margin lending rules and allow brokerages to roll over contracts and wait to close out accounts. The CSRC also announced it would lower the threshold for individual investors to trade on margin and expand funding channels for brokerages. Lu Jianxin and Pete Sweeney, "Timeline of China's Attempts to Prevent Stock Market Meltdown," Reuters, August 28, 2015.

[16] These companies comprised about 30 percent of the Shanghai market.

[17] James Kynge, "Prestige of the Communist Party Tumbles in the Great Fall of China," *Financial Times*, July 9, 2015. "At the critical time during the competition between bearish and bullish factors, such measures will motivate the whole market, which shows the authorities' resolve in stabilizing the market and will have immediate effects," an article in Xinhua News declared on July 6. "Early Bird Report 6-July-2015," Xinhua Finance Agency, July 6, 2015, http://en.xfafinance.com/html/Early_Bird/2015/114008.shtml. *People's Daily* also claimed that China was "capable and confident" that it would maintain a stable market, arguing that market risks were firmly under control. "China 'Capable, Confident' of Stabilizing Capital Market: People's Daily," Xinhua News, July 6, 2015, http://en.people.cn/business/n/2015/0706/c90778-8916145.html.

Rights" (SDR) basket of reserve currencies, but the rapidity of the decline was not expected. Some interpreted the devaluation as an effort to boost exports amid slowing growth, but others saw the movement as unintended and a reflection of a lack of confidence in the RMB. Indeed, 2015 and 2016 saw significant capital outflows from both foreign investors and domestic capital holders who were pursuing safety outside of China.[18] Later that year, the IMF would add the RMB to its SDR basket, the first addition to the basket since adoption of the euro. The decision was heralded as a statement of China's standing as a global economic power, but the push toward a "freely usable currency" also enabled capital flight, prompting eventual controls in 2016 and 2017 on "irrational" outbound investments and efforts to "protect 3 trillion" of reserves and defend the RMB against further drops.[19]

The so-called national team, principally comprising Central Huijin and the CSF, made over 1.3 trillion RMB from purchasing on China's two stock exchanges between June and September 2015, eventually holding shares in half of all listed firms.[20] Yet the large-scale deployment of state resources, in events that seem reminiscent of efforts by the Indonesian Banking Restructuring Agency during the AFC, facilitated collusion and looting in the midst of crisis. While intervention by the "national team" may have staved off further collapse, the use of state capital was not unproblematic. By the end of 2015, six out of twenty-one securities companies on the "national team" were under investigation for short-selling or insider trading. According to one person, "People at CITIC and other firms were calling up their friends saying, 'Tomorrow, I am buying [whatever firms].'"[21] Moreover, initial investments by the "national team" seemed to have moved the market, but subsequent investments were perceived as failures. Because state capital was essentially rescuing collapsing companies, "People were happy for the 'national team' to buy because they wanted to sell."[22] Essentially, after revealing

[18] Carlos Tejada, "5 Things to Know about China's Currency Devaluation," *Wall Street Journal*, August 10, 2015; Neil Gough and Keith Bradsher. "China Devalues Its Currency as Worries Rise about Economic Slowdown," *New York Times*, August 10, 2015.

[19] [19] "IMF Launches New SDR Basket Including Chinese Renminbi, Determines New Currency Amounts," International Monetary Fund Press Release 16/40, September 30, 2016, http://www.imf.org/en/News/Articles/2016/09/30/AM16-PR16440-IMF-Launches-New-SDR-Basket-Including-Chinese-Renminbi.

[20] Chen Li, Huanhuan Zheng, and Yunbo Liu, "The Hybrid Regulatory Regime in Turbulent Times: The Role of the State in China's Stock Market Crisis in 2015–2016," *Regulation & Governance* 16, no. 2 (2022): 392–408, https://doi.org/10.1111/rego.12340.

[21] Interview, private institutional investor, Shanghai, May 2017. See also Hou Qiang, "Securities Firms Fined for Profiteering amid Stock Market Chaos," Xinhua News, September 2, 2015.

[22] Interview, private institutional investor, Shanghai, May 2017.

that they would intervene on such a scale, the intervention then failed to move the market because it simply generated counterparties. Within a few months, Zhang Yujun, an assistant chairman of the CSRC who had played a critical role in the efforts of the "national team," was removed from office and under investigation by the Central Commission on Discipline Inspection (CCDI).[23]

During the crisis and in the months immediately following, the CCP turned on financial market participants—business and political elites—in actions that would presage a wider resurgence of state discipline in the financial sector. During the crisis, several high-profile finance professionals were detained. Li Yifei, chairwoman of the Man Group, a large global hedge fund, disappeared in late August 2015, with her husband reporting she had been detained. Ms. Li resurfaced and claimed she had been on a mountain meditation retreat. A few months later, Guo Guangchang of Fosun, nicknamed "China's Warren Buffet," was detained, not for the first time. Yim Fung, CEO of Guotai Junan International Securities in Hong Kong, was also reported missing by his company in 2015, and, as in the cases of Li and Guo, returned to work within a month.[24] In none of these cases were charges announced, and all of these high-profile individuals were either rumored or reported to be assisting regulators to understand how financial markets had become so volatile. Whether "assistance" meant technical explanations, for example on how margin-lending technology platforms worked or providing information about the actions of peers and competitors, was not confirmed.[25]

Not all financial elites were lucky enough to experience catch-and-release. Xu Xiang, dubbed the "hedge fund king," was taken into police custody in 2016 in a series of events that illustrate the logic of mutual endangerment. His hedge fund, Zexi Investment, had grown by nearly 800 percent between 2011 and 2016 and it had been left unscathed in the stock market crash that past summer, in fact growing spectacularly during the crisis. By the end of the summer, the annual return on his funds was more than 200 percent, but

---

[23] Yifan Xie and Wei Gu, "China Securities Official Is under Investigation," *Wall Street Journal*, November 15, 2015. Zhang Yujun died of cancer in 2021. He was never officially charged, and the CCDI never presented evidence against him.

[24] Sophia Yan, "Giant Chinese Brokerage Can't Find Its CEO," *CNN Money*, November 24, 2015.

[25] Opinion, "The Case of China's Missing Brokers," *Wall Street Journal*, December 8, 2015; Scott Cendrowski, "The 'Warren Buffet' of China Disappears," *Fortune*, December 11, 2015; Xie Yu, "'Missing' Fosun Chairman Guo Guangchang Back at Work after 'Helping Chinese Authorities with Investigation,'" *South China Morning Post*, December 14, 2015; Scott Cendrowski, "China's Anti-corruption Drive Nets Another Top Banker," *Fortune*, December 9, 2015.

a viral social media post accused Xu and his firm of abusing connections to manipulate stocks in their favor and to gain insider information on government actions. After initially being tipped off that the authorities were headed for him, Xu was captured in a police blockade on a bridge while attempting to flee.[26] In January 2017 Xu was sentenced to five and a half years in prison for market manipulation as well as fined a record 1.1 billion yuan.[27]

The CSRC moved to fine and punish the makers and operators of technology platforms ("brokerage access platforms") that enabled retail investors to open accounts without real-name registration, a violation of the Securities Act.[28] In early November, the CCDI announced that it was investigating Yao Gang, vice chairman of the CSRC for discipline violations. Yao, who headed the department that chooses which companies go public on the Chinese exchanges, had served in his position since 2009 and ranked as one of the top CCP officials at the CSRC. After announcement of the investigation, the CSRC removed Yao's profile from its website, and CSRC chairman Xiao Gang declared that both Yao and Zhang Yujun, the former assistant chairman relieved of his position following probes in September, were "negative examples."[29]

Before, during, and after the crisis, financial market participants interacted with the state and its agents in a cycle of risk-taking and punitive state responses. Market participants heeded the government's embrace of equity market expansion, but rather than markets allocating resources efficiently and providing discipline, short-termism and distrust shaped behaviors that ultimately looked like financial manipulation and looting, leading to further government interventions that exacerbated distrust and provided further

[26] Alex W. Palmer, "The Fall of China's Hedge-Fund King," *New York Times Magazine*, March 29, 2016.
[27] Xie Yu, "Once China's Hedge Fund Guru, Xu Xiang Sentenced to 5.5 Years in Prison for Market Manipulation," *South China Morning Post*, January 23, 2017.
[28] These were Hundsun Technology, Mecrt Corporation (Shanghai), and Hithink Flush Information company. The technology platforms also enabled hierarchical margin lending; once a borrower's account had declined in value by a certain amount, lenders could control the accounts to sell or buy, leading to faster changes in equities prices than regulators thought was technically possible—the digital equivalent of breaking the ticker-tape machine. The largest platform was HOMS, owned by Hundsun Technologies in Hangzhou, in which Alipay held a 20.6 percent stake. See Dinny McMahon, "Peer-to-Peer Lending Takes Off in China," *Wall Street Journal*, June 3, 2015; Chuin-Wei Yap, "China Crackdown on Margin Lending Hits Peer-to-Peer Lenders," *Wall Street Journal*, July 13, 2015; Jess McHugh, "China 'Black Monday' Timeline: The Chinese Stock Market Crash and How It Happened," *International Business Times*, August 24, 2015; Moshinsky, "China's National Team"; Yue Wang, "Hundsun Tech under Probe after China's Stock Bust," *Forbes*, July 13, 2015; interview, private institutional investor, Shanghai, May 2017.
[29] Xie and Gu, "China Securities Official."

opportunities for looting. As in Indonesia, mutual endangerment both contributed to the onset of a financial crisis and shaped dynamics during the crisis that made it difficult to manage. But the crisis dynamics in China were fundamentally different from those in Indonesia: the equities market crisis was relatively confined because of the small size of China's stock markets, and the CCP enjoyed broad control of cross-border capital flows to stabilize the RMB.

A Herd of Gray Rhinos: Debt and Threat in Xi's China

A larger threat to the regime's economic and political stability is a debt crisis that is also fundamentally a result of mutual endangerment. A great deal of scholarly and popular attention has surrounded China's public debt, mostly incurred by local governments that, for reasons I address in Chapter 6, rely on land finance and land-enabled borrowing to accelerate GDP growth and meet expenditure burdens (see Figure 7.1). The massive accumulation of corporate debt, however, has received less attention, certainly from social scientists. We have come to expect debt problems from state firms and

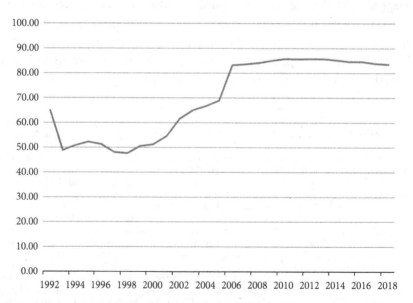

Figure 7.1 Debt-to-Asset Ratio, Listed Firms, 1992–2018
Source: China Securities Regulatory Commission, via CEIC.

nonperforming loans issued to the same, but why would nonstate firms, presumably facing market discipline, take on existential loads of debt, imperiling their financial solvency and potentially attracting the ire of the party-state, ever wary of financial instability?

The answer is that the relationships between large business groups and the state and within them are best characterized by mutual endangerment. Most, if not all, participants in these relationships have short time horizons and an acute sense of vulnerability, if not active threat. Individually, the actions by these participants amount to excessive risk-taking and looting that is quite costly for both the firms and society.

Estimating the total amount of corporate debt in China, as well as the debt of any individual firm, is difficult since many firms have hidden and off-balance-sheet debt because they have endeavored to raise funds illegally or have relied on the shadow-banking system or both. The Bank for International Settlements (BIS) estimates that total debt for Chinese nonfinancial corporates has gone from 105.3 percent of GDP in 2006 to 160.7 percent of GDP in 2020. Disentangling private from public debt is difficult because much of local government debt is assumed by local government financing vehicles, which are registered as companies, but BIS also estimates that "core debt" credited to the private, nonfinancial sector reached over 200 percent of GDP by 2016.[30] Following the financial crisis of 2015, the debt and external financing of large Chinese corporations came under scrutiny by the Xi Jinping government; Xi himself designated corporate debt as a "gray rhino," a systemic risk that, if it starts to move quickly, could become existential.[31] In May and June 2017, several firms—internationalized conglomerates, especially Fosun, Wanda, Anbang, and HNA—came under China Banking Regulatory Commission (CBRC) investigation for debt, especially financing of global acquisitions, including offshore financing and bonds and bank credits of subsidiary firms hidden from lenders to upper levels of the business systems.[32]

[30] Data from the Bank of International Settlements, 2021, https://www.bis.org/statistics/about_c redit_stats.htm?m=2673. "Core debt" includes debt securities, loans, and currency and deposits.

[31] Hong Yuran Wu, Guo Nan, and Leng Cheng, "China Asks Banks to Assess Credit Risks Linked to Firms Active in Overseas Deals," *Caixin Global*, June 22, 2017, https://www.caixinglobal.com/ 2017-06-22/china-asks-banks-to-assess-credit-risks-linked-to-firms-active-in-overseas-deals-101104621.html.

[32] "民企大佬海外并购急刹车   万达、复星、海航纷纷表态" (Overseas Mergers and Acquisitions of Private Enterprise Leaders Suddenly End; Wanda, Fosun, and HNA Express Their Views), *Renmin wang*, August 1, 2017, http://finance.people.com.cn/n1/2017/0801/c1004-29441 056.html. I was fortunate to be based in Shanghai from January through July 2017 and to benefit from

Table 7.1 Corporate Bonds for Select Firms, 2004–2017

	HNA	Fosun	Anbang	Wanda
Bonds (#)	174	97	22	17
Value	157 billion RMB	125 billion RMB	27.3 billion RMB	1.1 trillion RMB
Number Offshore	8	5	0	2
Total Financial Institutions Involved (onshore bonds only)	26	14	9	14

Source: Bond prospectuses collected via the WIND database and the National Association of Financial Market Institutional Investors.

A close examination of the financial activities of these four firms, as well as other large conglomerates, reveals much about the connection between partial liberalization and mutual endangerment. For each of these firms, I used China- and non-China-based databases as well as formal corporate filings in the Bureau of Industry and Commerce (工商局) to pull bond prospectuses for all known subsidiaries of major conglomerates (also gleaned from databases and corporate filings; see Appendix C). Bond prospectuses both indicate firm debt in bond markets and contain valuable, though incomplete, data on bank credit and other firm financials. Table 7.1 shows data on onshore and offshore bonds issued by the four large "gray rhino" firms. Figures 7.2 and 7.3 visualize the bank relationships for Wanda and HNA, as gleaned from prospectus disclosures. Though these data are not comprehensive, the pattern that emerges is one of financial dispersal and extensive borrowing from small and nonstate financial institutions as well as large state financial institutions.

The dramatic dispersion of financial connections and sheer size of borrowings, from financial institutions and in bond markets, illustrate the logic and political consequences of mutual endangerment. These firms did not come under CBRC investigation until late spring 2017, by which time executives of some of the firms (e.g., Fosun) had been detained and released multiple times, yet they were still accessing domestic and global markets

extensive conversations with observers of these firms and with some representatives from the firms themselves as well as general financial-sector participants and regulators at this critical time.

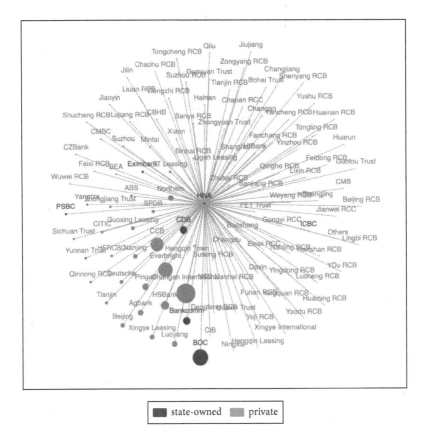

Figure 7.2 Lending Banks to HNA

for financial expansion. By many accounts, brief scrutiny of these firms that resulted from the financial crisis and the exodus of capital in 2016–17 brought a real surprise to regulators who were blindsided by the dispersal of financial connections and the systemic risks these firms posed. One official likened what he saw to an iceberg: "We realized we only saw the very top of a mountain of debt. There were many of these icebergs, and they could be deadly for the whole system. Once we noticed one, we saw them everywhere."[33]

Maneuvering the Chinese economy around the icebergs, and indeed dismantling the icebergs, would take years. Anbang and HNA were essentially nationalized, with both assets and debts assumed by various parts of the Chinese state. Dalian Wanda and Fosun both engaged in a directed

[33] Interview, CBRC official, Shanghai, May 2017.

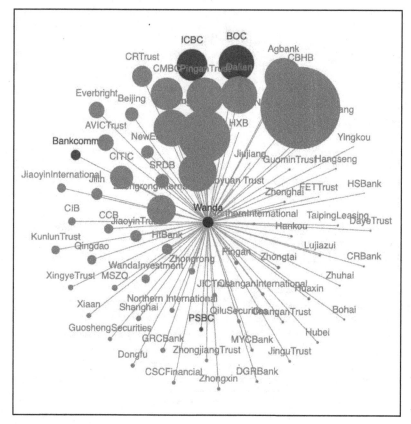

Figure 7.3 Lending Banks to Wanda

Source: Circle size is based on total loans or line of credit amount disclosed in bond prospectuses, 2000–2018. Bond prospectuses do not provide an exhaustive source of data on all loans or credit lines, and many banks appear anonymously in the prospectuses. See Appendix C.

unwinding, short-selling many domestic and global assets to reduce debt burdens. Eventually, in corporate transactions reminiscent of the Malaysian state reconfiguration of troubled assets, Wanda acquired special shareholders, including other large firms close to the Chinese state (e.g., Alibaba and Jingdong) and local state-owned enterprises (SOEs).[34] The excessive debt, facilitated by political connections and partial financial liberalization, appears to be a form of systemic looting, by which the savings of current and

---

[34] 李晓青 (Li Xiaoqing), "王健林的2017一次海外收购遇阻引发的万达集团生存之战" (Wang Jianlin's 2017: Wanda Group's Battle for Survival Caused by Overseas Acquisition Frustrations), February 20, 2018, https://www.thepaper.cn/newsDetail_forward_1999828.

future generations of Chinese households are transferred to corporations and individuals with little or no accountability. The debt crisis, among other things, prompted a reorganization of the state's role in the economy and another reconfiguration of the regulatory system. The potential for distrustful business elites to engage in behavior that is profoundly destructive for a political regime is a theme I return to in the concluding chapter.

Reclaiming Financial Control

In the years since the 2015–16 financial crisis, the CCP under Xi Jinping has made aggressive moves toward rebuilding the party-state's disciplinary power over business in a number of arenas. Efforts to extend state monitoring and control in the financial system have been most prominent, beginning in 2015–16, due to necessity and the crisis, and expanding more systematically in the following years. CCP efforts, like those during the crisis, have featured a combination of relying on the state's coercive apparatus and extending the regime's hand into financial markets and firm corporate governance. These efforts, collectively and individually, have been viewed as "crackdowns" on various parts of the Chinese economy, evidence of the "end of an era" of reforms, or the state "striking back" after decades of market ascendance.[35]

While I do not dispute the magnitude and direction of what Jeremy Wallace productively calls the "neopolitical turn" under Xi,[36] I see these efforts as primarily intended to exert discipline over state-business relations and in reaction to the threats generated by mutual endangerment. In Chapter 1, I argue that each of the forms of state-business relations I lay out is dynamic: mutual alignment yields endogenous pressures for more innovation, and mutual endangerment yields financial instability and calls for clamping down on business at the expense of economic growth. While the "neopolitical turn" has been accompanied by some ideological discussion, such as Xi's 2021 call for

---

[35] Nicholas R. Lardy, *The State Strikes Back: The End of Economic Reform in China?* (Washington, DC: Peterson Institute for International Economics, 2019); Carl Minzner, *End of an Era: How China's Authoritarian Revival Is Undermining Its Rise* (New York: Oxford University Press, 2018).

[36] Jeremy Wallace, "The New Normal: A Neopolitical Turn in China's Reform Era," in Karrie J. Koesel, Valerie Bunce, and Jessica Chen Weiss, eds., *Citizens & the State in Authoritarian Regimes: Comparing China and Russia* (New York: Oxford University Press, 2022), 31–58. See also John Yasuda, "Regulatory Visions and the State in East Asia: The Irrational Investor Problem in the Comparative Politics of Finance," *Comparative Political Studies.* Online first (2023). Doi: 10.1177/00104140231169015.

"common prosperity" and the regime's trumpeting of its model on the global stage, the post-2015 policies in pursuit of more state control over the Chinese economy originated primarily from the regime's insecurity via-à-vis business and the problems generated by mutual endangerment.

Shareholding

One highly visible manifestation of the regime's efforts to reconstitute financial discipline is the widespread presence of the state as shareholder and corporate governance participant. For a generation of scholars of the reform era, scholars of and participants in China's political economy have distinguished between state-owned and nonstate firms, theorizing about the dynamics of reform of the state sector and observing competitiveness in the private sector. Yet, especially after 2015, state capital has expanded beyond the majority state-owned sector, bringing the CCP along as monitor and shareholder in a large swath of firms in the broader economy and challenging the state-private dichotomy that has held sway over the Chinese political economy.

Figure 7.4 shows the rising prominence of central and local shareholding funds. We took the top ten shareholders of every firm listed on the Shanghai and Shenzhen stock exchanges for each year, 1993–2018. We then counted each time a shareholder is named and find the top twenty shareholders (measured by number of firms in which they hold shares rather than the size of the shares held) for each year. We examined the ownership structure for each shareholder to code as either a Big Four Bank (Bank of China, China Construction Bank, Agricultural Bank of China, or Industrial and Commercial Bank of China), a central shareholding firm, a local shareholding firm, a pension fund, private firm, or other. Figure 7.4 shows the number of firms by shareholder type. The figure visualizes several trends. First, private shareholders appear dominant in the late 1990s and early 2000s, after which the Big Four Banks appear to hold large numbers of firms after 2003. Second, central and local shareholding firms play an increasingly large role beginning in 2006; after 2012 and especially after the stock market crisis of 2015, central shareholding firms constitute the dominant shareholder on the Shenzhen and Shanghai exchanges.

The expansion of state capital has a strategic and upgrading logic as well as a risk management logic. As I have written elsewhere, the "financialization" of the state's role in the economy has accompanied industrial-policy efforts,

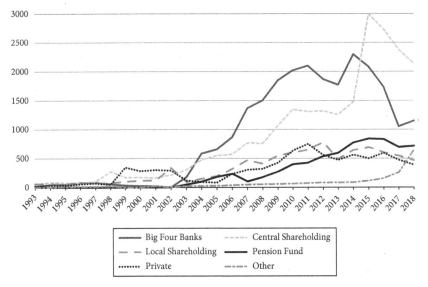

Figure 7.4 Number of Invested Firms by Shareholder Type for the Top Twenty Shareholders on the Shanghai and Shenzhen Stock Exchanges

Note: "Other" refers to Hong Kong–based investors.

Source: Data collected via WIND and analyzed by the author.

especially the Made in China 2025 plans to upgrade the Chinese economy and facilitate self-reliance and competition in frontier sectors.[37] China's industrial-policy efforts have received a good deal of attention, but the role of the state in corporate governance has focused on the monitoring of firms and has been extended to firms well beyond those involved in frontier technology sectors.

In November 2013, at the Third Plenum of the Eighteenth Party Congress, a Central Committee decision on "comprehensively deepening reform" formally encouraged the establishment of "state-owned capital operation companies" (国有资本运营公司) to shift from "managing enterprises" to "managing capital."[38] In July 2014, the first two official "state capital investment

---

[37] This section draws on material from Hao Chen and Meg Rithmire, "The Rise of the Investor State: State Capital in the Chinese Economy," *Studies in Comparative International Development* 55, no. 3 (2020): 257–77, https://doi.org/10.1007/s12116-020-09308-3. See also Margaret Pearson, Meg Rithmire, and Kellee Tsai, "China's Political Economy and International Backlash: From Interdependence to Security Dilemma Dynamics," *International Security* 47, no. 2 (Fall 2022): 135–76.

[38] State Council, "中共中央关于全面深化改革若干重大问题的决定" (Decision on Major Problems in the Deepening of Reform), November 15, 2013, http://www.gov.cn/jrzg/2013-11/15/content_2528179.htm.

companies" were established under the State-Owned Assets Supervision and Administration Commission (SASAC)—the managed SOEs COFCO (a food-processing company), and SDIC (an investment holding company).[39] A year later, a State Council directive on SOE reform explicitly encouraged state capital in private firms: "State-owned capital invests in non-state-owned enterprises in various ways" to "focus on public services, high-tech, eco-environmental protection, and strategic industries . . . and non-state-owned enterprises with large development prospects and strong growth potential."[40]

In February 2016, two new "state-owned capital operation enterprise" pilots were established within China Chengtong Holdings Group and China Reform Holdings, both asset management holding companies governed by SASAC. Both established multiple funds, with additional shareholders primarily drawn from other SOEs that provided capital for SOEs to buy listed private firms. By the end of 2018, these two pilots managed total assets of 900 billion RMB.[41] By 2022, twenty-three additional SOEs were designated as "state-owned capital investment companies" (国有资本投资公司) in order to, among other rationales, develop the "risk prevention role of the state economy."[42] Although the official language remains vague about the distinction between capital investment and operation, interviews suggest that capital operation firms may take a more active investment stance, perhaps managing distressed assets, whereas investment firms handle more passive investments.[43] A major economic rationale for extending state capital to the private sector has been to provide a source of financing to private firms in the context of the crackdown on shadow banking.[44] Ironically, perhaps, the CCP

[39] State capital investment companies are called 国有资本投资公司 in Chinese. "国务院国资委举办'四项改革'试点新闻发布会" (SASAC Holds Press Conference on the "Four Reforms"), July 15, 2014, http://www.sasac.gov.cn/n2588020/n2588072/n2591426/n2591428/c3731034/content.html.

[40] State Council, "关于深化国有企业改革的指导意见" (Guiding Opinions on Deepening the Reform of State-Owned Enterprises), September 13, 2015, http://www.gov.cn/zhengce/2015-09/13/content_2930440.htm.

[41] The website of China Chengtong Holdings Group lists these partners in the establishment of "China Structural Reform Fund Corporation Limited," http://www.cctgroup.com.cn/cctgroupen/about_us/group_profile/index.html; Li Yifang, "A 股股权转让大增的特征，原因及政策建议" (Increase in A Share Equity Transfer: Reason, Future, and Policy Recommendations) 上证研报 (Shanghai Securities Research Report), Number 8 (2019), 16.

[42] "5家中央企业正式转为国有资本欧子公司" (Five SOEs Formally Transformed into State Capital Investment Companies), June 21, 2022, http://www.gov.cn/xinwen/2022-06/21/content_5696886.htm. Other rationales include "deepening reform, developing world-class enterprises, and improving economic competitiveness, strength, and control."

[43] Interview, former CSRC official, August 2019.

[44] Xiao Gang, "Manage the Pace and Intensity of Risk Management and Promote the Healthy Development of the Asset Management Industry: Report for the 2019 China Wealth Management 50

seems to want capital to go to the private sector, but it has been intolerant of the risks that accompany financial liberalization, and therefore it is now offering itself as a source of finance.

As the central state has emphasized the need for state capital investment and operation, local governments have joined central shareholding funds and SOEs in pursuit of investments in the private sector. Beginning in the second half of 2017—after the establishment of central-level experimental state capital investment and operation enterprises but before the 2018 document providing official guidance on these firms—local SASACs began to establish state-owned capital investment and operation companies. Local investment companies have, in many cases, gone beyond minority investments, frequently engaging in "ownership transfers" of private, listed firms—essentially nationalization through open market equity purchases.

Most examples of private firms falling under state control involve distressed firms or large conglomerate firms under tremendous political and financial pressure. In many cases, firms experiencing a suspension in trading for a significant amount of time are eventually purchased by local SASACs, as was the case with a technology company in Anhui (Changxin Technology) and several others in Fujian in 2018. Those that welcomed state capital have argued that state investment or ownership helps distressed firms access capital and resources, whereas others (especially academic economists) have worried that such "mixed ownership reform" is inviting state capital into the private sector rather than the other way around. In the cases of large, distressed conglomerate firms, heavy pressure from regulators has forced companies such as HNA, Dalian Wanda, and Fosun to unwind some of their global purchases; HNA reportedly sold its 7.6 percent stake in Deutsche Bank to a group comprising a number of state shareholding firms, including CIC and CMIG, profiled below. Some of Anbang's insurance assets were taken over by local SOEs in Xiamen and Shenzhen after the company was nationalized and its chairman jailed in early 2018.[45]

Forum," Xinhua News, August 20, 2019, http://www.xinhuanet.com/money/2019-08/20/c_1124896 522.htm (accessed November 2019). Xiao Gang is former chairman of CSRC.

[45] Chen Yanqing (陈燕青), "地方国资入主民企再掀高潮: 今年超10家民营A股公司将变身国企" (Entry of Local State Capital into Private Enterprises Continues: More Than Ten Private A-Share Companies Will Become State-Owned This Year," *Tencent News: Finance*, October 9, 2018.

Crackdowns

In addition to the state's financial resources, the CCP has used the state's co-ercive powers to discipline business and political elites whose actions are perceived to be threatening to political and economic stability and legitimacy. This chapter has already made a number of references to detentions, arrests, anticorruption prosecutions, and even nationalizations, especially during the 2015–16 stock market crisis and the related aftermath. But the regime's efforts to tame mutual endangerment have been systematic as well as ad hoc, and they have relied on familiar means of governance, namely, campaigns. The CCP's focus on the financial sector and on economic "crimes" has both laid bare the dynamics of mutual endangerment and contributed to the short time horizons, distrust, and political vulnerability that have given rise to this form of state-business relations.

Although the anticorruption campaign has targeted political officials over illicit ties to business since its inception in 2013, regulatory officials became an explicit focus after the financial crisis. Zhang Yujun, mentioned above, and Yao Gang were the first financial regulatory officials to come under CCDI investigation in 2015, but between 2015 and 2021, at least thirty-four other officials, in banking, insurance, and securities regulation, met similar fates. At least six of these officials, all in Inner Mongolia's banking regula-tory offices, were publicly linked to Xiao Jianhua and his Baoshang Bank; and three were linked to Xu Xiang, the "hedge fund king" captured on a bridge in 2016.[46] Almost all of these officials were accused of taking bribes and/or abusing their positions of power for personal enrichment. Lai Xiaomin, who served on the CBRC between 1994 and 2008 and at the time of arrest was president of China Huarong Asset Management, one of the four state-owned asset management companies, was accused of receiving more than 1.7 billion RMB in bribes (more than $250 million), for which he received a death sen-tence in the largest bribery case in PRC history.[47]

Corruption and collusion in financial markets are not surprising, but the scale and logic of the relationships illustrate the shift from mutual alignment

---

[46] Data were collected from the CCDI website and media reports. See Appendix C for details.

[47] "华融公司原董事长赖小民被执行死刑" (Lai Xiaomin, Former Chairman of Huarong Company, Is Executed), January 29, 2021, https://www.ccdi.gov.cn/yaowen/202101/t20210129_235 027.html; "权威解读 | 赖小民案 案财物近17亿元已追缴" (Nearly 1.7 Billion Yuan of Property Involved in the Lai Xiaomin Case Has Been Recovered), https://www.ccdi.gov.cn/toutiao/202008/ t20200814_223735.html.

to mutual endangerment. These relationships are not built on "access money" exchanged for facilitating productive business efforts in an inhospitable business environment, but rather represent conspiratorial grand theft, by which political and business elites engage in a plunder of state resources in networks that become more difficult to escape with every illicit choice.

In addition to prosecutions and crackdowns, the CCP has made a concerted effort to rearticulate the party-state's institutional control over the financial sector. The Financial Stability and Development Committee (金融稳定发展委员会) was established in July 2017, as Xi Jinping himself expressed that the party's leadership over financial matters should be emboldened to address systemic risk and that "financial security is an essential part of national security."[48] The connection between the financial sector and "national security" was not new in 2017; Articles 19 and 20 of the 2015 National Security Law establish "economic security" and "financial stability" as pillars of national security, and Xi's government increasingly saw many aspects of economic organization as part of an expanded view of "comprehensive national security."[49] The securitization of financial governance marks a new turn in the CCP's management of capital. The CBRC and China Insurance Regulatory Commission were reorganized into a combined commission, and the Office of Financial Stability has begun to organize coordinating bodies at the local levels to reassert central control over a sector with inherent social risks.[50]

Conclusion: State Power and Insecure Capitalists

"Traffic lights" apply to all means of transportation on the road, and the same is true for capital. All types of capital cannot run amok. [We

---

[48] "全国金融工作会议在北京召开 习近平发表重要讲话" (Xi Jinping Delivers an Important Speech at the National Financial Work Conference Held in Beijing), July 15, 2017, https://news.qq.com/a/20170715/035661.htm.

[49] See Pearson, Rithmire, and Tsai, "China's Political Economy"; Sheena Chestnut Greitens, "Internal Security and Grand Strategy: China's Approach to National Security under Xi Jinping," statement before the US-China Economic & Security Review Commission, January 28, 2021, https://www.uscc.gov/sites/default/files/2021-01/Sheena_Chestnut_Greitens_Testimony.pdf; Helena Legarda, "China's New International Paradigm: Security First," Merics, June 15, 2021, https://merics.org/en/chinas-new-international-paradigm-security-first.

[50] "国务院金融稳定发展委员会成为并召开第一次会议" (The Financial Stability and Development Committee of the State Council Holds Its First Meeting), November 8, 2017, http://www.gov.cn/xinwen/2020-01/14/content_5469125.htm.

must establish] traffic lights for capital to prevent the savage growth
of some capital. We must fight against monopolies, profiteering, sky-
high prices, malicious speculation, and unfair competition. . . . To
curb the disorderly expansion of capital does not mean the absence
of capital, but the orderly development of capital. . . . [We must] support and guide norms of healthy capital development.

—Xi Jinping, 2022[51]

In addition to its own regulators and large, "mafia-like" business systems, the
CCP squarely trained its sights on local-level business actors, especially in
the 2018 launch of a campaign to "Sweep Away the Black and Eliminate Evil"
(扫黑除恶) The campaign was launched by the Office of the Leading Group
for the Special Struggle against Gangs and Evil (扫黑除恶专项斗争领导小
组办公室) to "normalize the fight against gangs and evil."[52] The campaign
is accompanied by volumes of propaganda, typical of campaigns, that focus
on violent organized crime and extortion, highlighting stories of hidden
bodies and family triads. But the campaign has also targeted economic
crimes, such as illegal finance and business and political actors forming "protective umbrellas" to shield themselves from scrutiny and prosecution.[53]
In some cases, local campaign enforcers go back decades to round up local
entrepreneurs for actions that some call "original sin," things businesspeople
simply had to do to work within a prohibitive institutional environment.

China under Xi has displayed all of the economic distortions and risks that
mutual endangerment can bring—systemic debt accumulation, looting of
large and small firms with destructive economic consequences, widespread
fraud and malfeasance, and corruption resembling grand theft. But, while
the New Order in Indonesia succumbed to these risks, the Chinese regime

[51] 习近平 （Xi Jinping), "正确认识和把握我国发展重大理论和实践问题" (The Correct
Understanding of the Major Theoretical and Practical Problems of China's Development), speech
at the Central Economic Work Conference, Beijing, December 2021, and reprinted in issue no. 10
of *Qiushi*, May 2022, http://www.qstheory.cn/dukan/qs/2022-05/15/c_1128649331.htm and English
translation at https://interpret.csis.org/translations/the-correct-understanding-of-major-theoreti
cal-and-practical-problems-of-chinas-development/.
[52] "检察机关推进扫黑除恶专项斗争：坚持'稳、准、狠'" (The Procuratorial Organs Promote
a Special Campaign against Gangsters and Evil: Adhere to "Stability, Accuracy and Ruthlessness"),
January 7, 2020, https://www.spp.gov.cn/spp/cffhjcznzxzsfwdjzdgz/202001/t20200107_452093.
shtml; "扫黑除恶从专项斗争转向常态化开展未来怎么做?" (What Should We Do in the Future
When the Anticrime Campaign Shifts from a Special Campaign to a Normal One?), Xinhua News
Agency, March 30, 2021, http://www.gov.cn/xinwen/2021-03/30/content_5596864.htm.
[53] See Ben Hillman, "Law, Order and Social Control in Xi's China," *Issues and Studies* 57, no. 2
(2021): 1–21.

has attempted to root out the deleterious effects of mutual endangerment through coercive state power and a reconfiguration of regulatory institutions. What does the theory of state-business relations advanced in this book tell us about whether the CCP can be successful?

On the one hand, we have seen how financial discipline, even with pervasive distrust, can facilitate productive economic growth. One version of China's future might be one in which the CCP reclaims disciplinary control over the private sector through an effective regulatory apparatus, state corporate governance participation, and monitoring through widespread state shareholding, or a combination thereof. But Malaysia's experience also shows us the risks attending such a return to mutual alignment; the "developmental paradox" produces a politically disciplined corporate sector that is unlikely to participate in what Xi diagnoses as the "disorderly expansion of capital," but also a corporate sector unable to take risks and dominated by state-connected behemoths with little capacity for innovation. This kind of stagnation would be at odds with other economic and political goals of the CCP under Xi, namely, the acceleration of technology-driven, innovation-driven economic growth to become a self-reliant economic superpower.

But there is also reason to imagine that a return to mutual alignment via state coercion and regulatory muscle may bring outcomes even worse than stagnation. Unlike in Malaysia, Chinese capitalists have decades of accumulated distrust of the party-state, and the uncertainty of economic elites has likely worsened as a result of the CCP's efforts to rescue the country from mutual endangerment. While such efforts may generate a short-term course correction, campaigns and crackdowns reinforce the sense of vulnerability that has long alienated capitalists from the regime. We can imagine that the present round of crackdowns, like those in the decades since the 1940s, may abate in favor of accommodations for capitalists when the regime requires investment and economic growth. But this new episode in the pattern of accommodation-reprisal holds the same implications for China's moral economy of capitalism, in which the CCP and capital need each other but mutually expect disorderly behavior. The "norms of healthy capital development" Xi seeks, in the context of precarious ties, may prove to be elusive indeed.

8

Conclusion

Power and Moral Economy in Authoritarian Capitalism

> I began to wonder after working in the company for several years: What is the point of trying to build the asset portfolio with proper understandings of risk and return? My colleagues were taking cuts of what they knew were bad loans, and my boss expected me to hand over my cuts, and he did not care. I wanted to survive and make money myself, and it was a joke to pretend like any of us cared about the bank's balance sheet.
>
> —Shanghai, June 2017

> The experiential lessons of history are captured by routines in a way that makes the lessons, but not the history, accessible to organizations and organizational members who have not themselves experienced the history.
>
> —Barbara Levitt and James G. March[1]

This book has examined state-business relations in three different Asian authoritarian regimes, all of which have presided over economic growth, industrialization, and vast modernization projects. Though their achievements vary, all three of these countries set forth from the mid-twentieth century with largely agrarian, mostly poor populations, and economies dominated by primary industry and foreign multinationals. What lessons do their shared and divergent experiences yield for intellectual and policy debates about the power of business, the role of the state in the economy, and the compatibility of capitalism and authoritarianism?

---

[1] Barbara Levitt and James G. March, "Organizational Learning," *Annual Review of Sociology* 14, no. 1 (1988): 320, https://doi.org/10.1146/annurev.so.14.080188.001535.

Precarious Ties. Meg Rithmire, Oxford University Press. © Oxford University Press 2023.
DOI: 10.1093/oso/9780197697528.003.0008

The Moral Economy of Authoritarian Capitalism

A core argument in the book is that cronyism as a category is insufficiently descriptive of state-business relations in authoritarian regimes. It fails to account for behaviors of business elites or their consequences for regimes. More specifically, designating state-business relations as crony, or corrupt, or even identifying specific political connections of firms tells us very little about what we might think of as the moral economy of authoritarian capitalism, or what working concepts of reciprocity and understandings of the purpose of economic activity are shared by participants in a political economy.[2] Here I ask why some political economies seem marred by pervasive fraud, with business elites appearing to loot their own firms, and, relatedly, why some "cronies" appear to quickly turn against political elites in times of crisis. The main answer is that these political economies are built on precarious ties—fundamental distrust between political and business elites.

Elites can be close—"cronies"—but distrust one another at the same time. In Indonesia and China, because of their historical experiences and deeply embedded social relationships, capitalist elites expect defection (betrayal, with costly, even existentially costly, effects) rather than reciprocity from political elites. They therefore structure their behavior, even their firms, with these expectations. They invest in mobile assets, hedge their economic positions, and pursue illicit relationships with political elites and other business elites as forms of insurance against defection, and relatively short time horizons shape their economic choices. My argument is not that every single Chinese Indonesian capitalist behaved this way and certainly not that every Chinese firm thinks this way, but rather that this worldview was sufficiently pervasive in both political economies to affect general norms of doing business. In their classic exploration of the organization of the firm, Levitt and March write that economic "action stems from a logic of appropriateness or legitimacy more than from a logic of consequentiality or intention. It involves matching procedures to situations more than it does calculating choices."[3] Many of my interlocutors, especially in China, emphasized that they never intended to become enmeshed in corrupt relationships and especially in actions that would destroy the value of their own firms. Rather,

---

[2] For other conceptualizations of moral economy, see James C. Scott, *The Moral Economy of the Peasant: Rebellion and Subsistence in Southeast Asia* (New Haven: Yale University Press, 1976); E. P. Thompson, *The Making of the English Working Class* (Harmondsworth: Penguin, 1972).

[3] Levitt and March, "Organizational Learning," 320.

as the quotation at the beginning of this chapter illustrates, these behaviors were so pervasive in the general business environment that they were impossible to avoid.

A large literature exists examining the political and economic preferences of firms, looking primarily at how different sectoral profiles, asset structures, and positions in global production affect those preferences.[4] I have argued that in the regimes under study here, political statuses and relations transcend all these factors as sources of preferences; in fact, sectoral choices, asset choices, and corporate forms are frequently endogenous to political status. I am not the first by far to observe that firm structures and choices are functions of the business environment. An early literature on business groups and vertical integration sees these phenomena as a "microeconomic response to well-known conditions of market failure in developing countries."[5] For the most part, scholars expect business groups to decrease in prominence over time with institutional strengthening and market development.[6] Yet such groups emerged in China after several decades of economic reforms, and, in both China and Indonesia, they became more prominent in the wake of financial liberalization. Even more puzzlingly, many were not seeking advantage in new markets and revenue streams as much as inverting basic expectations about what firms do by looting their own assets.

Institutional weaknesses such as incomplete bankruptcy laws or poor financial supervision are perhaps necessary conditions for mutual endangerment (especially asset expatriation and looting), but insufficient ones. We also require a rich accounting of political histories and experiences. Mutual endangerment only obtains when business elites have shared worldviews built on political vulnerability and distrust of political elites. While contemporary

---

[4] Jeffry A. Frieden, *Debt, Development, and Democracy: Modern Political Economy and Latin America, 1965–1985* (Princeton, NJ: Princeton University Press, 1991); Peter Alexis Gourevitch, *Politics in Hard Times: Comparative Responses to International Economic Crises* (Ithaca: Cornell University Press, 1986); David A. Lake, "Open Economy Politics: A Critical Review," *Review of International Organizations* 4, no. 3 (2009): 219–44. For a critical discussion, see Jeffrey A. Winters, "Power and the Control of Capital," *World Politics* 46, no. 3 (1994): 419–52; Meredith Woo-Cumings, *Race to the Swift: State and Finance in Korean Industrialization* (New York: Columbia University Press, 1991); Sylvia Maxfield and Ben Ross-Schneider, eds., *Business and the State in Developing Countries* (Ithaca: Cornell University Press, 1997).

[5] Nathaniel H. Leff, "Industrial Organization and Entrepreneurship in the Developing Countries: The Economic Groups," *Economic Development and Cultural Change* 26, no. 4 (1978): 666, https://doi.org/10.1086/451052.

[6] Unless, that is, they become more "entrenched" over time, erecting barriers to entry for new firms. See Randall Morck, Daniel Wolfenzon, and Bernard Yeung, "Corporate Governance, Economic Entrenchment, and Growth," *Journal of Economic Literature* 43, no. 3 (2005): 655–720, https://doi.org/10.1257/002205105774431252.

political economy has veered toward a focus on institutions and incentives, this research shows that classic conceptions of moral economy remain instructive to explain behavior, especially dramatic behavior, even in arenas like financial innovation and integration, seemingly the province of technocratic regulation. Moral economies, and "informal institutions" more broadly, are built on learned expectations of exchange over long periods of time, and they are not easily dislodged or transformed by changes to formal institutions.[7]

The Disruptive Power of Business

What do the experiences of these three regimes in authoritarian Asia contribute to debates about state-business relations and the power of capital? I began in the first chapter by rejecting conceptions of power in state-business relations in terms of inquiring which side wields more power, but this study does point to a form of power that business seems to hold over political elites that is undertheorized in social science literatures.

For generations, scholars have debated the relative importance of "structural" and "instrumental" power; business enjoys structural power in that it affects political choices through the sheer possibility that firms may withhold investment if political elites pursue courses of action that firms dislike. Dependence of political regimes of all kinds on private investment for economic growth and stability forces states to accommodate the interests of private capital.[8] Instrumental power, on the other hand, refers to the ability of corporate actors to affect policy and secure benefits through lobbying or other forms of particularistic bargaining. To be sure, we see both forms of power at work here. All three regimes liberalized their financial systems or

---

[7] Douglass C. North, "Economic Performance through Time," *American Economic Review* 84, no. 3 (1994): 359–68. See also Pepper D. Culpepper, "Institutional Change in Contemporary Capitalism: Coordinated Financial Systems since 1990," *World Politics* 57, no. 2 (2005): 173–99, http://dx.doi.org/10.1353/wp.2005.0016.

[8] For the classic statement, see Charles Lindblom, *Politics and Markets: The World's Political Economic Systems* (New York: Basic Books, 1977); Adam Przeworski and Michael Wallerstein, "Structural Dependence of the State on Capital," *American Political Science Review* 82, no. 1 (1988): 11–29, https://doi.org/10.2307/1958056. For a more contemporary take on global financial capital, see Winters, "Power and Control"; *Frieden, Debt, Development, and Democracy*. For a critical take, see Pepper D, Culpepper, "Structural Power and Political Science in the Post-crisis Era," *Business and Politics* 17, no. 3 (2015): 391–409, https://doi.org/10.1515/bap-2015-003; David Vogel, "Political Science and the Study of Corporate Power: A Dissent from the New Conventional Wisdom," *British Journal of Political Science* 17, no. 4 (1987): 385–408.

otherwise adopted "probusiness" reforms when they needed to mobilize investment and faced weak fiscal positions or changes in external economic conditions that inhibited state investment.[9] And, clearly, we see how particularistic access to the state or various political elites enabled firms and businesspeople to capture resources for themselves.

But there is an irony evident in contrasting the Malaysian case with China and Indonesia. In Malaysia, elite capitalists of all kinds, I argue, were not as vulnerable as their Indonesian and Chinese counterparts, yet they generally enjoyed less autonomy from state intervention in corporate governance, and the Chinese Malaysian capitalists have been unable to challenge decades of punitive economic policies aimed at redistribution based on ethnicity. In contrast, Suharto's ethnic Chinese cronies appear to have taken actions that wreaked havoc on the country's financial system, and the allegedly "co-opted" Chinese capitalists have similarly engaged in widespread debt accumulation and firm involution, generating what the Chinese Communist Party (CCP) itself believes to constitute "systemic risk" for the regime.

Chinese and Indonesian capitalists seem to possess, and Malaysian capitalists seem to lack, a form of power over political elites and regimes that does not demand accommodation or particular resources but rather threatens political disruption, even destruction. This form of power entails, but is not limited to, the dynamic of firms "too big to fail," whereby firms, or even entire sectors, require consistent political accommodations or resources because of their social importance and are thereby in conditions of "permanent state receivership."[10] Disruptive power describes the ability of firms to engage in actions that endanger specific political elites or even overall regimes. It differs from structural power, or at least classic expressions of the concept, in that it does not require the state to adopt probusiness policies to facilitate investment but rather to shift its political and economic interventions and orientations to address the social and political problems that flow from actions by business. Regime elites and ruling parties must either tolerate the social instability that comes from such disruption—protests against fraud and misallocation of resources, bankruptcies that threaten negative effects on economic bystanders, corruption revelations that imperil

---

[9] On states' dependence on mobile capital and on Indonesia's experience, see Jeffrey A. Winters, *Power in Motion: Capital Mobility and the Indonesian State* (Ithaca: Cornell University Press, 1996).

[10] Theodore J. Lowi, *The End of Liberalism: The Second Republic of the United States*, 2nd ed. (New York: Norton, 1979). I note that Culpepper sees this particular phenomenon as structural power. Culpepper, "Structural Power."

public trust and legitimacy, and so forth—or take actions that discipline the business actors.

We saw in Suharto's Indonesia how such actions were nearly impossible in the late New Order because Suharto's family and close associates were able (via instrumental power, perhaps) to block them. Business wielded the ultimate disruptive power, contributing to and accelerating a financial crisis that caused the regime to unravel. In China, when, at the outset of his term in 2013, Xi Jinping said that the "market will be the primary force in allocating resources," many observers inside China and out were convinced he was authentically committed to deepening reforms.[11] Yet reforms stalled in part because business actions were disruptive. As Chapter 6 details, financial liberalization facilitated fraud, looting, and asset expatriation, generating public outrage and macroeconomic risks that the CCP worried were existential. The party-state has been able to rein in some business actors and sectors via arrests, crackdowns, and campaigns, but it has also been unwilling to tolerate bankruptcies and market corrections that might provide more systematic and long-lasting sources of discipline in firms. Malaysia and China have adopted extensive state shareholding as a means of monitoring and, theoretically, disciplining firms, and we see in both cases how these new interventions interact with those countries' moral economies to create new incentives and behaviors to which the state will react in turn.

The analytical payoff of identifying different forms of business power is, again, not to declare which party wields more power but to understand the politics and policies that different forms of power bring about. Structural power is argued to lead to accommodation of capital, instrumental power to capture or rent-seeking, and disruptive power creates a politics of risk management that can overwhelm a regime (as it did during the New Order) or, under some circumstances, serve as an impetus for a reassertion and reconstruction of state power. Disruptive power can constrain political elites and ruling parties from taking measures they may prefer and force them to solve immediate problems in ways they do not prefer. I have presented the cases in the book to show the dynamic nature of disruptive power, and state-business

---

[11] See Arthur R. Kroeber, "Xi Jinping's Ambitious Agenda for Economic Reform in China," Brookings Institution, 2013, https://www.brookings.edu/opinions/xi-jinpings-ambitious-agenda-for-economic-reform-in-china/; Daniel H. Rosen, "China's Economic Reckoning: The Price of Failed Reforms," *Foreign Affairs* 100, no. 4 (2021): 20–29. I note here that many participants in China's financial markets, even as late as 2015–16, believed Xi would be increasingly liberal, viewing the anticorruption campaign as a necessary step to eliminate vested interests that block reform.

relations more generally. Both business and political elites, in authoritarian regimes and beyond, are engaged in constant efforts to improve their positions, and actions of adaptation and reaction cause political economy models to change shape over time. Mutual alignment produces dynamics of economic stagnation and repeated, frequently unsuccessful, efforts to overcome it. The dynamics of mutual endangerment are more destructive and explosive, leading to social and political combustion in the Indonesian case and to a dramatic reshaping of state control over the economy in the Chinese case.[12]

The Limits of Technocracy

Last, what does regime type have to do with state-business relations and development in Asia? While modernization theorists posit that democracy will be an outcome of economic development and modernization, the three regimes under study here have shaped narratives about the necessity of limited political competition for stability and development. Each regime certainly justified its monopoly on political power in those terms; the New Order and the Barisan Nasional both invoked the specter of ethnic violence, the threat of communism, and the crucible of conflict in the regime formation period, and the CCP's delivery of growth and political stability is core to its social contract with China's population.[13] Outsiders shaped these narratives as well. In the cases of Indonesia and Malaysia, especially the former, the rejection of communism endeared the regimes to Western—especially

[12] On this dramatic reshaping, see Margaret Pearson, Meg Rithmire, and Kellee Tsai, "Party-State Capitalism in China," *Current History* 120, no. 827 (2021): 207–13, https://doi.org/10.1525/curh.2021.120.827.207; Nicholas R. Lardy, *The State Strikes Back: The End of Economic Reform in China?* (Washington, DC: Peterson Institute for International Economics, 2019); Carl Minzner, *End of an Era: How China's Authoritarian Revival Is Undermining Its Rise* (New York: Oxford University Press, 2018).

[13] That the New Order was built on the events of September 30, 1965, is the core thesis in Roosa's book on the coup and violence. See John Roosa, *Pretext for Mass Murder: The September 30th Movement and Suharto's Coup D'État in Indonesia* (Madison: University of Wisconsin Press, 2006). On China, I do not subscribe to the idea that the regime depends on a "performance-based legitimacy," but its revolutionary mandate was indeed about modernization and stability. See Chalmers A. Johnson, *Peasant Nationalism and Communist Power: The Emergence of Revolutionary China* (Stanford: Stanford University Press, 1962); Elizabeth J. Perry, "Is the Chinese Communist Regime Legitimate?," in Jennifer M. Rudolph, Michael Szonyi, and Fairbank Center for East Asian Research, eds., *The China Questions: Critical Insights into a Rising Power* (Cambridge, MA: Harvard University Press, 2018), 11–17. More generally on democracy and development in Asia, see Dan Slater and Joseph Wong, *From Development to Democracy: The Transformations of Modern Asia* (Princeton, NJ: Princeton University Press, 2022).

American—makers of foreign policy and directors of international financial institutions. Whether or not the CCP promotes its model as one adaptable to other countries, it is undeniable that the Chinese experience offers at least an example of a non-Western "alternative" model of economic development that has captured the attention of policymakers, especially within authoritarian regimes, the world over.[14]

In some of these assessments, the state's management of development is imagined to be fundamentally technocratic rather than political. With the right advice and institutional design, authoritarian states can manage macroeconomic stability, "pick" the right "winners" in choosing which firms to support, and even harness the "right" kinds of corruption to facilitate economic exchange and, indeed, development.[15] If optimizing institutional design is mostly about economic or technocratic rules, do political rules and political systems matter?

The findings in this book illustrate just how much political status, norms, and inclusion do matter for state-business relations and, by extension, for economic outcomes. Structurally vulnerable capitalists in Indonesia, abetted by a corrupt political elite, involuted that country's experience with financial liberalization and embrace of global capitalism with disastrous consequences. China under the CCP presided over an enormous developmental success, but constructing functional advanced financial markets has proven elusive. Instead of providing efficiency and discipline, China's liberalized financial architecture has been fertile territory for arbitrage, fraud, and generally destructive forms of corruption. While I concur with scholars such as Raghuram Rajan and Luigi Zingales, who argue that these forms of "relationship-based capitalism" cannot be attributed to cultural propensities, I do not agree that "financial underdevelopment" alone is to be blamed.[16] The effects of financial development, no matter how sophisticated the regulatory

---

[14] Bradley R. Simpson, *Economists with Guns: Authoritarian Development and U.S.-Indonesian Relations, 1960–1968* (Stanford: Stanford University Press, 2008); Matthias Fibiger, *Suharto's Cold War: Indonesia, Southeast Asia, and the World* (New York: Oxford University Press, 2023); Daniel Bell, *The China Model: Political Meritocracy and the Limits of Democracy* (Princeton, NJ: Princeton University Press, 2016); Maria Repnikova, *Chinese Soft Power* (New York: Cambridge University Press, 2022); Kerry Ratigan, "Are Peruvians Enticed by the 'China Model'? Chinese Investment and Public Opinion in Peru," *Studies in Comparative International Development* 56, no. 1 (2021): 87–111, https://doi.org/10.1007/s12116-021-09321-0.

[15] Yuen Yuen Ang, *China's Gilded Age: The Paradox of Economic Boom and Vast Corruption* (New York: Cambridge University Press, 2020); Ross H. McLeod, "Soeharto's Indonesia: A Better Class of Corruption, " *Agenda* 7, no. 2 (2000): 99–112.

[16] Raghuram Rajan and Luigi Zingales, *Saving Capitalism from the Capitalists: Unleashing the Power of Financial Markets to Create Wealth and Spread Opportunity* (New York: Crown Business, 2003).

frameworks may be, depend on political expectations and identities; we have seen how alienated and vulnerable capitalists can sow destruction with access to liberalized financial systems.

This is not a book about state-business relations in democracies, and I do not advance any theory about how political trust works in open political systems, or beyond the cases I have analyzed in depth. But we might see how certain institutions that tend to feature in democracies, namely, rule of law guarantees for protection of property and persons, would be a solution to endemic distrust between political and economic elites. While it feels admittedly unsavory to conclude a book about fraud and the disruptive power of business by crying out for rights for capitalists, most social scientists would accept that giving any social or economic group a stake in a system and protection from the worst outcomes tends to moderate behaviors.

That societies, even capitalists themselves, may be better off with open and competitive political systems is not surprising; it is, after all, the foundation of classical historical understandings of capitalists as agents of expanding political inclusion, even democratization, in the Western world. In that process, it was not that economic elites mobilized to demand rights and inclusion for everyone; they desired those things for themselves, and demands from others followed with great struggle.[17] I have argued here that economic elites cannot be permanently co-opted and weakened by authoritarian political elites and parties, but rather dynamically pursue their interests in ways that will reshape regimes over time. Though they may not identify as a class or hold political preferences for democracy, it is incorrect to view their behaviors as necessarily buttressing the rule of authoritarian regimes, and it is too early to conclude their actions will not be the source of profound and systemic political change.

---

[17] Charles Tilly, *Democracy* (New York: Cambridge University Press, 2007); Didi Kuo, *Clientelism, Capitalism, and Democracy: The Rise of Programmatic Politics in the United States and Britain* (New York: Cambridge University Press, 2018); Francis Fukuyama, *The Origins of Political Order: From Prehuman Times to the French Revolution* (New York: Farrar, Straus and Giroux, 2011); Barrington Moore, *Social Origins of Dictatorship and Democracy; Lord and Peasant in the Making of the Modern World* (Boston: Beacon Press, 1966). For a sense of how more contemporary capitalists have facilitated democratization by withdrawing their support for authoritarian regimes, see Stephan Haggard and Robert R. Kaufman, *The Political Economy of Democratic Transitions* (Princeton, NJ: Princeton University Press, 1995).

APPENDICES

APPENDICE

Indonesian Conglomerate Firms

Chapter 3 contains several figures, tables, and text references to the organization, structure, assets, and relationships of large Indonesian firms. For these inferences, I triangulate several sources of descriptive data.

1) CISI Raya Utama, PT, *A Study on 300 Prominent Indonesian Businessmen, 1990.* Jakarta, 1990.

   Data on individual assets, history, family relations, ethnic identity

2) CISI Raya Utama, PT, *A Study on the Top-200 National Private Business Groups in Indonesia, 1989.* Jakarta, 1989.

   Data on subsidiaries, business activities, sales, assets, ownership, trends, and some information on origins and major connections

3) CISI Raya Utama, *A Study on the Top-300 National Private Business Groups in Indonesia, 1991–1992.* Jakarta, 1991.

   Data on subsidiaries, business activities, sales, assets, ownership, trends, and some information on the origins and major connections

4) Appendices in Andrew Rosser, *The Politics of Economic Liberalization in Indonesia: State, Market, and Power.* Richmond, Surrey, UK: Curzon, 2002.

   Data on bank ownership and securities firm ownership

5) Pusat Data Business Indonesia, *Conglomeration Indonesia: A Profile of Indonesian Largest Business Groupings Featuring Conglomeration Presence in Indonesia.* Jakarta, 1989.

   Data on subsidiaries, business activities, sales, assets, ownership, trends, and some information on origins and major connections

Figure A.1 Example of Data Entry for the Aneka Group, from (2) and (3)

26.

7. Business Trend   : G r o w i n g

8. Major Owner   : Mr. Santoso Amidjojo alias Jo Hui Tek

9. Top Executives   : a. Mr. Santoso Amidjojo alias Jo Hui Tek
                                b. Mr. Eddy Amidjojo
                                c. Mr. Hendarmin Siantar

10. Estimated Sales Turnover : 1987 - Rp 115 billion
                                1988 - Rp 130 billion

11. Estimated Net Assets   : 1988 - Rp 40 billion

12. Contact Address   : P.T. ANEKA DJAKARTA IRON STEEL

                                5th Floor, PUTERA Building
                                Jalan Gunung Sahari no. 39
                                Jakarta Pusat
                                Phones - (021) 630808, 621141, 654921
                                Telex   - 46755 JAKARTA IA
                                Cable   - JOTEK JAKARTA

R e m a r k s :

The ANEKA Group was established in 1970's by Mr. Santoso Amidjojo alias Jo Hui
Tek and his brother Mr. Johan Amidjojo. Initially the group was engaged only
in distribution on steel building material and metal products. Its business
has been expanding vertically as well as horizontally. Since the mid of 1970's
the group members have been expanding their business to steel building
material manufacturing, steel structure fabricating, and bicycle parts and
components manufacturing and bicycle assembling. Later on their business have
been expanding also to coal mining and rattan furniture manufacturing. We have
observed that their business has been growing moderately. The ANEKA Group is a
major national private business group in steel building material manufacturing, steel structure fabricating and bicycle parts and components manufacturing.

The group is led by Mr. Santoso Amidjojo (50 years) and assisted by his sons.
Based on the present Indonesian standard, the ANEKA Group is regarded as a
medium-size national private business group.

                              * * *

P.T. CISI Raya Utama

Data on the Top 100 Malaysian Firms

Chapter 4 contains tables, figures, and text insights on the degree of state shareholding and the board connections among the top one hundred firms listed on the KLSE from 2004 to 2018. This appendix briefly describes the sources of the data and my methods for measuring state shareholding over time.

Data Sources

I obtained the top one hundred firms by market capitalization by taking the top one hundred on the last trading day of the year; some firms drop in and out of the list year to year. Table B.1 lists these firms alphabetically. Historically Chinese-owned firms are in bold, and members of the G20 group of government-linked companies (GLCs) that participated in the GLC transformation program are indicated with an asterisk (*).

Shareholding information for those firms was obtained via Bursa Malaysia, Capital IQ, and the Bloomberg databases. Board membership data were obtained via BoardEx and the firms' annual reports. I then coded whether board members with government backgrounds served under Prime Ministers Mahathir (1981–2003), Badawi (2003–8), and/or Najib (2008–18).

Data Analysis

Figures 4.3 and 4.4 display data on state shareholding cumulatively over time (for all government-linked investment vehicles, or GLICs) and for the six largest GLCs). Table B.2 lists the names of the GLICs and GLCs that are designated as contributing to "state shareholding" and their average share of total market capitalization over 2004–2018.

Table B.1 Top One Hundred Firms by Market Capitalization on KLSE, 2004–2018 (Malaysia)

Firms That Appear on the List of the Top One Hundred Firms on the KLSE, 2004–2018
Aeon Co. (M) Berhad
AEON Credit Service (M) Berhad
AFFIN Bank Berhad*
AirAsia Group Berhad
AirAsia X Berhad
Alam Maritim Resources Berhad
Alliance Bank Malaysia Berhad
Allianz Malaysia Berhad
AMMB Holdings Berhad
Amway (Malaysia) Holdings Berhad
Ann Joo Resources Berhad
APM Automotive Holdings Berhad
Astro Malaysia Holdings Berhad
Axiata Group Berhad*
Bank Islam Malaysia Berhad
Batu Kawan Berhad
Berjaya Food Berhad
Berjaya Land Berhad
Berjaya Sports Toto Berhad
Bermaz Auto Berhad
BIMB Holdings Berhad*
Bintulu Port Holdings Berhad
Boustead Heavy Industries Corporation Berhad*
Boustead Holdings Berhad*
Boustead Plantations Berhad
British American Tobacco (Malaysia) Berhad
Bumi Armada Berhad
Bursa Malaysia Berhad
Cahya Mata Sarawak Berhad
CapitaLand Malaysia Trust
Carlsberg Brewery Malaysia Berhad
CIMB Group Holdings Berhad*
CSC Steel Holdings Berhad
Dagang NeXchange Berhad

Table B.1 Continued

Firms That Appear on the List of the Top One Hundred Firms on the KLSE, 2004–2018

Dayang Enterprise Holdings Berhad

Dialog Group Berhad

Digi.Com Berhad

DRB-HICOM Berhad

Dutch Lady Milk Industries Berhad

Eastern & Oriental Berhad

ECM Libra Group Berhad

Eco World Development Group Berhad

Eversendai Corporation Berhad

Far East Holdings Berhad

FGV Holdings Berhad

Fraser & Neave Holdings Berhad

Gamuda Berhad

Gas Malaysia Berhad

GDEX Berhad

Genting Berhad

Genting Malaysia Berhad

Genting Plantations Berhad

Globetronics Technology Berhad

Green Packet Berhad

GuocoLand (Malaysia) Berhad

Hap Seng Consolidated Berhad

Hap Seng Plantations Holdings Berhad

Hartalega Holdings Berhad

Heineken Malaysia Berhad

Hengyuan Refining Company Berhad

Hock Seng Lee Berhad

Hong Leong Bank Berhad

Hong Leong Capital Berhad

Hong Leong Financial Group Berhad

Hong Leong Industries Berhad

IGB Real Estate Investment Trust

IHH Healthcare Berhad

(*continued*)

Table B.1 Continued

Firms That Appear on the List of the Top One Hundred Firms on the KLSE, 2004–2018

IJM Corporation Berhad

IJM Plantations Berhad

Inari Amertron Berhad

IOI Corporation Berhad

IOI Properties Group Berhad

JAKS Resources Berhad

Jaya Tiasa Holdings Berhad

JCY International Berhad

Karex Berhad

Keck Seng (Malaysia) Berhad

KLCC Property Holdings Berhad

KNM Group Berhad

Kossan Rubber Industries Berhad

KPJ Healthcare Berhad

KSL Holdings Berhad

Kuala Lumpur Kepong Berhad

Landmarks Berhad

Lebtech Berhad

Lingkaran Trans Kota Holdings Berhad

Lion Industries Corporation Berhad

Lion Posim Berhad

Lotte Chemical Titan Holding Berhad

LPI Capital Berhad

M K Land Holdings Berhad

MAA Group Berhad*

Magnum Berhad

Mah Sing Group Berhad

Malakoff Corporation Berhad

Malayan Banking Berhad*

Malayan Cement Berhad

Malaysia Airports Holdings Berhad*

Malaysia Building Society Berhad*

Malaysia Marine and Heavy Engineering Holdings Berhad

Malaysian Bulk Carriers Berhad

Table B.1 Continued

Firms That Appear on the List of the Top One Hundred Firms on the KLSE, 2004–2018

Malaysian Pacific Industries Berhad

Malaysian Resources Corporation Berhad*

Maxis Berhad

MBM Resources Berhad

Media Chinese International Limited

Media Prima Berhad

MISC Berhad

MMC Corporation Berhad

MNRB Holdings Berhad

MSM Malaysia Holdings Berhad

Mudajaya Group Berhad

Mulpha International Berhad

My E.G. Services Berhad

Nestlé (Malaysia) Berhad

Oriental Holdings Berhad

OSK Holdings Berhad

Padini Holdings Berhad

Panasonic Manufacturing Malaysia Berhad

Parkson Holdings Berhad

Pavilion Real Estate Investment Trust

Pavilion REIT Management Sdn Berhad

PBA Holdings Berhad

Perdana Petroleum Berhad

Petron Malaysia Refining & Marketing Berhad

PETRONAS Chemicals Group Berhad

PETRONAS Dagangan Berhad

PETRONAS Gas Berhad

Pharmaniaga Berhad

Pos Malaysia Berhad

PPB Group Berhad

Press Metal Aluminium Holdings Berhad

Public Bank Berhad

Puncak Niaga Holdings Berhad

(*continued*)

Table B.1 Continued

Firms That Appear on the List of the Top One Hundred Firms on the KLSE, 2004–2018

QL Resources Berhad

REDtone Digital Berhad

RHB Bank Berhad

S P Setia Berhad

Sapura Energy Berhad

Sarawak Oil Palms Berhad

Scientex Berhad

Scomi Energy Services Berhad

Scomi Group Berhad

Serba Dinamik Holdings Berhad

Shangri-La Hotels (Malaysia) Berhad

Shin Yang Shipping Corporation Berhad

Sime Darby Berhad*

Sime Darby Plantation Berhad*

Sime Darby Property Berhad*

Southern Steel Berhad

Star Media Group Berhad

Subur Tiasa Holdings Berhad

Sunway Berhad

Sunway Construction Group Berhad

Sunway Real Estate Investment Trust

Supermax Corporation Berhad

Syarikat Takaful Malaysia Keluarga Berhad

Ta Ann Holdings Berhad

Talam Transform Berhad

Taliworks Corporation Berhad

Tan Chong Motor Holdings Berhad

Telekom Malaysia Berhad*

Tenaga Nasional Berhad*

TIME dotCom Berhad

Top Glove Corporation Berhad

TSH Resources Berhad

Uchi Technologies Berhad

UEM Edgenta Berhad*

Table B.1 Continued

Firms That Appear on the List of the Top One Hundred Firms on the KLSE, 2004–2018

UEM Sunrise Berhad*
UMW Holdings Berhad*
Unisem (M) Berhad
United Malacca Berhad
United Plantations Berhad
UOA Development Berhad
V.S. Industry Berhad
Velesto Energy Berhad
ViTrox Corporation Berhad
W T K Holdings Berhad
Wah Seong Corporation Berhad
WCT Holdings Berhad
Westports Holdings Berhad
White Horse Berhad
Yinson Holdings Berhad
YTL Corporation Berhad
YTL Hospitality REIT
YTL Power International Berhad
Zelan Berhad
Zhulian Corporation Berhad

Table B.2 GLICs and GLCs Designated as Contributing to "State Shareholding" (Malaysia)

Name	Average KLSE Share, 2004–2018 (%)
Bank Negara Malaysia	0.165
BNPP Asset Management Holding	0.011
Bursa Malaysia Berhad, ESOP	0.013
Employees Provident Fund of Malaysia	**10.013**
Felda Holdings Berhad	0.002
Gabungan Kesturi Sdn Berhad	0.020
Kerajaan Negeri Pahang	0.017
Khazanah Nasional Berhad	**5.850**
Kumpulan Wang Persaraan	**2.282**
Lembaga Kemajuan Perusahaan Pertanian Negeri	0.005
Lembaga Kemajuan Tanah Persekutuan	0.549
Lembaga Tabung Angkatan Tentera (LTAT)	**0.287**
Lembaga Tabung Haji, Endowment Arm	**0.669**
Ministry of Finance Malaysia	**0.063**
Pahang State Government shares	0.016
Pelaburan MARA Berhad	0.001
Penang Development Corporation	0.061
Penang State Government	0.000
Permodalan ASSAR Sdn Berhad	0.010
Permodalan Nasional Berhad	**10.422**
Pertubuhan Keselamatan Sosial	0.081
Petroliam Nasional Berhad	**8.004**
PMB Investment Berhad	0.003
PTB Unit Trust Berhad	0.000
Sabah State Government	0.004
Sarawak Economic Development Corp.	0.006
State Of Sarawak	0.136
WCT Berhad, Employees Provident Fund Board	0.004
Yayasan Sabah Group, Endowment Arm	0.004

Chinese Conglomerate Firm Data

Chapter 6 contains tables, figures, and text references to the corporate structures and assets of large Chinese conglomerate firms. Overall, a research team under my supervision used several data sources to obtain corporate-structure information and financial information on a total of 21 conglomerate firms. The twenty-one firms, listed in Table C.1, were chosen because their names repeatedly surfaced in fieldwork conversations in 2016–17 as large conglomerate firms that were privately owned.

I used several sources to collect information on these firms.

1) WIND information system, a database with information on firms and firm financials. Listed firms have financial information, and nonlisted firms have ownership information in WIND's 企业库.

2) The 企业库 became available in WIND in late 2019, including information on corporate filings available from the China Bureau of Industry and Commerce (工商局). These data include beneficial ownership, registered capital, and linked subsidiaries or invested firms.

Table C.1 Privately Owned Large Conglomerate Firms (China)

Name
复星 Fosun
安邦 Anbang
海航 HNA
新希望 New Hope
明天 Tomorrow
大连万达 Dalian Wanda
宝能 Baoneng
万向 Wanxiang
泛海 Oceanwide
亨通 Hengtong
三胞 Sanpower
华信 CEFC
忠旺 Zhongwang
恒大 Evergrande
新湖 Xinhu
杉杉 Shanshan
沙钢 Shagang
涌金 Yongjin
锦龙 Golden Dragon
世纪金源 Century Golden
香江 Xiangjiang

3) The WireScreen database holds the above information and became available to me in spring 2022. The data are not longitudinal, so the data in Chapter 6 are for 2019 and 2020, and I used WireScreen to triangulate and verify.
4) The National Association of Financial Market Institutional Investors (NAFMII), an industry association in China.

Subsidiaries and Corporate Structure

Data on subsidiaries and corporate structure obtained in the following way:

> We used WIND to look up the name of the primary firm, then to look up all information related to the shareholding firms until we found the ultimate beneficial owner. (All firms in China are owned by either a SASAC or a "natural person.") We also used WIND to obtain a list of all subsidiary companies and invested companies at > 30 percent and all of the subsidiaries and invested companies of those companies. Table 6.4 in Chapter 6 lists all these subsidiaries as well as how many layers of ownership exist in total. Figure C.1 shows an example of the ownership structure of New Hope Liuhu Ltd. To obtain the overall corporate structure, we followed the shareholder companies until we reached a natural person and obtained all information for companies down the hierarchy.

"Implicit subsidiaries" are companies that we believe are controlled by these conglomerates because they are listed as holding relevant assets in bond prospectuses but they do not appear in corporate filings in the 企业库.

Financial Information

Neither this appendix nor the text provides size as well as assets and revenues for any of these companies. The reason for this is that, as the book explains, many of these corporate organizations are structured to obscure their corporate organization and financials.

Figure C.1 New Hope Liuhe Ltd. (新希望六和股份有限公司)

（一）发行人及下属子公司获得主要银行的授信情况

发行人资信情况良好，与东莞银行、东莞农商行、广州农商行、兴业银行等
金融机构一直保持长期的良好合作关系，间接融资能力较强。截至2016年12月31
日，发行人共获得主要银行有效授信额度304.94亿元，已使用额度40.75亿元，未
使用授信额度264.19亿元。发行人获得主要银行的授信情况如下：

单位：亿元

金融机构名称	授信额度	已用额度
江门新会农商行	23.34	0
兴业银行	20	9.3
广发银行	18	0
交通银行	18	0
东莞银行	15	6.55
华兴银行	15	2
顺德农商行	15	0
南粤银行	12	0
浦发银行	12	0
江西银行	11	0

Figure C.2 Example: Jinlong Group–Dongguan Securities Co., Ltd.

Simply put, I do not have sufficient faith in public information on corporate organization, even through my manual data-collection efforts, to state such figures.

We did obtain information on bond market borrowings and, through bond prospectuses, on the relationships to banks gleaned from bond disclosures. These data are also imperfect. They do not capture anything close to the universe of bank relationships, and many bank names are anonymous in the bond prospectuses. (See Figures C.2 and C.3.) I pull, through NAFMII data and through WIND, all prospectuses issued by any subsidiary of a firm listed in Table C.1.

The bond prospect in Figure C.3 discloses the identity of the lending banks.

Offshore Activities

I use two main sources to examine the overseas activities of large conglomerate firms.

1) FactSet database on M&A transactions.
2) The International Consortium for Investigative Journalists (ICIJ) Offshore Leaks Database on offshore registered companies. These data include information on more than 800,000 "offshore entities" that are typically designed to obscure ownership and that are registered in tax havens. Overall, the database contains 4,655 entities identified as Chinese, 7,913 individual officers identified as Chinese, 661 Chinese "intermediaries" (law firms, accounting firms, etc.), and over 32,000 addresses associated with the above. As Figure C.4 shows, the data are rendered in

2014年末，公司主要银行借款情况如下：

单位：万元

借款金融机构	金额	起始日	到期日
银行 A	473,322	2014 年 6 月 16 日	2015 年 6 月 10 日
银行 B	233,746	2013 年 10 月 9 日	2014 年 10 月 8 日
银行 C	200,000	2013 年 10 月 22 日	2016 年 10 月 21 日
银行 D	140,419	2014 年 2 月 19 日	2015 年 2 月 17 日
银行 E	100,100	2014 年 7 月 30 日	2016 年 7 月 29 日
银行 F	97,827	2014 年 1 月 28 日	2015 年 1 月 27 日
银行 G	97,757	2014 年 2 月 11 日	2015 年 2 月 10 日
银行 H	85,000	2014 年 10 月 22 日	2016 年 10 月 21 日
银行 I	82,000	2014 年 9 月 23 日	2016 年 9 月 22 日
银行 J	80,000	2011 年 7 月 7 日	2016 年 7 月 6 日
银行 K	60,584	2014 年 10 月 15 日	2015 年 10 月 14 日
银行 L	57,130	2014 年 7 月 30 日	2015 年 7 月 31 日
银行 M	56,799	2014 年 7 月 25 日	2015 年 7 月 24 日
银行 N	55,000	2014 年 8 月 20 日	2016 年 8 月 19 日
银行 O	50,000	2014 年 7 月 30 日	2016 年 7 月 30 日
合计	1,869,683		

Figure C.3 Example: Evergrande Group–Evergrande Real Estate Group Co., Ltd.

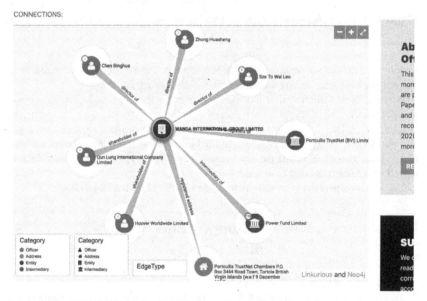

Figure C.4 ICIJ Offshore Leaks Database Entry for "Wanda International Group Ltd." (China)

pinyin rather than Chinese characters, but the firm pinyin names do not necessarily match the firm names in our Chinese data. Therefore, to find the "ICIJ appearances," I matched all addresses associated with the entities in the ICIJ database to any address found associated with any subsidiary of the twenty-one large firms listed in Table C.1. We first matched a single pinyin syllable, and then manually checked whether the full address matched.

APPENDIX D

Interview Data

The insights in the book are, in part, derived from interviews conducted with business actors, political officials, journalists, and academic or think-tank personnel who have expertise on the three countries under study. For the most part, these interviews occurred in Indonesia, Malaysia, and China, but some also took place in Singapore, Hong Kong, Boston, or New York between 2015 and 2020 for Indonesia and Malaysia and between 2007 and 2022 for China. Some data from the interviewees are cited in the book, but other meetings and field visits informed my arguments without being cited directly in the text.

IRB HUA16-0858 granted me approval for these interviews.

Table D.1 Indonesia Fieldwork

Dates	Private Sector	Public Sector
Jakarta (9/2016–1/ 2017) Sumatra (6/2017) Singapore (7/2015, 7/ 2016–1/2017)	Representatives from 23 large firms Representatives from 4 industry associations (Electronics, Palm Oil, Food and Beverage, Financial Technology) Publicly available interviews: Dato Sri Prof. Dr. Tahir (Mayapada Group) Shinta Kamdani (Sintesa Group) Mochtar Riady (Lippo Group)	Representatives from: Ministry of Trade Board of Investment President's Office Ministry of Finance Bank Indonesia

Note: The publicly available interviews are documented in Harvard Business School, "Creating Emerging Markets Project," https://www.hbs.edu/creating-emerging-markets/interviews/Pages/default.aspx?HBSGeographicArea=Southeast%20Asia.

Table D.2 Malaysia Fieldwork

Dates	Firms	Other
Kuala Lumpur (8/2016–1/ 2017, 9–10/2018)	24 large domestic firms Representative firms: Sunway, Maybank, Petronas, MUI, IOI, Sime Darby, 6 foreign-invested firms Financial investors, both domestic and foreign (including, e.g., Khazanah Nasional Berhad)	Academics and think-tank researchers UMNO party officials (2016 only) Ministry of Finance Bank Negara

Table **D.3** China Fieldwork: Firms

Firm Size	Geographic Distribution	Sectors Represented	Firm Ownership
Small and medium (0–50 employees): 76 Large (50–500 employees): 37 Very large (> 500 employees): 85	Guangdong (29) Shanghai (27) Beijing (9) Outside of China (9) Central Provinces (9) Western Provinces (8) Northeast Provinces (5)	Manufacturing Infrastructure Energy Mining & resource extraction Agriculture (research and development; dairy) Technology Real estate Hospitality Finance Insurance Entertainment Logistics Shipping and shipbuilding Power generation	Central SOEs (6) Other SOEs (4) Non-state owned (156)

Table **D.4** China Fieldwork: Officials

Ministry of Finance (8)
State Administration of Foreign Exchange (2)
China Securities Regulatory Commission (11)
China Insurance Regulatory Commission (5)
China Banking Regulatory Commission (8)
Ministry of Commerce (7)
National Development and Reform Commission (4)
People's Bank of China (3)

Glossary

Indonesia and Malaysia

"Alibaba." Business partnership in which Chinese and *pribumi* actors collude (Indonesia).

Assimilasi. Forced assimilation.

bangsa Indonesia. Indonesian people or nation.

Bapak Pembangkrutan. "Father of bankruptcy."

Bapak Pembanguan. "Father of development."

Bapindo. Bank Penbangunan state development bank (Indonesia).

Bappenas. Ministry of National Development Planning (Indonesia).

Bulog. Agency responsible for rice price stability (Indonesia).

bumiputeras. Ethnic Malay and, later, other indigenous peoples.

cukong. Elite Chinese businessmen.

demam bursa. "Stock market fever."

deposito berjangka. Long-term deposit.

deregulasi. Deregulation (Indonesia).

Gerakan (Parti Gerakan Rakyat Malaysia). Malaysian People's Movement Party.

Gestapu. September 30 Movement (Indonesia).

jockis. Jockeys.

Kelompok Politik—Panitia Perumus Kebidjaksanaan Penjelesaian Masalah Tjina. Political Bureau of the Committee for the Formulation of Chinese-Related Policies (Indonesia).

konglomerat. Conglomerate.

kumiai. Cooperative syndicate.

Melay Persatuan Cina Malaysi. Malaysian Chinese Association.

NEKOLIM. Neocolonialism and dependence.

Pakatan Rakyat. People's Pact.

Panitia Negara Urusan Tjina. State Committee for Chinese Affairs.

peranakan **Chinese.** Ethnic Chinese descended from the first waves of southern Chinese settlers to Southeast Asia.

pergerakan. "Age of movements" (Indonesia).

Pribumis. Indigenous business class.

priyayi. Javanese noble.

reformasi. Political reform.

Rukunegara. Basic Principles of the State (Malaysia).

sook ching. "Purification by elimination" (Malaysia).

totok. Recent migrants to Indonesia.

yayasans. Foundations.

China

ban'an fei 办案费. To pay fees.

baohu san 保护伞. "Protective umbrella."

biaoxian 表现. Feigned loyalty.

dacai, xiao yinhang 大财政, 小银行. Fiscal means.

dai hong maozi 戴红帽子. "Wearing the red hat" (private firm registered as a collective enterprise).

faren daibiao 法人代表. Legal representative.

ganqing 感情. Feelings.

Gongshang ju 工商局. Bureau of Industry and Commerce.

gongsi heying qiye 公私合营企业. Joint state-private enterprise.

guahu qiye 挂户企业. "Hang-on enterprise" (part of a state enterprise or a government organization).

guanxi 关系. Relationship.

Guohuo gongsi 国货公司. National Goods Company.

guojia dui 国家队. "National team."

guoyou ziben touzi gongsi 国有资本投资公司. State capital investment company.

guoyou ziben yunying gongsi 国有资本运营公司. State-owned capital operation company.

houtai laoban 后台老板. "Backstage boss."

hunye jingying moshi 混业经营模式. "Mixed financial operation."

Jinrong jianguan xietiao buji lianxi huiyi 金融监管协调部际联席会议. Joint Conference on Financial Supervision.

Jinrong wending fazhan weiyuanhui 金融稳定发展委员会. Financial Stability and Development Committee.

luan tanpai, luan fakuan, luan shoufei 乱摊派，乱罚款，乱收费. Arbitrary demands for contributions, fines, and fees.

maiban guanliao zibenjia 买办官僚资本家. Bureaucratic comprador capitalist.

Mingtian xi 明天系. Tomorrow System.

minying 民营. Private (firm).

minying qiye 民营企业. People-run enterprise (non-state-run firm).

minzu zibenjia 民族资本家. National capitalist.

quandi ritou 圈地热头. "Enclosures craze."

qunzhong yundong 群众运动. Mass mobilization campaign.

renqing 人情. Feelings.

rongzi pingtai 融资平台. "Financial platform" company.

sanfan wufan 三反五反. Three- and five-antis (campaign).

sanluan 三乱. Three chaotics.

saohei chu'e or *saohei* 扫黑除恶. "Sweep Away the Black and Eliminate Evil."

Saohei chu'e zhuanxiang lingdao xiaozu bangongshi 扫黑除恶专项斗争领导小组办公室. Office of the Leading Group for the Special Struggle against Gangs and Evil.

shencha diaocha 审查调查. Examination and investigation.

shiji kongzhi ren 实际控制人. Actual controller.

siying qiye 私营企业. Private enterprise.

tudi caizheng 土地财政. Land fiscalization.

wenfeng erdong 闻风而动. "Smell the wind and adapt."

xi 系. System.

xia hai 下海. "Jump into the sea" (of business).

xiao caizheng, da yinhang 小财政，大银行. Financial means.

yihang sanhui 一行三会. "One bank and three commissions."

yingchou 应酬. "Social engagement."

you jia toujia, you qin touqin 有家投家，有亲投亲. "To have a hometown is to invest in it, to have a family is to invest in it."

yusuan nei 预算内. Budgetary.

yusuan wai 预算外. Extrabudgetary.

Zhongguo siying qiye chouyang diaocha 中国私营企业抽样调查. National Private Enterprise Sample Survey.

Zhongyang jinrong gongzuo weiyuanhui 中央金融工作委员会. Central Financial Work Commission.

Bibliography

English-Language Sources

Abdelal, Rawi. 2007. *Capital Rules: The Construction of Global Finance.* Cambridge, MA: Harvard University Press.

Abdelal, Rawi. 2015. "The Multinational Firm and Geopolitics: Europe, Russian Energy, and Power." *Business and Politics* 17, no. 3: 553–76. https://doi.org/10.1515/bap-2014-0044.

Abdelal, Rawi, and Laura Alfaro. 2003. "Malaysia: Capital and Control." Harvard Business School Case 702-040.

Ades, Alberto, and Rafael Di Tella. 1997. "National Champions and Corruption: Some Unpleasant Interventionist Arithmetic." *Economic Journal* 107, no. 443: 1023–42. https://doi.org/10.1111/1468-0297.00204.

Akashi, Yōji. 1970. *The Nanyang Chinese National Salvation Movement, 1937–1941.* Lawrence: Center for East Asian Studies, University of Kansas.

Akerlof George, and Paul M. Romer. 1993. "Looting: The Economic Underworld of Bankruptcy for Profit." *Brookings Papers on Economic Activity*, no. 2: 1–73. https://doi.org/10.2307/2534564.

Albertus, Michael, Sofia Fenner, and Dan Slater. 2018. *Coercive Distribution.* New York: Cambridge University Press.

Alesina, Alberto, Salvatore Piccolo, and Paolo Pinotti. 2019. "Organized Crime, Violence, and Politics." *Review of Economic Studies* 86, no. 2: 457–99. https://doi.org/10.1093/restud/rdy036.

Allen, Franklin, Yiming Qian, Guoqian Tu, and Frank Yu. 2019. "Entrusted Loans: A Close Look at China's Shadow Banking System." *Journal of Financial Economics* 133, no. 1: 18–41.

Amstad, Marlene, and Zhiguo He. 2020. "Chinese Bond Markets and Interbank Market." Pp. 105–50 in *The Handbook of China's Financial System,* edited by Marlene Amstad, Guofeng Sun, and Wei Xiong. Princeton, NJ: Princeton University Press.

Amstad, Marlene, Guofeng Sun, and Wei Xiong, eds. 2020. *The Handbook of China's Financial System.* Princeton, NJ: Princeton University Press.

Anderson, Benedict. 2008. "Exit Suharto." *New Left Review*, no. 50 (March–April): 27–59.

Ang, Yuen Yuen. 2016. *How China Escaped the Poverty Trap.* Ithaca: Cornell University Press.

Ang, Yuen Yuen. 2020. *China's Gilded Age: The Paradox of Economic Boom and Vast Corruption.* New York: Cambridge University Press.

Aspinall, Edward. 2005. *Opposing Suharto: Compromise, Resistance, and Regime Change in Indonesia.* Stanford: Stanford University Press.

Aspinall, Edward, Meredith L. Weiss, Allen Hicken, and Paul D. Hutchcroft. 2022. *Mobilizing for Elections: Patronage and Political Machines in Southeast Asia.* New York: Cambridge University Press.

Bai, Chong-En, Chang-Tai Hsieh, and Zheng Michael Song. 2019. "Special Deals with Chinese Characteristics." NBER Working Paper no. 25839.

Baik, Jiwon, and Jeremy Wallace. 2021. "Slums amidst Ghost Cities: Incentive and Information Problems in China's Urbanization." *Problems of Post-communism* 70, no. 1: 11–26. https://doi.org/10.1080/10758216.2020.1860690.

Bartrand, Jacques. 2008. "Ethnic Conflicts in Indonesia: National Models, Critical Junctures and the Timing of Violence." *Journal of East Asian Studies* 8, no. 3: 425–49.

Bayly, C. A., and T. N. Harper. 2007. *Forgotten Wars: Freedom and Revolution in Southeast Asia*. Cambridge, MA: Belknap Press of Harvard University Press.

Bell, Daniel A. 2015. *The China Model: Political Meritocracy and the Limits of Democracy*. Princeton, NJ: Princeton University Press.

Bell, Jeffrey, Christine Dinh-Tan, and Philip Purnama. 1997. "Busang (A): River of Gold." Harvard Business School Case 798-002 (May).

Bell, Jeffrey, Christine Dinh-Tan, and Philip Purnama. 1997. "Busang (B): River of Gold." Harvard Business School Case 798-003 (October).

Bell, Jeffrey, Christine Dinh-Tan, and Philip Purnama. 1997. "Busang (C): River of Gold." Harvard Business School Case 9-798-004 (September).

Bellin, Eva. 2000. "Contingent Democrats: Industrialists, Labor, and Democratization in Late-Developing Countries." *World Politics* 52, no. 2: 175–205.

Bellin, Eva. 2002. *Stalled Democracy: Capital, Labor, and the Paradox of State-Sponsored Development*. Ithaca: Cornell University Press.

Belogurova, Anna. 2015. "The Malayan Communist Party and the Malayan Chinese Association: Internationalism and Nationalism in Chinese Overseas Political Participation, c.1920–1960." Pp. 125–44 in *Decolonization and the Cold War: Negotiating Independence*, edited by Leslie Hames and Elisabeth Leake. London: Bloomsbury.

Belogurova, Anna. 2019. *The Nanyang Revolution: The Comintern and Chinese Networks in Southeast Asia, 1890–1957*. New York: Cambridge University Press.

Bennett, Gordon A. 1976. *Yundong: Mass Campaigns in Chinese Communist Leadership*. Berkeley: Center for Chinese Studies, University of California.

Bernstein, Thomas P. 1967. "Leadership and Mass Mobilisation in the Soviet and Chinese Collectivisation Campaigns of 1929–30 and 1955–56: A Comparison." *China Quarterly*, no. 31: 1–47.

Bernstein, Thomas P. 2006. "Mao Zedong and the Famine of 1959–1960: A Study in Wilfulness." *China Quarterly*, no. 186: 421–45.

Bhagwati, Jagdish N. 1982. "Directly Unproductive, Profit-Seeking (DUP) Activities." *Journal of Political Economy* 90, no. 5: 988–1002.

Bigley, Gregory, and L. Pearce Jone. 1998. "Straining for Shared Meaning in Organization Science: Problems of Trust and Distrust." *Academy of Management Review* 23, no. 3: 405–21.

Blaydes, Lisa. 2010. *Elections and Distributive Politics in Mubarak's Egypt*. New York: Cambridge University Press.

Boeke, J. H. 1953. *Economics and Economic Policy of Dual Societies, as Exemplified by Indonesia*. New York: International Secretariat, Institute of Pacific Relations.

Booth, Anne. 1984. "Survey of Recent Developments." *Bulletin of Indonesian Economic Studies* 20, no. 3: 1–35.

Bremmer, Ian. 2010. *The End of the Free Market: Who Wins the War between States and Corporations?* New York: Portfolio.

Breznitz, Dan, and Michael Murphree. 2011. *Run of the Red Queen: Government, Innovation, Globalization, and Economic Growth in China*. New Haven: Yale University Press.

Brown, David. 1994. *The State and Ethnic Politics in Southeast Asia*. London: Routledge.

Brown, Jeremy, and Paul G. Pickowicz, eds. 2007. *Dilemmas of Victory: The Early Years of the People's Republic of China*. Cambridge, MA: Harvard University Press.

Brownlee, Jason. 2007. *Authoritarianism in an Age of Democratization*. New York: Cambridge University Press.

Calomiris, Charles W., and Stephen H. Haber. 2014. *Fragile by Design: The Political Origins of Banking Crises and Scarce Credit*. Princeton, NJ: Princeton University Press.

Carstens, Sharon A. 2005. *Histories, Cultures, Identities: Studies in Malaysian Chinese Worlds*. Singapore: Singapore University Press.

Case, William. 2002. *Politics in Southeast Asia: Democracy or Less*. Richmond, Surrey, UK: Curzon.

Case, William. 2017. "Stress Testing Leadership in Malaysia: The 1MDB Scandal and Najib Tun Razak." *Pacific Review* 30, no. 5: 633–54.

Chan, Sarah. 2017. "Assessing China's Recent Capital Outflows: Policy Challenges and Implications." *China Finance and Economic Review* 5, no. 3: 1–13. https://doi.org/10.1186/s40589-017-0048-0.

Chan, Shelly. 2015. "The Case for Diaspora: A Temporal Approach to the Chinese Experience." *Journal of Asian Studies* 74. no. 1: 107–28.

Chan, Shelly. 2018. *Diaspora's Homeland: Modern China in the Age of Global Migration*. Durham, NC: Duke University Press.

Chandler, Alfred D. 1977. *The Visible Hand: The Managerial Revolution in American Business*. Cambridge, MA: Belknap Press of Harvard University Press.

Chang, Ha-Joon. 1994. *The Political Economy of Industrial Policy*. New York: St. Martin's.

Chen, Hao, and Meg Rithmire. 2020. "The Rise of the Investor State: State Capital in the Chinese Economy." *Studies in Comparative International Development* 55, no. 3: 257–77. https://doi.org/10.1007/s12116-020-09308-3.

Chen, Kaiji, Jue Ren, and Tao Zha. 2018. "The Nexus of Monetary Policy and Shadow Banking in China." *American Economic Review* 108, no. 12: 3891–3936.

Chen, Ling. 2018. *Manipulating Globalization: The Influence of Bureaucrats on Business in China*. Stanford: Stanford University Press.

Chen, Wenhong. 2007. "Does the Colour of the Cat Matter? The Red Hat Strategy in China's Private Enterprises." *Management and Organization Review* 3, no. 1: 55–80.

Chen, Zhuo, Zhiguo He, and Chun Liu. 2020. "The Financing of Local Government in China: Stimulus Loan Wanes and Shadow Banking Waxes." *Journal of Financial Economics* 137, no. 1: 42–71.

Cheung Yin-Wong, and XingWang Qian. 2010. "Capital Flight: China's Experience." *Review of Development Economics* 14, no. 2: 227–47.

Chirot, Daniel, and Anthony Reid, eds. 1997. *Essential Outsiders: Chinese and Jews in the Modern Transformation of Southeast Asia and Central Europe*. Seattle: University of Washington Press.

Chng, Nancy, and Richard Borsuk. 2014. *Liem Sioe Liong's Salim Group: The Business Pillar of Suharto's Indonesia*. Singapore: Institute of Southeast Asian Studies.

Chua, Christian. 2004. "Defining Indonesian Chineseness under the New Order." *Journal of Contemporary Asia* 34, no. 4: 465–79.

Chwieroth, Jeffrey M. 2010. "How Do Crises Lead to Change? Liberalizing Capital Controls in the Early Years of New Order Indonesia." *World Politics* 62, no. 3: 496–527. https://doi.org/10.1017/S0043887110000110.

Clarke, Donald C. 2003. "Economic Development and the Rights Hypothesis: The China Problem." *American Journal of Comparative Law* 51, no. 1: 80–111.

Cliver, Robert K. 2015. "Surviving Socialism: Private Industry and the Transition to Socialism in China, 1945–1958." *Cross-Currents: East Asian History and Culture Review* 4, no. 2: 694–722. For online text, see https://cross-currents.berkeley.edu/sites/default/files/e-journal/articles/cliver.pdf, 139–64.

Cochran, Sherman. 2007. "Capitalists Choosing Communist China: The Liu Family of Shanghai, 1948–1956." Pp. 359–85 in *Dilemmas of Victory: The Early Years of the People's Republic of China*, edited by Jeremy Brown and Paul G. Pickowicz. Cambridge, MA: Harvard University Press.

Cochran, Sherman. 2014. *The Capitalist Dilemma in China's Communist Revolution*. Ithaca: Cornell University Press.

Cole, David C., and Betty F. Slade. 1990. "Financial Development in Indonesia." Development Discussion Paper no. 336. Cambridge, MA: Harvard Institute for International Development.

Cole, David C., and Betty F. Slade. 1996. *Building a Modern Financial System: The Indonesian Experience*. New York: Cambridge University Press.

Coleman, James S. 1994. *Foundations of Social Theory*. Cambridge, MA: Belknap Press of Harvard University Press.

Corsetti, Giancarlo, Paolo Pesenti, and Nouriel Roubini. 1998. "What Caused the Asian Financial and Currency Crisis? Part I: A Macroeconomic Overview." NBER Working Paper no. 6833 (December). "Part II: The Policy Debate." NBER Working Paper no. 6834 (December).

Crouch, Harold. 1979. "Patrimonialism and Military Rule in Indonesia." *World Politics* 31, no. 4: 571–87.

Culpepper, Pepper D. 2005. "Institutional Change in Contemporary Capitalism: Coordinated Financial Systems since 1990." *World Politics* 57, no. 2: 173–99.

Culpepper, Pepper D. 2011. *Quiet Politics and Business Power: Corporate Control in Europe and Japan*. New York: Cambridge University Press.

Culpepper, Pepper D. 2015. Structural Power and Political Science in the Post-crisis Era." *Business and Politics* 17, no. 3: 391–409. https://doi.org/10.1515/bap-2015-0031.

Dickson, Bruce J. 2000–2001. "Cooptation and Corporatism in China: The Logic of Party Adaptation." *Political Science Quarterly* 115, no. 4: 517–40.

Dickson, Bruce J. 2003. *Red Capitalists in China: The Party, Private Entrepreneurs, and Prospects for Political Change*. New York: Cambridge University Press.

Dickson, Bruce J. 2008. *Wealth into Power: The Communist Party's Embrace of China's Private Sector*. New York: Cambridge University Press.

Dikötter, Frank. 2016. *The Cultural Revolution: A People's History, 1962–1976*. New York: Bloomsbury.

Dimitrov, Martin K. 2009. *Piracy and the State: The Politics of Intellectual Property Rights in China*. New York: Cambridge University Press.

Diwan, Ishac, Adeel Malik, and Izak Atiyas, eds. 2019. *Crony Capitalism in the Middle East: Business and Politics from Liberalization to the Arab Spring*. New York: Oxford University Press.

Diwan, Ishac, and Marc Schiffbauer. 2018. "Private Banking and Crony Capitalism in Egypt." *Business and Politics* 20, no. 3: 390–409. https://doi.org/10.1017/bap.2018.1.

Doner, Richard F. 1991. *Driving a Bargain: Automobile Industrialization and Japanese Firms in Southeast Asia*. Berkeley: University of California Press.

Doner, Richard F., and F. Ansil Ramsay. 2018. "Competitive Clientelism and Economic Governance: The Case of Thailand." Pp. 237–76 in *Business and the State in Developing Countries*, edited by Sylvia Maxfield and Ben Ross-Schneider. Ithaca: Cornell University Press.

Doner, Richard F., Bryan K. Ritchie, and Dan Slater. 2005. "Systemic Vulnerability and the Origins of Developmental States: Northeast and Southeast Asia in Comparative Perspective." *International Organization* 59, no. 2: 327–61.

Eaton, Sarah, and Genia Kostka. 2017. "Central Protectionism in China: The 'Central SOE Problem' in Environmental Governance." *China Quarterly*, no. 231: 685–704.

Elkins, Caroline. 2022. *A Legacy of Violence: A History of the British Empire*. New York: Alfred A. Knopf.

Enoch, Charles, Barbara F. Baldwin, Olivier Frécaut, and Arto Kovanen. 2001. "Anatomy of Banking Crises: Two Years of Living Dangerously, 1997–1999." International Monetary Fund Working Paper WP/01/52. https://www.imf.org/external/pubs/ft/wp/2001/wp0152.pdf.

Fane, George, and Ross H. McLeod. 1999. "Lessons for Monetary and Banking Policies from the 1997–1998 Economic Crises in Indonesia and Thailand." *Journal of Asian Economics* 10, no. 3: 395–413.

Feith, Herbert, and Lance Castles, eds. 1970. *Indonesian Political Thinking, 1945–1965*. Ithaca: Cornell University Press.

Feng Tianli, and Guofeng Wang. 2010. "How Private Enterprises Establish Organizational Legitimacy in China's Transitional Economy." *Journal of Management Development* 29, no. 4: 377–93.

Fibiger, Matthias. 2023. *Suharto's Cold War: Indonesia, Southeast Asia, and the World*. New York: Oxford University Press.

Fisman, Raymond. 2001. "Estimating the Value of Political Connections." *American Economic Review* 91, no. 4: 1095–1102. https://doi.org/10.1257/aer.91.4.1095.

Fisman, Raymond, and Edward M. Miguel, eds. 2008. *Economic Gangsters: Corruption, Violence, and the Poverty of Nations*. Princeton, NJ: Princeton University Press.

Ford, Michele, and Thomas Pepinsky, eds. 2014. *Beyond Oligarchy: Wealth, Power, and Contemporary Indonesian Politics*. Ithaca: Southeast Asia Program, Cornell University.

Frieden, Jeffry A. 1991. *Debt, Development, and Democracy: Modern Political Economy and Latin America, 1965–1985*. Princeton, NJ: Princeton University Press.

Friedman, Jeremy Scott. 2015. *Shadow Cold War: The Sino-Soviet Competition for the Third World*. Chapel Hill: University of North Carolina Press.

Friedman, Jeremy Scott. 2021. *Ripe for Revolution: Building Socialism in the Third World*. Cambridge, MA: Harvard University Press.

Frost, Adam K., Zeren Li, and Yasheng Huang. 2021. "Anarchy and Capitalism in China's Cultural Revolution." Working paper. https://scholar.harvard.edu/adamkfrost/publications/anarchy-and-capitalism-chinas-cultural-revolution.

Fukuyama, Francis. 2011. *The Origins of Political Order: From Prehuman Times to the French Revolution*. New York: Farrar, Straus and Giroux.

Gale, Bruce. 1987. *1837: A 150-Year History of the Malaysian International Chamber of Commerce and Industry*. Kuala Lumpur: The Chamber.

Gallagher, Mary Elizabeth. 2005. *Contagious Capitalism: Globalization and the Politics of Labor in China*. Princeton, NJ: Princeton University Press.

Gambetta, Diego. 1993. *The Sicilian Mafia: The Business of Private Protection*. Cambridge, MA: Harvard University Press.

Gasiorowski, Mark J. 1995. "Economic Crisis and Political Regime Change: An Event History Analysis." *American Political Science Review* 89, no. 4: 882–97. https://doi.org/10.2307/2082515.

Geddes, Barbara. 1999. "What Do We Know about Democratization after Twenty Years?" *Annual Review of Political Science* 2: 115–44. https://doi.org/10.1146/annurev.polisci.2.1.115.

Gerschenkron, Alexander. 1962. *Economic Backwardness in Historical Perspective: A Book of Essays*. Cambridge, MA: Belknap Press of Harvard University Press.

Gold, Thomas, Doug Guthrie, and David L. Wank, eds. 2002. *Social Connections in China: Institutions, Culture, and the Changing Nature of Guanxi*. New York: Cambridge University Press.

Gomez, Edmund Terence. 1994. *Political Business: Corporate Involvement of Malaysian Political Parties*. Townsville, Queensland, Australia: Centre for South-East Asian Studies, James Cook University of North Queensland.

Gomez, Edmund Terence. 2006. "Malaysian Business Groups: The State and Capital Development in the Post-Currency Crisis Period." Pp. 119–46 in *Business Groups in East Asia: Financial Crisis, Restructuring, and New Growth*, edited by Sea-Jin Chang. New York: Oxford University Press.

Gomez, Edmund Terence. 2009. "The Rise and Fall of Capital: Corporate Malaysia in Historical Perspective." *Journal of Contemporary Asia* 39, no. 3: 345–81.

Gomez, Edmund Terence, and K. S. Jomo. 1997. *Malaysia's Political Economy: Politics, Patronage, and Profits*. New York: Cambridge University Press.

Gomez, Edmund Terence, Thirshalar Padmanabhan, Norfaryanti Kamaruddin, Sunil Bhalla, and Fikri Fisal. 2018. *Minister of Finance Incorporated: Ownership and Control of Corporate Malaysia*. Singapore: Palgrave Macmillan.

Goodwin, Jeff. 2001. *No Other Way Out: States and Revolutionary Movements, 1945–1991*. New York: Cambridge University Press.

Gourevitch, Peter Alexis. 1986. *Politics in Hard Times: Comparative Responses to International Economic Crises*. Ithaca: Cornell University Press.

Greitens, Sheena Chestnut. 2021. "Internal Security and Grand Strategy: China's Approach to National Security under Xi Jinping." Statement before the U.S.-China Economic & Security Review Commission. January 28. https://www.uscc.gov/sites/default/files/2021-01/Sheena_Chestnut_Greitens_Testimony.pdf.

Greitens, Sheena Chestnut, Myunghee Lee, and Emir Yazici. 2020. "Counterterrorism and Preventive Repression: China's Changing Strategy in Xinjiang." *International Security* 44, no. 3: 9–47.

Gunter, Frank R. 1996. "Capital Flight from the People's Republic of China, 1984–1994." *China Economic Review* 7, no 1: 77–96.

Gunter, Frank R. 2017. "Corruption, Costs, and Family: Chinese Capital Flight, 1984–2014." *China Economic Review* 43 (April): 105–17.

Guo, Kai, Ningxin Jiang, Fan Qi, and Yue Zhao. 2020. "RMB Internationalization: Past, Present, and Prospect." Pp. 229–51 in *The Handbook of China's Financial System*, edited by Marlene Amstad, Guofeng Sun, and Wei Xiong. Princeton, NJ: Princeton University Press.

Ha, Yong-Chool, and Myung-Koo Kang. 2010. "Creating a Capable Bureaucracy with Loyalists: The Internal Dynamics of the South Korean Developmental State, 1948–1979." *Comparative Political Studies* 44, no. 1: 78–108.

Hachem, Kinda. 2018. "Shadow Banking in China." *Annual Review of Financial Economics* 10, no. 1: 287–308. https://doi.org/10.1146/annurev-financial-110217-023025.

Hachem. Kinda, and Song Zheng. 2021. "Liquidity Rules and Credit Booms." *Journal of Political Economy* 129, no. 10: 2721–65.

Hacker, Jacob S., and Paul Pierson. 2010. *Winner-Take-All Politics: How Washington Made the Rich Richer—and Turned Its Back on the Middle Class.* New York: Simon & Schuster.

Haggard, Stephan. 2000. *The Political Economy of the Asian Financial Crisis.* Washington, DC: Institute for International Economics.

Haggard, Stephan, and Robert R. Kaufman. 1995. *The Political Economy of Democratic Transitions.* Princeton, NJ: Princeton University Press.

Haggard, Stephan, with Linda Low. 2000. "Appendix 2.1: The Political Economy of Malaysia's Capital Controls." Pp. 73–85 in Stephan Haggard, *The Political Economy of the Asian Financial Crisis.* Washington, DC: Institute for International Economics.

Hall, Peter A., and David W. Soskice, eds. 2001. *Varieties of Capitalism: The Institutional Foundations of Comparative Advantage.* New York: Oxford University Press.

Handelman, Stephen. 1995. *Comrade Criminal: The Theft of the Second Russian Revolution.* London: Michael Joseph.

Hanna, Donald. 2000. "Restructuring Asia's Financial System." Pp. 45–70 in *The Asian Financial Crisis: Lessons for a Resilient Asia,* edited by Wing Thye Woo, Jeffrey D. Sachs, and Klaus Schwab. Cambridge, MA: MIT Press.

Hara, Fujio. 1997. "Malayan Chinese and China: Conversion in Identity Consciousness, 1945–1957." Institute of Developing Economies Occasional Paper no. 33. Tokyo: Institute of Developing Economies.

Hardin, Russell. 2002. *Trust and Trustworthiness.* New York: Russell Sage Foundation.

Harper, T. N. 1998. *The End of Empire and the Making of Malaya.* New York: Cambridge University Press.

Heilmann, Sebastian. 2005. "Regulatory Innovation by Leninist Means: Communist Party Supervision in China's Financial Industry." *China Quarterly,* no. 181: 1–21.

Heilmann, Sebastian. 2018. *Red Swan: How Unorthodox Policy-Making Facilitated China's Rise.* Hong Kong: Chinese University Press.

Heilmann, Sebastian, and Elizabeth J. Perry, eds. 2011. *Mao's Invisible Hand: The Political Foundations of Adaptive Governance in China.* Cambridge, MA: Harvard University Asia Center.

Heilmann, Sebastian, and Elizabeth J. Perry. 2011. "Embracing Uncertainty: Guerrilla Policy Style and Adaptive Governance in China." Pp. 1–29 in *Mao's Invisible Hand: The Political Foundations of Adaptive Governance in China,* edited by Sebastian Heilmann and Elizabeth J. Perry. Cambridge, MA: Harvard University Asia Center.

Heurlin, Christopher. 2016. *Responsive Authoritarianism in China: Land, Protests, and Policy Making.* New York: Cambridge University Press.

Hicken, Allen. 2001. "Clientelism." *Annual Review of Political Science* 14, no. 1: 289–310.

Hill, Hal. 1996. *The Indonesian Economy since 1966: Southeast Asia's Emerging Giant.* New York: Cambridge University Press.

Hill, Hal. 1999. *The Indonesian Economy in Crisis: Causes, Consequences, and Lessons.* New York: St. Martin's Press.

Hill, Hal, and Harold Crouch, eds. 1990. *Indonesia Assessment 1990: Proceedings of Indonesia Update Conference, October 1990.* Canberra: Indonesia Project, Department of Economics and Department of Political and Social Change, Research School of Pacific Studies, Australia National University.

Hillman, Ben. 2010. "Factions and Spoils: Examining Political Behavior within the Local State in China." *China Journal*, no. 64: 1–18.

Hillman, Ben. 2021. "Law, Order and Social Control in Xi's China." *Issues and Studies* 57, no. 2: 1–21.

Hou, Yue. 2017. "Participating for Protection: Legislatures, Private Entrepreneurs, and Property Security in China." Unpublished manuscript.

Hou, Yue. 2019. "The Private Sector: Challenges and Opportunities during Xi's Second Term." *China Leadership Monitor*, no. 59 (March). https://www.prcleader.org/past-issues.

Hou, Yue. 2019. *The Private Sector in Public Office: Selective Property Rights in China*. New York: Cambridge University Press.

Hsieh, Chang-Tai, and Peter J. Klenow. 2009. "Misallocation and Manufacturing TFP in China and India." *Quarterly Journal of Economics* 124, no. 4: 1403–48. https://doi.org/10.1162/qjec.2009.124.4.1403.

Hsing, You-tien. 1998. *Making Capitalism in China: The Taiwan Connection*. New York: Oxford University Press.

Hsing, You-tien. 2010. *The Great Urban Transformation: Politics of Land and Property in China*. New York: Oxford University Press.

Huang, Robin Hui. 2018. "Online P2P Lending and Regulatory Responses in China: Opportunities and Challenge." *European Business Organization Law Review* 19, no. 1 (March): 63–92. https://doi.org/10.1007/s40804-018-0100-z.

Huang, Yasheng. 1996. *Inflation and Investment Controls in China: The Political Economy of Central-Local Relations during the Reform Era*. New York: Cambridge University Press.

Huang, Yasheng. 1999. *Why Is There So Much Demand for Foreign Equity Capital in China? An Institutional and Policy Perspective*. Cambridge, MA: Weatherhead Center for International Affairs, Harvard University.

Huang, Yasheng. 2003. *Selling China: Foreign Direct Investment during the Reform Era*. New York: Cambridge University Press.

Huang, Yasheng. 2008. *Capitalism with Chinese Characteristics: Entrepreneurship and the State*. New York: Cambridge University Press.

Hutchinson, Brian. 1997. "Rags & Riches: The Story Behind Bre-X's Spectacular Roller Coaster Ride." *The Calgary Herald*, March 29: B8.

Jain, Vishal, and Dileep M. Kumar. 2014. "Story of 'Asia's Banking Grandmaster': Tan Sri Dato' Sri Dr. Teh Hong Piow: A Case Study." *Research Journal of Social Science & Management* 3, no. 9: 72–81.

Jesudason, James V. 1989. *Ethnicity and the Economy: The State, Chinese Business, and Multinationals in Malaysia*. New York: Oxford University Press.

Jiang, Junyan, and Dali L. Yang. 2016. "Lying or Believing? Measuring Preference Falsification from a Political Purge in China." *Comparative Political Studies* 49, no. 5: 600–634.

Johnson, Chalmers A. 1962. *Peasant Nationalism and Communist Power: The Emergence of Revolutionary China*. Stanford: Stanford University Press.

Johnson, Chalmers A. 1982. *MITI and the Japanese Miracle: The Growth of Industrial Policy, 1925–1975*. Stanford: Stanford University Press.

Johnson, Simon, Rafael LaPorta, Florencio Lopez-de-Silanes, and Andrei Schleifer. 2000. "Tunnelling." *American Economic Review* 90, no. 2: 22–27.

Johnson, Simon, and Todd Mitton. 2003. "Cronyism and Capital Controls: Evidence from Malaysia." *Journal of Financial Economics* 67, no. 2: 351–82. https://doi.org/10.1016/S0304-405X(02)00255-6.

Kahin, George McTurnan. 1952. *Nationalism and Revolution in Indonesia*. Ithaca: Cornell University Press.

Kalyvas, Stathis. 2003. "The Ontology of 'Political Violence': Action and Identity in Civil Wars." *Perspectives on Politics* 1, no. 3: 475–94.

Kang, David C. 2002. *Crony Capitalism: Corruption and Development in South Korea and the Philippines*. New York: Cambridge University Press.

Kennedy, Scott. 2005. *The Business of Lobbying in China*. Cambridge, MA: Harvard University Press.

Khanna, Tarun, and Yishay Yafeh. 2007. "Business Groups in Emerging Markets: Paragons or Parasites?" *Journal of Economic Literature* 45, no. 2: 331–72. https://doi.org/10.1257/jel.45.2.331.

Khoo, Boo Teik. 2003. *Beyond Mahathir: Malaysian Politics and Its Discontents*. New York: Zed Books.

Khoo, Ying Hooi. 2016. "Malaysia's 13th General Elections and the Rise of Electoral Reform Movement." *Asian Politics & Policy* 8, no. 3: 418–35. https://doi.org/10.1111/aspp.12273.

Kim, Diana S. 2020. *Empires of Vice: The Rise of Opium Prohibition across Southeast Asia*. Princeton, NJ: Princeton University Press.

Kim, Eun-mi. 1997. *Big Business, Strong State: Collusion and Conflict in South Korean Development, 1960–1990*. Albany: State University of New York Press.

Koon, Heng Pek. 1992. "The Chinese Business Elite of Malaysia." Pp. 127–44 in *Southeast Asian Capitalists*, edited by Ruth McVey. Ithaca: Cornell University Press.

Kornai, János. 1992. *The Socialist System: The Political Economy of Communism*. Princeton, NJ: Princeton University Press.

Kostka, Genia, and Xiaofan Yu. 2015. "Career Backgrounds of Municipal Party Secretaries in China: Why Do So Few Municipal Party Secretaries Rise from the County Level?" *Modern China* 41, no. 5: 467–505.

Kroeber, Arthur R. 2013. "Xi Jinping's Ambitious Agenda for Economic Reform in China." Brookings Institution. https://www.brookings.edu/opinions/xi-jinpings-ambitious-agenda-for-economic-reform-in-china/.

Krueger, Anne O. 1974. "The Political Economy of the Rent-Seeking Society." *American Economic Review* 64, no. 3: 291–303. https://doi.org/10.2307/1808883.

Krugman, Paul. 1998. "What Happened to Asia?" http://web.mit.edu/krugman/www/DISINTER.html.

Kuhn, Philip A. 2008. *Chinese among Others: Emigration in Modern Times*. Lanham, MD: Rowman & Littlefield.

Kuntjoro-Jakti, Dorodjatun. 1981. "The Political-Economy of Development: The Case of Indonesia under the New Order Government, 1966–1978." PhD dissertation. University of California, Berkeley.

Kuo, Didi. 2018. *Clientelism, Capitalism, and Democracy: The Rise of Programmatic Politics in the United States and Britain*. New York: Cambridge University Press.

Kuran, Timur. 1995. *Private Truths, Public Lies: The Social Consequences of Preference Falsification*. Cambridge, MA: Harvard University Press.

Kydd, Andrew H. 2018. *Trust and Mistrust in International Relations*. Princeton, NJ: Princeton University Press.

Laclau, Ernesto. 1975. "The Specificity of the Political: The Poulantzas-Miliband Debate." *Economy and Society* 4, no. 1: 87–110. https://doi.org/10.1080/03085147500000002.

Lake, David A. 2009. "Open Economy Politics: A Critcial Review." *Review of International Organizations* 4, no. 3: 219–44.

Landry, Pierre F. 2008. *Decentralized Authoritarianism in China: The Communist Party's Control of Local Elites in the Post-Mao Era*. New York: Cambridge University Press.

Lardy, Nicholas R. 2019. *The State Strikes Back: The End of Economic Reform in China?* Washington, DC: Peterson Institute for International Economics.

Laurence, Henry. 2001. *Money Rules: The New Politics of Finance in Britain and Japan*. Ithaca: Cornell University Press.

Lee, Ching Kwan. 2007. *Against the Law: Labor Protests in China's Rustbelt and Sunbelt*. Berkeley: University of California Press.

Lee, Ching Kwan. 2017. *The Specter of Global China: Politics, Labor, and Foreign Investment in Africa*. Chicago: University of Chicago Press.

Lee, Doreen. 2016. *Activist Archives: Youth Culture and the Political Past in Indonesia*. Durham, NC: Duke University Press.

Lee, Kam Hing, and Poh Ping Lee. 2003. "Malaysian Chinese Business: Who Survived the Crisis?" *Kyoto Review of Southeast Asia*, no. 4. https://kyotoreview.org/issue-4/malaysian-chinese-business-who-survived-the-crisis/.

Lee, Poh Ping. 2016. "Malaysia in 2015: A Denouement of Sorts for the Prime Minister." *Asian Survey* 56, no. 1: 101–7.

Leff, Nathaniel H. 1978. "Industrial Organization and Entrepreneurship in the Developing Countries: The Economic Groups." *Economic Development and Cultural Change* 26, no. 4: 651–75. https://doi.org/10.1086/451052.

Legarda, Helena. 2021. "China's New International Paradigm: Security First." *Merics*, June 15, 2021. https://merics.org/en/chinas-new-international-paradigm-security-first.

Leighton, Christopher. n.d. "Revolutionary Rich: Red Capitalists under Mao." Manuscript.

Leutert, Wendy. 2016. "State-Owned Enterprise Mergers: Will Less Be More?" *China Analysis* (European Council on Foreign Relations), no. 197. https://ecfr.eu/wp-content/uploads/China_Analysis_%E2%80%93_Big_is_Beautiful.pdf.

Levitsky, Steven, and Lucan Way. 2010. *Competitive Authoritarianism: Hybrid Regimes after the Cold War*. New York: Cambridge University Press.

Levitt, Barbara, and James G. March. 1988. "Organizational Learning." *Annual Review of Sociology* 14, no. 1: 319–40. https://doi.org/10.1146/annurev.so.14.080188.001535.

Lewis, Christine. 2019. "Raising More Public Revenue in Indonesia in a Growth and Equity-Friendly Way." OECD Working Paper no. 1534 (February). https://doi.org/10.1787/a487771f-en.

Li, Chen. 2016. "Holding 'China Inc.' Together: The CCP and the Rise of China's Yangqi." *China Quarterly*, no. 228: 927–49. https://doi.org/10.1017/S0305741016001466.

Li, Chen, Huanhuan Zheng, and Yunbo Liu. 2022. "The Hybrid Regulatory Regime in Turbulent Times: The Role of the State in China's Stock Market Crisis in 2015–2016." *Regulation & Governance* 16, no. 2: 392–408. https://doi.org/10.1111/rego.12340.

Li, Tania Murray. 2018. "After the Land Grab: Infrastructural Violence and the 'Mafia System' in Indonesia's Oil Palm Plantation Zones." *Geoforum* 96: 328–37. https://doi.org/1016/j.geoforum.2017.10.012.

Liddle, R. William. 1996. "Indonesia: Suharto's Tightening Grip." *Journal of Democracy* 7, no 4: 58–72.

Lieberthal, Kenneth. 1980. *Revolution and Tradition in Tientsin, 1949–1952*. Stanford: Stanford University Press.

Lim, Guanie, Chen Li, and Emirza Adi Syailendra. 2021. "Why Is It So Hard to Push Chinese Railway Projects in Southeast Asia? The Role of Domestic Politics in Malaysia and Indonesia." *World Development*, vol. 138. https://doi.org/10.1016/j.worlddev.2020.105272.

Lim, Mah Hui. 1981. *Ownership and Control of the One Hundred Largest Corporations in Malaysia*. Kuala Lumpur: Oxford University Press.

Lin, Justin Yifu. 1992. "Rural Reforms and Agricultural Growth in China." *American Economic Review* 82, no. 1: 34–51.

Lin, Yi-min. 2017. *Dancing with the Devil: The Political Economy of Privatization in China*. New York: Oxford University Press.

Lindblom, Charles Edward. 1977. *Politics and Markets: The World's Political Economic Systems*. New York: Basic Books.

Ling, Sieh Lee Mei. 2018. "The Transformation of Malaysian Business Groups." Pp. 103–26 in *Southeast Asian Capitalists*, edited by Ruth McVey. Ithaca: Cornell University Press.

Liu, Adam Yao. 2018. "Building Markets within Authoritarian Institutions: The Political Economy of Banking Development in China." PhD dissertation. Stanford University.

Liu, Adam Yao, Jean C. Oi, and Yi Zhang. 2022. "China's Local Government Debt: The Grand Bargain." *China Journal*, no. 87: 40–71.

Liu, Hong, and Guanie Lim. 2019. "The Political Economy of a Rising China in Southeast Asia: Malaysia's Response to the Belt and Road Initiative." *Journal of Contemporary China* 28, no. 116: 215–31.

Looney, Kristen E. 2015. "China's Campaign to Build a New Socialist Countryside: Village Modernization, Peasant Councils, and the Ganzhou Model of Rural Development." *China Quarterly*, no. 224: 909–32. https://doi.org/10.1017/S0305741015001204.

Looney, Kristen E. 2020. *Mobilizing for Development: The Modernization of Rural East Asia*. Ithaca: Cornell University Press.

Looney, Kristen E., and Meg Rithmire. 2017. "China Gambles on Modernizing through Urbanization." *Current History* 116, no. 791: 203–9. https://doi.org/10.1525/curh.2017.116.791.203.

Low, Alex. 1997. "Indonesian Banking: An Exercise in Reregulation of Deregulation." *James Cook University Law Review* 4: 39–67.

Lowi, Theodore J. 1979. *The End of Liberalism: The Second Republic of the United States*. 2nd ed. New York: Norton.

Lu, Xi, and Peter Lorentzen. 2016. "Rescuing Autocracy from Itself: China's Anti-corruption Campaign." Working paper. University of San Francisco.

Lü Xiaobo, and Pierre F. Landry. 2014. "Show Me the Money: Interjurisdiction Political Competition and Fiscal Extraction in China." *American Political Science Review* 108, no. 3: 706–22.

Luhmann, Niklas. 2017. *Trust and Power*. Translated by Christian Morgner and Michael King. Malden, MA: Polity Press.

Lust-Okar, Ellen. 2009. "Competitive Clientelism in the Middle East." *Journal of Democracy* 20, no. 3: 122–35. https://doi.org/10.1353/jod.0.0099.

MacFarquhar, Roderick. 1974. *The Origins of the Cultural Revolution: Contradictions among the People, 1956–1957*. New York: Columbia University Press.

MacFarquhar, Roderick, and Michael Schoenhals. 2006. *Mao's Last Revolution*. Cambridge, MA: Belknap Press of Harvard University Press.

MacIntyre, Andrew J. 1993. "The Politics of Finance in Indonesia: Command, Confusion, and Competition." Pp. 123–64 in *The Politics of Finance in Developing Countries*, edited by Stephan Haggard, Chung H. Lee, and Sylvia Maxfield. Ithaca: Cornell University Press.

MacIntyre, Andrew J. 2003. *The Power of Institutions: Political Architecture and Governance*. Ithaca: Cornell University Press.

MacIntyre, Andrew J., T. J. Pempel, and John Ravenhill, eds. 2008. *Crisis as Catalyst: Asia's Dynamic Political Economy*. Ithaca: Cornell University Press.

Mackay, Donald. 1997. *The Malayan Emergency, 1948–60: The Domino That Stood*. Washington DC: Brassey's.

Mackie, J. A. C., ed. 1976. *The Chinese in Indonesia: Five Essays*. Honolulu: University Press of Hawai'i.

Mahathir, Mohamad bin. 1970. "The Malay Economic Dilemma." Pp. 32–61 in Mohamad bin Mahathir, *The Malay Dilemma*. Singapore: Asia Pacific Press.

Mahathir, Mohamad bin. 1970. "What Went Wrong?" Pp. 4–15 in Mohamad bin Mahathir, *The Malay Dilemma*. Singapore: Asia Pacific Press.

Mahathir, Mohamad bin. 1998. *The Way Forward*. London: Weidenfeld & Nicholson.

Mahoney, James, and Dietrich Rueschemeyer, eds. 2003. *Comparative Historical Analysis in the Social Sciences*. New York: Columbia University Press.

Malhi, Amrita. 2018. "Race, Debt, and Sovereignty: The 'China Factor' in Malaysia's GE14." *Round Table* 107, no. 6 : 717–28.

March, James G. 1962. "The Business Firm as a Political Coalition." *Journal of Politics* 24, no. 4: 662–78. https://doi.org/10.2307/2128040.

Markus, Stanislav. 2015. *Property, Predation, and Protection: Piranha Capitalism in Russia and Ukraine*. New York: Cambridge University Press.

Mattingly, Daniel C. 2020. *The Art of Political Control in China*. New York: Cambridge University Press.

Mauzy, Diane K. 1993. "Malaysia: Malay Political Hegemony and 'Coercive Consociationalism.'" Pp. 106–27 in *The Politics of Ethnic Conflict Regulation*, edited by John McGarry and Brendan O'Leary. London: Routlegde.

Maxfield, Sylvia. 1990. *Governing Capital: International Finance and Mexican Politics*. Ithaca: Cornell University Press.

Maxfield, Sylvia, and Ben Ross-Schneider, eds. 1997. *Business and the State in Developing Countries*. Ithaca: Cornell University Press.

McLeod, Ross H. 1992. "Indonesia's New Banking Law." *Bulletin of Indonesian Economic Studies* 28, no. 3: 107–22.

McLeod, Ross H. 1996. "Indonesia's Economic Performance: An Assessment." *Journal of Asian Business* 12, no. 4: 71–83.

McLeod, Ross H. 2000. "Soeharto's Indonesia: A Better Class of Corruption." *Agenda* 7, no. 2: 99–112.

Mehmet, Ozay. 1986. *Development in Malaysia: Poverty, Wealth, and Trusteeship*. London: Croom Helm.

Melvin, Jess. 2018. *The Army and the Indonesian Genocide: Mechanics of Mass Murder*. New York: Routledge.

Mertha, Andrew C. 2005. "China's 'Soft' Centralization: Shifting *Tiao/Kuai* Authority Relations." *China Quarterly*, no. 184: 791–810.

Mertha, Andrew C. 2017. "'Stressing Out': Cadre Calibration and Affective Proximity to the CCP in Reform-Era China." *China Quarterly*, no. 229: 64–85.

Miliband, Ralph. 1969. *The State in Capitalist Society*. New York: Basic Books.

Minzner, Carl. 2018. *End of an Era: How China's Authoritarian Revival Is Undermining Its Rise*. New York: Oxford University Press.

Moore, Barrington. 1966. *Social Origins of Dictatorship and Democracy: Lord and Peasant in the Making of the Modern World*. Boston: Beacon Press.

Morck, Randall, Daniel Wolfenzon, and Bernard Yeung. 2005. "Corporate Governance, Economic Entrenchment, and Growth." *Journal of Economic Literature* 43 (3): 655–720. https://doi.org/10.1257/002205105774431252.

Moss, David A. 2002. *When All Else Fails: Government as the Ultimate Risk Manager.* Cambridge, MA: Harvard University Press.

Nahm, Jonas. 2021. *Collaborative Advantage: Forging Green Industries in the New Global Economy.* New York: Oxford University Press.

Naughton, Barry M. 1994. "Chinese Institutional Innovation and Privatization from Below." *American Economic Review* 84, no. 2: 266–70.

Naughton, Barry M. 2009. "Understanding the Chinese Stimulus Package." *China Leadership Monitor,* no. 28.

Naughton, Barry M., and Kellee S. Tsai, eds. 2015. *State Capitalism, Institutional Adaptation, and the Chinese Miracle.* New York: Cambridge University Press.

Nolan, Peter. 2012. *Is China Buying the World?* Cambridge: Polity.

Nonini, Donald. 2015. *Getting By: Class and State Formation among Chinese in Malaysia.* Ithaca: Cornell University Press.

North, Douglass C. 1994. "Economic Performance through Time." *American Economic Review* 84, no. 3: 359–68.

O'Brien, Kevin J., and Lianjiang Li. 1999. "Selective Policy Implementation in Rural China." *Comparative Politics* 31, no. 2: 167–86.

Oi, Jean Chun. 1999. *Rural China Takes Off: Institutional Foundations of Economic Reform.* Berkeley: University of California Press.

Oksenberg, Michel. 1970. "Getting Ahead and Along in Communist China: The Ladder of Success on the Eve of the Cultural Revolution." Pp. 304–47 in *Party Leadership and Revolutionary Power in China,* edited by John Wilson Lewis. New York: Cambridge University Press.

Olson, Mancur. 1982. *The Rise and Decline of Nations: Economic Growth, Stagflation, and Social Rigidities.* New Haven: Yale University Press.

Ong, Lynette H. 2012. *Prosper or Perish: Credit and Fiscal Systems in China.* Ithaca: Cornell University Press.

Ong, Lynette H. 2014. "State-Led Urbanization in China: Skyscrapers, Land Revenue and 'Concentrated Villages.'" *China Quarterly,* no. 217: 162–79.

Ong, Lynette H. 2022. *Outsourcing Repression: Everyday State Power in Contemporary China.* New York: Oxford University Press.

Ong, Lynette H. 2022. *The Street and the Ballot Box: Interactions between Social Movements and Electoral Politics in Authoritarian Contexts.* New York: Cambridge University Press.

Ongkili, James P. 1985. *Nation-Building in Malaysia, 1946–1974.* New York: Oxford University Press.

Osburg, John. 2013. *Anxious Wealth: Money and Morality among China's New Rich.* Stanford: Stanford University Press.

Osburg, John. 2018. "Making Business Personal: Corruption, Anti-corruption, and Elite Networks in Post-Mao China." *Current Anthropology* 59, no. S18: S149–S159.

Parris, Kristin. 1993. "Local Initiative and National Reform: The Wenzhou Model of Development." *China Quarterly,* no. 134: 242–63.

Pearson, Margaret M. 1991. *Joint Ventures in the People's Republic of China: The Control of Foreign Direct Investment under Socialism.* Princeton, NJ: Princeton University Press.

Pearson, Margaret M. 1997. *China's New Business Elite: The Political Consequences of Economic Reform*. Berkeley: University of California Press.

Pearson, Margaret M. 2005. "The Business of Governing Business in China: Institutions and Norms of the Emerging Regulatory State." *World Politics* 57, no. 2: 296–322.

Pearson, Margaret M., Meg Rithmire, and Kellee Tsai. 2021. "Party-State Capitalism in China." *Current History* 120, no. 827: 207–13. https://doi.org/10.1525/curh.2021.120.827.207.

Pearson, Margaret M., Meg Rithmire, and Kellee Tsai. 2022. "China's Political Economy and International Backlash: From Interdependence to Security Dilemma Dynamics." *International Security* 47, no. 2: 135–76.

Pei, Minxin. 2006. *China's Trapped Transition: The Limits of Developmental Autocracy*. Cambridge, MA: Harvard University Press.

Pei, Minxin. 2016. *China's Crony Capitalism: The Dynamics of Regime Decay*. Cambridge, MA: Harvard University Press.

Pempel, T. J., ed. 1999. *The Politics of the Asian Financial Crisis*. Ithaca: Cornell University Press.

Pempel, T. J. 2021. *A Region of Regimes: Prosperity and Plunder in the Asia-Pacific*. Ithaca: Cornell University Press.

Peng, Winnie Qian, K. C. John Wei, and Zhishu Yang. 2011. "Tunneling or Propping: Evidence from Connected Transactions in China." *Journal of Corporate Finance* 17, no. 2: 306–25.

Pepinsky, Thomas B. 2008. "Capital Mobility and Coalitional Politics: Authoritarian Regimes and Economic Adjustment in Southeast Asia." *World Politics* 60, no. 3: 438–74.

Pepinsky, Thomas B. 2009. *Economic Crises and the Breakdown of Authoritarian Regimes: Indonesia and Malaysia in Comparative Perspective*. New York: Cambridge University Press.

Pepinsky, Thomas B. 2015. "Interpreting Ethnicity and Urbanization in Malaysia's 2013 General Election." *Journal of East Asian Studies* 15, no. 2: 199–226.

Pepper, Suzanne. 1999. *Civil War in China: The Political Struggle, 1945–1949*. 2nd ed. Lanham, MD: Rowman & Littlefield.

Perry, Elizabeth J. 2007. "Studying Chinese Politics: Farewell to Revolution?" *China Journal*, no. 57: 1–22.

Perry, Elizabeth J. 2008. "Chinese Conceptions of 'Rights': From Mencius to Mao—and Now." *Perspectives on Politics* 6, no. 1: 37–50.

Perry, Elizabeth J. 2011. "From Mass Campaigns to Managed Campaigns: 'Constructing a New Socialist Countryside.'" Pp. 30–61 in *Mao's Invisible Hand: The Political Foundations of Adaptive Governance in China*, edited by Sebastian Heilmann and Elizabeth J. Perry. Cambridge, MA: Harvard University Asia Center.

Perry, Elizabeth J. 2018. "Is the Chinese Communist Regime Legitimate?" Pp. 11–17 in *The China Questions: Critical Insights into a Rising Power*, edited by Jennifer Rudolph, Michael Szonyi, and Fairbank Center for Chinese Studies. Cambridge, MA: Harvard University Press.

Perry, Elizabeth J. 2021. "Missionaries of the Party: Work-Team Participation and Intellectual Incorporation." *China Quarterly*, no. 248 (S1): 73–94.

Perry, Elizabeth J., and Xun Li. 1997. *Proletarian Power: Shanghai in the Cultural Revolution*. Boulder, CO: Westview Press.

Peterson, Glen. 2012. *Overseas Chinese in the People's Republic of China*. London: Routledge.

Pierson, Paul. 2000. "Increasing Returns, Path Dependence, and the Study of Politics." *American Political Science Review* 94, no. 2: 251–67.

Pincus, Jonathan, and Rizal Ramli. 1998. "Indonesia: From Showcase to Basket Case." *Cambridge Journal of Economics* 22, no. 6: 723–34. https://doi.org/10.1093/cje/22.6.723.

Posner, Elliot. 2005. "Sources of Institutional Change: The Supranational Origins of Europe's New Stock Markets." *World Politics* 58, no. 1: 1–40. http://dx.doi.org/10.1353/wp.2006.0021.

Poulantzas, Nicos. 1969. "The Specificity of the Political." *New Left Review*, no. 1/58: 67–78.

Prawiro, Radius. 1998. *Indonesia's Struggle for Economic Development: Pragmatism in Action.* New York: Oxford University Press.

Przeworski, Adam, and Michael Wallerstein. 1988. "Structural Dependence of the State on Capital." *American Political Science Review* 82, no. 1: 11–29. https://doi.org/10.2307/1958056.

Purcell, Victor. 1948. *The Chinese in Malaya.* New York: Oxford University Press.

Purcell, Victor. 1965. *South and East Asia since 1800.* Cambridge: University Press.

Purdey, Jemma. 2006. *Anti-Chinese Violence in Indonesia, 1996–1999.* Honolulu: University of Hawai'i Press.

Puthucheary, James. 1960. *Ownership and Control in the Malayan Economy: A Study of the Structure of Ownership and Control and Its Effects on the Development of Secondary Industries and Economic Growth in Malaya and Singapore.* Singapore: Eastern Universities Press.

Rahman, Tunku Abdul. 1969. *May 13: Before and After.* Kuala Lumpur: Utusan Melayu Press.

Rajan, Raghuram, and Luigi Zingales. 2003. *Saving Capitalism from the Capitalists: Unleashing the Power of Financial Markets to Create Wealth and Spread Opportunity.* New York: Crown Business.

Ratigan, Kerry. 2021. "Are Peruvians Enticed by the 'China Model'? Chinese Investment and Public Opinion in Peru." *Studies in Comparative International Development* 56, no. 1: 87–111. https://doi.org/10.1007/s12116-021-09321-0.

Ratigan, Kerry, and Leah Rabin. 2020. "Re-evaluating Political Trust: The Impact of Survey Nonresponse in Rural China." *China Quarterly*, no. 243: 823–38.

Razak, Abdul. 1972. "Foreword." Pp. in 1–15 in *The Second Malaysia Plan, 1971–1975*, edited by Hussein Syed Alatas. Singapore: Occasional Paper no. 15, Institute of Southeast Asian Studies.

Reid, Anthony. 1997. "Entrepreneurial Minorities, Nationalism, and the State." Pp. 33–71 in *Essential Outsiders: Chinese and Jews in the Modern Transformation of Southeast Asia and Central Europe*, edited by Daniel Chirot and Anthony Reid. Seattle: University of Washington Press.

Repnikova, Maria. 2022. *Chinese Soft Power.* New York: Cambridge University Press.

Reuter, Ora John, and Jennifer Gandhi. 2011. "Economic Performance and Elite Defection from Hegemonic Parties." *British Journal of Political Science* 41, no. 1: 83–110. https://doi.org/10.1017/S0007123410000293.

Riady, Mochtar. 2017. *My Life Story.* Singapore: Wiley.

Rithmire, Meg. 2014. "China's 'New Regionalism': Subnational Analysis in Chinese Political Economy." *World Politics* 66, no. 1: 165–94.

Rithmire, Meg. 2015. *Land Bargains and Chinese Capitalism: The Politics of Property Rights under Reform.* New York: Cambridge University Press.

Rithmire, Meg. 2017. "Land Institutions and Chinese Political Economy: Institutional Complementarities and Macroeconomic Management." *Politics & Society* 45, no. 1: 123–53.

Rithmire, Meg. 2022. "Going Out or Opting Out? Capital, Political Vulnerability, and the State in China's Outward Investment." *Comparative Politics* 54, no. 3: 477–99. https://doi.org/10.5129/001041522X16244682037327.

Rithmire, Meg, and Hao Chen. 2021. "The Emergence of Mafia-Like Business Systems in China." *China Quarterly*, no. 248: 1037–58. https://doi.org/10.1017/S0305741021000576.

Robison, Richard. 1986. *Indonesia: The Rise of Capital*. Sydney: Allen & Unwin.

Robison, Richard, and Vedi R. Hadiz. 2004. *Reorganising Power in Indonesia: The Politics of Oligarchy in an Age of Markets*. London: RoutledgeCurzon.

Roosa, John. 2006. *Pretext for Mass Murder: The September 30th Movement and Suharto's Coup d'État in Indonesia*. Madison: University of Wisconsin Press.

Rosen, Daniel H. 2021. "China's Economic Reckoning: The Price of Failed Reforms." *Foreign Affairs* 100, no. 4: 20–29.

Ross-Schneider, Ben, and Sylvia Maxfield. 1997. "Business, the State, and Economic Performance in Developing Countries." Pp. 3–35 in *Business and the State in Developing Countries*, edited by Sylvia Maxfield and Ben Ross-Schneider. Ithaca: Cornell University Press.

Rosser, Andrew. 2002. *The Politics of Economic Liberalisation in Indonesia: State, Market and Power*. Richmond, Surrey, UK: Curzon.

Sabel, Charles F. 1993. "Studied Trust: Building New Forms of Cooperation in a Volatile Economy." *Human Relations* 46, no. 9: 1133–70. https://doi.org/10.1177/001872679304600907.

Saravanamuttu, Johan. 2003. "The Eve of the 1999 General Elections: From the NEP to *Reformasi*." Pp. 1–24 in *New Politics in Malaysia*, edited by Francis Loh Kok Wah and Johan Saravanamuttu. Singapore: Institute of Southeast Asian Studies.

Sargeson, Sally. 2011. "The Politics of Land Development in Urbanizing China." *China Journal*, no. 66: 145–52.

Sato, Yuri. 1994. "The Development of Business Groups in Indonesia: 1967–1989." Pp. 101–53 in *Approaching Suharto's Indonesia from the Margins*, edited by Takashi Shiraishi. Ithaca: Cornell University Press.

Schelling, Thomas C. 1984. *Choice and Consequence*. Cambridge, MA: Harvard University Press.

Schleifer, Andrei, and Robert W. Vishny. 1993. "Corruption." *Quarterly Journal of Economics* 108, no. 3: 599–617.

Schwarz, Adam. 1990. "Caveat Rupiah: Indonesian System's Weaknesses Revealed by Forex Loss." *Far Eastern Economic Review* 149, no. 38: 105–6.

Scott, James C. 1972. "Patron-Client Politics and Political Change in Southeast Asia." *American Political Science Review* 66, no. 1: 91–113. https://doi.org/10.2307/1959280.

Scott, James C. 1976. *The Moral Economy of the Peasant: Rebellion and Subsistence in Southeast Asia*. New Haven: Yale University Press.

Seabrooke, Leonard. 2006. *The Social Sources of Financial Power: Domestic Legitimacy and International Financial Orders*. Ithaca: Cornell University Press.

Segal, Adam. 2003. *Digital Dragon: High-Technology Enterprises in China*. Ithaca: Cornell University Press.

Sheng, Andrew. 1992. "Bank Restructuring in Malaysia, 1985–88." Pp. 124–48 in *Financial Regulation: Changing the Rules of the Game*, edited by Dimitri Vittas. Washington, DC: The World Bank, EDI Development Studies.

Shih, Victor C. 2008. *Factions and Finance in China: Elite Conflict and Inflation*. New York: Cambridge University Press.

Shih, Victor C. 2010. "Local Government Debt: Big Rock-Candy Mountain." *China Economic Quarterly* 14, no. 2: 26–32.

Shih, Victor C., Christopher Adolph, and Mingxing Liu. 2012. "Getting Ahead in the Communist Party: Explaining the Advancement of Central Committee Members in China." *American Political Science Review* 106, no. 1: 166–87.

Shin, Yoon Hwan. 1989. "Demystifying the Capitalist State: Political Patronage, Bureaucratic Interests, and Capitalists-in-Formation in Soeharto's Indonesia." PhD dissertation, Yale University.

Shum, Desmond. 2021. *Red Roulette: An Insider's Story of Wealth, Power, Corruption and Vengeance in Today's China*. New York: Scribner.

Sicular, Terry. 1998. "Capital Flight and Foreign Investment: Two Tales from China and Russia." *World Economy* 21, no. 5: 589–602.

Siddiquee, Noree Alam, and Habib Zafarullah. 2022. "Absolute Power, Absolute Venality: The Politics of Corruption and Anti-corruption in Malaysia." *Public Integrity* 24, no. 1: 1–17.

Sidel, John Thayer. 2021. *Republicanism, Communism, Islam: Cosmopolitan Origins of Revolution in Southeast Asia*. Ithaca: Cornell University Press.

Simpson, Bradley R. 2008. *Economists with Guns: Authoritarian Development and U.S. - Indonesian Relations, 1960–1968*. Stanford: Stanford University Press.

Skinner, G. William, and Edwin A. Winckler. 1969. "Compliance Succession in Rural Communist China: A Cyclical Theory." Pp. 410–38 in *A Sociological Reader on Complex Organizations*, compiled by Amitai Etzioni. 2nd ed. New York: Holt Rinehart and Winston.

Slater, Dan. 2003. "Iron Cage in an Iron Fist: Authoritarian Institutions and the Personalization of Power in Malaysia." *Comparative Politics* 36, no. 1: 81–101.

Slater, Dan. 2010. *Ordering Power: Contentious Politics and Authoritarian Leviathans in Southeast Asia*. New York: Cambridge University Press.

Slater, Dan, and Erica Simmons. 2010. "Informative Regress: Critical Antecedents in Comparative Politics." *Comparative Political Studies* 43, no. 7: 886–917.

Slater, Dan, and Joseph Wong. 2022. *From Development to Democracy: The Transformations of Modern Asia*. Princeton, NJ: Princeton University Press.

Smith, Graeme. 2015. "Getting Ahead in Rural China: The Elite-Cadre Divide and Its Implications for Rural Governance." *Journal of Contemporary China* 24, no. 94: 594–612.

So, Wai-yip Bennis. 2002. "The Policy-Making and Political Economy of the Abolition of Private Ownership in the Early 1950s: Findings from New Material." *China Quarterly*, no. 171: 682–703.

Soesastro, M. Hadi. 1989. "The Political Economy of Deregulation in Indonesia." *Asian Survey* 29, no. 9 (1989): 853–69.

Solinger, Dorothy J. 1993. *China's Transition from Socialism: Statist Legacies and Market Reforms, 1980–1990*. Armonk, NY: M.E. Sharpe.

Solnick, Steven Lee. 1998. *Stealing the State: Control and Collapse in Soviet Institutions*. Cambridge, MA: Harvard University Press.

Soltes, Eugene. 2019. "The Frequency of Corporate Misconduct: Public Enforcement versus Private Reality." *Journal of Financial Crime* 26, no. 4: 923–37. https://doi.org/10.1108/JFC-10-2018-0107.

Somers Heidhues, Mary F. 1964. *Peranakan Chinese Politics in Indonesia*. Ithaca: Southeast Asia Program, Cornell University.

Sorace, Christian, and William Hurst. 2016. "China's Phantom Urbanisation and the Pathology of Ghost Cities." *Journal of Contemporary Asia* 46, no. 2: 304–22.

Spiller, Pablo T. 1990. "Politicians, Interest Groups, and Regulators: A Multiple-Principals Agency Theory of Regulation, or 'Let Them Be Bribed.'" *Journal of Law and Economics* 33, no. 1: 65–101.

Steinfeld, Edward S. 1998. *Forging Reform in China: The Fate of State-Owned Industry*. New York: Cambridge University Press.

Stern, Rachel E., and Kevin J. O'Brien. 2012. "Politics at the Boundary: Mixed Signals and the Chinese State." *Modern China* 38, no. 2: 174–98.

Stoler, Ann Laura. 1995. *Capitalism and Confrontation in Sumatra's Plantation Belt, 1870–1979*. 2nd ed. Ann Arbor: University of Michigan Press.

Sun, Guofeng. 2019. "China's Shadow Banking: Bank's Shadow and Traditional Shadow Banking." BIS Working Paper no. 822. https://www.bis.org/publ/work822.pdf.

Sun, Guofeng. 2020. "Banking Institutions and Banking Regulations." Pp. 9–37 in *The Handbook of China's Financial System*, edited by Marlene Amstad, Guofeng Sun, and Wei Xiong. Princeton, NJ: Princeton University Press.

Tagliacozzo, Eric. 2005. *Secret Trades, Porous Borders: Smuggling and States along a Southeast Asian Frontier, 1865–1915*. New Haven: Yale University Press.

Tai, Yuen. 2000. *Labour Unrest in Malaya, 1934–1941: The Rise of the Workers' Movement*. Kuala Lumpur: Institute of Postgraduate Studies and Research, University of Malaya.

Tajima, Yuhki. 2014. *The Institutional Origins of Communal Violence: Indonesia's Transition from Authoritarian Rule*. New York: Cambridge University Press.

Tan, Yeling, and James Conran. 2022. "China's Growth Models in Comparative and International Perspective." Pp. 143–66 in *Diminishing Returns: The New Politics of Growth and Stagnation*, edited by Lucio Baccaro, Mark Blyth, and Jonas Pontusson. New York: Oxford University Press.

Taylor, Jeremy E. 2019. "'Not a Particularly Happy Expression': 'Malayanization' and the China Threat in Britain's Late-Colonial Southeast Asian Territories." *Journal of Asian Studies* 78, no. 4: 789–808.

Thompson, E. P. 1972. *The Making of the English Working Class*. Harmondsworth: Penguin.

Tilly, Charles. 1990. *Coercion, Capital, and European States, AD 990–1990*. Cambridge, MA: Basil Blackwell.

Tong, James W. 2009. *Revenge of the Forbidden City: The Suppression of the Falungong in China, 1999–2005*. New York: Oxford: Oxford University Press.

Truex, Rory. 2014. "The Returns to Office in a 'Rubber Stamp' Parliament." *American Political Science Review* 108, no. 2: 235–51.

Truex, Rory, and Daniel L. Tavana. 2019. "Implicit Attitudes toward an Authoritarian Regime." *Journal of Politics* 81, no. 3: 1014–27.

Tsai, Kellee S. 2002. *Back-Alley Banking: Private Entrepreneurs in China*. Ithaca: Cornell University Press.

Tsai, Kellee S. 2005. "Capitalists without a Class: Political Diversity among Private Entrepreneurs in China." *Comparative Political Studies* 38, no. 9: 1130–58.

Tsai, Kellee S. 2006. "Adaptive Informal Institutions and Endogenous Institutional Change in China." *World Politics* 59, no. 1: 116–41.

Tsai, Kellee S. 2007. *Capitalism without Democracy: The Private Sector in Contemporary China.* Ithaca: Cornell University Press.

Tsai, Lily L. 2007. *Accountability without Democracy: Solidary Groups and Public Goods Provision in Rural China.* New York: Cambridge University Press.

Twang, Peck Yany. 1998. *The Chinese Business Elite in Indonesia and the Transition to Independence, 1940–1950.* New York: Oxford University Press.

van der Kamp, Denise S. 2021. "Blunt Force Regulation and Bureaucratic Control: Understanding China's War on Pollution." *Governance* 34, no. 1: 181–209.

van der Kamp, Denise S., Peter Lorentzen, and Daniel Mattingly. 2017. "Racing to the Bottom or to the Top? Decentralization, Revenue Pressures, and Governance Reform in China." *World Development* 95 (July): 164–76.

Varshney, Ashutosh. 2008. "Analyzing Collective Violence in Indonesia: An Overview." *Journal of East Asian Studies* 8, no. 3: 341–59.

Vickers, Adrian. 2005. *A History of Modern Indonesia.* New York: Cambridge University Press.

Vogel, David. 1987. "Political Science and the Study of Corporate Power: A Dissent from the New Conventional Wisdom." *British Journal of Political Science* 17, no. 4: 385–408.

Vogel, Steven Kent. 2018. *Marketcraft: How Governments Make Markets Work.* New York: Oxford University Press.

Volkov, Vadim. 2002. *Violent Entrepreneurs: The Use of Force in the Making of Russian Capitalism.* Ithaca: Cornell University Press.

Walder, Andrew G. 1986. *Communist Neo-traditionalism: Work and Authority in Chinese Industry.* Berkeley: University of California Press.

Walder, Andrew G. 2009. *Fractured Rebellion: The Beijing Red Guard Movement.* Cambridge, MA: Harvard University Press.

Wallace, Jeremy L. 2014. *Cities and Stability: Urbanization, Redistribution, & Regime Survival in China.* New York: Oxford University Press.

Wallace, Jeremy L. 2016. "Juking the Stats? Authoritarian Information Problems in China." *British Journal of Political Science* 46, no. 1: 11–29.

Wallace, Jeremy L. 2020. "The New Normal: A Neopolitical Turn in China's Reform Era." Pp. 31–58 in *Citizens & the State in Authoritarian Regimes: Comparing China and Russia,* edited by Karrie J. Koesel, Valerie J. Bunce, and Jessica Chen Weiss. New York: Oxford University Press.

Wallace, Jeremy L. 2023. *Seeking Truth and Hiding Facts: Information, Ideology, and Authoritarianism in China.* New York: Oxford University Press.

Walter, Carl E. 2020. "Convergence and Reversion: China's Banking System at 70." *Journal of Applied Corporate Finance* 32, no. 4: 34–43.

Walter, Carl E., and Fraser J. T. Howie. 2011. *Red Capitalism: The Fragile Financial Foundation of China's Extraordinary Rise.* Hoboken, NJ: Wiley.

Wang, Gungwu. 1959. *A Short History of the Nanyang Chinese.* Singapore: Eastern Universities Press.

Wang, Gungwu. 1970. "Chinese Politics in Malaya." *China Quarterly,* no. 43: 1–30.

Wang, Gungwu. 2001. *Don't Leave Home: Migration and the Chinese.* Singapore: Times Academic.

Wang, Gungwu, and Jennifer Wayne Cushman. 1988. *Changing Identities of the Southeast Asian Chinese since World War II.* Hong Kong: Hong Kong University Press.

Wang, Shaoguang, and Angang Hu. 1999. *The Political Economy of Uneven Development: The Case of China*. Armonk, NY: M. E. Sharpe.

Wang, Yingyao. 2015. "The Rise of the 'Shareholding State': Financialization of Economic Management in China." *Socio-economic Review* 13, no. 3: 603–25. https://doi.org/10.1093/ser/mwv016.

Wang, Yuhua. 2017. "Betting on a Princeling." *Studies in Comparative and International Development* 52, no. 4: 395–415.

Wang, Yuhua, and Bruce J. Dickson. 2022. "How Corruption Investigations Undermine Regime Support: Evidence from China." *Political Science Research and Methods* 10, no. 1: 33–48.

Wank, David L. 1996. "The Institutional Process of Market Clientelism: *Guanxi* and Private Business in a South China City." *China Quarterly*, no. 147: 820–38.

Wank, David L. 1999. *Commodifying Communism: Business, Trust, and Politics in a Chinese City*. New York: Cambridge University Press.

Wedeman, Andrew Hall. 2003. *From Mao to Market: Rent Seeking, Local Protectionism, and Marketization in China*. New York: Cambridge University Press.

Wedeman, Andrew Hall. 2012. *Double Paradox: Rapid Growth and Rising Corruption in China*. Ithaca: Cornell University Press.

Weiss, Meredith L. 2006. *Protest and Possibilities: Civil Society and Coalitions for Political Change in Malaysia*. Stanford: Stanford University Press.

Weiss, Meredith L. 2013. "Malaysia's 13th General Elections: Same Result, Different Outcome." *Asian Survey* 53, no. 6: 1135–58.

Weiss, Meredith L. 2020. "Legacies of the Cold War in Malaysia: Anything but Communism." *Journal of Contemporary Asia* 50, no. 4: 511–29. https://doi.org/10.1080/00472336.2019.1709128.

Wells, Jennifer. 1997. "Greed, Graft, and Gold." *Mclean's* 110, no. 9: 38–45.

Westad, Odd Arne. 2003. *Decisive Encounters: The Chinese Civil War, 1946–1950*. Stanford: Stanford University Press.

White, Tyrene. 2006. *China's Longest Campaign: Birth Planning in the People's Republic, 1949–2005*. Ithaca: Cornell University Press.

Whitfield, Lindsay. 2018. *Economies after Colonialism: Ghana and the Struggle for Power*. New York: Cambridge University Press.

Whiting, Susan H. 2001. *Power and Wealth in Rural China: The Political Economy of Institutional Change*. New York: Cambridge University Press.

Whiting, Susan H. 2011. "Values in Land: Fiscal Pressures, Land Disputes and Justice Claims in Rural and Peri-urban China." *Urban Studies* 48, no. 3: 569–87.

Winters, Jeffrey A. 1994. "Power and the Control of Capital." *World Politics* 46, no. 3: 419–52. https://doi.org/10.2307/2950688.

Winters, Jeffrey A. 1996. *Power in Motion: Capital Mobility and the Indonesian State*. Ithaca: Cornell University Press.

Winters, Jeffrey A. 2011. *Oligarchy*. New York: Cambridge University Press.

Winters, Jeffrey A. 2013. "Oligarchy and Democracy in Indonesia." *Indonesia*, no. 96: 11–33.

Wong, Christine P. W. 2011. "The Fiscal Stimulus Programme and Public Governance Issues in China." *OECD Journal on Budgeting* 11, no. 3: 1–22.

Wong, Christine P. W., Christopher John Heady, Wing Thye Woo, and Asian Development Bank. 1995. *Fiscal Management and Economic Reform in the People's Republic of China*. Hong Kong: Oxford University Press for the Asian Development Bank.

Wong, Siu-lun. 1988. *Emigrant Entrepreneurs: Shanghai Industrialists in Hong Kong*. New York: Oxford University Press.

Woo, Wing Thye, Bruce Glassburner, and Anwar Nasution. 1994. *Macroeconomic Policies, Crises, and Long-Term Growth in Indonesia 1965–90*. Washington DC: World Bank Comparative Macroeconomic Series.

Woo, Wing Thye, Jeffrey D. Sachs, and Klaus Schwab, eds. 2000. *The Asian Financial Crisis: Lessons for a Resilient Asia*. Cambridge, MA: MIT Press.

Woo-Cumings, Meredith. 1991. *Race to the Swift: State and Finance in Korean Industrialization*. New York: Columbia University Press.

World Bank. 2002. "Private Capital Flows to Emerging Markets." Pp. 41–53 in *Global Development Finance: Financing the Poorest Countries*.

Wright, Tom. 2018. *Billion Dollar Whale: The Man Who Fooled Wall Street, Hollywood, and the World*. New York: Hachette.

Xiao, Geng. 2004. "People's Republic of China's Round-Tripping FDI: Causes and Implications." ADB Institute Discussion Paper no. 7 (July).

Xiao, Yuan. 2016. "Making Land Fly: The Institutionalization of China's Land Quota Markets and its Implications for Urbanization, Property Rights, and Intergovernmental Politics." PhD dissertation, MIT.

Xiao-Planes, Xiaohong. 2014. "Buy 20 Years." *European Journal of East Asian Studies* 13, no. 2: 214–39.

Yang, Dali L. 1996. *Calamity and Reform in China: State, Rural Society, and Institutional Change since the Great Leap Famine*. Stanford: Stanford University Press.

Yang, Jisheng. 2020. *The World Turned Upside Down: A History of the Chinese Cultural Revolution*. Translated by Stacy Mosher and Guo Jian. New York: Farrar, Straus and Giroux.

Yasuda, John K. 2018. *On Feeding the Masses: An Anatomy of Regulatory Failure in China*. New York: Cambridge University Press.

Yasuda, John K. 2022. "The Irrational Investor: Stock Markets, Regulatory Paternalism, and the Developmental State in East Asia." Chinese Politics Research in Progress Working Paper.

Yasuda, Nobuyuki. 1991. "Malaysia's New Economic Policy and the Industrial Co-ordination Act." *Developing Economies* 29, no. 4: 330–49.

Ye, Min. 2014. "China Invests Overseas: Regulation and Representation." *Modern China Studies* 21, no. 1: 173–204.

Ye, Min. 2014. *Diasporas and Foreign Direct Investment in China and India*. New York: Cambridge University Press.

Ye, Min. 2020. *The Belt Road and Beyond: State-Mobilized Globalization in China, 1998–2018*. New York: Cambridge University Press.

Yeoh, Emilie. 2008. "Requiem for a Dream: The Rise and Fall of a Communal Economic Revival Movement." Pp. 210–73 in *China in the World: Contemporary Issues and Perspectives*, edited by Emile Kok-Kheng Yeoh and Joanne Hoi-Lee Loh. Kuala Lumpur: Institute of China Studies, University of Malaya.

You, Jong-sung. 2021. "The Changing Dynamics of State-Business Relations and the Politics of Reform and Capture in South Korea." *Review of International Political Economy* 28, no. 1: 81–102.

Zhang, Qi, and Mingxing Liu. 2013. "The Political Economy of Private Sector Development in Communist China: Evidence from Zhejiang Province." *Studies in Comparative International Development* 48, no. 2: 196–216.

Zhang, Qi, and Mingxing Liu. 2019. *Revolutionary Legacy, Power Structure, and Grassroots Capitalism under the Red Flag in China*. New York: Cambridge University Press.

Zhang, Qi, Dong Zhang, Mingxing Liu, and Victor Shih. 2021. "Elite Cleavage and the Rise of Capitalism under Authoritarianism: A Tale of Two Provinces in China." *Journal of Politics* 83, no. 3: 1010–23.

Zhou, Taomo. 2019. *Migration in the Time of Revolution: China, Indonesia, and the Cold War*. Ithaca: Cornell University Press.

Zhou, Xueguang. 2010. "The Institutional Logic of Collusion among Local Governments in China." *Modern China* 36, no. 1: 47–78.

Zweig, David. 1997. *Freeing China's Farmers: Rural Restructuring in the Reform Era*. Armonk, NY: M.E. Sharpe.

Zysman, John. 1983. *Governments, Markets, and Growth: Financial Systems and the Politics of Industrial Change*. Ithaca: Cornell University Press.

Primary Source Materials

China

陈银峰 (Chen Yinfeng). 2009. "论中国的金融监管与金融反腐败" (On Chinese Financial Regulation and Financial Anti-corruption). 商场现代化(学术版).第9期: 52–53.

China Minsheng Investment Group (CMIG). 2015. "中民投的远景和第一步, 对话董文标" (The Background and the First Steps of CMIG: A Conversation with Dong Wenbiao), November 12. https://www.cm-inv.com/cn/ourtalk/1012.htm.

China Minsheng Investment Group (CMIG). 2019. "中民投于中国长城开展全民合作" (CMIG and China Great Wall Begin Collaboration on All Fronts). March 1. https://www.cm-inv.com/cn/companyNews/2299.htm. Accessed May 2019.

China Private Economy Yearbook: 1994–2013 (中国私营经济年鉴).) 1994–2013. Beijing: Zhonghua gongshang lianhe chubanshe.

中国证券监督管理委员会 (China Securities Regulatory Commission). 2011. "证监会查处江苏三友信息披露违法行为" (CSRC Investigates and Punishes Jiangsu Sanyou's Illegal Information Disclosure Behavior). December 9.

崔鸿雁 (Cui Hongyan). 2012. "建国以来我国金融监管制度思想演进研究" (Research on the Evolution of China's Financial Supervision System since the Founding of the State). 复旦大学经济学院博士学位论文. 5月.

崔琳 (Cui Lin). 2019. "统一监管还是分业监管: 基于不完全契约的视角" (Integrated Regulation or Separated Regulation: An Anarchy from the Perspective of Incomplete Contract Theory). 金融评论. 第6期: 68–85, 122.

段志国 (Duan Zhiguo). 2016. "分权背景下的地方金融监管权研究" (Research on Local Financial Supervision against the Backdrop of Decentralization). 中央财经大学法学院博士学位论文. 5月. PhD Dissertation, Central University of Finance and Economics. (中央财经大学, Beijing.

何德旭 (He Dexu). 2003. "金融监管: 世界趋势与中国的选择: 兼论中国银监会的设立" (Regulatory Supervision, Global Trends, and China's Choices: Also on the Establishment of China's Banking Regulatory Commission). 管理世界. 第9期: 52–61.

关丹中华商会 (Kuantan Chinese Chamber of Commerce). 1993. Speech by Vice Minister of Industry and Commerce. February.

郎咸平 (Lang Xianping). 2001. 新财富 (New Wealth Magazine). April 成都商报 (Chengdu Commercial Newspaper). July 2003.

李传芳 (Li Chuanfang), 董芷林 (Dong Zhilin), 杨之立 (Yang Zhili). 2015. "追忆我的伯父'大右派;'李康年" (Recalling My Uncle "The Great Rightist." Li Kangnian). 世纪 (Century). 第3期 : 12–16.

李怡芳 (Li Yifang). 2019. A 股股权转让大增的特征，原因及政策建议" (Increase in A Share Equity Transfer: Reason, Future, and Policy Recommendations). 上证研报 (Shanghai Securities Research Report). Number 8.

刘鸿儒 (Liu Hongru). 2009. "回顾我国金融体制改革的历程" (Reviewing the History of China's Financial System Reform). 百年湖. 第5期: 22–28.

"投之家幕后嫌犯卢智建被警方抓获" (Lu Zhijian, Suspect behind Investment House, Is Arrested by Police). 2018. September 13. http://finance.sina.com.cn/money/bank/dsfzf/2018-09-13/doc-ihkahyhw6442228.shtml.

Meizhou city gazetteer (1979–2000) (梅州市志). 2011. Beijing: Fangzhi chubanshe.

中国人民银行济南分行课题组 (People's Bank, Ji'nan Branch, Research Group). 2005. "'一行三会'体制下的金融宏观调控与监管协调的综合效能研究" (Research on the Comprehensive Effectiveness of Financial Macro-control and Regulatory Coordination under the System of One Bank and Three Commissions). 金融研究. 增刊.

国务院 (State Council). 2013. "中共中央关于全面深化改革若干重大问题的决定" (Decision on Major Problems in the Deepening of Reform). November 15. http://www.gov.cn/jrzg/2013 11/15/content_2528179.htm.

国务院 (State Council). 2015. "关于深化国有企业改革的指导意见" (Guiding Opinions on Deepening the Reform of State-Owned Enterprises). September 13. http://www.gov.cn/zhengce/2015-09/13/content_2930440.htm.

苏龙飞 (Su Longfei). 2013. "明天帝国: 影子金融大亨肖建华的资产版图" (Tomorrow Empire: Asset Map of Xiao Jianhua). 新财富. 4月: 38–73 and http://www.xcf.cn/new fortune/fmgs/201304/t20130407_426444.htm.

孙国峰 (Sun Guofeng). 2012. 第一排: 中国金融改革的近距离思考 (China's Financial Reforms: Through Eyes of a Front-Bencher). 北京: 中国经济出版社.

Suzhou Municipal Gazetteer: 1986–2005 (苏州市志). 2014. Nanjing: Jiangsu fenghuang kexue jishu chubanshe.

唐立久 (Tang Lijiu) and 张旭 (Zhang Xu). 2005. 解构德隆 (Deconstructing Delong). 杭州: 浙江人民出版社.

王浩 (Wang Hao), 王红林 (Wang Honglin)，王立升 (Wang Lisheng)， and 周皓 (Zhou Hao). 2018. "影子银行：中国利率市场化双轨改革机制" (Shadow Banking: China's Dual-Track Reform Mechanism to Liberalize Interest Rates). 清华五道口金融学院. January 5. http://www.pbcsf.tsinghua.edu.cn/portal/article/index/id/2188.html. Accessed July 2021.

王立锋 (Wang Lifeng). 2018. "我国金融监管框架优化路径研究" (Research on the Path to Optimize China's Financial Regulatory Framework). 中央党校博士学位论文. 7月. PhD Dissertation, China Central Party School (中国中央党校, Beijing.

王年一 (Wang Nianyi). 1988. 大动乱的年代 (A Decade of Great Upheaval). 郑州；河南人民出版社.

王永宁 (Wang Yongning). 2012. "'一行三会'监管协调机制的有效性问题" (On the Effectiveness of the Coordinating Mechanisms for Financial Supervision in China). 山东大学学报 (哲学社会科学版). 第4期: 54–58.

吴晓灵 (Wu Xiaoling). 2017. "防控金融风险 注重金融安全" (Preventing and Controlling Financial Risks with a Focus on Financial Security). 清华五道口全球金融论坛上的讲话. June 3. http://www.pbcsf.tsinghua.edu.cn/portal/article/index/id/1187.htmlnational.

习近平 (Xi Jinping). 2021. "正确认识和把握我国发展重大理论和实践问题" (The Correct Understanding of the Major Theoretical and Practical Problems of China's Development). December. Speech at the Central Economic Work Conference, Beijing, and reprinted issue in no. 10 of the May 2022 issue of *Qiushi*. http://www.qstheory.cn/dukan/qs/2022-05/15/c_1128649331.htm and English translation at https://interpret.csis.org/translations/the-correct-understanding-of-major-theoretical-and-practical-problems-of-chinas-development/.

邢桂君 (Xing Guijun). 2008. "我国金融控股公司监管研究" (Research the Supervision of Chinese Financial Holding Companies). 金融与经济. 第6期.

易纲 (Yi Gang). 2019.中国金融改革思考录 (Thoughts on China's Financial Reform). 北京: 商务印书馆.

曾筱清 (Zeng Xiaoqing), 李萍 (Li Ping), 吕婷婷 (Lu Tingting). 2003. "金融改革与金融监管的互动分析及其立法建议" (Analysis of the Reciprocal Relationship between Financial Reform and Financial Regulatory Control: Some Related Legislative Issues). 中央财经大学学报. 第3期.

张承惠 (Zhang Chengwei). 2016. "关于我国金融监管框架重构的思考与建议" (Thoughts and Suggestions on the Reconstruction of China's Financial Supervisory Framework). 重庆理工大学学报. 第30卷, 第9期: 1–5.

张德江 (Zhang Dejiang). 2016. "在纪念荣毅仁同志诞辰100周年座谈会上的讲话" (Speech at the Symposium Honoring the One Hundredth Anniversary of the Birth of Comrade Rong Yiren). April 26. http://www.xinhuanet.com//politics/2016-04/26/c_1118744840.htm.

周逢民 (Zhou Fengmin). 2012. "中央与地方政府金融监管模式选择" (The Choice of China's Model of Central and Local Financial Supervision). 金融发展评论. 第5期: 70–75.

周学东 (Zhou Xuedong). 2020. 中小银行金融风险主要源于公司治理失灵: 从接管包商银行看中小银行公司治理的关键 (The Financial Risks of Small and Medium Banks Mainly Stem from the Failure of Corporate Governance: The Baoshang Bank). 中国金融. 第15期: 19–21. http://www.cqvip.com/qk/96434x/202015/7102558854.html.

朱民 (Zhu Min). 2017. 功能监管是未来方向，金融委发挥协调作用" (Functional Supervision Is the Future Direction and the Financial Commission Will Play a Coordinating Role). 清华五道口金融学院. 11月, 24号. http://www.pbcsf.tsinghua.edu.cn/portal/article/index/id/1317.html. Accessed February 2020.

Indonesia

Assaat. 1957. "The Chinese Grip on Our Economy." Speech to the All-Indonesian Importers Congress. March 1956. Badan Pekerdja KENSI Pusat (Central Working Committee of the All-Indonesia National Economic Congress). Djakarta: Djambatan. Pp. 51–62 in *Indonesian Political Thinking, 1945–1965*, compiled by Herbert Feith and Lance Castles. Ithaca: Cornell University Press, 1970.

Badan Penyahayan Perbankan Nasional (BPPN). 1999–2002. *Laporan Tahunan*. Jakarta. Indonesia Banking Restructuring Agency Annual Reports.

Economist Conference: Roundtable with the Government of Indonesia. 1995. Proceedings, Paper, Summary, and Conclusion. March 19–21. Grand Hyatt, Jakarta. NUS Closed Stacks.

"Guidance on the Chinese Issue." 1967. *Sekkab*. Indonesian National Archives.

Kelompok Politik—Panitia Perumus Kebidjaksanaan Penjelesaian Masalah Tjina (Political Bureau of the Committee for the Formulation of Chinese-Related Policies). 1967. August 6. Sekkab. Indonesian National Archives.

Laporan Ekonimi. 1991. Various issues. MCA. Seminar on Privatisation. Kuala Lumpur. May 12.

Sekkab. 1965–71. Materials in the Indonesian National Archives related to the Chinese issue. Indonesia National Archives, Jakarta.

Suta, I Putu. 2004. *BPPN: The End*. Jakarta: Yayasan Sad Satria Bhakti.

Newspapers

Jakarta Globe (English). Daily. 2008–

Jakarta Post (English). Daily. 1983–

Tempo (English). Weekly. 1971–

SWA. Biweekly business magazine. 1985–

Malaysia

ASEAN Briefing. 1990. "Outlook on the Malaysian Economy 1990." Development Bank of Singapore, no. 13 (January).

Bee, YB Encik Tiah Eng (MP Kluang Utara). 1973. November 28. Malaysia Chinese Association. "A Collection of Speeches by MCA Members of Parliament Delivered at the Dewan Rakyat on the Mid-Term Review of the Second Malaysia FYP , 1971–75." NUS Singapore-Malaysia Collection.

Boh, Enche Khaw Kai (Minister of Local Government and Housing and MCA Vice President). 1968. "Why You Should Join the MCA." Collected MCA Pamphlets. NUS Singapore-Malaysia Collection, March 15.

The Central Bank and the Financial System in Malaysia: A Decade of Change, 1989–1999. 1999. Kuala Lumpur: Bank Negara Malaysia.

Chee, Lim Fung. 1980. Seminar on Political Challenges of the Eighties for the Chinese Community. Kuala Lumpur. May 25. NUS Singapore-Malaysia Collection.

The Chinese Community towards & beyond 1990 in Multi-racial Malaysia: A Political Seminar. 1987? Kuala Lumpur: Ibu Pejabat MCA.

Collected MCA Materials. 1987. June 28. NUS Singapore-Malaysia Collection.

Daniel, G. P. 1995. *Dr. Ling Liong Sik and the Politics of Ethnic Chinese Unity*. Selangor Darul Ehsan, Malaysia: Times.

Economic Planning Unit. *The Second Malaysia Plan, 1971–1975*. https://www.epu. gov.my/en/economic-developments/development-plans/rmk/second-malay sia-plan-1971-1975.

Economic Planning Unit. *Third Malaysia Plan 1976–80*. https://www.epu.gov.my/sites/ default/files/2021-05/FirstOutlinePerspective.pdf.

Economic Planning Unit. *Seventh Malaysia Five Year Plan, 1996–2000* (Putrajaya). https://www.epu.gov.my/en/economic-developments/development-plans/rmk/seve nth-malaysia-plan-1996-2000 and Economic Planning Unit, "Eight Malaysia 2001– 2005" (Putrajava). https://www.epu.gov.my/en/economic-developments/developm ent-plans/rmk/eight-malaysia-plan-2001-2005.

Economic Planning Unit. *Eight Malaysia 2001–2005*. https://www.epu.gov.my/en/econo mic-developments/development-plans/rmk/eight-malaysia-plan-2001-2005.

Economic Planning Unit. *Tenth Malaysia 10th MP* (Putrajava). https://www.epu.gov.my/ en/economic-developments/development-plans/rmk/tenth-malaysia-plan-10th-mp.

Hamid, Ahmad Sarji Abdul, ed. 1993. *Malaysia's Vision 2020: Understanding the Concept, Implications, and Challenges*. Petaling Jaya, Selangor Darul Ehsan, Malaysia: Pelanduk Publications.

Hun, YB Enick Richard Ho Ung (MCA MP Sitiawan). 1973. November 29. Malaysia Chinese Association. "A Collection of Speeches by MCA Members of Parliament Delivered at the Dewan Rakyat on the Mid-Term Review of the Second Malaysia FYP, 1971–1975." NUS Singapore-Malaysia Collection. Malaysian Chinese Association.

Hussein, Tun Haji Abdul Razak bin Dato'. 1969. *The May 13th Tragedy: A Report*. Kuala Lumpur: National Operations Council.

Khen, Michael Yeoh. 1987. "The Chinese Political Dilemma." June 12. *The Chinese Community towards & beyond 1990 in Multiracial Malaysia*. NUS Singapore-Malaysia Collection.

Kok, Lim San. 1971. "Some Aspects of the Malayan Chinese Association, 1949–69." *Journal of the South Seas Society* 26, no. 2: 31–48.

Koon, Kew Yin. 2012. *Malaysia: Road Map for Achieving Vision 2020*. Petaling Jaya: Strategic Information and Research Development Centre.

Mahathir, Mohamad. 2000. "Malaysia: Bouncing Back from the Brink." Speech delivered at the World Economic Forum Annual Meeting in Davos, Switzerland. January 29, 1999. Pp. in 49–56 in *Selected Speeches of Dr. Mahathir Mohamad*, vol. 2: *Managing the Malaysian Economy*, edited by Hashim Makaruddin. Subang Jaya, Selangor: Pelanduk.

Malaysian Chinese Association. 1973. "A Collection of Speeches by MCA Members of Parliament Delivered at the Dewan Rakyat on the Mid-Term Review of the Second Malaysia FYP, 1971–1975." NUS Singapore-Malaysia Collection.

Malaysian Chinese Association. 1974. Economic Congress Materials. March. NUS Singapore-Malaysia Collection.

Malaysian Chinese Association. 1974. 25th Anniversary Souvenir Publication. NUS Singapore-Malaysia Collection.

Malaysian Chinese Association. 1985. Political Seminar: Democracy and the MCA. "The Role of the MCA: Towards the Next Century." MCA Collected Speeches. October 2. NUS Singapore-Malaysia Collection.

Malaysian Chinese Association. 1991. Seminar on Privatisation. May 12. Kuala Lumpur. NUS Singapore-Malaysia Collection.

Malaysian Chinese Chamber of Commerce. 1978. 马来西亚中华工商联合会. 全国华人经济大会. 报告录. Speech by the Chairman at the Malaysian Chinese Economic Conference. Report on Conference Proceedings. April 9. Federal Hotel.吉隆坡 (Kuala Lumpur): 马来西亚中华工商联合会. NUS Singapore-Malaysia Collection.

Ngian, Chin Hon (MCA Sec Johore). 1974. "The Advancement of Life Chances of Have-Nots with Special Reference to the Chinese Have-Nots." March 3. MCA Economic Congress. NUS Singapore-Malaysia Collection.

Pan, Dr. Neo Yee. 1974. "The Role of Chinese Business in the Context of Our National Objectives." March 3. MCA Economic Congress. NUS Singapore-Malaysia Collection.

Penang Chamber of Commerce. 2013. *110th Anniversary Publication*, 2013. NUS Singapore-Malaysia Collection)

霹雳华人矿务公会卅七周年纪念特刊 (Perak Chinese Mining Association). 1972. 曾文福, 主编霹, 37th Anniversary Publication. 伊藤: 霹雳华人矿务公会.

霹雳嘉应会館九十五周年纪念特刊 (Perak Kaying Association). 1995. (华声: 砂劳越华人社团联合总会会讯 (Newsletter of the Confederation of Chinese Association Sarawak). July.

美里诏安会馆五十一周年纪念特刊 (Persatuan of Chawan Miri 51st Anniversary). 2001. Sarawak.

Putrajaya Committee on GLC High Performance. 2015. *GLC Transformation Programme Graduation Report*. https://www.pcg.gov.my/media/1118/glctp-vol1-graduation-report.pdf.

Sin, Tun Tan Siew (President of Malaysian Chinese Association). 1965. "The Role of the MCA in Malaysia." Speech to the Historical Society of the University of Malaya. September 10. NUS Singapore-Malaysia Collection.

Sin, Tun Tan Siew. "The Challenge Ahead." 1968. Speech at the MCA General Assembly. Kuala Lumpur. March 23. NUS Singapore-Malaysia Collection.

Sin, Tun Tan Siew. 1974. Foreword. MCA 25th Anniversary Souvenir Publication. NUS Singapore-Malaysia Collection.

Wah, Loh Kok. 1982. "The Politics of Chinese Unity in Malaysia: Reform and Conflict in the Malaysian Chinese Association 1971–73." ISEAS Occasional Paper no. 70. NUS Singapore-Malaysia Collection.

Yeoh, Emile Kok-Kheng. 2008. "Communal Economic Movement of Chinese Overseas: A Malaysian Case." ICS Working Paper Series no. 2008–16. Kuala Lumpur: Institute of China Studies, University of Malaya.

Yong Poh Kon. 1980. "Economic Challenges of the 1980s." Paper prepared for the Seminar on Challenges of the 1980s. MCA, May 25.

Index